Joking Asides

ELLIOTT ORING

Joking

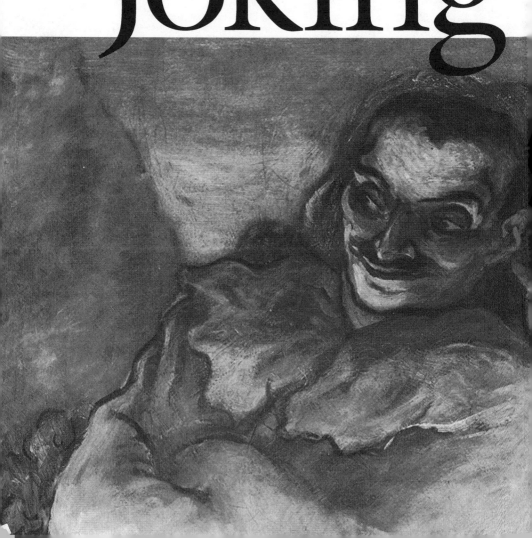

Asides

The Theory, Analysis, and Aesthetics of Humor

UTAH STATE UNIVERSITY PRESS

Logan

© 2016 by the University Press of Colorado

Published by Utah State University Press
An imprint of University Press of Colorado
5589 Arapahoe Avenue, Suite 206C
Boulder, Colorado 80303

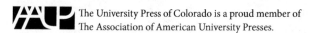 The University Press of Colorado is a proud member of
The Association of American University Presses.

The University Press of Colorado is a cooperative publishing enterprise supported, in part, by Adams State University, Colorado State University, Fort Lewis College, Metropolitan State University of Denver, Regis University, University of Colorado, University of Northern Colorado, Utah State University, and Western State Colorado University.

∞ This paper meets the requirements of the ANSI/NISO Z39.48-1992 (Permanence of Paper).

ISBN: 978-1-60732-491-1 (paperback)
ISBN: 978-1-60732-492-8 (e-book)

Library of Congress Cataloging-in-Publication Data
Names: Oring, Elliott, 1945– author.
Title: Joking asides : the theory, analysis, and aesthetics of humor / by Elliott Oring.
Description: Logan : Utah State University Press, 2016.
Identifiers: LCCN 2015041274| ISBN 9781607324911 (pbk.) | ISBN 1607324911
  (pbk.) | ISBN 9781607324928 (ebook) | ISBN 160732492X (ebook)
Subjects: LCSH: Wit and humor—History and criticism. | Jewish wit and
  humor—History and criticism. | Wit and humor—Psychological aspects.
Classification: LCC PN6147 .O76 2016 | DDC 809.7—dc23
LC record available at http://lccn.loc.gov/2015041274

Cover image: "Crispin and Scapin," Honoré Daumier, 1858–1860.

For
Frank de Caro, who is sitting at his desk,
and
Norman Klein, who probably isn't

Contents

Preface

Every universe, our own included, begins in conversation.
—MICHAEL CHABON

This volume of essays is meant to continue a conversation that I began in my previous volumes on humor (Oring 1992, 2003) and ultimately to continue that conversation initiated by the Greek philosophers who first contemplated the nature of laughter. As this conversation has been going on for some 2,500 years, I don't expect it to end anytime soon. Nothing is likely to be definitively resolved in the study of humor, least of all by this collection of essays. The essays merely proffer hypotheses, respond to proposals by other scholars, and suggest ways that humor generally, and jokes specifically, operate for different groups in different times and in different media. The essays generate more problems than solutions, and this is to be expected. They are intended not to foreclose lines of thought and discussion but to stimulate them.

The essays coalesce around different issues. Chapter 1, "What Freud Actually Said about Jokes," revisits Sigmund Freud's famous work *Jokes and Their Relation to the Unconscious*. This book was particularly important in framing fundamental questions about the psychology of humor for subsequent generations of scholars, and this essay suggests that important elements of this psychology have been misapprehended. Chapter 2, "Parsing the Joke: The General Theory of Verbal Humor and Appropriate Incongruity"; chapter 3, "Blending and Humor"; chapter 4, "On Benign Violations"; and chapter 5, "Humor and the Discovery of False Beliefs" closely examine four different theories of humor. In each case, they are found wanting. It seems that every new theory, new philosophy, or new discipline eventually gives rise to claims that it has unlocked the secret of humor. Henri Bergson's "Laughter: An Essay on the Significance of the Comic," published in 1900, stemmed from his philosophy of vitalism (*élan vital*). That same year, Sigmund Freud published *The Interpretation of Dreams,* and his book on jokes followed five years later. In the later decades of the twentieth century, the Semantic Script Theory of Humor and the General Theory of Verbal Humor came out of script-based semantics, Conceptual Integration Theory out of cognitive linguistics, False-Belief Theory out of cognitive and evolutionary psychology, and Benign Violation Theory out of nowhere in particular.[1] All of these theories claim to have solved the problem of what humor is and how it works.

As a folklorist, I was first drawn to matters of humor through jokes, because jokes are traditional aesthetic forms and because repertoires of jokes coalesce about groups of people and may serve to say something about how the individuals in these communities see themselves and the world around them (Oring 1973, 1981, 1983, 1984, 1994). I was interested in jokes as cultural and psychological phenomena. In order to interpret them, however, I had to have some sense of what humor is and how it operates. I characterized jokes and humor more generally as based on the perception of an *appropriate incongruity;* that is, "the perception of an appropriate interrelationship of elements from domains that are generally regarded as incongruous" (Oring 1992, 2). In other words, humor depends upon perceiving a conflation of incongruous words, behaviors, visual forms, or ideas that nevertheless seem appropriately related. This notion, if not the term, has been around at least since the late eighteenth century (Beattie 1778). I have spelled out and applied this notion in numerous essays but most thoroughly in "Appropriate Incongruity" (Oring 1992, 1–15) and "Appropriate Incongruity Redux" (Oring 2003, 1–12). The virtues of the formulation *appropriate incongruity* are that: (1) the notion is clear and concise; (2) it is rooted in previous conceptualizations of humor; (3) it provides a method for the close analysis of various humorous forms and behaviors; (4) it is "experience near"; that is, the people whose humor I study can generally grasp it; and (5) it is imprecise. This last would not at first seem to be a virtue, but in fact, adhering to rigid formulations of what constitutes a joke or humorous expression can lead analysis astray. My critique of the General Theory of Verbal Humor in chapter 2 provides a good illustration of how a degree of imprecision may allow for a clear grasp of how a joke works when more formal approaches seem to miss the mark.

Chapters 6 through 10 focus on humor in particular historical and cultural contexts. Chapter 6, "Framing Borat," is the only essay that addresses the topic of humor in popular culture. The film *Borat: Cultural Learnings of America for Make*

Benefit for Glorious Nation of Kazakhstan was released in 2006 and was wildly popular in the West but was banned in Russia and most Arab countries. It garnered both praise and criticism. The criticisms centered on the way that certain groups described or encountered in the course of the film were made objects of ridicule. This chapter attempts to sort out some matters in dealing with the targets of humor and the moral uproar such ridicule inevitably provokes. Chapter 7, "Risky Business: Political Jokes under Repressive Regimes," explores the explanations that have been offered of those political jokes that engender severe penalties from the powers that be. Consequently, such jokes are told circumspectly. In German they have been called *Flüsterwitze*—whispered jokes—and they circulated in Franco's Spain, Nazi Germany, and most prominently in the Soviet Union and Iron Curtain countries. Chapter 8, "Listing toward Lists: Jokes on the Internet," explores the presentation of jokes as lists rather than as discrete dialogic or narrative texts. Of course, plenty of discrete joke texts do appear on the Internet, but the joke list is particularly widespread, although relatively rare in oral and literary culture. Chapter 9, "What Is a Narrative Joke?" attempts to address the question of when a joke can be regarded as a narrative. If a joke is not a one-liner or cast in the form of a riddle, a Wellerism, or a Shaggy Dog Story, it is often termed a "narrative joke." In other words, "narrative joke" actually serves as a residual class to label those texts that do not fit neatly into other categories. Most jokes are actually dialogues rather than sequences of action. The chapter attempts to define a narrative joke, identify some of the ways narratives are constructed within jokes, and make some observations on aspects of the form's development. Chapter 10, "Demythologizing the Jewish Joke," returns to questions I first posed more than thirty years ago (Oring 1983, 1992, 112–21): What are "Jewish jokes," and how did Jews come to be identified with this particular genre? The chapter challenges received wisdom about what such jokes are and how they function in the hopes of getting the study of the Jewish joke, and Jewish humor more generally, on a firmer historical footing.

The final two chapters deal with a largely overlooked topic in the study of jokes—aesthetics. Chapter 11, "From the Ridiculous to the Sublime: Jokes and Art," questions the exclusion of jokes from the category of art. It suggests that some philosophers of aesthetics have been too quick to exclude the joke from their consideration. The joke, in fact, may have more to teach philosophers about art than philosophers have to teach about jokes. Chapter 12, "Contested Performance and Joke Aesthetics," explores an encounter between two accomplished joke tellers in an effort to understand how they apprehend the qualities that make for a good joke and a good joke performance. The data show that aesthetics is very much on jokers' minds when they tell a joke. These performers think carefully about their jokes—their structure, phraseology, and rhythms—indicating that jokes cannot simply be written off as "one-shot affairs" (Carroll 2003, 358).

These essays were inspired by the books and essays of a host of scholars and writers. Their names and works can be found in the works cited list at the end of the volume. Although the conversation on humor and laughter has been going on for millennia, the distribution of comments and responses has been uneven. Interest in humor and laughter has waxed and waned. The commentary increased substantially over the last century, and in the last thirty years—with contributions by psychologists, literature scholars, linguists, philosophers, anthropologists, and folklorists—it has positively exploded. The online archiving and publication of journals, and the online posting of manuscripts and published essays by individual authors, has made it easy to access this literature and to be overwhelmed by it. I trust this volume, printed on acid-free paper and bound between two tangible covers, will nevertheless find its way into the hands of both serious scholars and thoughtful readers. Hopefully, these essays will provoke reflection and stimulate response. After all, without response, there is no conversation.

I am indebted to colleagues who consented to read and comment on essays included in this volume: Salvatore Attardo, Christie Davies, Władysław Chłopicki, Frank de Caro, Christian Hempelmann, Robert Mankoff, and John Morreall. I have also benefited from conversations with other colleagues, a few, unfortunately, no longer with us: Mahadev Apte, Alan Dundes, Henry Glassie, Bill Ivey, Greg Kelley, Barbara Kirshenblatt-Gimblett, Norman Klein, Michaela Lang, Jay Mechling, Wolfgang Mieder, Victor Raskin, Gregory Schrempp, Tim Tangherlini, Barre Toelken, Peter Tokofsky, Donald Ward, and Bert Wilson. My deepest thanks go to informants who provided materials and contextual data for materials included in this volume: Jan Brunvand, Judy Brunvand, Vilen Chernyak, Robert Cochran, Boris Faynberg, Maya Kaufman, Abe Kotlyar, Esther Lebovich, Alex Levoff, Natalie Olson, and Victor Raskin.

Friends and relatives remain a constant source of inspiration and amusement: Victor Astapov, Anastasiya Astapova, Bruce Carpenter, Inta Carpenter, Kerstin Danielson, Larry Danielson, Benjamin Fass, Bob Georges, Mary Georges, Genevieve Giuliano, Jess Hordes, Naomi Hordes, Rosan Jordan, Judit Katona-Apte, Tadashi Nakamura, Jon Olson, Alejandro Omidsalar, Claire Oring, Katie Oring, Mark Oring, Nathan Power, Fred Reinman, Gloria Reinman, Kathleen Stocks, Tok Thompson, Hrag Varjabedian, and Hannele Wilson. Many thanks go to Robin DuBlanc for her smart, yet restrained, copyediting. I continue to rely on Norman Klein and Kathleen Stocks for their proofreading, and they usually have their work cut out for them. Errors that remain in the book are, unfortunately, mine.

Most of the essays in this volume are new, but several have been previously published in whole or in part. "Chapter 2, "Parsing the Joke: The General Theory of Verbal Humor and Appropriate Incongruity," appeared in *Humor: International Journal of Humor Research* 24 (2011): 203–22 © 2011 Mouton de Gruyter. Chapter 6, "Framing Borat," appeared in a shorter version as "Borat and the Targets of Cinematic Comedy," in *Electronic Journal of Communication/La revue electronique de communication* 18 (2008), http://cios.org/www/ejc/EJCPUBLIC/018/2 /018412.html. Chapter 7, "Risky Business: Political Jokes under Repressive Regimes," was published in *Western Folklore* 63 (2004): 209–36 © 2004 Western States Folklore Society. Chapter 8, "Listing toward Lists: Jokes on the Internet," was included in *Folk Culture in the Digital Age*, ed. Trevor J. Blank (Logan: Utah State University Press, 2012), 98–118 © 2012 Utah State University Press. Chapter 12, "Contested Performance and Joke Aesthetics," was included in *The Individual and Tradition: Folkloristic Perspectives*, ed. Ray Cashman, Tom Mould, and Pravina Shukla (Bloomington: Indiana University Press, 2011), 365–85 © 2011 Indiana University Press.

Joking Asides

CHAPTER ONE

What Freud Actually Said about Jokes

A good joke is the one ultimate and sacred thing which cannot be criticised.
—G. K. CHESTERTON

No scholar who has even the slightest connection to the study of humor can be unaware of Sigmund Freud's book *Jokes and Their Relation to the Unconscious.* First published in 1905, the book was revolutionary in its understanding of jokes, the comic, and humor and extended the domain of psychoanalytic theory from symptoms, dreams, and slips of the tongue to the arena of the aesthetic. One has to give some credit to Deuticke, Freud's publisher, for taking on the project. After all, Deuticke had sold only some 350 copies of *The Interpretation of Dreams,* published five years earlier (Freud 1960, 8:xx). As it turned out, it would take Deuticke another five years to sell all copies of the first edition of the dream book, and a second edition of the joke book would not appear until seven years after the first.[1]

Even though Freud's book on jokes is widely recognized, it is not necessarily widely read. Yet even those who have never read Freud's book would probably be able to give a reasonable, if brief, account of Freud's theory of jokes. Undoubtedly, such accounts would sound very much like what popular writers and scholars present in their own books and essays. Max Eastman, for example: "Witty jokes, like myths and dreams and daydreams, slips and errors, art and poetry, are frequently employed as vehicles of expression by repressed impulses . . . Jests often liberate the surging wishes prisoned in us. They remove our lid of culture, and let us be, in fun at least and for a second, animals" (Eastman 1936, 250–51).[2] This view is not peculiar to popular writers on humor alone (although I would hesitate

3

to characterize Eastman's book as merely popular). One can find elements of his view repeated in the works of the most serious and dedicated humor researchers. For example, Joel Sherzer: "Humor and laughter . . . in the case of Freud, [are] an expression of latent, especially sexual repressions and aggressions" (Sherzer 1990, 96); Christopher Wilson: "The joke, then, is assumed to offer pleasure by temporarily reducing the tension of repression; and might also be gratifying in reducing the tension of the impulse itself—'in allowing unconscious elaboration of a repressed wish'" (Wilson 1979, 95); John Morreall: "Joking (like dreaming) serves as a safety valve for forbidden feelings and thoughts, and when we express what is usually inhibited, the energy of repression is released in laughter" (Morreall 1983, 111).

Psychoanalysts characterize Freud's theory of jokes in a similar fashion. Norman Holland: "Freud's recognition of the similarity and style between jokes and dreams (and, to a lesser extent, symptoms and slips of the tongue) meant that he could establish a relation between funniness and unconscious mental processes generally . . . A joke allows the id's impulses to thread their way through the ego's defenses" (Holland 1982, 47, 52); Martin Grotjahn: "According to Freud, laughter occurs when psychic energy is stimulated, then temporarily repressed, and finally freely and suddenly released without guilt or conflict . . . An aggressive intent must be stimulated, then repressed from consciousness into the unconscious; there it must be carefully disguised by the work of the unconscious censorship and finally allowed to emerge again—now in the disguise of a joke which expresses the hostile aggressive intent successfully . . . The dream symbolizes and fulfills symbolically a wish; wit expresses an aggressive trend in disguise" (Grotjahn 1970,162). And finally, Alan Dundes: "One element of emotional maturity is the ability to accept restrictions on pleasure-seeking (id) drives and to redirect the energies into secondary gratifications (sublimation). These energies must find some secondary outlet. One most effective substitute gratification is wit, especially as an aggressive expression . . . Even the spoken aggression may be further ameliorated by being couched in symbolic terms" (Dundes 1987, 42, 44).

One could cite many other examples (Schaeffer 1981, 12; Neve 1988, 37; Nilsen 1988, 344; Ziv and Gadish 1990, 248; Norrick 2001, 205; Lefcourt 2001, 36, 39; Billig 2005, 151). It should also be noted that these quotations have been lifted from more detailed descriptions of Freud's work in which nuances, complications, and ramifications are discussed at greater length and in greater depth. Nevertheless, I would contend that these descriptions of Freud's theory of jokes are representative and correct in their essentials. Jokes are like dreams and slips of the tongue. They all allow for the expression of thoughts repressed in the unconscious, and their articulation in jokes serves as a kind of release and relief necessary for both the psychological and physiological functioning of the individual (Keith-Spiegel 1972, 20–21; Goldstein, Suls, and Anthony 1972, 160; Rothbart 1977, 90; Charney 1983, 2:111; Apter 1982, 191; Morreall 1983, 28; Ziv 1984, 20, 48; Morreall 1987, 111; Dundes 1987, 44; Haig 1988, 23; Wyer and Collins 1992, 664; Davis 1993, 7, 81; L. Rappaport 2005, 19–20; Billig 2005, 169–71; Morreall 2008, 222–24; Kuipers 2008, 362; Hurley, Dennett, and Adams 2011, 44).[3]

But to what extent are jokes like dreams? In Freud's view, dreams are wish fulfillments. The wishes they fulfill are those which have been repressed—have been made inaccessible to consciousness—and that would greatly disturb the dreamer were they to become conscious. These wishes—the latent thoughts underlying the dream—are disguised in the language of the dream. This language utilizes a set of transformational rules that make the dream thoughts unrecognizable: *condensation, displacement, pictorial representation*, and *secondary revision*.[4] Freud calls these transformations the "dream-work," the work that the psyche must do to convert the unconscious thoughts into a dream. Were the latent dream thoughts—which are largely sexual and aggressive in nature—recognizable to the dreamer, they would disturb sleep. In the dream, however, the wishes are fulfilled while remaining unrecognizable. The function of the dream, in Freud's view, is to fulfill these wishes in order to preserve sleep (Freud 1953, 5:644, 678).

In *Jokes and Their Relation to the Unconscious*, Freud first attempts to unravel the techniques of jokes. He distinguishes between the *joke envelope* (*witzige Einkleidung*, actually "joking costume") and the *joke thought* (*Gedankenwitz*). The envelope is what makes a thought a joke. It is the product of joke techniques. To understand the techniques of a joke one must engage in the joke's *reduction*, a process that gets rid of the joke by minimally changing its mode of expression but retaining its underlying thought. For example, Freud reduces the following witticism by Felix Unger, professor of jurisprudence and president of the Supreme Court, to its underlying thought. "I drove with him *tête-à-bête*." *Tête* means "head," *tête-à-tête* means "in private conversation," and *bête* means "beast" or "brute" in French. The joke means, "I drove with X *tête-à-tête*, and X is a stupid ass." The joke depends upon the change of the initial phoneme in *tête* to the one in *bête*. Freud describes the technique of this joke as "condensation accompanied by slight modification" (Freud 1960, 8:23–25, 93). Condensation, however, is also one of the operations of the dream-work. Freud goes on to identify other joke techniques—displacement, indirect representation, allusion, unification, faulty reasoning, absurdity, representation by the opposite—all of which are cognates or subcategories of mechanisms of the dream-work. Freud, in fact, calls the techniques that transform a thought into a joke the *joke-work*, based on his previous analysis of dreams (8:54). For Freud, there is a significant correspondence between jokes and dreams.

In 1899, when Freud's friend Wilhelm Fliess was reading page proofs of *The Interpretation of Dreams*, he commented that the dream examples that were analyzed seemed too full of jokes. Freud responded: "All dreamers are insufferably witty, and they have to be, because they are under pressure, and the direct way is barred to them. If you think so, I shall insert a remark to that effect somewhere. The ostensible wit of all unconscious processes is closely connected with the theory of jokes and humour" (Freud 1954, 297). It is unlikely, however, that Fliess's comment first awakened Freud to the analogy between dreams and jokes. First, Freud's response to Fliess's observation seems fully formed and the result of previous reflection rather than off the cuff. Second, two years before, in June 1897, when Freud was deep in the analysis of his own dreams, he wrote to Fliess that he had "recently made a collection of significant Jewish stories [jokes]" (211). Third, in a footnote in *Studies on Hysteria*, first published in 1895, Freud comments on the analysis of a patient's hallucinations. Although he did not explicitly label them "jokes," he remarked nevertheless that they "called for much ingenuity" (Freud 1955, 2:181n1).

The distinction between the joke thought and the joke envelope is an important one for Freud, although it is rarely emphasized in reviews of and commentaries on his work (but see Billig 2005, 155). In his book, Freud distinguishes other aspects of jokes as well. He notes the difference between "verbal jokes" and "conceptual jokes," that is, between jokes that rely on their linguistic formulation and those that are independent of such formulations (Freud 1960, 8:91). Freud also distinguishes between "innocent jokes" and "tendentious jokes" (8:90–91). The innocent joke is an end in itself and serves no other particular aim. Innocent jokes, however, are not necessarily trivial or lacking in substance. They may actually convey a significant thought. What defines the innocent joke is that it is not tendentious. The pleasure it produces is purely aesthetic and fulfills no other aim in life. The tendentious joke, however, serves purposes beyond entertainment that are inaccessible to the innocent joke. According to Freud, there are two purposes a joke may serve: "It is either a *hostile* joke (serving the purpose of aggressiveness, satire, or defence) or an *obscene* joke (serving the purpose of exposure)." Such purposes can be fulfilled by both conceptual and verbal jokes as these joke species have no necessary connection with their purposes (8:96–97). It should become obvious from what follows that there is in reality only one purpose, and obscenity is a subset of hostility or aggressiveness.

The obscene joke is itself a transformation of what might be called an "archetypical scene," although Freud never uses this term. Freud sees the obscene joke as related to *smut*—the bringing to prominence in speech of sexual facts and relations. The purpose of smut is typically, Freud claims, to excite a woman and to serve as a means of seduction. If the woman resists, that speaker's purpose is inhibited, and what began as seductive speech is transformed into something hostile and cruel. The resistance of a woman is almost guaranteed when another man is present. But in such cases, the hostility is maintained against the woman, and this interfering third party is converted into an *ally* who is bribed into laughter by the "effortless satisfaction of his own libido" aroused by the obscenities. It is typically the appearance of a barmaid that initiates smutty speech in a tavern (Freud 1960, 8:99–100).[5]

I am not sure where Freud acquired his ethnographic information about smutty speech, through reading or by visiting taverns during his vacations in the countryside. The point is that he regards smut as the basis for understanding the obscene joke. The obscene joke, in Freud's view, is essentially domesticated smut that takes place in higher levels of society. Whereas the presence of a woman at lower levels of the social order would arouse smutty speech, at higher social levels smut is not tolerated except to the extent that it is enclosed within the envelope of a joke. Those who could never bring themselves to laugh at coarse smut, however, can laugh when a joke comes to their aid. Even then, an obscene joke would be exclusive to the company of men and not permitted in the presence of ladies (Freud 1960, 8:99–101).

The same can be said for jokes that have a hostile purpose. Where the expression of open hostility is inhibited, it may still be articulated in the form of a joke. Thus the joke about Serenissimus (the name used by the German press for a royal personage) who, upon seeing a man who strongly resembled his royal person, asked: "'Was your mother at one time in service at the Palace?'—'No, your Highness;' was the reply, 'but my father was'" (Freud 1960, 8:68–69).[6] The reply circumvents an inhibition against insulting a monarch. Freud identifies four categories of tendentious joke: the *obscene joke,* which is directed against a woman; the *hostile joke* proper, which is directed against persons more generally; the *cynical joke,* which is directed against a social institution; and the *skeptical joke,* which is directed against the strictures of knowledge and reason themselves (8:108, 115). In other words, all tendentious jokes are hostile jokes. It is only their targets and manner that vary.

Freud sees the joke process—at least the tendentious joke process—in very much the same terms as he sees the smut process. It involves *three* people: the one who makes the joke, the one who is the target of the joke (who may not be present), and the one for whom the joke is made and who laughs at it. Freud is concerned with the question of why the one who makes the joke does not laugh—or at least, does not laugh in the same way as the one to whom the joke is told. Freud holds that the joke teller needs the one who hears the joke to stimulate his own laughter. Although he feels pleasure, the joker does not laugh, according to Freud, because of the expenditure of energy made by the joker in the creation of the joke, an expenditure that the third person—the listener—does not have to make. Thus, there is no overall saving of energy by the joker; the energy that would have been saved by circumventing the inhibition is expended in the joke-work (Freud 1960, 8:150). This is the case for jokes that are of the joker's own invention. In the case of what are today called "canned jokes," the joker is merely passing on the joke and is already aware of both its thought and its formulation—what it says and how it says it. The joker cannot be seduced by the joke envelope. Canned jokes must be novel in order to succeed (154). And that is why the joker needs the third person—because he is unable to laugh at the joke himself. "We supplement our pleasure by attaining the laughter that is impossible for us by the roundabout path of the impression we have of the person who has been made to laugh" (155–56). Laughter is contagious.

After his consideration of the purposes of jokes, Freud inquires into the sources of pleasure they provide. These are twofold: the pleasure afforded by the techniques of the joke employed in the joke envelope, and the pleasure that results from the inhibited thought expressed in the joke. Innocent jokes are pleasurable solely for their techniques (Freud 1960, 8:118). Tendentious jokes are doubly pleasurable: for their technique and for the inhibited thoughts they express. The pleasure of the tendentious joke results from an economy in the energy that is expended in the inhibition of the sexual or aggressive thought that is revealed in the joke. The joke, through its techniques, circumvents that inhibition and brings the thought to mind.[7] The energy that had been involved in maintaining the inhibition thereby becomes superfluous and is experienced as pleasure and ultimately released in laughter (119, 147–48). Furthermore, the pleasure of a tendentious joke is greater when an *internal* inhibition is overcome, such as the inhibition against the naming of sexual parts and functions, rather than an external one, such as the inhibition against exacting revenge on a royal personage for a received insult (118).

The argument for the pleasure underlying the innocent joke is a little more subtle since it would appear that there is no obvious inhibited thought that is overcome and consequently no psychical energy to be made superfluous. Freud, however, maintains that any joke, by virtue of its technique, links words and ideas together in nonsensical sequences that are inhibited by "serious thought" (Freud 1960, 8:120). But because these joke techniques still result in something that makes *some* kind of sense, the thoughts they contain become permissible and are protected from criticism. This again results in an economy of psychical expenditure, as the inhibition against nonsense is bypassed and the energy dedicated to the strict maintenance of sense is liberated. Such economies engender pleasure in even the most innocent of jokes (127–30).[8]

A joke thus promotes a thought and guards it against criticism. Consequently, the joke envelope is a formation of considerable power. When brought into association with a hostile purpose, as in a tendentious joke, it bribes the listener with a yield of pleasure and turns that person into a co-conspirator in the aggression. Suppose a person wants to insult someone but feelings of propriety stand in opposition to this wish. A change in the person's mood might produce an insult, but that would result in unpleasure because of the violation of social conventions. But a joke constructed from the words and thoughts of the insult might not meet with the same resistance as a direct insult. The joke makes the insult possible but the pleasure that results is a product of the pleasure produced by the joke technique (Freud calls this the fore-pleasure [1960, 8:137]) and the additional pleasure of the inhibited aggression (136). In some sense, a tendentious joke, with its technical and aggressive components, is somewhat like a nuclear bomb. A chemical explosion is needed to bring the fissile material to critical mass to trigger the much greater nuclear denotation. People who laugh at a tendentious joke do not strictly know what they are laughing at—the chemical or the nuclear reaction (102, 132).

Nevertheless, it certainly doesn't require much reflection to discern that the kinds of thoughts underlying the jokes that Freud is talking about are well within ordinary awareness. In another of Felix Unger's witticisms, the aggression is again clear enough. In remarking on the author of a series of essays in the Vienna newspaper about the relations of Napoleon with Austria, Unger said, "Is that not the *roter Fadian* that runs through the story of the Napoleonids?" (Freud 1960, 8:22–24). *Roter* means "red" and *Faden* means "thread," so the entire phrase suggests a scarlet thread or theme that runs through the newspaper articles and ties them together. But the author of these pieces was known to have red hair, and *Fadian* means "dull person," so the criticism of both the essays and the author were transparent. The joke conveyed that these were mind-numbing essays produced by an uninspired (and red-haired) author. Unlike a dream, this joke formation is in no way impenetrable. Its message could have been deciphered with relative ease by almost any literate person in Vienna at that time. If the thoughts underlying jokes are accessible to anyone with the requisite social, cultural, and linguistic knowledge, what exactly are the relations of jokes to the unconscious in Freud's theory? Are jokes really like dreams or are they fundamentally different?

The formation of a dream depends on residue from the day's thoughts and activities being dragged into the unconscious and conjoined with an unconscious wish. This material is transformed by means of the dream-work and represented,

TABLE 1.1. Comparing dreams and jokes

	Dream	Joke
Source	Unconscious wish	Preconscious thought
Inhibition	Repression	Suppression
Mechanism	Dream-work	Joke-work
Format	Images	Words
Message	Unintelligible	Intelligible
Context	Asocial	Social
Personnel	One person	Three people
Outcome	Prevent unpleasure	Produce pleasure
Purpose	Preserve sleep	Preserve civility

for the most part, in images. Censorship will not permit the conscious mind to become aware of the unconscious wish except as an unrecognizable formation produced by the dream-work. That unrecognizable formation is what we remember of our dreams. It is what Freud calls the dream's "manifest content"—which we know as an absurd collage lacking logic; coherence; wholly familiar characters, activities, and settings; or meaning (1960, 8:61).

Jokes, as we have seen, make use of the joke-work, which employs mechanisms that parallel those of the dream-work. But in the case of jokes, a *conscious* or *preconscious* thought is dragged into the unconscious and transformed and then released back into consciousness. The techniques of the dream-work and the joke-work are the transformational rules of unconscious thought. The thought that is transformed in the unconscious by the joke-work is not an unconscious one, and it is fully recoverable after its transformation has been effected. In this respect, a joke is *unlike* a dream. A dream remains unintelligible without arduous analysis. "It is a completely asocial mental product" that has nothing to communicate to the dreamer, nor to anyone else. The joke, however, is the most social of all the pleasure-producing mental functions and has a requisite "condition of intelligibility." According to Freud, "A dream is a wish that has been made unrecognizable; a joke is developed play" (1960, 8:179). The comparison between jokes and dreams is summarized in table 1.1.

The real similarity between dreams and jokes lies only in the strong analogy between the dream-work and the joke-work. It was this analogy that brought Freud to his interest in and understanding of jokes. The analogy does not lie only in the similarity of their technical methods, however, but in the fact that a thought is dragged into the unconscious and undergoes *unconscious revision* in both cases. The dream-work and the joke-work are, in a sense, the *grammar* of the unconscious responsible for the creation of both dreams and jokes. In almost every other respect, however, dreams and jokes differ substantially. Jokes originate in the preconscious. The preconscious is not the unconscious. The preconscious consists of knowledge, memories, and habits of thought that are outside immediate awareness but accessible to consciousness (Laplanche and Pontalis 1973, 325–27); it is what today would be called by psychologists "long-term memory" (Hurley, Dennett, and Adams 2011, 105). The dream thought is repressed; the joke thought is suppressed. The dream is mainly constructed in images (a result of regression) and the joke in words. The dream is unintelligible without protracted psychological analysis; the joke's thought is seized upon in an instant. The dream is a solitary production and, for the most part, uncommunicable; it begins and ends with the dreamer. The joke, however, demands communication and thrives in social interaction. Ultimately, the dream serves to prevent the arousing of unpleasure in an effort to maintain sleep; the joke is dedicated to the production of pleasure in the effort to preserve civilized life.[9]

I think the notion that jokes serve as a "safety valve" (Dundes 1987, 44; Morreall 1987, 111) that allows for the reduction of "tension" (e.g., Wilson 1979, 95; Haig 1988, 23; L. Rappaport 2005, 19) created by impulses that well up from the unconscious is off base. Freud's theory of jokes is not really a "release" or "relief" theory. Of course, any theory that ties humor to laughter will to some extent involve release since energy is, in fact, released in laughter. But to show that energy is released in laughter does not imply a release theory unless that release is the *point* of the humor and not merely a consequence of it.

People have a full set of means at their disposal for the expression of unconscious sexual and aggressive thoughts. There are identifications with characters and actions in literature, film, or sport. There are the numerous waking fantasies to which we all, at times, give ourselves over, as well as regular nighttime dreams. There is even the possibility of outright assault. With jokes, however, the matter is different. It may be true that the ultimate source of our sexual and aggressive impulses is the unconscious. Certainly, any expression of sex or aggression is linked to the unconscious in the sense that it draws energy from it (Freud 1960, 8:101), although individuals might not recognize that their lust and rage are—from Freud's perspective—connected to the lust and rage they felt as infants and originally directed toward their parents. As Freud says, "Nothing that takes form in the mind can ultimately keep away" from the impulses sequestered in the unconscious (133). But jokes—unlike dreams and slips of the tongue—are largely recognized for what they are. They are not simply the result of unconscious forces seeking release and relief. When people produce a hostile joke, they usually know quite well what they are doing.

The energy that is released in a joke that creates pleasure and engenders laughter, according to Freud, is *not* the energy of an unconscious impulse. Rather, it is energy that has been devoted to the inhibition of such forms of expression in the task of maintaining a well-ordered society (Freud 1960, 8:118).[10] These forms of inhibition, of course, are well known to us: do not murder, do not assault, do not blaspheme, do not spout profanities, be sexually modest, be polite. Indeed, in civilized societies these inhibitions are often codified in law, and they are explicitly taught and absorbed in the course of a moral education from early childhood. So the energy that produces the pleasure in jokes, according to Freud, is that energy that is mobilized and stands in a *constant state of vigilance* against certain forms of behavior and expression. The source of pleasure is *not* energy that is escaping from the unconscious, although the unconscious may be implicated in some ultimate sense, as it is with everything we think, say, and do. The unconscious impulses are a constant. Joke telling is situational.[11]

A hostile intention precedes the making of a joke, and that intention is recognized for what it is. The person who responds to an insult from a royal person is fully aware of the anger he has been made to feel and his desire for revenge. These thoughts are not repressed. They are formed in the conscious mind. What the joke makes possible is not the expression of a hostile thought but the expression of a hostile thought that would be criticized or otherwise penalized if expressed *openly*. A joke deals with a thought that is *conscious* and is seeking a *socially acceptable* means of expression. Both smut and the obscene joke are perfectly conscious expressions. Both the smutty talker and joke maker know perfectly well what they are doing. An obscene joke, however, can find a path into upright society in a way that smut cannot (Freud 1960, 8:99–100). In sum, the joke emerges not as a manifestation of unconscious forces seeking release but as a literary construction that authorizes the communication of conscious, though prohibited, thoughts in public settings. When viewed in this light, Freud's theory does not appear as a theory of release and relief at all. More than anything else, it deserves, I believe, to be regarded as a *rhetorical theory* of the joke. Freud almost says as much: "Where argument tries to draw the hearer's criticism over on to its side, the joke endeavors to push the criticism out of sight. There is no doubt that the joke has chosen the method which is psychologically more effective" (133).

The first three-quarters of *Jokes and Their Relation to the Unconscious* is devoted to an analysis of jokes and the formulation of a theory. In the last quarter, Freud extends his discussion to the comic and humor. The category *humor* might be thought to include wit, jest, and the comic. These terms, however, do not map directly onto German terminology, especially the terminology in the nineteenth and early twentieth centuries. There was a difference between wit and jokes [*Witz*] on the one hand and humor [*Humor*] on the other. Wit and jokes could be caustic and mocking and emanate from a sense of superiority. True humor, however, is based on a sense of kinship with all of humanity (Richter 1973, 88, 91). Humor is noble in a way that witticisms, the comic, and jokes are not.[12]

Freud's dissertation on jokes is relatively clear. His foray into the comic is difficult, dense, and full of expressions of uncertainty about the classification of the materials as well as about his observations and analyses (e.g., Freud 1960, 8:181, 211, 212, 214, 227). The intention here, however, is not to completely unravel Freud's sense of the comic. It is only necessary to grasp his basic approach in order to amplify and clarify his theory of jokes and the source of their pleasure.

The comic, unlike jokes, is found rather than made. And it is found primarily in the words and actions of human beings. It is found in animals and things only by extension (Freud 1960, 8:181). If jokes require three people (the joke maker, the object or target of the joke, and the person to whom the joke is directed), the comic requires only two: the person who engages in the comic action or expression and the person who observes it. The first type of comic action that Freud explores is naïveté. Unlike the joke maker, the naïve person does not overcome an inhibition. The naïve person is simply unaware of the inhibition; for him it does not exist. Naïve action or expression occurs regularly in children and uneducated adults (182). There may be a similarity between naïve speech and jokes in terms of their wording and content, but the psychological mechanisms are different. No pleasure is obtained by the naïve person from his naïve expression. The techniques that are employed to overcome inhibition in jokes are completely absent. The naïve person can produce nonsense or smut because there is no internal resistance impeding their production (185). Simply fulfilling an unconscious impulse does not produce laughter. It is only in the overcoming of an inhibition that utterances and actions become funny.

When a person sees or hears someone do or say something naïve, it affects him as a joke would. The inhibition, which *does* exist for the observer, is lifted simply through the act of seeing or listening. The psychical energy devoted to maintaining the inhibition becomes superfluous and produces pleasure and is discharged in laughter. The only difference in the response to the naïve as opposed to the response to a joke is that the second person—the observer—must understand that the inhibition does not exist in the first person. In the absence of that understanding, the second person might respond with indignation rather than with pleasure and laughter. Thus a certain degree of empathy is necessary in grasping the comic aspect of the naïve. The first person's state of mind must be taken into account (Freud 1960, 8:186).

The comic of action, as in the exaggerated actions of a clown, is also discussed by Freud. He argues that a person encountering an exaggerated action automatically compares it to the action the observer would have made in achieving the same end. Even grotesque facial features and bodily postures are evaluated in terms of the effort necessary to re-create these grimaces and bearings. Freud posits an *ideational mimetics,* that is, the notion that ideas have neuromuscular consequences. They give rise to innervations of the muscles that anticipate a genuine movement that is never, in fact, realized. When one witnesses an exaggerated movement, one puts oneself in the place of that person making the movement and has an inclination to make the same movement. When the observer suddenly perceives that the expenditure of energy to make that movement is unnecessary, the energy that has been mobilized to make it becomes superfluous and is free to be discharged in laughter (Freud 1960, 8:190–94). The same might be said of mental characteristics. Mental characteristics become comic when a person has expended too little energy in confronting a problem or situation. The difference between what one would expend oneself on the problem and what one expends in empathizing with the first person's insufficient effort becomes available for discharge in laughter. Freud goes on to discuss other types of comedy: the comedy of situation, caricature, parody, travesty (following Lipps [1922]), but it is unnecessary to examine these here. What is critical is grasping Freud's understanding of the comic as an exercise in relative expenditures of psychical energy: "The source of comic pleasure [is always] . . . a comparison between two expenditures both of which must be ascribed to the preconscious" (Freud 1960, 8:208).

At the very end of his book, Freud turns to the matter of humor. He reiterates that distressing emotions can interfere with the comic as well as with jokes. Humor, however, occurs when there is an inclination to release a distressing emotion, but the emotion is dismissed at the moment of its being produced (Freud 1960, 8:228). There is the story, for example, of the criminal led out to his execution on a Monday who comments, "Well, this week's beginning nicely." The fate of the man might well arouse pity, but this pity is immediately extinguished when it is recognized that the man himself dismisses his situation as inconsequential rather than being overcome by it. As Freud remarks: "There is something like magnanimity . . . in the man's tenacious hold upon his customary self and his disregard of what might overthrow that self and drive it to despair" (229). It is the emotion that is at first aroused, but which finds itself misplaced, that produces both pleasure and laughter (229–30). The various types of humor depend upon the particular emotion that is made superfluous: pity, anger, pain, tenderness, and so on, and these types are constantly being extended (231–32). Unlike the comic, humor can remain a solo affair and can occur entirely within a single person. The presence or participation of another person is not necessary and would add nothing to it. And the pleasure an observer might derive from that person's situation would be comic rather than humorous pleasure (229).

We are now in a position to understand the formula that Freud presents at the conclusion of *Jokes and Their Relation to the Unconscious*: the pleasure in jokes arises from an economy of expenditure upon inhibition, the pleasure in the comic from an economy of expenditure upon ideation (the psychical energy invested in ideas), and the pleasure in humor from an economy of expenditure upon feeling (Freud 1960, 8:236). Jokes, the comic, and humor are about *savings* in the expenditure of energy; and they are distinguished from one another in terms of the sources of the energy that is saved. Whether one finds Freud's formula illuminating, useful, or convincing is another matter entirely. But it should be clear that Freud's thesis is not fundamentally about the release of forces welling up in the unconscious. The proposition "that humor can serve to reduce aggressive (and sexual) drives is the most widely tested hypothesis in the field of humor research" may be true, but it is not true that this proposition is "one of the central themes of Freud's theory" (Goldstein, Suls, and Anthony 1972, 161). Jokes, the comic, and humor are not analogues of dreams, slips of the tongue, or hysterical symptoms. Jokes, the comic, and humor all have their origins in the preconscious; dreams, slips of the tongue, and symptoms originate in the unconscious.

I do not believe that this exposition of Freud's theory of jokes is based on a particularly nuanced reading of Freud. I think, in fact, it is rather straightforward, although it has been necessary to skip over or simplify a number of issues. Nor would I claim that Freud could *never* see a joke as successfully camouflaging an unconscious thought.[13] This discussion, it should be noted, is put forward neither as a defense of Freud's propositions nor as a critique of them. I am not a champion of Freud's theory of jokes (Oring 1992, 16–28; 2003, 27–40, 41–57), although I admire the comprehensive scope of his inquiry, the boldness of his thought, the originality of his ideas, and the perspicacity of some of his observations and guesses. I do think, however, that the central idea informing Freud's theory has largely been misread. The thrust of Freud's theory seems clear. One need only examine the corpus of examples that Freud employs to realize that nothing about jokes is truly unconscious except for the *means* by which a joker converts a thought into the form of a joke. That is the fundamental relation of jokes to the unconscious featured in the title of Freud's famous book.

CHAPTER TWO

Parsing the Joke

The General Theory of Verbal Humor and Appropriate Incongruity

In baiting a mousetrap with cheese, always leave room for the mouse.
—SAKI

Thirty years have passed since the publication of Victor Raskin's *Semantic Mechanisms of Humor* in which he proposed his Semantic Script Theory of Humor (SSTH). The "Main Hypothesis" of this theory was:

> A text can be characterized as a single-joke-carrying text if:
> (a) The text is compatible fully or in part, with two different scripts;
> (b) The two-scripts with which the text is compatible are opposite. (V. Raskin 1985b, 99)

In addition to the notion of compatibly opposite scripts, jokes effect a switch from one script to another by means of a trigger or mechanism (114).

Raskin took some pains to distance his theory of humor from formulations that were generally termed "incongruity theories" (V. Raskin 1985a, 39; Attardo and Raskin 1991, 331)—that is, from the likes of Arthur Koestler's *bisociation* theory: "perceiving of a situation or idea . . . in two self-consistent but habitually incompatible frames of reference" (Koestler 1964, 35); from Jerry Suls's *incongruity-resolution* theory: the generation of an incongruity and the "finding of a satisfactory resolution" of that incongruity (Suls 1976, 41); and from my own *appropriate incongruity* formulation: "the perception of an appropriate interrelationship of elements from domains that are generally regarded as incongruous" (Oring 1992, 2).

I always regarded SSTH as a variant of incongruity theory, more specifically of those incongruity theories that emphasize both a notion of incongruity and a linkage between those incongruous categories. Certainly, it would seem that script oppositeness is an analogue of incongruity and compatibility is an analogue of appropriateness. Salvatore Attardo would later come to the same conclusion (Attardo 1997, 395).

GTVH AND KNOWLEDGE RESOURCES

In 1991, Attardo and Raskin revised Semantic Script Theory into the General Theory of Verbal Humor (GTVH). While GTVH retained the notion of oppositions and compatible scripts from SSTH, and something of the notion of the trigger, what distinguished GTVH from SSTH was its hierarchical "model of joke representation" in terms of six "Knowledge Resources informing the joke" (KRs). The six Knowledge Resources are: Language (LA), Narrative Strategy (NS), Target (TA), Situation (SI), Logical Mechanism (LM), and Script Opposition (SO).

These Knowledge Resources can be illustrated by examining variants of the same joke. Below is the anchor joke. Six variants of the joke follow, jokes that differ, supposedly, from the anchor by one of the six Knowledge Resources.[1]

Joke 1 (anchor): How many Poles does it take to screw in a light bulb?
Five. One to hold the light bulb and four to turn the table he's standing on.

The first variant of the anchor differs in Language (LA) alone. It is a paraphrase of the anchor joke and varies in terms of word choice, syntactic construction, and other features that appear in the surface of the text. This LA variant does not begin with the "How many" of the anchor joke and replaces "Poles" in the anchor joke with "Polacks." Hence joke 2: "The number of Polacks needed to screw in a light bulb? Five—one to hold the bulb and four to turn the table he's standing on."

If a joke varies from the anchor joke in Narrative Strategy (NS), the form of the joke differs. It might be cast as a one-liner, a poem, a proverb, a plotted narrative, or some other genre. Since the anchor is in riddle form, the variant is in a different form. Joke 3: "It takes five Poles to screw in a light bulb: one to hold the light bulb and four to turn the table he's standing on." There is no question and answer. It is expository.

A joke varies from the anchor joke in terms of its Target (TA) if it is directed at some stereotyped individual or group. Thus, Poles are known to be stupid in American jokelore. A group that was stereotypically regarded as smart or greedy would not serve as well in a variant of the anchor joke, but another group that

TABLE 2.1. Knowledge resource values in jokes 1–7

	LA	NS	TA	SI	LM	SO
(1) Anchor	LA 1	riddle	Poles	light bulb	figure/ground	stupidity
(2)	LA 2	riddle	Poles	light bulb	figure/ground	stupidity
(3)	LA 1	expository	Poles	light bulb	figure/ground	stupidity
(4)	LA 1	riddle	Irish	light bulb	figure/ground	stupidity
(5)	LA 1	riddle	Poles	car wash	figure/ground	stupidity
(6)	LA 1	riddle	Poles	light bulb	false analogy	stupidity
(7)	LA 1	riddle	Poles	light bulb	figure/ground	dirtiness

Source: Attardo and Raskin 1991, 322.

is also associated with stupidity might serve as a substitute for the Poles. Joke 4: "How many Irishmen does it take to screw in a light bulb? Five. One to hold the light bulb and four to turn the table he's standing on." Irishmen are stereotypically stupid in British jokelore and they once held, and to some degree retain, a similar place in American jokelore. TA is the only optional Knowledge Resource, according to GTVH. Not every joke will have a TA.

If a joke varies from the anchor joke in terms of Situation (SI), the characters, actions, and objects described are different, although the Logical Mechanism remains the same. Hence joke 5: "How many Poles does it take to wash a car? Two. One to hold the sponge and one to move the car back and forth." Instead of light bulbs and tables, the variant deals with washing a car.

If a joke varies in terms of its Logical Mechanism (LM), the means employed to create the script compatibility is different. In the anchor joke the LM is characterized as "figure-ground reversal." What is supposed to remain stationary is moved and what is moved is supposed to remain more or less stationary. The variant, therefore, cannot allude to a figure-ground reversal. Joke 6: "How many Poles does it take to screw in a light bulb? Five. One to hold the light bulb and four to look for the right screwdriver."

If a joke varies in terms of its Script Opposition (SO), it means that the opposition of the variant is different from that of the anchor joke. Since GTVH identifies the Script Opposition of the anchor joke as "dumbness"—that the Pole is too stupid to know how to do something correctly—the Script Opposition in the variant cannot be about stupidity. The variant, consequently, is constructed around dirtiness, another regular attribute of Poles in American jokelore. Joke 7: "How many Poles does it take to screw in a light bulb? Five. One to take his shoes off, get on the table, and screw in the light bulb, and four to wave the air deodorants to kill his foot odor." The anchor and the six variants were summarized by Attardo and Raskin and are represented in table 2.1.

GTVH makes several claims about the Knowledge Resources of jokes: (1) the KRs identify the relevant components of the joke (Attardo and Raskin 1991, 328); (2) the KRs can be hierarchically ordered so that SO→LM→SI→TA→NS→LA represents the order of these KRs in terms of their degree of abstraction (321); (3) jokes will be regarded as more similar when they share lower-level KRs, and they will be considered less similar when they share only higher-level ones; (4) the selection of a higher-order KR is more likely to influence available choices of a lower-level KR than vice versa; (5) the order of the KRs is a model of joke generation in a logical, linguistic sense but is *not* a representation of the stages of joke production—it follows a meaning to sound scheme that is characteristic of linguistic representations of ordinary language (310, 314, 324–27).

John Morreall has challenged the hierarchical aspect of GTVH, suggesting that its similarity to transformational-generative grammars of language is deficient because it does not provide algorithms that generate jokes and only jokes. Consequently, it is an abstraction without much explanatory power (in Attardo and Raskin 1991, 339–40). Attardo and Raskin responded to this criticism by stating that their model has many of the virtues of the generative paradigm with few of the vices. GTVH was not a psychological theory and had no interest in or applicability to joke creation. The theory was only supposed to be "*the general basis, format, and template for analysis*" of jokes (341).[2]

My questions about GTVH, consequently, are less about its theoretical status than its ability to serve as a template for analysis. I will start with the simplest question: how well do the Knowledge Resources capture the essential components of the joke? Certainly, Language (LA) is present in every oral or printed instantiation of a verbal joke. While GTVH is largely focused on printed texts, it would not be too much of an extension to include relevant paralinguistic features of oral texts. In addition, jokes—particularly canned jokes—are stylized kinds of communications. It is surprising that as a linguistic theory, GTVH has not inspired much research into the characteristics of joke language. Narrative Strategy (NS) also seems unobjectionable as an aspect of jokes—even if the term *narrative* is unfortunate—but GTVH has not inspired much close work on the various joke genres. Even if we may speak easily about riddle jokes, one-liners, Wellerisms, narrative jokes, and Shaggy Dog Stories, the attempt to enumerate and define the properties of these genres has yet to be undertaken. Again, this is a problem that seems particularly open to linguistic analysis and yet remains largely unexplored. The definition of the various narrative strategies should not be left to Evan Esar (1952), although his catalogue might serve as a starting point for such a classification of genres.

When it comes to the Knowledge Resource of Target (TA), the issue is more complicated. GTVH acknowledges that not all jokes have Targets. Indeed, TA is a component of jokes that is rooted in sociological rather than linguistic knowl-edge. Many jokes—but not all—have characters, but not every character is a Target. GTVH employs the word *stereotype* to characterize what turns a joke character into a Target.[3] For example, in the joke about the number of Poles it takes to screw in a light bulb, the Pole is a Target because in American jokes there is a preexisting notion that Poles are stupid. Still, the notion of Target is not well defined. It cannot simply refer to stereotypical characters that appear in jokes because such characters could appear in jokes contrary to stereotype. For exam-ple, one could tell a joke about a Polish character who behaves cleverly. A joke might easily be recognizable as such despite the fact that the character was not behaving according to type.[4] Conversely, an American might, for example, tell a joke about a Croatian whose behavior appears stupid. This joke might be rec-ognized as a joke even if there were no previous stereotypes of Croatians for the joking parties.[5] Would the Croatian, in the absence of an established stereotype, be a Target or just a character?

Attardo (2001, 23–24) revised the concept of Target as the "butt" of the joke, suggesting that a joke in which there is no aggression has no Target. But what of jokes that employ a stereotype that might easily be regarded as positive—for example, Frenchmen as sophisticated lovers. Would Frenchmen be Targets? If Targets are restricted to stereotypes, they would be; but if a Target is defined in terms of some previous negative attitude toward the character or some negative behavior directed toward the character within the joke itself, they would not be. This raises the question of whether an animal can be a Target. If something nega-tive happens to an elephant in a joke, does the elephant become a Target? Attardo wants to exclude the possibility of nonhuman Targets (24). But the question is not an idle one, and the concept of Target has to be delineated more precisely if it is to be regarded as a component of jokes—even if it is considered to be only an optional one.

One would think that all jokes involve Situation (SI). Jokes must be "about something": activities, "participants, objects, instruments" (Attardo and Raskin 1991, 303). Of course, some jokes lack all of those things. As Attardo points out, the joke "Can you write shorthand? Yes, but it takes me longer" presupposes a writing shorthand situation that is, however, left entirely in the background (Attardo 2001, 34). "*Traduttore—Traditore!* [Translator—Traitor!]" (Freud 1960, 8:34) is perhaps even sparer when it comes to what Attardo and Raskin (1991, 303) call the "props" of the joke. One may be able to say what these jokes are about—shorthand or translation—but they include no characters, activities, or objects at all. The word *situation* itself suggests a place, a topos; and for fictive genres, such places are usually inhabited. If these jokes cannot be characterized in terms of

Situation, they can be characterized in terms of *topic*. All jokes have topics, but it does not seem as though all jokes have Situations. Perhaps SI, like TA, should also be considered an optional component of the joke.

In the first formulation of GTVH, the Logical Mechanism was illustrated rather than defined. Attardo and Raskin describe the LM of joke 1, the anchor joke, as "figure-ground reversal," with the ground initially identified as static and the figure as active (Attardo and Raskin 1991, 303–7). What winds up being static and dynamic in the joke is the reverse of expectations—it is the table that turns rather than the wrist of the person holding the bulb. The LM would seem to be the means—using GTVH terminology—by which an opposition is made compatible (Attardo 2001, 25). The means to screw in the light bulb is hardly an efficient one, but the necessary rotation might, nevertheless, serve to accomplish the task. The LM is not logical, as Attardo and Raskin recognize, but pseudo-logical, paralogical, or otherwise spurious (Attardo and Raskin 1991, 307; Attardo 2001, 25; Oring 2003, 5–9). Logical Mechanisms were explored in some depth by Sigmund Freud—he called them the "techniques" of the joke—but his formulation of what they consisted of was quite different from those that were to emerge from GTVH (Freud 1960, 8:16–89).

I agree with Christie Davies on a number of important points about jokes, but I disagree with his statement that it is futile to attempt to identify and classify the LMs of jokes. He does not believe that general conclusions or testable hypotheses can be drawn from such a list. He wants GTVH to abandon the category of LM altogether because it does nothing for the theory (C. Davies 2004, 379). While I am entirely in favor of theory-driven hypotheses, I am equally in favor of generalizations that emerge from a close study of the materials themselves. Often, startling results emerge from naïve, nontheoretical questions while theory-driven ones flap and fail. At present we cannot know whether scrutiny of the means by which jokes create "compatible oppositions" or "appropriate incongruities" will lead to general conclusions or testable hypotheses. It is easy to demonstrate that different jokes can be formed in very similar ways. Can those ways be specified and enumerated? We need to understand as much as possible about how jokes do their work. Whether joke techniques can be reduced to a fixed number of clearly delineated principles is an open question.

I do share something of Davies's doubts about Logical Mechanisms, not so much because they are not logical but because they are not mechanisms. The means by which jokes are created are often embedded deeply in the joke. The compatibility of scripts often depends on an inference that is made from very specific formulations in the text or context. They are not mechanisms in the sense that they are distinct parts of the joke that can be easily identified or manipulated.[6]

A joke mechanism cannot be thought of as analogous to the balance wheel or mainspring of a watch. In this sense, I might identify with Davies's antipathy to the Logical Mechanisms in GTVH. But to the extent that I am interested to know as much as possible about how jokes work, I want the techniques of the joke to be specified as clearly as possible—with or without a theoretical impetus.[7]

There have been lists compiled of LMs (Paolillo 1998, 270–71; Attardo 2001, 27; Attardo, Hempelmann, and Di Maio 2002, 18), but the lists are far from complete and the mechanisms are not well defined. For example, one of the mechanisms is called "the garden path," and it is supposed to characterize those jokes that prime an initial sense of the material that is later revealed to be the wrong sense. Example: "Should a person stir his coffee with his right hand or his left hand? Neither. He should use a spoon" (Attardo and Raskin 1991, 306). But almost every joke might be characterized as "garden path" under this definition. Puns (unhelpfully termed *Cratylisms* in GTVH), which are regarded as a different mechanism, also establish a primary meaning for a word only to switch it to some less salient meaning. "'Pretty swell joint you have here,' the doctor said as he examined his patient's knee." The initial sense of *swell* meaning "good" and *joint* suggesting an "establishment" is replaced by "swollen"—and therefore "not good"—once we understand the statement is made by a doctor about a patient's knee joint and not about a bar or restaurant. Is this a pun or a garden path mechanism? The LM that has been termed "figure-ground reversal" in the Polish joke might be reconceived as "exaggerated inefficiency" (exaggeration being another mechanism in the LM catalogue). The "figure-ground" terminology is borrowed from Gestalt psychology and applies to such figures as the Rubin vase, which looks like human profiles when the black color is foregrounded and like a vase when the white color is foregrounded. I am not sure that this is the appropriate term for the mechanism of the Polish joke because in the illusion, what is perceived changes completely depending on what is considered to be foreground and background. This is not the case in the Polish joke. It is only the relation between expected movement and stasis that changes. The overall perception does not change. Attardo (2001, 27) subsumes figure-ground as a type of reversal, and this seems correct, but it might be better termed static-dynamic reversal. The objections I am raising to the conceptualization of LMs are not necessarily fatal to the enterprise of identifying, defining, and naming joke mechanisms. I believe, however, that the task remains to be done, and the current lists of LMs are premature. If the mechanisms of joking can be specified, it will prove a major triumph for humor studies.

Script Opposition (SO) is carried over into GTVH from SSTH and is characterized as the most abstract KR. According to the main hypothesis of GTVH, a text can be humorous only if it possesses a Script Opposition in which there is compatibility or overlap between the opposed scripts. How is that SO to be identified? Is there an unassailable method for identifying the relevant oppositions in jokes?

GTVH analyzes the anchor Polish joke (joke 1) as follows:

LA = text of joke
NS = riddle joke
TA = Poles
SI = light-bulb joke
LM = figure-ground
SO = dumbness, stupidity (Attardo and Raskin 1991, 322).

NS seems to be a riddle in that the joke is presented as a question and answer (if that is enough to define the riddle).[8] This analysis, however, seems problematic on several points. To reduce the SI of the joke to "light-bulb joke" reduces the characters, activities, and objects to only a single aspect of the Situation. We might regard screwing in a light bulb as the topic of the joke, but it hardly characterizes anything that comes after the question. The answer involves four men turning a table with one man standing upon it. Surely this is part of the Situation as well.

This is an important point because in Attardo and Raskin's analysis of the anchor joke and the six variants, there would appear to be *several* variants that differ from the anchor joke in terms of SI. Joke 6, for example, "How many Poles does it take to screw in a light bulb? Five, one to hold the light bulb and four to look for the right screwdriver," might be justifiably called a "light-bulb joke," but only to characterize the topic of the joke. As far as the Situation is concerned, it is different from the anchor joke about four men turning a table. In other words, this joke varies from the anchor joke not only in its LM, as Attardo and Raskin maintain, but in its SI as well. In fact, it differs in three KRs: it has a different LA, a different SI, and a different LM.[9]

Consider joke 7, which is supposed to vary from the anchor joke only in terms of SO: "How many Poles does it take to screw in a light bulb? Five. One to take his shoes off, get on the table, and screw in the light bulb, and four to wave the air deodorants to kill his foot odor." This joke also varies from the anchor joke, but on the basis of four KRs, not one. It varies in LA, SI, LM, and SO. That it varies in LA is obvious; that it varies in SI is also obvious because it concerns deodorants and the activity of waving; that it varies in LM should be obvious because it in no way depends on a figure-ground reversal; and it varies in the SO because it is made to evoke the idea of dirtiness rather than stupidity.

This is not a minor problem in categorization. Much depends on it. Attardo and Raskin have claimed that GTVH's hierarchy of KRs has to some extent been empirically verified. In an experiment published by Ruch, Attardo, and Raskin (1993), students were asked to rate the similarity of joke variants to an anchor joke. They employed three sets of seven jokes for their trials, one anchor joke and six variants in each set. They used the Polish jokes presented here, chicken jokes, and blonde jokes. The anchor joke for each set: "How many Poles does it take to screw in a light bulb? Five. One to hold the light bulb and four to turn the table he's standing on"; "Why did the chicken cross the road? It wanted to get to the other side"; and "What do you call it when a blonde dyes her hair brown? Artificial intelligence." Each of the variants in the sets purportedly varied from its anchor on the basis of a single KR alone. The hope was that students would find the jokes that varied by a single KR at the lower end of the hierarchy more similar to the anchor joke than jokes that varied from the anchor joke by a single KR at the upper end of the hierarchy. But again, the jokes in all the sets did not vary by a single KR from the anchor. The jokes that supposedly varied by only LM or SI or SO actually differed by more than one KR. There was also the added problem that Poles, blondes, and chickens were considered the TAs of the jokes. But as the chicken could not be considered a "stereotype" or the "butt" of the joke (Attardo and Raskin 1991, 301; Attardo 2001, 23), the chicken should not have been considered a TA at all, which further upset the parametric analysis of the experimental joke materials.[10]

So the experiment on GTVH was flawed from its beginning. The experimental methodology may have been fine, but the experimental materials were hopelessly compromised. My major concern, however, is not the experiment itself. My concern is that GTVH was not able to generate an accurate analysis of jokes, whether for an experimental purpose or not. If GTVH is a "template for analysis," as has been claimed (Attardo and Raskin 1991, 341), what kind of analysis does it offer?

GTVH AND APPROPRIATE INCONGRUITY

Let us return to the analysis of joke 1. As previously indicated, GTVH regards the basic SO in this joke as stupidity or, to put it in oppositional terms, stupidity versus intelligence (Attardo and Raskin 1991, 307). The LM Attardo and Raskin have termed "figure-ground reversal." Now, how does this opposition emerge from the joke? Presumably, the grossly inefficient behavior of the Poles physically turning the table causes a switch from an intelligent script that had been presumed to operate to a stupid script that has been revealed.[11] The Logical Mechanism is the figure-ground reversal, which is stupid on the one hand but is nevertheless workable since it could, at least theoretically, screw in the bulb. But is this the only way of parsing the joke?

How many Teamsters does it take to screw in a light bulb?

Five. One to hold the light bulb and four to turn the table he's standing on.

In this case we do not regard the behavior of the Teamsters as the result of stupidity. We are more likely to view it as a means to create more work so that more people can be employed at high salaries than are really necessary for the job. In other words, there may be no single interpretation for the activity in the joke. The reason we regard the Polish example as a stupidity joke is because Poles are regarded as stupid. Stupidity is in and of itself not an attribute of four men turning a table. Stupidity depends upon prior information about Polish attributes—a Polish script. The reason we do not regard the Teamsters as stupid is that we have access to a Teamster script.

We could create a number of variant jokes with different characters that would cause us to evaluate the reason for turning the table in a different way: for example, weight watchers turn the table to lose weight, weight lifters to build muscle, furniture movers to move furniture, Chinese eunuchs because the rituals of the emperor's court are excessively elaborate.[12] It is the inferences that are made about the joke characters (I would not call them "Targets") that "rationalize" the table-turning behavior. There is nothing that is inevitably stupid about it. Consequently, there is a challenge to the Knowledge Resource hierarchy that GTVH proposes since in GTVH terms, *it is not the SO that determines the TA, but the TA that determines the SO.* Parameters that are higher in the Knowledge Resource hierarchy do not "determine the parameters" below them as GTVH has maintained (Attardo 2001, 27).

Let us reconsider joke 1 from the perspective of appropriate incongruity. Recall that this perspective claims that all humor depends upon the perception of an incongruity that can nevertheless be seen as somehow appropriate. If these terms seem vague, it is because they need to capture what is going on in the joke without any precommitment to the categories of a formal theory. What can be perceived as incongruous in this joke? What can be perceived as appropriate? We should note that there is really more than one incongruity in the joke. The first is that the question presumes that it might be a different number for Poles than for other people. This is a minor incongruity that quickly collapses into the incongruity that follows. The number needed—five—is far in excess of the single person presumed to be sufficient for the task. When the description of the activities of that seemingly unnecessary number of people is given, the first incongruity is made appropriate. After all, the bizarre means of screwing in a light bulb might work in principle. What difference does it make to the accomplishment of the task whether the man's wrist turns or the man himself? This image of screwing in a light bulb with four men turning a table is actually humorous in the same way that a Rube Goldberg contraption, such as the "Self-Operating Napkin," is humorous.[13] In Goldberg's cartoons, simple tasks are accomplished by inordinately complicated devices. Yet the cartoons never explain why these devices were created. Certainly, they require much more effort than the direct performance of the task. With the Polish joke, however, the hearer is confronted with the second incongruity of why anyone should resort to such a convoluted method of light-bulb installation. What makes this incongruity appropriate is the idea that Poles are stupid and cannot grasp that a more direct method of screwing in a light bulb exists. Polish stupidity makes the extravagant procedure of light-bulb change appropriate.

What at first sight seemed to be a close analogy between the "compatibly opposed scripts" of GTVH and "appropriate incongruity" is not close at all when applied to the analysis of specific texts. From the perspective of appropriate incongruity, the Polish joke contains two incongruities and two levels of appropriateness. More important, stupidity is the means by which the final incongruity is made appropriate.

These are very different accounts of the joke. According to the appropriate incongruity analysis, stupidity makes appropriate or "resolves" the incongruity between the excessive behavior and what might be accomplished more directly.[14] It should be considered the equivalent of the LM in GTVH terms. It should not be considered the SO (Attardo 2001, 25). After all, the incongruous procedure employed is understood only when the stupidity script of the Poles is invoked. Appropriate incongruity regards the basic incongruity or opposition not as between smart and stupid but rather as between what might be called excessive and sufficient activity. Indeed, it is clear that excessive versus sufficient is relevant to a majority of light-bulb jokes (Attardo and Raskin 1991, 329).[15] Stupidity is relevant only to Polish and certain other (Italian, Irish) variants—but again, not as the basic opposition but as the means by which the incongruity between the excessive and the sufficient activity is made appropriate. How excess and sufficiency are reconciled in other light-bulb jokes—that is, the means by which appropriateness is achieved—depends upon attributes of the joke character (GTVH would call it the "Target"): in the Polish joke variant, excess depends upon stupidity; in the Teamster variant, on union labor practices; in the eunuch variant, on the elaborateness of imperial court ritual.[16]

Is there any way to decide between these two ways of parsing jokes? How might GTVH handle the following joke?

> Two Poles come out of a restaurant after eating dinner. One of them is bald. Just then a seagull flies overhead and defecates on the bald man's head. The friend is

upset and exclaims, "Oh, that's awful. Let me get some toilet paper." The bald Pole mutters, "Don't bother! He's probably a quarter of a mile away by now."

Although this joke employs a different Narrative Strategy—it is not a riddle but has a story line—GTVH would analyze this joke in the same way as the Polish light-bulb joke. It would regard the Script Opposition as stupidity versus intelligence. After all, why would the bald man think the toilet paper was for the bird rather than for himself? He is Polish; therefore he is stupid. But stupidity is not a basic aspect of the incongruity or the means of making that incongruity appropriate. Had the joke not identified the men as Polish but had merely described two men coming out of the restaurant, the joke would remain intact and work perfectly well. Listeners would be hard pressed to construct a motive for the man's focus on the bird's bottom rather than his own head, but that in no way destroys the joke. Does identifying the men as Polish improve the joke because it provides a motivation for his misunderstanding the intended purpose of the toilet paper? Perhaps, but that is not the issue. What is important is that the joke works perfectly without having to intuit a reason for the man's bizarre response (Oring 2003, 34–38).[17]

GTVH and the appropriate incongruity perspective would agree that many Polish jokes are about stupidity but would differ on what is meant by "about." The appropriate incongruity perspective would characterize stupidity as the *theme* of a great number of Polish jokes rather than the basic opposition underlying all of them. Stupidity is repeatedly invoked to make "sense" of a variety of incongruous behaviors.[18] It is not the basic opposition unless the joke is viewed from a very great distance. Even then, it is not the opposition that produces the joke.

How did the Polack break his arm raking leaves?
He fell out of the tree.

Again, GTVH would see the basic Script Opposition as stupidity versus intelligence. The appropriate incongruity perspective would see the incongruity between raking leaves in the tree versus raking leaves on the ground. As leaves can be found in both places, the activity of raking them is appropriate to both positions. That the man is Polish and stupid provides a rationale of why he should pursue the fruitless and more dangerous course, but this is an added factor. The joke would still exist if a generic man were substituted for the Pole. Again, we would not understand the motivation for the character's actions, and we might regard the joke as silly, but we would perceive and understand this as a joke.

While I believe that stupidity serves to make incongruities appropriate in the majority of Polish jokes, sometimes intelligence versus stupidity *is* the underlying opposition or incongruity.

What has an IQ of 500?
Poland.

Unlike the light-bulb and leaf-raking jokes, this joke presents the issue of intelligence explicitly—not merely intelligence, but inconceivably high intelligence. The highest IQs generally range in the mid- to high 100s. In the presumption that someone has an IQ of 500, there is already an incongruity between that number and the limits of real IQ. Even those who might not be familiar with IQ ranges would know that 500 was an extremely high number. The answer—Poland—is also incongruous. First of all, nations do not have IQs. At best, they could be said to have average IQs. It would be even more inconceivable, however, for a nation to have an average IQ of 500. Furthermore, as the nation with this extraordinary IQ is Poland, and Poles are typically regarded as stupid in jokelore, the incongruity is even more pronounced. If the incongruity is to be made appropriate, the number 500 cannot be regarded as an individual score or an average score. It must be regarded as a *sum*. Given that there are millions of Poles, the IQ of each would have to be inconceivably low to add up to 500. So here is a Polish joke in which intelligence and stupidity do constitute the basic incongruity or opposition in the joke. The mechanism by which this incongruity is made appropriate depends on the different ways a number may be composed: as an average or a sum. Composed in one way, it is associated with enormous intelligence; composed another way, it is associated with gross stupidity.

What accounts for this radical difference in conceptualization of the joke by GTVH and the appropriate incongruity perspective? Some of the problems of GTVH are inherited from SSTH.

Who was that gentleman I saw you with last night?
That was no gentlemen. That was a senator. (V. Raskin 1985b, 25)

Raskin suggested that the ambiguity in this joke is that "gentleman" can mean both a "man" and a "man of quality" and that the second speaker in the joke makes believe that the first was referring to a man of quality rather than to just a man. While the word *gentleman* can be used in both senses, this joke does not depend on this double meaning. The joke works just as well if the first speaker intended a man of quality rather than just a man, and it would be possible to load the first sentence to suggest that a man of quality was in fact intended. For example, "Who was that distinguished, finely dressed, well-mannered gentleman I saw you with last night? That was no gentleman. That was a senator." This form of the joke does not depend on the ambiguity of "gentleman" so much as it does on the ambiguity of "senator." A senator is supposedly a "man of quality" because of his election, station, privilege, and responsibilities. However, as the joke suggests, senators are not men of quality by virtue of their character. What appears on the surface is betrayed by what is underneath. Senators hold the status of gentleman but do not comport themselves as such.[19]

SSTH also suggested that jokes effect a switch from one script to another by means of a semantic switch-trigger. According to the theory, there were two basic types of triggers: *ambiguity* and *contradiction* (V. Raskin 1985b, 114). This characterization is not quite accurate. Contradictions do not so much trigger the switch from one script to another as they trigger the *search* for a connection to a second script.

"Is the doctor at home?" the patient asked in his bronchial whisper.

"No," the doctor's young and pretty wife whispered in reply. "Come right in." (100)

In this joke, the "contradiction"—the incongruity—is that the doctor's wife whispers her reply and invites the patient into the house although the doctor is absent. Why does she do so? The hearer is then invited to search for an alternative interpretation of the event that accommodates the wife's behavior given the circumstances. As Raskin has pointed out, a sexual script can be found that is compatible with the initial medical script: the doctor's wife is young and pretty, and whispering is appropriate to both illness and conspiracy. Thus, the patient's question can be reframed as a sexual solicitation with which the wife's reply is compatible (117–26). That is the ambiguity. Ambiguity is not really another type of trigger. It is simply a term that serves to label elements in a joke text that are open to an alternate interpretation. In the doctor's wife joke, the whisper allows for an alternate interpretation of the event. Thus, contradiction and ambiguity are not types of triggers. Contradiction is what signals that a search for a second interpretation is necessary. Ambiguity is the presence of an alternative interpretation of the joke material. This is a very general formulation of the joke, not the characterization of a specific mechanism. Contradiction and ambiguity are not types of triggers but stages in the switch from one script to another. They are the recognition that incongruities encountered in jokes are usually followed by a search for appropriateness. It is not surprising that this whole typology of switch-triggers was abandoned in the revision of SSTH to GTVH, but the failure to identify the problems in SSTH simply allowed such problems to be inherited by the later theory.

The biggest problem with SSTH that was fully adopted by GTVH is the notion of "opposition": a plus/minus kind of formalization characteristic of linguistic analysis. In SSTH, Raskin identified the Script Oppositions in thirty-two jokes. Most of these were not presented as true oppositions—for example, writer versus

postman, collision versus impression—although it was argued that their oppositional nature could be recognized if the scripts were "paraphrased" (V. Raskin
1985b, 107–8).[20] The opposition writer versus postman, for example, can be recast
as the opposition writer versus non-writer (or postman versus non-postman).
SSTH and GTVH further argue that most Script Oppositions in jokes evoke
"binary categories which are essential to human life," such as good versus bad, life
versus death, obscene versus non-obscene, money versus no money; high stature
versus low stature (114; Attardo 2001, 20). These life oppositions are categorized
under still more abstract oppositions: normal versus abnormal, actual versus
non-actual, possible versus impossible. These three higher-order oppositions are
themselves subcategories of an even higher-order opposition: real versus unreal
(V. Raskin 1985b, 107–14). This conceptualization of opposition is several degrees
removed from the *operation* of actual joke texts.

One can always find oppositions in fiction—not only in jokes (Lévi-Strauss
1955). That is part of the problem. Some oppositions will be irrelevant to the joke,
some will be relevant, and some will be fundamental; but even those that are fundamental may play very different roles. Consider a Soviet-era joke analyzed by
SSTH:

> Two dogs meet on the Polish-Czechoslovakian border in 1956. The Czech dog asks,
>   "What are you going to Czechoslovakia for?"
> "To eat a little. And why are you going to Poland?"
> "To bark a little." (V. Raskin 1985b, 47)

Little effort is required to recognize a number of oppositions in this joke: Poland
versus Czechoslovakia, north versus south, food versus freedom, eat versus bark,
bark versus complain, animal versus human. Some are irrelevant to the joke, such
as north versus south. Some are relevant but not fundamental, for example, animal
versus human. The hearer accepts that dogs behave like humans and communicate
in speech. That is part of the joke premise. Nevertheless, the idea of dogs behaving like humans contributes to the interpretation of "bark" later in the joke. The
Czechoslovakia and Poland opposition is subordinated to the opposition between
food and freedom, as it was understood by tellers and hearers that Czechoslovakia
had more material goods than Poland, but Poland offered a little more room for
anti-government expression. Raskin saw the basic opposition of the joke as barking versus complaining. When projected into the more abstract space of real versus unreal, the opposition became "a dog can bark versus a dog can complain"
(V. Raskin 1985b, 108, 110). Certainly, this is an opposition exceedingly relevant
to the joke, but it is not its basic opposition. As the joke unfolds, it is accepted
that a dog should go to Czechoslovakia—or anywhere—to eat if that is where

the food is. But there is an incongruity in the response of the dog who is heading to Poland to bark, because barking is what dogs do and should be able to do anywhere. This incongruity is made appropriate by the double meaning of "barking" as a short explosive animal cry and as a form of expression—here a complaint. This double meaning resolves the incongruity of why a dog must go somewhere to bark. The basic incongruity is not between barking and complaining but between a place-specific activity (eating) and a non-place-specific activity (barking). That barking can also be interpreted to mean complaining—an interpretation that is promoted by the fact that the dogs are acting and speaking like humans—makes the incongruity appropriate because barking in that second sense then becomes a place-specific activity as well. That the joke does not fundamentally depend upon the opposition between "barking" and "complaining" is evidenced by the fact that a joke would exist were it told about two *people* who met on the border with one going to Czechoslovakia to eat and the other going to Poland to complain.

TEXTS AND TEMPLATES

The attempt to impose an abstract template on a corpus of jokes may cloud the process of analysis. Once it is felt that one knows what parts a joke should have, the identification of these parts can become a rote procedure, with the jokes being plugged into pre-established categories. The analyst is insulated from the properties of the joke by the categories and terminology. What is analyzed is no longer the joke but the terminology and categories of the template into which the joke has been cast. Research that has come out of GTVH has employed logical and mathematical symbols, graphs, sets, matrices, and functions. There is nothing wrong with the attempt to employ such formal means of representation, but they are unlikely to be useful if the representations of the jokes they provide are erroneous to begin with. Furthermore, they are likely to mask the analyses of jokes for those unfamiliar with these tools and their applications. For many, they are not easily accessible and consequently do not invite close criticism.

What I find ironic is that if I, as a folklorist and anthropologist, were asked for an appraisal of what was going on in Polish jokes as a whole, I might answer that they are about intelligence versus stupidity and about dirtiness versus cleanliness. It would then be important to know the role these concepts played in the culture and how the jokes frame and comment on these categories. This would be basic to a cultural analysis of the jokes. These oppositions would bear on the potential *meanings* of the jokes to the people who tell and hear them (Oring 1981, 87–130). But were I asked how the jokes *operate*, how they work to produce humor, these oppositions would play a different role.

Understanding how a joke works depends upon scrutiny of the joke. It involves going *serially* through the joke, noting where incongruities arise and how they are made appropriate.[21] There are no preconceptions about the kinds of incongruities that will necessarily arise, where they will arise, or how appropriateness is established. GTVH theorists are linguists who should be concerned with how jokes emerge in the course of an unfolding written or oral text. They should be concerned with where an incongruity is registered and how its appropriateness is recognized. What is surprising is that my analysis of jokes seems closer to language than theirs, and their analysis seems closer to culture than mine. Despite their brevity, jokes can be incredibly complex affairs. They require close scrutiny and careful analysis. Their parts are not as distinct and identifiable as the parts of a simple machine. Abstract models of jokes are not in and of themselves the problem. They must, however, prove faithful to how a joke works to produce humor.

CHAPTER   THREE

Blending and Humor

Who in the rainbow can draw the line where the violet tint ends and the
orange tint begins? Distinctly we see the difference of the colors, but where
exactly does the one first blendingly enter into the other? So with sanity and
insanity.

—HERMAN MELVILLE

The Semantic Script Theory of Humor (SSTH), introduced in the last chapter,
received its first complete exposition in the penultimate decade of the twentieth
century (V. Raskin 1985b). By the time of its reformulation as the General Theory
of Verbal Humor (GTVH) six years later (Attardo and Raskin 1991), another linguistic approach to the analysis of humor had emerged. This theory emerged from
cognitive linguistics rather than script-based semantics and went under the name
of "Conceptual Integration Theory" or, more commonly, "Blending Theory."

Cognitive linguistics is concerned with the conceptual underpinnings of language behavior. From the point of view of cognitive linguists, language is not a
formal system of rules that a speaker need master in an effort to represent meaning in spoken or written messages (Fesmire 1994, 150). Cognitive linguistics is
concerned with a system of cognitive operations that are not peculiar to linguistic
organization alone. In fact, these operations are responsible for the creation of
"grammar, conceptualization, discourse, and thought itself" (Fauconnier 2003,
1:542; Brône, Feyaerts, and Veale 2006, 204). Cognitive linguistics holds language
to be *embodied*; which is to say that language is used by humans with particular
sorts of bodies and brains, who have specific goals, and use them in distinct physical and social situations (Bergen and Binsted 2015). Language employs models
and frames that are coordinated with encyclopedic information and demands
creative extrapolations between knowledge domains.

The cognitive operations underlying language behavior are usually unconscious, but they are easily demonstrable in even the most basic areas of language use. For example, the sentence "Hal loaded the hay into the wagon" can be refigured as "Hal loaded the wagon with hay." In the first sentence it is the content—the hay—that is focused upon in the object of the sentence, and in the second sentence it is the container—the wagon—that is focused upon. The switch between sentences that emphasize the content or the container can be performed with other verbs as well: "Jared sprayed water on the roses" and "Jared sprayed the roses with water." However, this alternation cannot be done with all verbs: "Amy poured water into the glass" cannot be turned into "Amy poured the glass with water." Whether the utterances are convertible into one another depends upon whether the verb can specify both the way content is moved and how the container has been changed as a result. *Load* is a word that suggests not only that something has been moved into something else but that what has been moved is appropriate to the container so that it can function appropriately. One can load a camera with film or a gun with bullets, but one cannot "load" a camera or gun with water or hay. "Load" also suggests that the container is transformed by the movement. A wagon loaded with hay is in a different state than a wagon with no hay or just a bale of hay in it. When the state of the container is regarded as changed, it can be expressed as the direct object: "loaded the wagon with hay." The reason that one does not say "poured the glass with water" is that the verb *pour* is indifferent to the state of the container. "Pour" says something about the motion of a liquid. Thus, one can say "poured water into the glass." But one can pour water anywhere and onto or into anything. The verb is unconcerned with where the liquid winds up—that is, with the state of the container. So the verb does not mesh with a construction that affects the state of the container. Thus, "poured the glass with water" does not compute. "Fill" has the opposite problem. It is a verb that is focused on the state of the container but is utterly indifferent to the means by which the change of state is brought about. So one can "fill the glass with water" but not "fill water into the glass" because "fill" specifies nothing about the motion of some content (Pinker 2007, 34–51).

Whether this example is fully grasped or not, it should nevertheless convey a sense of how form, space, motion, causation, and intention can affect the use of verbs as they are figured in sentences. Beneath the units of language and their elaboration in utterances lies a world—a hidden world—of perception and thought. Cognitive linguistics, in other words, is concerned with the conceptual underpinnings of language and not the formal properties of the linguistic system as such.

Cognitive linguistics is a broad field, and Blending Theory emerges from a concern with how language is used creatively and spontaneously in real-time expression and communication (Fauconnier 2001).[1] Basically, blending theorists hold that novelty in language—at all levels of language, from grammatical construc-tions to complex literary texts—results from the blending of elements from dif-ferent conceptual domains. It grows out of the discovery that metaphor, far from being a tangential and merely colorful aspect of language, lies at its very heart. Metaphors are pervasive in language and can be so basic, in fact, that they often are not even recognized. For example, ideas are *objects* ("I *gave* you that idea"); linguistic expressions are *containers* ("It's difficult to *put* my idea *into* words"); and communication is *sending* ("It's hard to get that idea *across* to him") (Lakoff and Johnson 1980, 10–11).

The discovery of the centrality and pervasiveness of metaphor in ordinary lan-guage led to Conceptual Metaphor Theory, the analysis of the ways metaphors work. Metaphors are employed to structure and extend understanding from one domain to another. If "Life is a journey," then life may be short or long, have many twists and turns, one can tarry or hurry along, one may come to crossroads where choices have to made, and so on. The domain being mapped, in this case "life," is called the *target* domain, and the domain doing the mapping, the "journey," is called the *source* domain. Not only are terms from the source mapped onto the target—for example, one may "stumble" in life—but the logic is as well. The two domains are said to share "inferential structure" (Coulson 2001, 163). As journeys have destinations and timetables, life should as well. Novel constructions may be easily formulated and understood (Grady, Oakley, and Coulson 1999, 103), such as knowing when in the course of life to "get out of the weather" or to "stop and smell the roses" along the way.

Conceptual Metaphor Theory was felt by some linguists to be limited, however. Metaphors are not a one-way street. It is not simply a matter of mapping of a source onto a target. In metaphors there is a mapping *between* domains. Metaphoric constructions often produce something that is not present in either the source or target domains—what is called *emergent structure* (Fauconnier 1997, 150–58; Fauconnier and Turner 1998, 138–42; Coulson 2001, 166). Such structures emerge through the *blending* of semantic domains.

An example frequently used by blending theorists to illustrate this idea is the metaphorical expression "The surgeon is a butcher." The expression is meant to suggest that the surgeon in question is incompetent (Grady, Oakley, and Coulson 1999, 103–6). How does this meaning arise from this metaphorical construction? Conceptual Metaphor Theory cannot explain it. There is nothing in the domain of butcher to suggest incompetence in performance; thus, the notion of incom-petence cannot result from simply mapping the domain of butcher onto surgeon. According to blending theorists, the idea of incompetence emerges from the blend of the two occupational domains of surgeon and butcher.

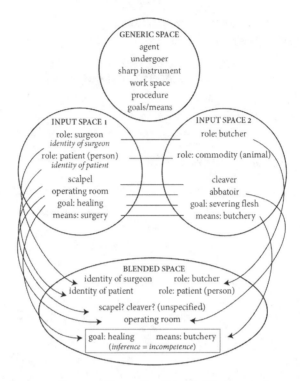

FIGURE 3.1. Conceptual Integration Network: "The Surgeon Is a Butcher" (after Grady, Oakley, and Coulson 1999, 105)

Figure 3.1 shows how blending accounts for the meaning of incompetence in the surgeon/butcher metaphor. Rather than a straightforward mapping from the domain of butchery onto the domain of surgery, as Conceptual Metaphor Theory would have it, Blending Theory makes use of the notion of *mental spaces*. These are subsets of knowledge domains that are used short term in specific transient situations (Fauconnier 1997, 11; Grady, Oakley, and Coulson 1999, 102).[2] Blending theorists analyze metaphor in terms of these mental spaces. In "The surgeon is a butcher," there are two *input spaces*: a *generic space* and a *blended space*. Input space 1 is related to the domain of surgeons and is filled with elements of role (the surgeon and patient), the specific identities that fill these roles (that is, the specific surgeon and patient), the tools of the surgeon's trade (scalpel), the venue of the work (operating room), the surgeon's goals (healing), and the means by which these goals are achieved (surgery). Input space 2 is related to the domain of butchers. It includes the role of the butcher, the role of the butcher's subject (an animal), the instruments (knives, cleavers), the venue of the work (abattoir), the butcher's goal (severing flesh), and the means by which this goal is achieved (butchery). Note that "The surgeon is a butcher" is likely to be uttered about a specific surgeon in relation to a specific patient. That is why the roles of the surgeon and patient in input space 1 in the diagram are filled by specific individuals. Input space 2 is not about a specific butcher so no identity need be specified. Similarly, the object of the butcher's activity is some generic animal, not some specific animal. While there is some resemblance between what is recruited from inputs spaces 1 and 2—what is called partial cross-space mapping (indicated by solid horizontal lines)—there is no exact correspondence between the elements of the input spaces. In fact, what is called the generic space—in the circle at the very top of the diagram—is what the two input spaces have in common: an agent, an undergoer (the object of the agent's activity), a sharp instrument, a work space, and a procedure that comprises both goals and means (103). The elements of the generic space are often of a higher degree of abstraction than the elements of the input spaces themselves (e.g., agent rather than the specific agents of surgeon or butcher).

The blended space is comprised of elements from the input spaces such that a new structure can emerge that is characteristic of neither input space. In the blend of "The surgeon is a butcher," the means and goals of the butcher are incompatible with the means and goals of the surgeon. The surgeon is meant to heal through the use of precise instruments whereas the butcher is meant to kill and rend the flesh of animals with relatively coarse instruments (such as a cleaver). The blend suggests that the particular goals of the surgeon are pursued with the means of a butcher. This leads to the inference that the surgeon is incompetent (Grady, Oakley, and Coulson 1999, 106), an inference made from the elements enclosed by the rectangle in the diagram of the blended space.

While it does seem possible to infer the meaning of incompetence from the blended space, the problem seems to be that other meanings might be inferred as well. For example, (1) the surgeon is brutal, (2) the surgeon is a murderer, (3) the surgeon specializes in amputation, (4) the surgeon works in unsterile environments, (5) the surgeon lacks compassion, (6) the surgeon looks at a human and sees only meat.[3] The problem is not that one cannot infer incompetence from the elements in the blend. The problem is how competing inferences are rejected or suppressed. Given that new structure may emerge in the blend, how does only a single inferential structure emerge?

The answer is that it does not. Context has a lot to do with how a statement like "The surgeon is a butcher" is interpreted. It cannot unequivocally be interpreted to mean the surgeon is incompetent although this may, over time, have developed as its prototypical or conventional meaning. If "The surgeon is a butcher" is uttered by a patient lying in a hospital in reference to a particularly hideous scar on her abdomen, the statement may be inferred to be a criticism directed at a surgeon who did not devote the necessary time and effort to minimize the mark on the patient's body. The surgeon was not so much incompetent as uncaring (Brandt and Brandt 2005, 219–24). Suppose, however, that someone meets a friend on the street whom she hasn't seen in some time and asks why her limp is so much worse than it was when they met six months before. The friend answers that her knee was operated on and the problem is now much worse than before. If she concludes her account with the statement "The surgeon is a butcher," the interpretation might well be that the surgeon is incompetent. This context would not support the hypothesis of an uncaring surgeon. There is no reason to suppose that the surgeon deliberately set out to reduce the functionality of the knee. Context would suppress such an interpretation in favor of the inference that the surgeon was not sufficiently skilled to perform the operation properly. Finally, suppose that one accompanies a friend to a surgeon's office and the surgeon begins outlining with a marking pen on the patient's body where the necessary cuts will have to be made during surgery. During this time, the surgeon is focused on the marking task without speaking to the patient at all. If the patient were to casually comment to the friend in the room, "The surgeon is a butcher," it would not suggest that the surgeon was incompetent or even uncaring, but that the surgeon was relating to the patient at that moment as to a piece of meat. The patient was perhaps likening the surgeon's drawing to the outlines of beef cuts in diagrams of cows that sometimes hang in butcher shops. The surgeon, on hearing the comment, might even apologize or laugh. But the message would not be the same as in the other scenarios.[4]

One seeming problem with blending analyses is that there is no account of the range of emergent structures that are possible within a blend and no articulation of the means by which some of these are highlighted or suppressed. Why should I not, for example, interpret the statement "That woman is a dog" to mean that she is playful, affectionate, loyal, and likes to be taken out, and why should I not interpret the statement "That woman is a fox" to mean that she is hairy, short-legged, mates only in winter, and likes chicken? Context would seem one obvious suppression mechanism. There might well be others: world knowledge, or the type or complexity of the inferences, or even the nature of the input spaces that are blended (Krikmann 2009, 20). Cognitive linguists are interested in "selection," the means by which focus is directed toward elements that are relevant in the interpretation of metaphor (Brône and Feyaerts 2003, 12–13). It is strange, however, that these concerns are ignored in the analysis of one of Blending Theory's most prominent and frequently cited examples (Glucksberg 1998, 42; Coulson 2001, 166; Kyratzis 2003, 4–6; Kövecses 2005, 267–70; Dore 2007).

My concern here is merely to show that the analysis of "The surgeon is a butcher" seems incomplete and post hoc. That is to say, one already knows what the metaphor means and one analyzes the input material to arrive at the prefigured destination.[5] But to my understanding, that is not what cognitive linguists say they want to do. Cognitive linguistics regards language as "ecologically situated," which is to say that language creation and comprehension depend upon the physical and social contexts of its use (Fesmire 1994, 153; Pollio 1996, 244; Fauconnier and Turner 1998, 157). They claim to want to understand how people manage to create blends that can fulfill their communicative intentions in real time. The question is not so much whether one can succeed in the retrospective analysis of a metaphor as succeed in a prospective analysis of one (Gibbs 2000, 349).[6] In truth, whether Blending Theory allows linguists to account for "online" creative speech is not really my concern. I am not a linguist (which should not be construed in the same way as Richard Nixon's statement "I am not a crook"), and their objectives are not necessarily mine. Blending analysis, however, seems to proceed without a precise method.

Of course, certain jokes and cartoons can be characterized in terms of blending. A blending analysis offered of figure 3.2 points to the fine-dining and barnyard-feeding input spaces. In the blend, the farmer cross-maps to a waiter, the pig a customer, the trough a table, and the swill fine restaurant fare. This analysis further suggests that the pig can speak in the cartoon because of background knowledge about the behavior of customers in restaurants. As customers can speak and summon waiters, so can the pig. The speaking pig, it is claimed, is part of the emergent structure of the blend (Coulson 2005a, 108–10).

While this cartoon clearly depends upon the intermingling of restaurant and barnyard domains, I don't think one can safely attribute the fact that the pig can speak to an emergent structure in the blend. In the cartoon, only the pig's speech establishes that a blend of restaurant and barnyard domains exists at all. Were the pig silent, no blend could be perceived. It seems perverse to regard the pig's speech as an emergent structure of the blend when that speech is what creates the blend in the first place. It takes a cause and turns it

"Garcon!"

FIGURE 3.2.

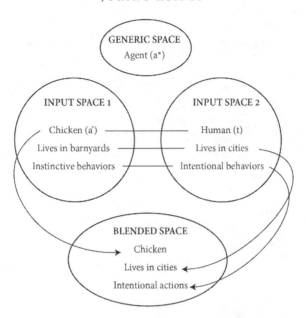

FIGURE 3.3.

into its own effect.[7] When animals speak in jokes and cartoons, there is a de facto blend between animal and human domains. This kind of blend in and of itself is not sufficient to produce humor, however. There are many texts—mythological texts, for example—that depend on a blend of inputs from human and animal domains that do not seem to be humorous in either intention or effect.

Consider another blending analysis made by a blending theorist of a classic children's joke.

Why did the chicken cross the road?
To get to the other side.

Seana Coulson, the cognitive linguist who analyzed this joke stated, "Chickens aren't found on streets and customarily are not construed as having directional intentions. The resolution, in the answer, is so obvious it's funny." Figure 3.3 shows the generic space in the joke simply as an agent. Input space 1 consists of chickens that live in barnyards and their instinctive behaviors. Input space 2 includes humans who live in cities and their intentional actions. The blend results in a chicken that lives in cities and has intentional actions. Coulson added, furthermore, that the humor of the joke disappears when it is reformulated so that the chicken is not framed as a person but is unambiguously a chicken. "Why did the chicken cross the barnyard? To get some scraps" is not funny at all (Coulson 2005b, 3; see also Kyratzis 2003, 6–7).

Unfortunately, this entire analysis is off base. In the first place, cities have nothing to do with any input space for this joke. The joke asks why the chicken crossed the *road*—not why it crossed Broadway, the Champs Elysée, or the Ringstrasse.[8] Roads run through rural landscapes and chickens can be found crossing them on a regular basis. Nor does human intentionality play much of a part in the construction of the joke. In fact, the counterexample "Why did the chicken cross the barnyard? To get some scraps" illustrates this quite clearly. Here specific intentions are attributed to a chicken. The chicken sensed food across the yard and went to get it. That was the chicken's intention. There is no anomaly in imputing intentions to chickens. Chickens do not move through space randomly (random movement would suggest a lack of intention), and when a chicken flies over a fence into a neighboring yard, one might reasonably presume that it intended to do so, although identifying its specific goal might prove elusive. In other words, we regularly accept the intentionality of chickens when the intention—the goal-seeking behavior—is described, such as scraps, sex, or safety. In fact, a joke would remain if a human agent were substituted for the chicken: "Why did the farmer cross the road? To get to the other side."

This classic joke depends upon the expectation that a "why" question about a particular effect merits the description of a particular cause or intention. The incongruity in the joke is not that a chicken had an intention, but that that intention—"to get to the other side"—is simply another way of describing the action that is the object of inquiry. If one crosses the road, one gets to the other side and vice versa. That is why the answer is both incongruous and appropriate. It reveals an intention, but that intention provides no more information than was contained within the question.

If the analysis of the joke is wrong, the description of the proposed blend is wrong as well. This joke does not depend on merging the mental spaces of chickens and humans or countryside and cityscape. It depends upon what constitutes a satisfactory answer to who, what, where, when, why, or how questions. Underlying the joke is the request for specific historical information, for which tautology is incongruously but appropriately substituted. Some other jokes of this type:

"I see there's a funeral in town today."
"Yeah."
"Who died?"
"I'm not sure, but I think it's the one in coffin." (Keillor 2005, 94)[9]

EXAM QUESTION: "Why did the North go to war against the South in 1861?"
STUDENT ANSWER: "To fight."

EXAM QUESTION: Identify six Arctic mammals.
STUDENT ANSWER: Four seals and two polar bears.

"Why has John remained a bachelor?"
"Because he is still unmarried."

How far can a dog run into a forest?
Only half way. After that he'll be running out of the forest. (Rothbart and Pien
    1977, 37)[10]

The information in the answers to these questions is for the most part a priori. It is not clear how these kinds of jokes would be analyzed in terms of blending.[11]

Nevertheless, these types of jokes have something to contribute to linguistic theories of humor. Rachel Giora (1991) has suggested that jokes depend upon surprise and that surprise is created by the *marked informativeness* of the punchline. "'Did you take a bath?' a man asked his friend who just returned from a resort. 'No,' his friend replied, 'only towels'" (472). Given all the things that can be done at a resort—bathing, swimming, or sitting in the sun, stealing towels is the least expected and therefore the most informative. That response is almost inaccessible and therefore is markedly informative in relation to the question of what one does at a resort (473). The why-did-the-chicken-cross-the-road joke and other tautological jokes that resemble it, however, challenge the principle that marked informativeness characterizes the punchline of jokes that depend on semantic ambiguity. The ambiguity of who, what, where, when, why, and how—what might be called *wh* ambiguity jokes—violates the principle of marked informativeness. Jokes manage to appear even when—especially when—a punchline would seem to be markedly uninformative.[12]

Demonstrating the failure of a cognitive linguist to correctly analyze the why-did-the-chicken-cross-the-road joke is not meant to serve as an attack on Blending Theory per se. Anyone can misconstrue a joke, and I do not mean to suggest that cognitive linguists in general, or blending theorists in particular, usually misconstrue jokes or that they are worse at joke analysis than anyone else.[13] What my criticism of the blending analysis is meant to show, however, is that Blending Theory does not necessarily identify the properties essential to joke creation or comprehension, and that when a joke has been misinterpreted, there is nothing in Blending Theory that will identify or correct the error. Blending does not provide an analysis of a joke but is superimposed on an analysis that is undertaken outside the blending framework. If that first analysis is deficient, the formulation of the blend will likely be deficient as well.

Do all jokes equally lend themselves to blending analyses? Consider the joke about the man who turns to his wife, after the airliner has safely landed, and complains about the money they have wasted on flight insurance. The joke depends on his not recognizing that for his insurance to pay off, he and his wife would have had to be killed in an airplane crash. Is the joke created from a blend of lottery and life-insurance spaces? The man treats his flight insurance like a lottery ticket. He hopes that a small investment with luck will turn into a large payout. An insurance-policy holder is cross-mapped onto a lottery-ticket holder, the policy is mapped onto the ticket, and the lottery winnings are mapped onto the policy payout. Unlike in a lottery, however, the large payout in the insurance sphere comes only with the death of the "ticket" holder. The problem with this analysis is that there is no clear indication of a lottery or other betting space as a separate input to the blend. Invoking it would seem to serve the benefit of Blending Theory rather than the categories of the joke itself. In fact, it might be argued that insurance policies are already firmly within a betting or lottery space even if it is others, rather than the insured, who collect when the slim odds play out. The joke is easily analyzed in terms of appropriate incongruity, however. It is appropriate that the man might wish to earn a large payout for a small premium payment. It is incongruous to wish for that payment if it depends on his own death.

What about the following joke?

PATIENT: "How much to have this tooth pulled?"
DENTIST: "Ninety dollars."
PATIENT: "Ninety dollars for just a few minutes work?"
DENTIST: "I can do it slower if you like." (Keillor 2005, 184)

It might be argued that this joke depends on a blend of patient and dentist input spaces. One cannot recruit much in the way of knowledge about dentists and patients other than the patient's desire to pay less and the dentist's expectation of adequate compensation for the work performed. Also, dentistry is generally regarded as an unpleasant and painful procedure. That information alone, however, does not account for the joke. The joke depends, rather, on the ways a rate of pay can be reckoned. A rate of pay will go down if the money paid for a unit of work goes down. But a rate of pay will also go down if the time it takes to earn a fixed amount of money goes up. The patient suggests the rate of pay is too high ("ninety dollars for just a few minutes work") and might be lower. The dentist agrees that the rate of pay can be lower, but only by increasing the time it takes to perform the job ("I can do it slower"). The overall cost to the patient, however, would not change. Furthermore, since the job that is being paid for is a dental procedure, the pain the patient will endure with the second means of rate reduction will be prolonged. What may seem attractive as an economic calculation is unattractive as a medical one.

One might, I suppose, argue that this joke depends upon a blend of economic and medical input spaces in which the time it takes to do a job must be evaluated differently. In the medical space, time is related not only to what the patient must pay but to what the patient must endure. But again, the imposition of a blend framework seems forced. One wonders whether this is really how the mind works in constructing or comprehending the joke. What is taking place in the joke is easily analyzed in terms of appropriate incongruity. The dentist's willingness to work slower appropriately reduces his rate of compensation as the patient suggests. Incongruously, however, it would at once increase the patient's level of suffering.[14]

"If you buy a goldfish, I'll throw in the aardvark."

FIGURE 3.4. HERMAN © LaughingStock International Inc. Reprinted by permission of UNIVERSAL UCLICK for UFS. All rights reserved.

In a *Herman* cartoon by Jim Unger, a man stands over a table in a pet store where some small fish are swimming about in a tank (see figure 3.4). Next to him stands the proprietor with an aardvark in his arms. The proprietor says, "If you buy a goldfish, I'll throw in the aardvark" (Unger 2007, 108). It might be argued that there is a blend of input spaces of the pet store and other kinds of stores—department stores, for example—where customers are offered free merchandise when they purchase some particular product. Thus, one might receive a free lipstick with the purchase of a featured perfume. The problem with such an analysis is that such promotions are as characteristic of pet stores as any other store. Buy a kitten and get a free scratching post. Buy an aquarium and get a free goldfish. There is nothing humorous about such offers in pet stores. If the blend, on the other hand, is conceived as one of domestic and wild input spaces, still no joke emerges. Pet stores frequently offer exotic forms of wildlife for sale.

The joke is easily grasped in terms of appropriate incongruity, however. It is incongruous to offer an exotic and ungainly mammal to promote the sale of a small, inexpensive, and familiar fish. The aardvark would likely prove a disincentive, rather than an incentive, to make the purchase. The appropriateness of the incongruity depends on the fact that incentives are regularly offered to promote sales in all kinds of stores.

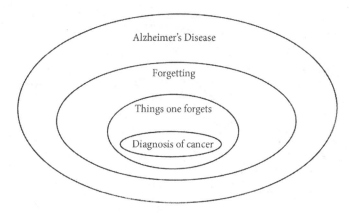

Alzheimer's Disease

Forgetting

Things one forgets

Diagnosis of cancer

FIGURE 3.5.

The two jokes below don't seem to immediately lend themselves to blending analysis at all. They do not seem to depend on the mixing together of two distinct semantic domains but rather to operate on some deviation within a single domain:

> DOCTOR: You have cancer and you have Alzheimer's.
> PATIENT: At least I don't have cancer. (Keillor 2005, 183)

> There are two rules for succeeding in business. The first one is "Never tell them everything you know." (177)

The first joke (see figure 3.5) does not depend on a blending of Alzheimer's and cancer domains. The joke proceeds from within the domain of Alzheimer's. Alzheimer's is a disease that involves severe memory impairment. Thus, the set of things one forgets is within the domain of Alzheimer's and the diagnosis of cancer is within the domain of things that one might forget. Note that cancer is strictly optional and theoretically could be replaced by any number of serious medical conditions. The joke is easily and completely analyzable as an appropriate incongruity. It is incongruous that the patient should be thankful that he does not have cancer immediately after hearing that very diagnosis, but it is appropriate since he has also been diagnosed with a disease that is characterized by a severe memory impairment.

The second joke, about the rules of business (see figure 3.6), again seems to proceed from within a single domain. The first rule on the list contains within it the rationale for failing to enunciate the second rule, whose disclosure was implied.[15] In this respect, it is like the Alzheimer's joke. This joke is also easily explained in terms of appropriate incongruity, but blending would be hard put, I think, to offer an uncomplicated description of how this joke works.

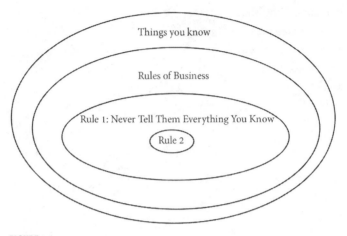

FIGURE 3.6.

There may be other ways to graphically represent these two jokes, but it is hard to image a diagram with two distinct input spaces and a blended space. Incongruity does not have much status in Blending Theory, and blending theorists do not invoke incongruity in their analyses of jokes. In their exposition of Conceptual Integration Theory, Gilles Fauconnier and Mark Turner remark that incongruity can make blends more visible, but blends need not be incongruous (Fauconnier and Turner 1998, 141).[16] Although incongruity is certainly tricky to operationalize, it would seem that the analysis of what makes a blend humorous depends on just such a difficult notion. Blending theory makes no use of appropriateness either in characterizing humor, but to some extent cross-domain mapping may subsume such a notion without specifically calling attention to it (137).

It is important to distinguish blending analyses of jokes from blending analyses of metaphors. Metaphors are by definition blends, as *X is a Y (in Z)* conjoins aspects of domain X with domain Y in some context Z, which is assumed or optionally identified. Jokes also conjoin domains but only sometimes by blending them. Often the domains are merely *linked*—perhaps by a single term—rather than blended. In the joke about the dentist and the patient, the patient and the dentist domains are linked by virtue of the two ways of conceptualizing variation in a rate of pay. While a rate of pay is itself a blend of time and money, it is not the blend created in the joke. Rate of pay, rather, is broken down into alternative computations. These alternatives—reduce pay and keep time constant or keep pay constant and increase time—are what create an appropriate linkage between the patient's suggestion that the rate of pay is too high and the dentist's incongruous offer to lower it.

I am not suggesting that Blending Theory is utterly incapable of offering an analysis of the jokes presented above. However, the joke examples employed to demonstrate the power of blending should not be chosen by the analyst. Blending needs to be applied to difficult rather than easy cases. Then one can assess whether the blending analysis (1) accurately represents the joke, and (2) is simple and straightforward enough to persuade that it models the means by which jokes are produced or, at least, comprehended.

In approaching humor, Blending Theory looks at the contribution that input spaces make to a blend and to the structure that emerges from that blend. Blending theory seems unconcerned, however, with the *means* by which relations are regularly established in humor. The field of humor studies is interested in attempting to identify the "techniques" or "mechanisms" that are repeatedly employed in the creation of a humorous stimulus.

> A Jew meets his friend on the street and is asked how he is. "What can I say? My business is failing and I'm afraid that I may have to declare bankruptcy."
>
> "Don't worry," says his friend, "things could be worse."
>
> "On top of that, my wife is very sick and needs a major operation, and I don't know where I can find the money to pay for it. I don't know what's going to happen."
>
> "Don't worry," says the friend, "things could be worse."
>
> "And my son has met a Gentile girl and is talking about leaving the faith and converting to Catholicism."
>
> "Don't worry," says the friend, "things could be worse."
>
> "Things could be worse? Things could be worse? My livelihood is in jeopardy, my wife may be dying, and my son is planning to convert. How could things be worse?"
>
> "They could be happening to me."

From the point of view of appropriate incongruity, a listener to this joke is at first asked to accept the friend's claim that "things could be worse" as proffered consolation. After all, although things are bad, things could always be worse. As the litany of afflictions grows, however, it seems incongruous that the friend's formulaic expression could possibly offer any comfort. When the friend is ultimately challenged on this point, the incongruity of his claim is found to be appropriate. It is not that the situation is not severe, but that severity is relative. The worst calamities are those that directly affect the self.

An incongruity is made appropriate in this joke through a shift in point of view. Any number of jokes employ the same technique to establish the appropriateness of their incongruities.

"Do you take off your glasses because you think it makes you look better?"

"No, because it makes you look better." (Keillor 2005, 263)

From the perspective of an outside observer, the removal of eyeglasses might be interpreted as an attempt to improve overall facial appearance. A suggestion—an accusation, really—is made that the action might be motivated by some petty vanity on the part of the eyeglasses wearer. Yet the wearer suggests that the glasses have been removed in order to improve the appearance of the interlocutor. But this is incongruous because glasses are worn to improve vision. To remove them, in most instances, would impair vision. Nothing should look better with impaired vision. This incongruity can be regarded as appropriate, however, if what is being perceived is regarded as ugly. In such a case, a visual impairment might be the preferred sensory condition. The change in point of view allows the eyeglasses wearer to deny she is concerned with her own looks and to substitute the suggestion that she is more concerned with the looks of her interlocutor. This is an example of "ready repartee" (Freud 1960, 8:68) or "trumping humor" (Veale, Feyaerts, and Brône 2006, 312–19) in which an aggressive statement is slightly modified and turned back against its speaker.[17]

When there is a shift in the subject, the perspective is shifted as well, and so is the interpretation of the object or event in question.[18] The shift makes appropriate an incongruity once the subjectivity that informs it is grasped. Nevertheless, merely shifting perspective is not sufficient to create humor. If it were, Akira Kurosawa's 1950 film *Rashomon* would be a comedy as it gives accounts of an event from distinct viewpoints. The shift in perspective must also serve to make an incongruity appropriate in a manner that is clearly spurious (Oring 2003, 5–9). We do not take off our glasses to endure the ugliness of an acquaintance. We do not tell a suffering friend that things could be worse because we can imagine them happening to ourselves. Multiple perspective is often employed in humor creation, but the identification of it as a technique would seem to stand outside the purview of Blending Theory.[19] Blending theory seems concerned only with input and blended spaces. The identification of the techniques or mechanisms of humor is still in a fairly primitive state in humor studies, but few would suggest that the identification, analysis, and categorization of these mechanisms are without significance for the field (Freud 1960, 8:16–89; Oring 1992, 10–12; 2011b; Berger 1997; Paolillo 1998; Attardo, Hempelmann, and Di Maio 2002).[20]

Blending theory seems to be able to handle some of those jokes that Freud would have described as resulting from the techniques of condensation, multiple use of the same material, or double meaning (Freud 1960, 8:41–42). But it would seem to fail in accounting for jokes that are based upon what Freud calls "displacement," that is, "the diversion of a train of thought, the displacement of the psychical emphasis on to a topic other than the opening one" (51). Freud's example:

> An impoverished individual borrowed 25 florins from a prosperous acquaintance, with many asseverations of his necessitous circumstances. The very same day his benefactor met him again in a restaurant with a plate of salmon mayonnaise in front of him. The benefactor reproached him: "What? You borrow money from me and then order yourself salmon mayonnaise? Is that what you've used my money for?" "I don't understand you," replied the object of the attack; "if I haven't any money I can't eat salmon mayonnaise, and if I have some money I mustn't eat salmon mayonnaise. Well, then, when am I to eat salmon mayonnaise?" (49–50)

This joke seems to fall beyond the pale of a blending analysis. No domains are blended. The borrower presumes the right to spend the borrowed money on a delicacy at a time he has more fundamental needs to satisfy. The answer to his final question should be, "You should not indulge in luxuries until after *you* have *earned* money sufficient to pay for your *basic necessities*." The borrower is right that without money he cannot buy delicacies, and with borrowed money he should not. But he is wrong in thinking that he is justified in spending the money—regardless of its source and intended purpose—on whatever he pleases. One might suggest that there is a blend between the domains of "one's own money" and "other people's money," but such a blend is not in itself humorous. A number of bankers and money managers now sit in prison for blending exactly these two input spaces. It is only the borrower's appropriately incongruous argument that turns the confounding of the domains into a joke.

In an issue of the journal *Humor* devoted to cognitive linguistics, Salvatore Attardo makes two points that are directed not at Blending Theory but at cognitive linguistics as a whole. The first is that cognitive linguistic approaches to humor seem to involve mainly and merely notational differences from previous linguistic approaches (Attardo 2006, 341). Certainly, the way Blending Theory lays out an analysis of a joke looks different from the General Theory of Verbal Humor or appropriate incongruity. And indeed, there has been much in linguistic studies that seems only to be a reinvention of the wheel.[21] That is not my central concern. There are cognitive linguistic analyses of humor that are both interesting and on the money (e.g., Bergen and Binsted 2003; Veale, Feyaerts, and Brône 2006).

My biggest reservation about Blending Theory is that a full analysis of a joke is necessary before it can be cast into a blend structure. In other words, there is nothing that I do not have to do in analyzing a joke that a blending theorist does not have to do if the blend analysis is ultimately to serve as a credible representation of the joke in question. Before a blend can be described for a joke, an ordinary, nontheoretical processing of the joke must first be performed. If that first non-blend analysis is inaccurate, the blend analysis will not be accurate either, as could be seen with the chicken-crossing-the-road joke. Blending Theory cannot independently provide a proper analysis of a joke. I would go a step further. If blending is a secondary analysis imposed on some primary analysis, why presume that it represents the means by which jokes are created and understood? Perhaps there is some other representation of the joke that not only describes the elements that comprise it but proposes why the text in question *is* a joke.[22]

Another of Attardo's objections to cognitive linguistic approaches is that they fail to distinguish between humor and pretty much all other linguistic activity (Attardo 2006, 344). Indeed, Blending Theory has been applied to a wide range of linguistic expressions: to the semantic analysis of nominal compounds, predicating and non-predicating adjectives, privative adjectives, counterfactuals, and metaphors (Fauconnier 1997; Coulson 2001). It is probably applicable to almost everything, which seems a fault of the theory rather than a virtue. As Attardo states, "If we want to use humorous examples to illustrate a given linguistic theory, that's great for the linguistic theory, but it does nothing for the understanding of humor" (Attardo 2006, 344). I wholeheartedly agree. We must be able to distinguish between humorous and nonhumorous expression, and theories that do not or cannot differentiate between the two seem to be of limited use. However, we cannot leave it only to cognitive linguists or blending theorists to conceptualize the difference. We must attempt to delineate the difference as well. What, for example, is the difference between a serious metaphor and a joke?

It has been suggested that the difference depends on (1) the semantic distance between the categories involved in the joke or metaphor (Freud 1960, 8:120; Morrissey 1990, 124–25; Attardo 2006, 345), or on (2) the degree of multistep inferential processing necessary to understand the joke or the metaphor (Pollio 1996, 243; V. Raskin 2008, 12–13).[23] In other words, jokes link domains of greater semantic distance than metaphors, or jokes require more inferential processing than metaphors. I am suspicious of both hypotheses. Shakespeare's "Thou art the grave where buried love doth live" (Sonnet 31) seems harder to process than many a joke. I regularly stumble over Shakespeare, but only rarely over a joke. How much inferential processing is required to interpret "The surgeon is a butcher" as "The surgeon is incompetent"? Is it less than the inferential processing deployed in grasping the joke about the chicken crossing the road? Why should the joke necessitate a greater degree of inferential processing?

Attardo (2007) has questioned the notion that humor depends on greater semantic distance. After all, how does one even measure semantic distance?[24]

It may be possible to challenge the semantic distance argument more directly. Metaphors are generally not reversible. "My job is a jail" is difficult to recast as "My jail is a job."[25] But this is only sometimes true. "The surgeon is a butcher" can be inverted—"The butcher is a surgeon"—although the grounds of the metaphor change. This latter formulation is likely to attribute positive properties to the butcher, whereas in the first metaphor, negative properties were attributed to the surgeon (Glucksberg 1998, 41). "The butcher is a surgeon" is an expression that might be provoked by an observation of a butcher's dexterous, economical, and artistic carving of a side of beef.[26]

Consider another case. Someone boasts, "My lawyer is a shark" and his interlocutor responds, "My shark is a lawyer." The first formulation is a serious metaphor, the second a humorous response. It would seem, therefore, that the difference between metaphor and humor cannot simply be attributed to the semantic distance between the categories invoked in the respective figures. One may, on certain occasions, turn a metaphor into humor without a change in semantic categories or distance at all.

Why should one formulation of these semantic categories be a metaphor while its inverse registers as a joke? Metaphors, it has been argued, are not comparisons but class inclusion assertions (Glucksberg 1998, 40–41). That is to say, when someone proclaims his lawyer to be a "shark," hearers understand that the word does not refer to the fish but to a superordinate category of vicious, predatory, aggressive, and tenacious creatures of which the shark is but an example. The lawyer is then understood to possess some or all of these qualities. However, when someone states that his shark is a lawyer, one searches in vain for characteristics of lawyers that may be attributed to a shark. Sharks do not hold degrees, are not argumentative, don't obfuscate, charge exorbitant fees, appear in court, or fail to return phone calls. In those qualities that sharks and lawyers do share—viciousness, aggressiveness, and tenaciousness—the shark far exceeds the lawyer; so to say, "My shark is a lawyer" adds nothing to the understanding of sharks. Even those with the greatest antipathies to lawyers would be unlikely to seriously maintain that lawyers are more aggressive or bloodthirsty than sharks. Lawyers may figuratively attack, dismember, and devour; but sharks do so literally. "My lawyer is a shark" is a statement that is true figuratively. "My shark is a lawyer" is not true even figuratively. It is an assertion that a literal shark is literally a lawyer. The statement is clearly incongruous, but it can be regarded as appropriate because some of the characteristics of sharks and lawyers are held to be similar. If a shark were literally assigned the occupation of bookkeeper or firefighter, the assignment would simply be puzzling. But the assignment of the occupation lawyer is not puzzling because some of the attributes of a shark present themselves as appropriate to that particular profession.[27]

It is important to note that in the "My shark is a lawyer" witticism, the source and target domains are the same as in the "My lawyer is a shark" metaphor. That is, in "My shark is a lawyer," the shark is still the source domain. Even though the metaphor and witticism are inversions of one another, nothing can be inferred about sharks from the witticism, although we may infer something about lawyers: lawyers are figuratively, though humorously, sharks. Given that the semantic domains for the two expressions are the same, and the source and target are the same, and the distances between the source and target are the same, how would Blending Theory distinguish between the two lawyer/shark formulations?

I repeat a suggestion that I made some years ago. The difference between metaphor and humor is that the incongruities in metaphors must be seriously engaged and the connections between source and target legitimately established. Metaphors are puzzles to be solved. Humor, however, does not demand the discovery of legitimate connections between the incongruous domains invoked. The connections detected are appropriate but spurious. They have psychological, not logical, validity. In humor, there is no authentic resolution (Oring 1992, 14; 1995; 2003, 4–8).[28]

Another way to characterize the difference between metaphor and humor is that an analysis of a metaphor demands the identification of its *meaning*. An analysis of "Juliet is the sun" must propose ways in which Juliet is the sun for Romeo. If no conceivable connections can be detected, the expression is unlikely to be granted metaphorical status. "Roses are the bartenders of the vegetable world" has the grammar of a metaphor but does not have metaphorical status unless some legitimate relationship between roses and bartenders can be discerned. But this is not true of jokes or humor generally. To discover the means by which utterances, images, or behaviors comprise humor is only to recognize that it is humor. Whether blending, incongruity, or some other theory is invoked to characterize humor, the result is not a meaning but merely the formulation of an ideational structure—the structure that identifies it as a joke. Metaphors are fundamentally semantic constructions. They exist as metaphors to the extent that a meaning can be proposed for them. Humor, however, is a syntactic affair. To be sure, it depends on semantic domains, but it is the particular *arrangement* (the original sense of the word "syntax") of those domains that creates humor. To be able to characterize something as humorous is not necessarily to know what it means. The identification of a meaning, if there is one, requires a further level of analysis. To use the terminology of blending, the emergent structure in a humorous expression is always a spuriously appropriate incongruity. Those incongruous input spaces must be perceived as spuriously appropriate. In fact, it might be argued—again presuming the language of Blending Theory—that all humor shares this single emergent structure.[29] It is this structure that characterizes the blend as humor rather than something else—metaphor, dream, art, or fantasy. Of course, some jokes may extend beyond their boundaries and connect with our knowledge of the world at large and thus create meaning (see Oring 2003, 27–40, 85–96). But the primary sense of a joke is a spuriously appropriate incongruity, not a statement about the world.[30]

An example of an emergent structure that extends beyond this self-contained joke structure has been identified in a blend analysis of the joke about the Menendez computer virus:

> Menendez brothers virus: Eliminates your files, takes the disk space they previously occupied, and then claims it was a victim of physical and sexual abuse on the part of the files it erased.

This joke depends upon knowing that Erik and Lyle Menendez murdered their parents. They inherited their parents' money and property, which they spent on an extravagant lifestyle. When they were finally charged with the crime, they maintained the killing was in self-defense because over the years they had been physically and sexually abused by their parents. The blend in the joke is of two input spaces drawn from the domain of the actual crime and the domain of computer viruses (see figure 3.7).

The situation of the killing is related to the computer domain, and every element in the blend is drawn from the computer input except for the very last element—sexual abuse. Sexual abuse is pertinent only to the social space, but it is included in the blended space with the other elements from the computer space.[31] "The possibility of an abused virus arises only in the blended space where it enjoys a short-lived existence." So the joke depends upon recognizing analogies between the human space and the computer space except for the physical and sexual abuse, which is "chimerical" in the blend (Coulson 2001, 181).

I would maintain that the primary emergent structure of this text is an appropriate incongruity: it is incongruous that a computer virus could claim to be the victim of physical or sexual abuse, but it is appropriate given the strong analogies between the behaviors of the Menendez brothers and the behavior of a computer virus in all the other areas. But there is another structure that emerges from this blend. It is maintained that the ridiculousness of attributing physical or sexual abuse to a blend that is otherwise made up of only computer elements transfers back to input 1. As it is ridiculous in the blend that a virus could claim to be abused, so it is ridiculous that the Menendez brothers could justify their homicides by claiming physical and sexual abuse. To use a term of Sigmund Freud's, the blend is "tendentious"; it is has purpose beyond that of making a joke (Freud 1960,

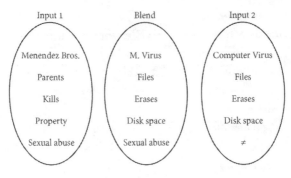

FIGURE 3.7.

8:90). It expresses something serious about the world. Because the Menendez brothers claimed physical and sexual abuse as the motive for killing their parents, the absurdity of the virus claiming abuse is projected back into the social domain. The Menendez brothers' claim in the social space, consequently, is equally absurd (Coulson 2001, 181–83). As the cognitive linguist claims, "The links in the component spaces in a frame network allow us to capture an important component of the meaning of this joke that would be overlooked by conventional cognitive science approaches to cross-domain mapping. The rhetorical topic of this joke is not the target domain of computer viruses, but the social source" (183).

What is being referred to here is an emergent structure of the blend that expresses something about the social world input from which the blend is in part derived. This is so. If I were to use the terminology of Blending Theory, I would call this a "secondary" emergent structure. The first emergent structure is the joke itself—the spuriously appropriate incongruity. The secondary structure is an important meaning of the joke, as the analyst notes, but if it is a meaning that would be missed by conventional cognitive science, it is hardly a meaning likely to be missed by folklorists, anthropologists, or sociologists who study humor. They are very much attuned to and interested in the potential meanings of jokes and other forms of humor (e.g., Oring 1981, 1984, 1992, 2003; Dundes 1987; C. Davies 1990, 1998, 2002).

There is one last point I would mention, which concerns the term *blending* itself. To blend means more than to combine; but to "intimately or harmoniously combine so that their individuality is obscured in the product" (*Oxford English Dictionary*). This does not seem to be the case with humor. A joke may be a harmonious whole, but the elements that comprise it never really lose their distinctive qualities.

The cartoon described below can be reckoned in terms of blending wild-animal feeding and family-restaurant dining. A lion family is sitting in a restaurant and examining the menu as humans do. The caption "Can I have a pony?" spoken by the young lion has a different meaning in the human and animal domains. In the human world it is a request to the parents for a pet. In the animal kingdom it is a request for a meal. While the meaning of pony as food in the cartoon probably registers later than its meaning as pet, one domain does not obliterate or trump the other. Both the food and pet meanings—and thus the animal and human domains—remain active in understanding the cartoon and persist in its contemplation. The divers components are never obscured; the spaces never truly blend. Even though there may be a shift in perception, it is the continual dissonance, I would argue, that makes the cartoon funny. No single or novel meaning of "pony" emerges.

A principle of Blending Theory is that a good blend "must enable an understander to unpack the blend and to reconstruct its inputs" (Fauconnier and Turner 1998,163). What is true for metaphors and other blended constructions is especially true for humor. In fact, humor is never blended in the sense defined above. Metaphors are resolved in the discovery of a particular meaning; humor is not. Humor depends on the recognition of an irresolvably dissonant structure. Metaphors can become conventional or "dead" when their input spaces are overlooked or forgotten. As long as the appropriate incongruity is preserved, jokes remain jokes, even if they might be regarded as "stale."

The entry of cognitive linguists into humor analysis has been characterized by one commentator as an "invasion" (Krikmann 2009, 26). There is an implication that cognitive linguistics has solved or is capable of solving all the problems in the analysis of humor. That part of cognitive linguistics that goes under the name of "Blending Theory," however, seems to have several of its own problems in its application to humor. First, the theory offers no method for humor analysis. Humor must be first analyzed outside a blending framework before it can be put into a blend framework. Blending analysis is thus a post hoc affair. If the initial analysis of a joke is incorrect, a blending template is unlikely to correct it. Second, blending is applicable to the analysis of some jokes, but it is not clear that all jokes readily lend themselves to such analysis.[32] Third, Blending Theory is not interested in the techniques that are repeatedly employed in the creation of jokes and other forms of humor. Fourth, appropriate incongruity analyses of jokes are likely to provide clearer guides to the analysis of humor than Blending Theory, and the process of registering incongruities and looking for appropriate relations seems simpler and more intuitive for the online processing of humor. Fifth, Blending Theory does not distinguish humor from other kinds of blends—most notably the blends effected in the production of metaphor and art. Sixth, what counts as discovery in cognitive linguistics is often the recasting of well-known ideas in linguistic terminology. For example, "The rhetorical topic of this joke is not the target domain . . . but the social source"—which is to say a joke can have social meaning. Seventh, *blending* is perhaps not the best word to characterize what is going on in the construction and comprehension of humor. The dissonance that persists in humor does not seem adequately represented by the meaning of the word *blend*.

The question that those in humor studies must ask is what Blending Theory contributes to the analysis and understanding of humor. Whether blending reflects a revolution in the properties of mind achieved in the Upper Paleolithic (Fauconnier and Turner 2002, v), or whether blending is applicable to a variety of linguistic constructions in which humor theories have no interest and about which they have nothing to say is not the central issue. Blending theory must *add value* to the study of humorous forms, expressions, and behaviors. It must illuminate areas that remain opaque to current theories and methods. It is not in generalities that blending will prove itself, but in specificities.

CHAPTER FOUR

On Benign Violations

Levin saw it was a joke, but he could not smile.
—LEO TOLSTOY

A general theory of humor, Benign Violation Theory, was recently proposed by A. Peter McGraw and Caleb Warren. The theory claims that humor depends upon a sense of violation of a moral principle that, at the same time, is regarded as benign, nonthreatening, and consequently acceptable. The violation of a principle can be viewed as benign if there is another principle operating that suggests it is acceptable, there is only weak commitment to the violated principle, or the violation is psychologically distant (McGraw and Warren 2010, 1142). The theory is illustrated with a Venn diagram in figure 4.1.

The right circle is the domain of the violation; the left circle is the domain of the benign. The intersection of the domains is the area of the benign violation, wherein resides things humorous (McGraw and Warner 2014, 10, 64–66, 208–9).[1] The work of McGraw and his collaborators draws upon the earlier work of Thomas C. Veatch (1998). Veatch's terminology is somewhat different from theirs. He speaks of the perception of a violation [V] and a simultaneous perception of that violation as normal [N]. Humor resides in that dual perception: [N + V] (163–66).

The corollaries of this theory are that if a person is too attached to a violated moral principle, there will be no humor. The violation will not be regarded as benign and cannot be normalized. Conversely, if no violation is perceived or there is not the slightest commitment to the violated principle, the principle is not a

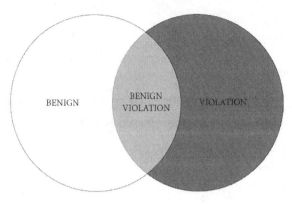

FIGURE 4.1.

moral one and humor will not be perceived either (Veatch 1998, 169; McGraw and Warren 2010, 1142).

New theories of humor invariably depend upon ignoring previous theoretical formulations or acknowledging them only in passing. While McGraw and Veatch both make some reference to incongruity theory, they do not give it its due or they actively misrepresent it. McGraw and his collaborators suggest that incongruity theory depends simply upon "a mismatch" between reality and expectations (McGraw, Williams, and Warren 2013, 5). Unintentionally killing a loved one might be incongruous but is unlikely to be funny (McGraw and Warren 2010, 1141). Similarly, Veatch argues that there are many absurd and incongruous situations that are not funny, such as the belief that two is the same as four. Likewise, he claims that Noam Chomsky's famous sentence "Colorless green ideas sleep furiously" is incongruous but hardly a joke (Veatch 1998, 185). When discussing Victor Raskin's Semantic Script Theory of Humor, Veatch simply subsumes the oppositions Raskin sees as fundamental to most jokes—life/death, money/no money, sexual/nonsexual—within his own theory of normal violations while overlooking the more fundamental idea of *script overlap*, which determines whether something is or is not funny (Veatch 1998, 193; V. Raskin 1985b, 99). Raskin's theory can easily be viewed as a form of incongruity theory, although he took some pains to distance himself from it (V. Raskin 1985a, 39; Attardo 1997, 395). More to the point, there is absolutely no mention or citation of my own formulation of *appropriate incongruity*, despite its striking resemblance to benign or normal violation and its similar use of oxymoronic phraseology (Oring 1973, 1975, 1992, 2003). The resemblance is not only in the character of the phrasing, however. A violation, according to Veatch, is of a principle that a perceiver believes. The principle defines the way things are supposed to be (Veatch 1998, 167). Such violations become funny if they can be simultaneously perceived as normal or benign. Appropriate incongruity depends on the perception of an appropriate relationship of elements from domains that are generally regarded as incongruous (Oring 1992, 2). In other words, humor is perceived when something does not quite fit (a violation?) but is nevertheless, at some level, appropriate (normal or benign?). These characterizations of humor—benign violation and appropriate incongruity—would on the surface appear enough alike so that the purported new theory would not merely dismiss incongruity theory but characterize it accurately and explore the similarities and differences between them.

From the appropriate incongruity perspective, two equals four is incongruous and unfunny *unless there is something to make that incongruity appropriate.* The situation of a woman who goes into a coffee shop, orders a whole cake, and tells the waitress to serve it cut in two pieces rather than four because she is on a diet is funny. Here two *does* equal four because two halves of a cake equals four quarters of a cake. What is incongruous is that the woman thinks that by eating fewer pieces she is consuming fewer calories. What is appropriate is that eating fewer pieces of a pastry is generally thought to result in lower caloric intake. The woman's rationale for eating two pieces is, of course, spurious since she will be eating the whole cake no matter how many pieces it is divided into.

I will stipulate to the unfunniness of Chomsky's famous sentence.[2] But what is to be made of "Colorless green ideas sleep furiously except when they have to get up in the middle of the night to pee"? This sentence should strike Veatch as equally or even more inharmonious, since it would seem to heap yet another semantic absurdity upon an already established sequence. Yet this variation of the sentence is funny, and appropriate incongruity can explain why. The semantically incongruous sentence becomes appropriate because people—especially older people—frequently have to get up in the middle of the night to urinate, which interrupts their sleep. The incongruous sentence becomes appropriate as some part of it—furiously sleeping ideas—is likened to sleeping human beings. Were McGraw or Veatch to argue that the reference to "peeing" is slightly risqué and constitutes a benign moral violation, one could simply substitute the phrase with "except when they have to get up to let out the cat." In the case of Chomsky's sentence, appropriate incongruity can explain why adding yet another absurdity to a string of absurdities creates humor. I am not entirely sure that Benign Violation Theory (henceforth BVT) is equally up to the task.

Despite the similarities, there are differences between BVT and an appropriate incongruity perspective. What constitutes a violation in BVT might be a physical threat, an assault on personal dignity, or some infringement of social or linguistic norms. "Anything that is threatening to one's sense of how the world 'ought to' be will be humorous, as long as the threatening situation also seems benign" (McGraw and Warren 2010, 1142). Any and all of these are considered *moral* violations, and moral violations arouse emotion. A moral violation is a violation of a principle about which a person cares. A moral violation is aversive, while the normalizing aspect is non-aversive. Levity results from the mixing of the two emotional responses (Veatch 1998, 164, 167; McGraw and Warren 2010, 1142). Consequently, BVT is an emotional theory of humor. Incongruity theories generally, and appropriate incongruity specifically, are not emotional theories.[3] Humor results from a *cognitive* dissonance. Some of the behaviors, images, and events that foster humor may arouse emotion. But this is separate from what is fundamental to a perception of humor. The perception of an appropriate incongruity is not emotional but intellectual.

BVT faces a problem that an appropriate incongruity perspective avoids. While it is easy to show why something humorous might be cognitively perceived as incongruous yet appropriate, BVT requires the *additional* demonstration that these perceptions necessarily register on an emotional level. It seems harder to demonstrate that *any* violation of expectations about how the world operates would necessarily arouse an emotional reaction beyond great or mild surprise. In other words, a linguistic joke, which depends upon violations of the phonological, morphological, syntactic, semantic, or pragmatic rules of ordinary discourse, would have to be shown to arouse negative emotions. Furthermore, it would have to be shown that an individual who responded to an ethnic, sexual, or linguistic joke with the same level of amusement had equal levels of negative emotion aroused in each case. The case would be even harder for BVT should a linguistic joke elicit more humor than an ethnic or sexual one.

A second problem is that in BVT, violations are of the *subjective moral order.* This means that what are considered benign violations vary with the individual. All humor researchers know that there is considerable variability in the responses to jokes. People find things funny at different times and in different situations, and scholars of humor must address these differences in the explanation of particular cases. But the introduction of the subjective moral order into the body of BVT suggests that the moral order may be so variable and contingent as to be unascertainable. McGraw and Warner report that Veatch claimed that he laughed at the following joke for over an hour: "Q: Why did the monkey fall from the tree? A: Because it was dead" (McGraw and Warner 2014, 8). There was no report of what subjective violation of moral principle Veatch was responding to in that joke or his degree of commitment to that principle. BVT is left with explaining what change in Veatch's personal moral calculus could trigger such an intense response in that particular instance.[4]

Although the appropriate incongruity perspective is not rooted in emotion, it does not neglect the question of the relation of humor to emotion. Emotion is not integral to the perception of humor, however: it stands, rather, as a force that may diminish or augment the humor aroused by the perception of an appropriate incongruity. Emotion may inhibit the perception of humor. Certain characters, topics, groups, or outlooks may be too emotionally charged to serve as targets for play (Freud 1960, 8:144; Oring 1992, 12). Humor demands a suspension of emotional attachments—"a momentary anesthesia of the heart," as Henri Bergson put it (Bergson 1956, 63–64). A joke may not be appreciated or even grasped if one is too emotionally invested in what is being joked about. So emotion is not irrelevant to the perception of humor. It can serve to quash the humor that might otherwise be produced by the perception of an appropriate incongruity.

Emotion may on occasion enhance the perception of humor. Although Sigmund Freud was not an incongruity theorist per se (he was well aware, however, of how jokes are structured), he made a definite distinction between what he called the *joke envelope* and the *joke thought*. The joke envelope—its form of expression—is purely an intellectual affair; it is a construction employing a variety of linguistic and conceptual techniques. The thought expressed—or revealed—in the course of the joke is another matter entirely. A valuable thought could be ensconced in a feeble envelope, or a well-crafted envelope might contain an insipid thought (Freud 1960, 8:92). The pleasure afforded by a joke that is simply a product of its formal techniques, according to Freud, is modest. But when a joke taps into certain suppressed thoughts, the amount of pleasure obtained from the joke is vastly increased (8:96). Although I do not believe that suppressed thoughts—aggressive or sexual thoughts for Freud—are the only kinds that can increase a joke's funniness, the point is that such emotionally charged thoughts can augment the pleasure obtained from the joke envelope.[5] A joke that targets a nondescript character—a generic fool—may become funnier when it targets a particular individual or group against whom the hearer harbors some animus, as both Veatch and McGraw recognize (Veatch 1998, 181; McGraw and Warner 2014, 124). So incongruity theorists do not ignore emotion. But they do not build emotion into the fundamental equation of what makes something humorous. Emotion can enhance or constrain the appreciation of humor, but humor is not at root an emotional process.

Once BVT has committed itself to seeing humor as an emotional rather than an intellectual process, it proceeds to pronounce on the emotions of joke tellers and joke appreciators in the absence of evidence and sometimes in contravention of known facts. For example, Veatch asserts that those who laugh at puns are generally bookish people who take pleasure in manipulating language forms and are more likely to care when linguistic proprieties are violated (Veatch 1998,

174). I would suggest that it might best be left to empirical investigation to decide which groups are more prone to employ puns and to laugh at them with lesser or greater gusto.

Veatch also claims that adults do not laugh at elephant jokes (Veatch 1998, 194–95). This cycle of jokes, according to Veatch, is a "relentless, repetitive series" hilarious to ten-year-olds and some adults. (Yet he laughed for over an hour at the elephant-type joke about the monkey falling from a tree.) Children laugh at elephant jokes, he asserts, because they often involve images of dirtying one's food ("How do you know an elephant has been in the refrigerator? There are foot-prints in the butter dish") and violate ideas about keeping things in their place. These contentions about elephant jokes, however, are belied by the available evidence. It would have helped if Veatch had read some of the published literature on elephant jokes (e.g., Cray and Herzog 1967; Abrahams and Dundes 1969; Oring 1992, 16–28).[6] When elephant jokes first became popular in the early 1960s, they were *not* children's jokes. Children, for the most part, would not have understood them. The cycle seems to have first emerged among high school and college-age students and spread widely as newspapers reported the jokes and publishers assembled and purveyed collections of them. They were not originally a part of children's culture.

BVT is also not very welcoming of computer-generated humor. I am not certain why. Perhaps BVT proponents assume that programmers have not indexed the emotional valences of the various terms and concepts into the encyclopedias that the joke programs access so that the humor produced cannot be the result of vio-lations with emotional import. Whatever the reason, computer-generated humor is regarded as necessarily "dumb" and overwhelmingly based on puns (McGraw and Warner 2014, 50–51). I do remember the following joke reported years ago at a conference of the International Society for Humor Studies when humor-generating programs were still in their infancy: "Mother Teresa is the Adolf Hitler of being good." This joke was not anticipated by the programmers. After the fact, one can imagine how the computer might have arrived at this joke. It does not depend on a pun, and it is not particularly dumb. In any event, a "dumb" joke is still a joke, and a theory of humor is required to account for it. A theory of humor cannot be a theory of only those examples a theorist happens to appreciate.

Because violations necessarily arouse emotions, according to BVT, advocates of the theory are often forced to comment on the emotional dispositions of those who find certain jokes funny. Thus, those who laugh at dead-baby jokes (see Dundes 1979) are more psychologically distant from the violated moral princi-ple, which in this case involves the killing or mutilating of babies. Veatch knew a woman who appreciated dead-baby jokes until she became a mother herself.

At that point, she could no longer appreciate a joke about a baby and an electric fan because she once saw her own child tottering toward an electric fan.[7] Veatch maintains that those who do not laugh at such jokes have a greater commitment to the violated moral principle than those who do, although it is not clear how this hypothesis would be validated (Veatch 1998, 173–74). Is it really being suggested that those who respond positively to such jokes are less concerned about the killing and maiming of babies? It does not require BVT or any kind of emotional theory of humor to argue that horrific ideas and images might, for some people, arouse enough emotion to suppress the appreciation of a joke. Yet, one possible interpretation of dead-baby jokes is that they are a reaction to the sentimentalized imagery and overly protective and indulgent behaviors of middle-class parents toward their infants and toward children more generally. It is not only the attitudes and behaviors of individuals in the general population but the attitudes conveyed in the surfeit of images and expressions that appear in television news, television programming more generally, and commercial advertisements. Such a hypothesis proposes that dead-baby jokes were a form of resistance against an overly child-centered society and not an indication of an individual's dispositions toward the maiming or killing of children. In any event, it would require something akin to a slaughter of innocents to test Veatch's suggestion that tellers of dead-baby jokes were more likely to murder or mutilate babies or permit babies to kill or mutilate themselves.

Veatch suggests that feminists do not laugh at sexist jokes (Veatch 1998, 172). I am not certain what the basis for this assertion is, although a woman who publicly identified herself as a feminist might feel obligated on general principles to reject, at least openly, all humor that targets female characters.[8] As far as men's and women's responses to "sexist humor," however, one experiment indicated that although men appreciated blonde jokes more, the difference in the mean appreciation scores for men and women was not statistically significant.[9] In fact, certain types of women appreciated the blonde jokes more than some men, and some men found the jokes more offensive than did some women (Greenwood and Isbell 2002, 346–47). Conversely, men laugh at feminist humor although they may not rate it as highly as women do. Nevertheless, men can and do appreciate feminist humor, even those with significantly lower commitment to feminist messages and with lower feminist sympathies (Gallivan 1992).[10] The complexity, rather than the simplicity, of the relationship between joke teller and joke target in reckoning joke funniness has also been supported in other experiments (Abrams and Bippus 2011, 2014).[11] Rather than suggest that humor is fundamentally emotional, it would seem to make more sense to see emotion as something brought to humor evaluation.

Veatch might respond that it is not the violation of a general moral principle that results in funniness or offense but the violation in a particular instance. The moral order is *subjective,* and, consequently, a person may be more or less morally involved (Veatch 1998, 174–75). This leaves the determination of moral principles, their violation, the aversive emotions aroused by them, and the degree to which they may be made benign or normalized to an utterly variable metric to be decided on a case-by-case basis. Recall the report that Veatch laughed at "Q: Why did the monkey fall from the tree? A: Because it was dead" *for over an hour,* although I am skeptical of the length of time claimed for the response. The appropriate incongruity perspective would focus on aspects of *context* surrounding particular humorous events that enhance or reduce the perception of an incongruity and its appropriateness as well as attending to those external emotional factors that might heighten or reduce the humorous response (Oring 2008, 196–203).

Humor theories are first and foremost obligated to be able to identify the differences between humorous and nonhumorous stimuli. Secondarily, there is the question of why some jokes, statements, and events are funnier than others. The latter is a different question, since all of these stimuli are regarded to some degree as funny and consequently are presumed to share some common element. The difference in responses to humor cannot be attributed to a property the humorous stimuli share. They can be attributed only to either differences of *degree* in the shared property or to *extrinsic* factors—that is, to something independent of benign violation or, for that matter, of appropriate incongruity. BVT claims that things are funnier when they are more complex, pleasurable, familiar, and intense. By increased complexity, Veatch means that there are more hidden violations in the humor stimulus (Veatch 1998, 181). There is no evidence that this is the case. It is not at all clear that stuffing linguistic, sexual, political, and logical violations into the same joke, for example, makes it funnier than a joke that trades on only one of these themes.

Incongruity theories have not attended particularly to explanations of increased and decreased funniness. There has been a suggestion that jokes that are *reversible*—that can be understood in radically different ways—are funnier, although there is no evidence to support this notion (R. Raskin 1992, 182). It has also been suggested that a humorous stimulus is funnier when the distance between incongruous domains is greater, or when there are a number of incongruities rather than only a single one (Freud 1960, 8:120; Deckers and Buttram 1990, 53–64). The idea that certain jokes are more *sophisticated* than others—that is, depend on negotiating a greater chain of inferences—is intriguing (V. Raskin 2008, 12–13; see also Freud 1960, 8:100).[12] Of course, there must be some outer limit for what a mind can process in registering an appropriate incongruity. Jokes must be deciphered almost instantly to be found amusing. Having to work too long at a joke reduces it to a puzzle, and while that work might eventually reveal why the expression in question is in fact a joke, the amusement provoked by the joke will be greatly diminished.[13] Unfortunately, joke sophistication and the other hypotheses have not been rigorously pursued, but these hypotheses do not presume anything about emotion; the hypotheses are entirely cognitive.

As for extraneous factors, even Veatch identifies a number of them. Humor appreciation may vary depending on the brevity, the amount of surprise, or the comprehension difficulty of the humorous stimulus (Veatch 1998, 188–91). All sorts of other factors might affect the funniness of a joke: the distance or closeness of the people among whom it is shared, the setting and circumstances— bar or classroom—in which it is told, and perhaps the extent to which a canned joke is related or unrelated to the conversation in which it is embedded (Oring 2003, 85–96). The quality of the thought underlying a joke or a certain joke technique may enhance its humor. Simple textual changes to a joke can have significant effects, as when rewording a punchline changes its comic effect although the overall sense of the joke remains the same. Jokes and other forms of humor are often *performed,* and the quality of a performance can vary significantly. The number of extraneous factors that might affect joke appreciation is potentially large, which is why they are not usually included in a general theory of humor. BVT seems to hold that most of the variation in funniness, and hence appreciation, is attributable to gradations of the emotional intensities of violations and/ or the strengths of their normalizing interpretations, but the evidence for this is scanty (Veatch 1998, 18; McGraw and Warner 2014, 60). What, for instance, constitutes a strong normalizing interpretation; what makes a violation more or less benign? There is no good reason to assume that variations in emotion are not adequately handled outside a theory of humor. The characterization of what Veatch calls the "cognitive representation" of a humor stimulus should be sufficient for a theory of humor without presuming that the emotional disposition attached to the representation is the essential factor (Veatch 1998, 165). Although everyone would acknowledge that language behavior may be impelled by emotion and has emotional effects, I don't know that linguistic theory is improved by suggesting that language is fundamentally emotional. Language is largely deemed a cognitive affair.

It might seem at first that Veatch's theory is identical to that of McGraw and his colleagues. There is a possible difference, however. Veatch's proposed theory requires a cognitive representation with emotional concomitants. McGraw's requires only a sense of a moral violation that is benign. He does not speak of a cognitive representation and consequently, humor might be something that is felt and reacted to purely on an emotional level even in the absence of an explicit cognitive representation. Incongruity theory requires such cognitive representations since it is a cognitive theory. Furthermore, because it is a cognitive theory, it accounts for the fact that those who are amused by something can often—though not always—approximately describe what it is that amuses them. They can identify elements they notice, elements that, I would argue, can be articulated with a concept of appropriate incongruity.

We encounter hundreds of benign violations every day that do not elicit amusement. If a woman's checkbook shows a balance of $4,456.88 but her bank statement says $4,456.97, she may be somewhat surprised, but if she is not obsessively compulsive about the account balance, she will reconcile her records with the bank statement total and not worry about searching for the source of the 9¢ discrepancy. After all, the bank's computer is likely to give the more accurate figure. There is a violation but a benign one, possibly due to a simple arithmetic error on her part. The situation is not likely to provoke amusement. Later, when looking at her checkbook, she discovers that she wrote a check for $128.01 but recorded it as $128.10; a simple inversion of the 0 and 1. If this discovery causes her slight amusement, it is because of the appropriateness of the incongruity. The recognition of the benign violation itself—the 9¢ discrepancy—caused none.

A man crosses the street against the light. He knows that it is contrary to the law and understands perfectly well that traffic laws are meant to protect both pedestrians and drivers. But he is alone at night crossing a small street with nary a car in sight. He knows that he is violating the law, but he is also aware that it will affect no one. It is a benign violation. He crosses the street, but he is not amused as he does so.

If linguistic violations are sufficient to cause humor in a joke, the question is why people do not laugh every time someone misspeaks. We all make dozens of errors while speaking, writing, or typing, but only a few of these cause amusement. There are, of course, some errors of speech that we don't even notice, but many that we do notice we *overlook*, fully aware that speaking errors are common—in fact, likely. Still, they violate our linguistic expectations and often they are violations not unlike those that occur in linguistic jokes. They should constitute, according to BVT, benign moral violations. Why, then, are they not a constant source of amusement?

The same may be said for small violations of social norms. If someone knocks a knife from the dinner table while dining in a restaurant, it is a small violation. One is supposed to keep the tableware on the table. One may pick it up and ask the waiter for a new utensil. But it is not usually a matter of amusement unless one of the parties at dinner says something like "Good thing you don't work at the plutonium-processing facility at Oak Ridge" to make it funny.[14] The possible counterexamples to BVT seem endless.

McGraw might shake off these counterexamples; he is "weary" of having to deal with them (McGraw and Warner 2014, 11). But he also favors what are called "black swan arguments"—that is, all one has to do to disprove a statement is to find one example that contradicts it. One black swan demolishes the claim that all swans are white (167–68). Invariably, in the study of humor, certain examples come up that are problematic for any theory. But as an advocate of black swan arguments, McGraw should be obligated, weary or no, to address examples contrary to BVT. There would seem to be many.

Benign violation theorists believe that incongruity theory has focused too much on verbal humor and that it should attend to a wider range of humorous forms and behaviors. They claim that incongruity theory cannot deal with jokes that fail in some situations or receive different evaluations by different test subjects (Veatch 1998, 193–94; McGraw and Warner 2014, 51). Of course, incongruity theory *can* deal with such differences; it simply cannot deal with them entirely within the theory of what makes something humorous (and neither can BVT). There are too many contingencies that bear on particular humorous expressions.

As a folklorist, I have focused on verbal jokes because they constitute a form of folklore. Linguists have concentrated on such jokes because these scholars are necessarily concerned with verbal communication. Indeed, humor theorists should focus on both verbal and other humorous stimuli. However, there is a basis for arguing that verbal jokes are particularly important specimens for humor analysis. The superiority of jokes versus behavioral and situational humor relates to the matter of context. When an analyst reports on the humorous behaviors of others, there is no certainty that all the relevant aspects of context will be apprehended. There may be background knowledge of the group being observed that is not known to or understood by the observer. There may be elements of the social situation that the analyst is missing. McGraw and Warner refer to examples of newscasters bursting into laughter in the middle of stories about war zones or political scandals and proclaim that there is nothing humorous about such moments (McGraw and Warner 2014, 71). Although I know that there are many situations in which laughter is not a reaction to the perception of humor, I would contend that in the case of the newscasters there is nothing humorous *only as far as we can see.* I imagine that in many instances the newscasters might well be able to explain what it was that struck them as funny.

The matter of context can be illustrated by referring to a "sidewalk neuroscience experiment" conducted by Robert R. Provine (2000, 9). Provine had his students record 1,200 "laughter episodes" and look at what had been said just before the laughter occurred. Only 10–20 percent of pre-laugh comments were estimated to be even remotely humorous. Some of these nonhumorous pre-laugh comments are listed below:

Typical Statements:	*Typical Questions:*
I'll see you guys later.	It wasn't you?
Put those cigarettes away.	Does anyone have a rubber band?
I hope we all do well.	Oh, Tracey, what's wrong with us?
It was nice meeting you too.	Can I join you?
We can handle this.	How are you?
I see your point.	Are you sure?
I should do that, but I'm too lazy.	Do you want one of mine?
I try and lead a normal life.	What can I say?
I think I'm done.	Why are you telling me this?
I told you so.	What is that supposed to mean? (40–41)
I was completely horrified.	
There you go!	
I know!	
Must be nice!	
Look, it's Andrei!	

Granted, these comments and questions are not what one might normally think of as humorous and laughter provoking. Below, however, are eleven of the first twelve punchlines in direct discourse from a contemporary joke book:

Punchlines
It's the plumber.
What do you think? I'm saying grace.
Can't rightly say. I never caught one yet.
Sorry, I'm in sales not management.
The guy I'm looking for is the one who left the stall open.
About 12 cars and a caboose.
He got the pope as his chauffer.
Meow.
Wake up George, we're rich.
The alligator ate them all.
I just want my wife to see what happens to a man who doesn't drink, smoke, or gamble. (R. Edwards 1993)

On the surface, many of these punchlines would not appear to be humorous either. They prove humorous only when we know and understand what preceded them. They are humorous within the context of the joke, and it may be the case that many of the comments and questions that Provine's assistants recorded were also humorous in the context of the interaction that preceded them and in the context of the history of the relationship of the participants. I am not suggesting that the nonhumorous statements Provine cites were the punchlines of truncated jokes. I do not dispute the notion that laughter is often social and affiliative rather than a response to humor. My point is less a criticism of Provine's methodology than a suggestion about how important grasping the social context of interaction is in understanding spontaneously generated humor. One can sit with a group of people and not be able to figure out what it is that they are laughing about. "You had to be there" may not be enough to unravel the mystery. Sometimes you not only had to be there, you had to be there from the beginning of the relationship of the participants. That is why it is dicey to employ high-context humor as examples in humor analysis unless the analysts are certain that they fully grasp the relevant context.

Verbal joke texts and drawn cartoons are low-context humor. Of course, the contexts in which jokes are told and the situations in which someone points to a cartoon in a magazine may affect the perception and appreciation of humor. But cartoons in magazines and jokes in joke books are intended primarily for solitary consumption. They are for the most part self-contained. All that is needed to grasp the humor, beyond general cultural knowledge, is present in the text.[15] Unlike the spontaneous joking and laughter among a group of friends, it is less likely that there are contextual matters that the analyst is missing.

It is instructive to look at BVT's approach to the analysis of canned jokes (of which there are very, very few). Veatch's analysis of the riddle "Q: When is a door not a door? A: When it is ajar" (Veatch 1998, 200–201) is, unsurprisingly, virtually the same as the one offered by appropriate incongruity (e.g., Oring 1973, 362; 1992, 2). The riddle question proposes an incongruity—indeed, a logical contradiction—that is made appropriate by invoking a pun. The riddle answer concludes that a door can be *ajar* and *a jar*. The first is the state of a door; the second is not a door at all. The riddle answer is, of course, *spurious* because a word must retain a single, specified meaning when employed in reasoning. Veatch claims that the blatant violation of reasoning in this joke is a moral violation, "if only a mild one" (Veatch 1998, 201). I am not sure if a logical contradiction should be considered only a mild violation. Furthermore, though the pun injects some measure of appropriateness to the logical contradiction of a "door that is not a door," it hardly "normalizes" it. How could a pun, which is recognized by all who hear it as paralogical, "predominate" and be felt to be "more consciously real and correct" than the logical contradiction itself (167)? Those who understand the joke do not accept that the logical contradiction has been domesticated. Rather, they hold the incongruity, its "solution," and the speciousness of that "solution" in mind at the same time. To the extent that Veatch recognizes this problem, he argues that puns are not really very funny and people often groan at puns rather than laugh at them (204).[16] All in all, it is not clear what is gained by adding the notion of moral violation to the analysis of this joke or what is achieved by claiming the necessity of the arousal of emotion. It would seem to be enough to claim that the emotion that is necessarily aroused is that of *amusement* at the cognitive perception of an appropriate incongruity. All other attendant emotions are just that—attendant. They are responses to the contents of the joke or aspects of the humorous situation and not at the core of what makes something funny.

Another joke discussed by Veatch is:

Q: What's black and white and red all over and can't turn around in a doorway?

A: A nun with a javelin through her head.

Veatch notes that many principles are violated here, among them the sanctity of human life and the sanctity of those who devote themselves to holiness. There is also the violation that someone with a spear through her head should be concerned about turning around in a doorway. She should have more important things to deal with (Veatch 1998, 196). To be precise, the joke does not indicate that the nun is *concerned* about being unable to turn around in a doorway. The conditions of the riddle question—this is an example of a riddle joke—establish that not being able to turn around in a doorway is a factor that needs to be addressed in a solution, along with the black, white, and red. This riddle is itself derived from the older riddle "What's black and white and red all over?—A wounded nun" (alternately, an embarrassed zebra, a skunk with diaper rash, among others), which circulated decades ago. That joke was itself a takeoff on the "What's black and white and red all over?—A newspaper" riddle, which appears in many folk-riddle collections and in numerous popular publications throughout the twentieth century (Barrick 1974, 253–55). These more recent riddles are parodies, with *red* regarded solely as a color and not as a pun (read), as in the newspaper archetype. The wounded nun and the nun with a javelin through her head are parody riddles of the sick-joke strain. What is common to all of these jokes, however, is that they violate the sense that riddles are traditionally supposed to be resolved by identifying an integrated, coherent, and familiar object or event (Oring 1992, 20); rather, they identify an ersatz, unlikely, or implausible object or event. Understanding the incongruity and the appropriateness in all of these riddles is a cognitive achievement, and there is little to be gained by suggesting they all depend on moral violations that arouse emotion. The wounded nun variants employ an image that might provoke an emotional response, but it seems difficult to argue that all the black-and-white-and-red-all-over parodies about zebras and skunks depend upon arousing emotion. In the case of the wounded nun, emotion is an extra. It is brought to the joke through its imagery, but it is not in itself the source of the humor.

Both Veatch and McGraw are fully aware that amusement does not necessarily excite laughter, nor is laughter necessarily a response to amusement (Veatch 1998, 198–99; McGraw et al. 2012, 8; McGraw and Warner 2014, 78). There are many other situations in which humans laugh. Hysterical laughter, triumphant laughter, the laughter of relief, and chemically induced laughter are not likely to be responses to amusement. Much social laughter of the kind that Provine identified in his sidewalk experiments is communicative—social signaling—rather than a reaction to humor. Sympathetic laughter and simulated laughter likewise seem primarily communicative. Joyous laughter, such as the laughter emitted in the course of play, is expressive, but it seems more an expression of general pleasure than amusement. Play is fun but not necessarily funny, and there seems to be some distance between the two.

BVT theorists put quite a premium on laughter as an indicator of humor. Indeed, Veatch, McGraw, and McGraw's collaborators argue that the ability of BVT to account for peekaboo or tickling puts it ahead of all other humor theories (Veatch 1998, 197–98, 205–7; McGraw and Warner 2014, 11; McGraw et al. 2012, 2).[17] I have been cautious about trying to use the laughter of young children as compelling evidence for a particular theory of humor (Oring 2003, 3–4). We often cannot ask children, let alone infants, what they are laughing about; and we should not expect to understand the answer they might give us. Tickling is claimed to be "a violation of physical integrity and comfort" that involves a pain sensation as well as a "normal" touch sensation. In other words, tickling would seem to involve a perception of an attack (violation) in the absence of any real threat (normal/benign). These BVT theorists also point to the fact that you cannot tickle yourself. McGraw cites an experiment that shows that if a person uses a mechanical device, and the control apparatus is delayed or otherwise dissociated from the person's hand motion, one can tickle oneself (Veatch 1998, 205–6; McGraw and Warner 2014, 11).

I am not confident that the response to tickling is the same as the sense of amusement at a joke. Furthermore, there seems to be a kind of tickling that is clearly an attack: when someone digs into someone else's ribs or chest in a forceful although not really painful way. Then there is the kind of tickling that stems from the application of a feather to the sole of one's foot, the back of one's neck, or the nostril of one's nose. This kind of touch is not equivalent to just any light touch; it would cause withdrawal were it administered while someone were asleep. My impression is that this latter type of tickling is of a kind that one *can* perform on oneself, although it is not likely to elicit laughter, whether performed by oneself or by another. Any laughter response that might be aroused by this type of tickling is more likely to be subjects laughing at their own reaction to the sensation rather than laughing at the sensation itself.

Generally what is interesting about tickling from the point of view of humor research is that as it is difficult to tickle yourself, it is likewise difficult to laugh at a joke you tell yourself. It seems one might make a joke at which one laughs, and laughs heartily, but this is generally in the presence of others. How often people spontaneously create humor at which they laugh when they are alone is worth exploring. Sometimes people do laugh in their dreams, but it is not clear how frequently this occurs.

If Veatch is the theoretician of BVT, McGraw and his collaborators are its research division. In three sets of experiments, they tried to test the benign violation hypothesis (McGraw and Warren 2010; McGraw et al. 2012; McGraw, Williams, and Warren 2013). The first set consisted of five experiments. In the first experiment, subjects were asked about four scenarios to see whether a moral violation version proved to be more humorous than one that did not involve a moral violation. They were yes-or-no questions. For example, a situation was described in which a father told his son to cremate his body after his death and do whatever he wanted with the ashes. In one version the son buries the ashes, and in the other he snorts the ashes. Subjects were asked to rate whether they thought the scenario was "wrong" and whether the scenario made them laugh. The degree of laughter was not assessed. The other scenarios involved selling a daughter's virginity versus selling her jewelry on eBay; a mother pocketing the money in the tip jar or adding money to the jar at her daughter's wedding; and Jimmy Dean hiring a rabbi versus a farmer as the spokesperson for the company's pork products. In each case a far greater percentage of respondents found the violation version "wrong" as opposed to the control version. The violation versions also received more "made me laugh" assessments (McGraw and Warren 2010, 1143).

Not explained, however, is why the violation version of using a rabbi as the spokesperson for Jimmy Dean pork products was considered wrong by only 22 percent of test subjects but rated as laughable by 62 percent. Only 12 percent of subjects saw the scenario as *both* wrong and laughable—less than half the rate for the other three scenarios. In other words, the violation version that received the lowest "wrong" rating of all the four scenarios received the highest "made me laugh" rating. This particular result is not discussed.

In the second experiment in the first set, subjects on a university campus were approached and asked to read either the burying or snorting-the-ashes scenario from the first experiment. The research assistants then rated those people who smiled or laughed as displaying amusement. The research participants then were asked to agree or disagree with whether the scenarios were "wrong," "not wrong," or "both wrong and not wrong." Subjects were more likely to display amusement at the violation version of the scenario. Those who rated the situation as "both wrong and not wrong" were significantly more likely to show amusement than those who rated the scenario as only "wrong" or only "not wrong" (McGraw and Warren 2010, 1144).

Of course, if the experiments had asked whether the behaviors were "incongruous" or "appropriate" or both, they might have come up with similar results. McGraw and Warren presume that violations—any violations—of expectations elicit negative emotions. Some do. But in the absence of a comparison with materials that do not depend upon behaviors strongly marked as true moral violations, a meaningful assessment of what provokes humor is hard to come by. Would the snorting-the-ashes scenario be regarded as more amusing than the following scenario? An Irishman walks into a bar in Cork and asks the bartender the quickest way to Dublin. When the bartender asks, "Are you walking or driving?" the man says he is driving. The bartender says, "That's the quickest way" (Keillor 2005, 127). Whatever violations are resident in this joke, they are hardly likely to rise to the level of emotion that attaches to snorting one's father's ashes.[18]

The third experiment in this set asked student subjects to rate a scenario in which a man rubs a kitten against his naked genitals. In one version the kitten purrs and seems to enjoy the contact; in the other it whines and does not. The expectation was that those subjects exposed to the second case would be less inclined to find it amusing since there is a violation of a norm with nothing to make that violation seem acceptable, that is, benign. Subjects were asked whether they thought the behavior was wrong and whether they were amused or disgusted. Most students rated both scenarios wrong (72 percent) and disgusting (94 percent). More subjects were amused by the scenario in which the kitten seemed to enjoy the contact over the one in which it didn't (61 percent versus 28 percent). Participants were more likely to report being amused *and* disgusted when the kitten enjoyed the contact (56 percent versus 22 percent), suggesting that amusement did not supplant the feeling of disgust but coexisted with it (McGraw and Warren 2010, 1144–45).

What all this suggests is that disgusting images, like other images, can be used in the creation of humor. Numerous joke books attest to this fact (e.g., Legman 1968, 1975). While in some instances the arousal of emotion may impede the perception of humor, emotionally charged images and ideas can also be used to create humor. Freud observed that a hostile or obscene thought can become tolerable when ensconced in joke form. The joke draws pleasure from a source that, for social reasons, would otherwise be inaccessible. "We can only laugh when a joke has come to our help" (Freud 1960, 8:101).

In other words, disgusting or otherwise tabooed ideas or images become *acceptable within a humorous frame.* "A soldier swears fidelity to his wife, but after months at the front without relief he has intercourse with a pig. On his return his wife asks, 'Have you been faithful to me, honey?' 'I sure have.' 'In a pig's ass, you have.' 'Damn them German spies!'" (Legman 1968, 215). While an act of bestiality is at the center of this joke, the joke revolves around the incongruity of the soldier mentioning German spies, which seems to have nothing to do with anything that has transpired. But his wife's dismissive expression "in a pig's ass" exactly refers to the act he was trying to hide. So it is appropriate that he feels that spies must have informed his wife about his sexual behavior. The joke does not hinge on emotion aroused by the act of bestiality but on the literal and metaphorical sense of the wife's expression. Technically, it depends on a pun. Any emotion aroused by the bestial act is, at best, an addition to the pleasure of the joke (Freud 1960, 8:101–2). Emotion doesn't produce the humor. The recognition of an appropriate incongruity does.[19]

The fourth experiment in the set conducted by McGraw and Warren contrasts the levels of disgust and amusement reported by subjects to scenarios in which a church offers a raffle ticket for a new Humvee to anyone who joins versus a credit union that offers the same reward. Subjects were categorized as churchgoers or nonchurchgoers, on the presumption that the former would be more committed to the violated norm and thus find the church raffle scenario less amusing than nonchurchgoers. While both groups almost equally reported being disgusted by the idea of a raffle ticket for a Humvee being offered for joining a church, non-churchgoers were more likely to report being both amused *and* disgusted (69 percent versus 35 percent). McGraw and Warren contend that a strong commitment to the sanctity of the church by churchgoers made them less likely to be amused by the scenario.

It is worth noting that 28 percent of churchgoers reported being disgusted even by the credit union scenario, although none of the nonchurchgoers were. Also, 16 percent of the churchgoers were disgusted *and* amused by the credit union scenario, almost half the percentage of churchgoers disgusted and amused by the church scenario. Furthermore, 44 percent of nonchurchgoers and 59 percent of churchgoers were amused by the harmless credit union scenario. Since there was no clear moral violation to contend with in the credit union case, one wonders what exactly caused their amusement (McGraw and Warren 2010, 1145–46).

If we take McGraw and Warren's fourth experiment at face value, it shows that strong commitment to a moral principle may arouse emotion that interferes with the perception or appreciation of humor. This, however, is a notion that humor theorists of all stripes—from Bergson and Freud to contemporary incongruity theorists—recognize (e.g., Oring 1992, 12; Morreall 1999, 18). It does not advance BVT since the experiment does not show that humor is produced by a benign violation. What it shows is that something that arouses too much emotion is likely to interfere with the ability to find a particular text, image, or behavior amusing.

The fifth experiment in the first set concerns the matter of psychological distance. It is maintained that a violation will seem more benign—and thus more amusing—when it is distanced from the perceiver. BVT theorists are fond of repeating Mel Brooks's dictum: "Tragedy is when I cut my finger. Comedy is when you walk into an open sewer and die" (Veatch 1998, 173; McGraw and Warren 2010, 1146; McGraw et al. 2012, 1).[20] Subjects were given a priming task of plotting far or near points on a graph. Then they were given scenarios to read of a man having sex with a chicken before cooking and eating it versus a man marinating a chicken before cooking and eating it. Most subjects reacted with disgust to the man having sexual intercourse with the chicken regardless of whether they had completed the near or far priming task (86 percent versus 83 percent). But subjects who were primed with the far-distance plotting task were more likely to be disgusted *and* amused than those who were primed with the near-distance task (64 percent versus 28 percent) (McGraw and Warren 2010, 1146–47).

What is demonstrated is that psychological distance, or priming for psychological distance, increases the likelihood of humor perception when dealing with disgusting images. But this is only the inverse of the fourth experiment, which showed that emotional commitment—lack of distance—reduces humor. Conditions that increase or reduce the emotional power of an image or behavior affect the perception of amusement. When emotion is increased—by selecting for ideological commitments like church sanctity, for example—amusement is reduced. When emotional arousal is decreased by creating psychological distance from disturbing ideas and images, humor perception is increased. In other words, amusement may not register in the presence of too much emotion. Again, theorists of many stripes would recognize this principle, but they would not necessarily agree that humor was fundamentally emotional in nature. Rather, emotion is something that promotes or impedes humor perception. Although sunshine can motivate someone to go for a walk and rain may deter him, weather conditions are not what produce the ability to walk.

BVT claims it can account for experimental results that other humor theories cannot. A second set of five experiments was designed to determine whether serious violations ("tragedies") and mild violations ("mishaps") result in differences in the amusement perceived when the stimulus material is at greater or lesser psychological distances. The prediction was that distant tragedies would prove more amusing than recent tragedies, as distance reduces the severity of the violation. Mishaps, however, would be funnier when they were linked to recent events because the violation was mild and consequently benign. These experiments ranged from asking subjects what incidents in their lives became more humorous or less humorous as time passed to presenting them with incidents (e.g., hit by a car, stubbed your toe) that occurred either yesterday or five years in the past and then asking them to indicate which they would consider more humorous. Temporal distance was not the only distance examined. Experiments were conducted to determine whether more severe or milder violations were found more or less amusing at differing social distances (stranger versus friend), hypothetical distances (fake versus genuine), and spatial distances (perceptually far or near). In all instances, subjects found more distant tragedies and less distant mishaps more amusing (McGraw et al. 2012).[21]

The authors realized that the first three experiments were open to criticism because the manipulation for distance was too obvious to the experimental subjects (McGraw et al. 2012, 5). It might also be added that in these three experiments, the question of *interestingness* was not considered. One might have asked another set of respondents whether they would find personal mishaps that occurred yesterday versus five years ago or mishaps befalling a friend or a stranger more relatable in casual conversation *irrespective* of whether they were perceived as humorous. In the course of a conversation, if someone tells a story about a minor mishap, one cannot respond with a five-year-old or recent story about a stubbed toe unless there is something about the event that is interesting and relevant. One justification for telling a story about stubbing one's toe is that it is amusing. A simple report of stubbing one's toe, however, is not amusing. It must be *made* amusing. Were there a benign violation in a report of stubbing one's toe, and were such reports naturally to produce humor, accounts of stubbed toes would permeate our daily conversation. So when McGraw et al. (2012, 4) asked whether stubbing one's toe or getting hit by a car was more or less amusing, what the subjects may have been hearing and responding to was whether they were more or less likely to be able to *make* an account of such events amusing. Too often, researchers assume that the responses subjects provide in psychological experiments and to sociological surveys are answers to the questions they have asked. I think they might be wrong a good percentage of the time.[22]

In the experiment testing whether mishaps were more likely to be humorous when they befall a friend than a stranger, subjects were presented with stories in which a young woman texted Haiti 90999 200 times versus five times, thinking that her texts caused other people to donate money for disaster relief. Only later did she discover that in the first case $2,000 and in the second case $50 would be charged to her phone bill. The $2,000 loss was found more amusing when it was described as happening to a stranger, and the $50 loss was more amusing when it occurred to a close friend. While McGraw et al. feel that other humor theories might be able to explain a tragedy being more amusing when it occurs to strangers, they believe that only BVT can explain the increase in humor when a mishap is attributed to friends (2013, 4–5). But what is presented to the subjects is not simply a big loss (tragedy) versus a little loss (mishap). Subjects are presented with a *story* of a woman who did not know what she was doing; while thinking she was encouraging others to support relief efforts, she was actually donating her own money. What would have been the case if the experiment had asked subjects whether they found it more or less amusing if they learned that a stranger lost $2,000 and a friend had lost $50 and vice versa? The degree of violation would remain the same. The loss of $50 remains relatively benign, although it is still a violation. What would be missing, however, would be the account explaining the reason for the loss—the individual's cluelessness about the consequences of her texting. In other words, what would be missing would be a story with a structure of appropriate incongruity. A woman acts to raise money for relief efforts. It is incongruous that she does not realize that she is donating her own money, but it is appropriate since texting usually serves as a means of communication and not expenditure. What is added or subtracted from the structure of appropriate incongruity in the story is the emotion attached to friends versus strangers. The story is more humorous when it occurs to close friends without seriously damaging them. Emotion inhibits finding amusement in accounts in which friends are seriously damaged. But the humor is not generated by a benign violation. Whatever emotion is aroused is an adjunct of the tale that an appropriate incongruity perspective can straightforwardly analyze. Had McGraw et al. asked the subjects which of the stories was more interesting, I suspect they would have found the same results except that a severe loss to a friend would also prove interesting. The reason the severe version is found less amusing when it happens to a friend is that amusement provides pleasure and one does not—or should not—extract pleasure from a friend's misfortune. The sympathetic reaction suppresses the humor in the tragic case.

So the first three experiments in this series might simply show that tragedies retain their interest because of the nature of the event. They are interesting right after the occurrence and may hold interest far into the future. They may become the subject of humor once emotions aroused by the event—assuming they have been aroused—have sufficiently subsided. People, however, are ready to find mishaps more interesting and perhaps amusing because of their connection to familiar people and immediate events. Freud spoke about "topicality" as a source of pleasure in jokes and noted that there are certain jokes that provoke much laughter when they first appear because they allude to people and events of interest. When that interest ceases, however, the jokes lose a good deal of their pleasure and currency (Freud 1960, 8:122). Freud cited the example of a host who served a pudding known as a roulade, which demanded some skill in its preparation. When a guest inquired whether the pudding had been made at home, the host replied, "Yes, indeed. A home-roulade." At the time, the question of "home rule" was a headline in all the newspapers. A topical reference, according to Freud, adds pleasure to a joke or witticism much as a sexual or aggressive thought adds pleasure, although perhaps not to the same degree (94, 122). So while emotion can interfere with finding humor in a tragedy until some psychological distance has been acquired, mishaps may gain in humor from a connection to familiar people and recent events because they tap additional sources of pleasure.[23] It is not that humor is the result of affect provoked by a benign violation; it is that certain ideas, behaviors, and events may charge a humorous story or saying with additional energy.

There is only one experiment in the third set, and it is perhaps the most sophisticated experiment in the whole series. Using three humorous tweets—e.g., "JUS BLEW DA ROOF OFF A OLIVE GARDEN FREE BREADSTICKS 4 EVERYONE"—that were sent before Hurricane Sandy struck the northeast coast of the United States on October 29, 2012, McGraw, Williams, and Warren (2013) conducted an online survey of evaluations of these tweets from the day before the storm hit until ninety-nine days after the event. One hundred respondents were surveyed at each of ten time points. They were asked to rate whether the tweets were funny, humorous, upsetting, offensive, boring, irrelevant, or confusing (funny and humorous, upsetting and offensive, boring and irrelevant were collapsed into single indices).[24]

Results showed that the funniness rating for the tweets was high the day before the storm hit but fell following the storm and then rose to new highs about thirty-six days after the disaster, only to fall to new lows ninety-nine days after the event. McGraw, Williams, and Warren argue that while other humor theories might explain why humor appreciation fell immediately following the disaster—the offensiveness index rose after the extent of the storm's destruction became known—only BVT could explain why, when the humor finally became acceptable again weeks later, it then fell off considerably in the following months. From the point of view of BVT, humorous evaluations of the tweets rose when the severe violation following the storm was transformed into a benign violation a month later. After that point, however, apathy set in. Increased temporal distance from the disaster made the event seem "completely benign" (McGraw, Williams, and

Warren 2013, 5). Presumably, "completely benign" means there was no longer any real sense of a violation and consequently no humor.[25]

This explanation seems unconvincing. Although the offensiveness rating of the tweets rose in the week following the storm, and fell off when people found the tweets humorous thirty-six days later, the offensiveness rating ninety-nine days after the event was basically the same as it had been at thirty-six days. In fact, the rating rose slightly (McGraw, Williams, and Warren 2013, 4). If the tweets were still perceived as offensive, how would this suggest apathy or a situation that was "purely benign"? I would suggest, as I did above, that apathy is not simply a matter of an offensiveness rating, because humor is not simply a matter of affect aroused by what has been called a benign violation. In fact, ninety-nine days later the event probably ceased to be interesting to anyone other than those who had lived through it or were still recovering from it. As Freud would have said, it was no longer topical. It could no longer rely on that *extra* charge infused by recent events. "Home-roulade," while still a joke, is less funny when home rule is no longer a topic of conversation. Humorous tweets about Hurricane Sandy are less funny when everyday attention has turned to other matters and even to other crises and disasters. Humor can draw energy from emotionally charged ideas. This is not to say, however, that humor is fundamentally an emotional affair.[26]

BVT argues that incongruity theory cannot explain why psychological distance would result in different degrees of amusement. This, of course, is *not* the case. Appropriate incongruity theorists can and do use psychological distance to explain variations in the humor response as they would use other extrinsic factors: context, topicality, brevity, surprise, timing, prosody, phraseology, and truth. Because BVT argues that the perception of humor depends upon emotion, it focuses exclusively on highly charged images in its experiments: bestiality, human remains, disaster, disfigurement, immorality. It ignores the numerous examples of humor that do not depend on viscerally emotional ideas. "A guy in the garment industry has a son who asks him, 'Daddy, what kind of flower is that?' The father says, "What am I, a milliner?"' This is a joke and, presuming you know what a milliner is, a fairly decent joke. It employs no charged ideas or images. I would bet that it would rate higher in amusement than many of the charged scenarios used in the various experiments conducted by McGraw and his colleagues (see Earleywine and Mankoff 2013). An appropriate incongruity perspective can describe the source of this joke's humor quite easily (Oring 2003, 14–16). I would be interested to hear BVT's account of this joke. (Again, if the account is precisely the same, one has to wonder why the emotional component of the theory is at all necessary.)

When BVT emphasizes the cognitive representations of jokes—as Veatch does in his analysis of the when-is-a door-not-a-door riddle—the theory is really a clone of the appropriate incongruity perspective. That is to say, what is called a benign violation looks very much like an appropriate incongruity. When BVT commits to the notion that emotion necessarily underpins all these cognitive categories and is responsible for the sense of amusement, it has exceeded what is warranted by the data. Emotion *is* relevant to understanding humor. One can easily factor emotion into the humor equation in any number of instances. What is not clear is that one can always factor emotion out of it.

CHAPTER FIVE

Humor and the Discovery of False Beliefs

Art thou but a dagger of the mind, a false creation,
Proceeding from the heat-oppressed brain?
—WILLIAM SHAKESPEARE

The most recent effort at a theory of humor is the one proposed by psychologists Matthew M. Hurley and Reginald B. Adams and philosopher Daniel C. Dennett in their book *Inside Jokes: Using Humor to Reverse-Engineer the Mind* (2011). This is perhaps one of the most comprehensive and closely argued theoretical proposals since Sigmund Freud's *Jokes and Their Relation to the Unconscious*.[1] Their proposal has three components: (1) the theory itself, (2) the cognitive psychology that underlies the argument, and (3) an evolutionary account of how humor and laughter came to be. The theory itself is rather compact, although the terms in which it is rendered require some explanation.

THE THEORY

Humor occurs when: An active element in a mental space that has covertly entered that space (for one reason or another), and is taken to be true (i.e., epistemically committed) within that space, is diagnosed to be false in that space—simply in the sense that it is the loser in an epistemic reconciliation process; and (trivially) the discovery is not accompanied by any (strong) negative emotional valence. (Hurley, Dennett, and Adams 2011, 121)

While the terminology might at first sight seem off-putting to those not familiar with the language of cognitive science, all the terms can be clearly defined and the propositions straightforwardly explained. A *mental space* is a small conceptual arena that is constructed in the mind for purposes of local understanding and action as people think and talk (Fauconnier and Turner 2002, 40). If I say, "Next year, Melissa will take her bar exam," I have constructed a space of *next year*, a space that not only has a time dimension but will be presumed to resemble *this year* in many, but not all, of its attributes. For example, it will resemble this year in that it will be supposed that the United States will still be a country with a government and a legal system, law schools, and a bar exam. It will not be like this year, however, primarily because Melissa will be taking her exam and will be an attorney if she passes the exam, although she is not an attorney this year. Within the mental space for "next year," the space of "taking the bar exam" is constructed and populated with presumptions based on previous knowledge: it is an exam that aspiring attorneys, not physicians, take; it is difficult; it is something one usually takes after the completion of a law degree; it is a prerequisite for practicing law, and so on. There may be many other elements that come to inhabit this space, depending, in part, on the richness of our knowledge about legal training and accreditation and on the course of the conversation or behaviors taking place. In other words, a mental space is a provisional mental territory that is constructed and loaded with aspects of knowledge in order to understand what is being said, to construct one's own responses to what is being said, and within which one's own behaviors are planned and the behaviors of others are interpreted and predicted. One does not necessarily load the "bar" space with *all* the knowledge that one may possess about the bar exam. Rather, knowledge is loaded *as needed* for the task at hand. It may be necessary to call up to working memory only that the bar is a difficult law exam that requires preparation and is generally taken after graduating law school in order to respond to one's interlocutor, "Is she graduating from law school next year?" or "Will she be taking preparatory courses?"

An element (belief) is *active* if that element resides in *working memory* and not just long-term memory. You believe that you are reading a book right now. You also believe that brewed coffee is bitter. The first belief is active and in working memory; but unless you happen to be tasting coffee at the moment, or thinking about or being asked about the taste of coffee, the latter belief is not active. It is a part of long-term memory. Long-term memory beliefs are dispositions to have working-memory beliefs under particular circumstances (Hurley, Dennett, and Adams 2011, 104–5). We may activate the belief about coffee bitterness if a colleague offers us sugar with our coffee and we actively consider or state that it is the bitter taste we relish.

The proposition that the belief must enter the mental space *covertly* is to claim that the belief is not under active, conscious consideration. It is below the level of normal awareness. It is a tacit assumption within a particular mental space (Hurley, Dennett, and Adams 2011, 118). People are constantly engaged in a time-pressured *heuristic search* that generates presumptions about what they will experience next. Information is assimilated into our mental spaces without much in the way of careful inspection (117). Many of our presumptions prove to be correct—or at least, nothing explicitly contradicts them—but the process is also prone to error (12). If you indicate that you went to a restaurant, my mental space is likely to assume the presence of tables, chairs, menus, tableware, food, drink, cooks, waiters, and other diners. It does not assume aardvarks or nuclear reactors. If you tell me that an aardvark got loose in a restaurant, we might discuss how people come to possess aardvarks and why someone would bring one into a restaurant. But then the matter of aardvarks in the restaurant mental space is not covert but a matter of attention and deliberation. If you tell me, however, that you spilled a glass of water or wine on the table in a restaurant, I would not have to ponder the question of where a glass of water or wine could possibly have come from. Drinks and glassware inhabit the restaurant mental space covertly.

Epistemic commitment to a belief means that one takes the belief as true. The belief can be trusted, inferences drawn from it, and actions taken on its basis (Hurley, Dennett, and Adams 2011, 111). If one is epistemically committed to a belief, one is not pondering its likelihood or *wary* of its truth.[2] Epistemic belief A in working memory can run up against epistemic belief B in working memory such that B undermines the validity of A—that is, it shows belief A to be false. Actually, in an epistemic conflict of this type, different results are possible: (1) the conflict remains unresolved, (2) a creative insight dissolves what is only an apparent conflict, or (3) one of the beliefs survives and the other is obliterated (112), which is to say, it is the loser in a process of epistemic reconciliation. It is discovered to be false. Finally, in the context of humor, the discovery of a false belief must not be accompanied by any strong negative emotion that might overpower and suppress the mirth that would normally accompany this discovery.

In sum, people will find humor when a false belief that covertly inhabits their working memory is discovered to be false so long as this discovery does not arouse undue negative emotion. Also, because humans have what is called the *intentional stance* or a *theory of mind*—they can attribute a range of mental states to others—they can find mirth in the discovery of covert false beliefs in others and in others' discoveries of their own false beliefs (Hurley, Dennett, and Adams 2011, 145). Mirth, it must be added, is the pleasure in discovering a mistake in active belief structures.[3] This pleasure, it will be seen, is the reward necessary to advance the search for error, and it is indispensable within an evolutionary paradigm. Counterexamples to this theory would be those in which beliefs are:

"(1) active, (2) heuristically created, (3) committed, and (4) contradicted but not funny" (201).

There is a lot more to be said about the cognitive behaviors that underlie this theory—which for the sake of convenience will be labeled False-Belief Theory, or FBT—but nothing that is really necessary to grasp the overall approach.[4] The cognitive processes underlying the theory are spelled out at length in *Inside Jokes* and to attempt to discuss them here would be to reproduce a great deal of dense, though cogent, argument and detailed example. Not being a cognitive scientist, I will stipulate to the portrait of human cognition and emotion that Hurley, Dennett, and Adams present and leave it to others more versed in the field to register their approbation or disapproval. (I will not be quite as reticent when it comes to considering the evolutionary argument, however.) In any event, if FBT doesn't do the job in characterizing and analyzing humor today, the evolutionary argument is moot. My engagement with the theory stems from the effort to understand jokes and other forms of humor. My concern is whether the theory answers the questions I have and explains the examples of humor that are the objects of my attention.

The authors emphasize that humor is not a property of objects or events. It does not reside in jokes but in the human mind. Consequently, the focus on jokes and other humor stimuli is likely to produce tunnel vision (Hurley, Dennett, and Adams 2011, 16–19). The first statement is true: humor is not the property of objects or events per se. Humor is rooted in a perception of objects and events (Oring 1992, 2). All humor theorists know this, even if they sometimes fail to make the point explicit. The second proposition is not true. While humor theorists direct their attention to jokes and other humorous stimuli, they do so because studying the stimuli is likely to reveal *what it is that the mind must perceive* in order to register amusement and conjure up laughter. They do not and cannot address the mind directly.

Some examples might serve to concretize what has hitherto been a fairly abstract discussion.

> Two goldfish were in their tank. One turns to the other and says, "You man the guns, I'll drive." (Hurley, Dennett, and Adams 2011, 42).

With the description of goldfish in a tank, the mental space that is created presumes a fish tank. Goldfish primes the sense of tank as an aquarium. The punchline overturns this belief: the fish are situated in what can only be reckoned as a mechanized vehicle employed in armored combat. The pun on tank tricks us to commit to a fish-tank belief "when the word 'tank' is still not completely unambiguous." Until the punchline, there is nothing in the mental space to challenge the sense of the fish being in an aquarium. But once the punchline is uttered, we discover this committed belief to be false (110, 119).

Another punning example:

HARRY: Did Melissa pass the bar?

JANE: Have you ever known Melissa to pass a bar?

This example would seem to be exactly analogous to the first. Auditors or readers of this joke discover their commitment to the belief that "bar" refers to a law exam and "pass" to exam success to be false (what is termed a first-person belief). The punchline suggests that "bar" is taken to refer to a drinking establishment and "pass" to walking past. Suppose for a moment that I were Harry and you were Jane. Then the false belief would not be my commitment to a false belief about what "bar" and "passing" refer to, since I am the one doing the referring, but my false belief about what you would take the sense of "bar" and "pass" to be. I still retain the belief that "pass the bar" refers to success in a law examination. It is only my expectation that you will take the same meaning that proves to be false (a third-person belief). I would expect that Hurley, Dennett, and Adams would have to regard the joke text and the joke in the social exchange as cognitively two different jokes uncovering two different false beliefs: the first a false belief concerning my commitment to the meaning of "passing the bar" (first-person humor), the second a false belief about your commitment to the meaning of the term (third-person humor).[5]

In the second example, it is important to note that I almost immediately register your response as not genuine. I do not believe that you really believe my question about "passing the bar" refers to walking past a drinking establishment. That is why I do not correct your misunderstanding but rather smile, laugh, or just shake my head. I take your understanding to be appropriate but illegitimate and believe that you know it is illegitimate as well. I understand that you understand you have deliberately taken the term in some other sense while grasping my intended sense at the same time.

Here is a joke example not rooted in a pun:

Taking his seat in his chamber, the judge faced the opposing lawyers. "I have been presented by both of you with a bribe," the judge began. Both lawyers squirmed uncomfortably. "You, Attorney Leoni, gave me $15,000. And you, Attorney Campos, gave me $10,000."

The judge reached into his pocket and pulled out a check, which he handed to Leoni. "Now then, I am returning $5,000, and we are going to decide this case solely on its merits." (Hurley, Dennett, and Adams 2011, 151)

Hurley, Dennett, and Adams maintain that this joke depends upon the first-person belief that the lawyers will be reprimanded for engaging in bribery. This belief is aroused by the lawyers "squirming uncomfortably" at the judge's revelation of the offered bribes, and the auditors or readers of the joke expect the judge to prove himself immune to bribery. The punchline exposes these beliefs as false, and it shows the lawyers' expectation that they would gain some advantage from their bribes to be false as well (152).

Although the false beliefs that would likely be engendered in the telling of this joke are identified, something significant is left out of the account. More is going on than the discovery of a few false beliefs. The joke hinges on a recognition that the judge's return of bribe money only serves to demonstrate that he is corrupt, *and* his keeping $10,000 in bribes from each lawyer allows him to judge the case impartially. Without taking these factors into account a great deal of what makes the above text a joke is eliminated. But these are the elements that are central in recognizing a *structure of ideas* and not simply a negation of beliefs (although beliefs are negated). That structure of ideas is *appropriate incongruity* (which is related to incongruity resolution but not identical with it [Oring 1992, 1–15; 2003, 1–12]). In the joke there are two incongruities. The first is that the judge announces the bribes but then returns only a portion of the money to one of the attorneys. Why? Because he is equalizing the bribes from the attorneys in order to be able to decide the case impartially. That is appropriate because no attorney will garner any favor from the judge since his bribe is equal to the bribe of the other attorney. The second incongruity is that the judge claims to be acting impartially in the interest of justice, but in fact he is operating within a larger frame of corruption because he is accepting bribes. Again, this is appropriate since the judge has kept an equal amount of bribe money from each attorney, so the payments should not serve to sway the judge's decision one way or the other. Anyone who is amused by this joke and is asked to identify what makes it funny would probably point in some awkward fashion to the elements that comprise this structure. ("The judge is a crook but he acts as if he is even-handed.") Hurley, Dennett, and Adams strongly assert that humor does not reside in an act of interpretation and reinterpretation of a text or situation, only in the recognition of a covert false belief (Hurley, Dennett, and Adams 2011, 208–11). But if the humor in the joke is dependent only on the falsification of the beliefs that the attorneys would be reprimanded for their bribes and that the judge is honest, why would the text not remain a joke if the judge had not returned the money to Mr. Leoni but straightforwardly stated, "These bribes are now known to both of you and so are unlikely to sway me one way or the other. I will judge the case on its merits"? The same beliefs are falsified. The expectation that the attorneys will be reprimanded does not prove to be true; the expectation that the judge is immune to bribery is also falsified. But this would not seem to be much of a joke. Similarly, if the judge announced the bribes and said, "Thank you for your contributions to my children's college fund, but let us proceed with the case," the same beliefs would be falsified, but we might be amused only by the irony in the judge's characterization of his bribe taking. What actually serves to create the original joke, I would argue, hinges on *how* judicial impartiality can be rooted in blatant corruption, not simply on the revelation that the attorneys will not be reprimanded or that the judge is dishonest.

The same observations would apply to the jokes about the goldfish in a tank and Melissa passing the bar. Again Hurley, Dennett, and Adams identify a mistaken commitment to a belief about the denotations of words that proves to be false, but it is important to register that those words make some sense in at least two domains. In the case of goldfish, a "tank" suggests an aquarium, and in the case of guns and driving, it points to an armored vehicle. In a fictional world, fish could be situated in such a vehicle. At the same time, while it may be recognized that an armored vehicle may prove a valid substitute for an aquarium in a linguistic equation, it is not a *legitimate* substitute in a conceptual equation. Fish live in water and do not have the limbs to manipulate machinery. The substitution of an armored vehicle for an aquarium is recognized as specious. It is not that the initial sense of the meaning of *tank* proves "false" and the second "true." The second is recognized as equally false. It is characteristic of jokes that what makes an incongruity appropriate is that the appropriateness is seen to be spurious and illegitimate (Oring 1992, 2–3; 2003, 5–8).[6] It is not just the belief that *tank* refers to an aquarium that is mistaken but also that an armored vehicle, on the basis of the feeble thread of phonological identity, is in some way an acceptable surrogate for an aquarium in a mental space containing goldfish.[7] In the joke about the judge and lawyers, the appropriateness of the judge's action equalizing the bribes to level the field is also recognizable as spurious—one cannot claim a commitment to justice and the rule of law while accepting payoffs.

Another example:

What did the 0 say to the 8?
"Nice belt." (Hurley, Dennett, and Adams 2011, 201)

FBT would argue that we are mistaken in the presumption that 0 and 8 are two different numbers. An 8 is really a 0 with an additional item of apparel. One does not, however, accept that an 8 is a 0, but one accepts that an 8 could be seen as a 0 girded around the middle. The second interpretation does not nullify a belief about the difference between integers.[8]

The false-belief theorists think that the punchline of a joke serves only to reveal a false belief. An incongruity arises in a joke and the punchline points to a belief whose falseness gives rise to that incongruity. But the punchline leads to a reconceptualization of what has come before. It does not lead to a falsification in a logical sense of the term. In jokes, both A and ~A can be "false" (Oring 1973, 366; 1981, 125–26; 1992, 81–93).[9]

> OLE: Hello? Funeral Home?
>
> FUNERAL HOME: Yes?
>
> OLE: My wife Lena died.
>
> FUNERAL HOME: Oh, I'm sorry to hear that. We'll send someone right away to pick up the body. Where do you live?
>
> OLE: At the end of Eucalyptus Drive.
>
> FUNERAL HOME: Can you spell that for me?
>
> OLE: How 'bout if I drag her over to Oak Street and you pick her up dere. (Keillor 2005, 230)

There are no incongruities in the setup of this joke. What is revealed in the punchline is that Ole does not know how to spell the name of the street on which he lives. We may presume that he does, but the punchline exposes this belief as false. It also shows that Ole would be willing to drag his dead wife over to a street that he can spell in order for the funeral home to pick up the body. This is appropriate in that it solves the spelling problem because "Oak" is easier to spell than "Eucalyptus." (Ole is not the only one with a spelling problem, however; the funeral home also has a problem with the spelling of the street name and makes the question of its spelling overt, which should create a problem for FBT.) But Ole's solution is incongruous because one does not drag the body of a dead relative around the neighborhood to avoid spelling a street name. If Ole had responded to the spelling request with "U-k-a-l-i-p-t-u-s," the belief that he could spell the name of the street on which he lives would likewise be invalidated, but the sense of the joke—if there still was one—would be entirely changed. If Ole had responded, "Er, no, but I can meet you at Oak Street and show you where my house is," would there still be a joke? If Ole had responded, "It's between Oak and Pine where it meets Ash," we might suspect that Ole can't spell his street's name because he gives his street's location in relation to streets that are easier to spell, but we would still not be at the level of the original joke text. In other words, the nature of Ole's response is crucial to making the text a joke, and not merely by its awakening a joke recipient to the fact that Ole can't spell the name of his own street.

Hurley, Dennett, and Adams claim that FBT builds on incongruity-resolution theory, but this is somewhat misleading. They demote incongruity theory for being descriptive rather than explanatory (Hurley, Dennett, and Adams 2011, 46, 50), although description can be a form of explanation (Kaplan 1964, 329). I think that incongruity theorists of every stripe would admit that they do not know why certain types of incongruity provoke amusement and laughter. But that is neither here nor there. Isaac Newton did not know why masses attracted one another. He theorized that they did attract, however, and described that attraction in rather precise terms.

Hurley, Dennett, and Adams invoke some tired examples of incongruities from the work of the nineteenth-century philosopher Alexander Bain to demonstrate that incongruities are not inherently humorous (Hurley, Dennett, and Adams 2011, 48). For the most part, however, incongruity theories do not claim that incongruity in and of itself is humorous. As Hurley, Dennett, and Adams admit, some of Bain's examples "could be put in contexts where they would indeed strike us as funny" (49). Had such "contexts" been explored, perhaps they would have pointed to something about the kinds of incongruities that provoke amusement. In fact, FBT is not based in incongruity theory. The only thing that FBT acknowledges is that an incongruity is what alerts the mind to a commitment to a false belief (201, 288, 293). A contradiction in a mental space is encountered that is resolved in the diagnosis of that false belief. The belief becomes the loser in an epistemic reconciliation process described above. But Hurley, Dennett, and Adams completely neglect the matter of the perception of the *appropriateness* of an incongruity: what needs to be perceived if the exchange between the judge and the attorneys, for example, is to be regarded as amusing.

FBT offers a couple of counterexamples to incongruity theory. "What is the speed of dark?" (Hurley, Dennett, and Adams 2011, 51). Hurley, Dennett, and Adams characterize this sentence as a "non sequitur," but it does not seem to be one in either the logical or even the colloquial sense of the term. Because we can ask about the speed of light—and since the development of modern physics the term *speed of light* is invoked all the time in scientific and even casual discourse—it would not at first sight seem amiss to ask about the speed of its perceived opposite.[10] Would there be something fundamentally wrong in asking about the speed of a gas versus the speed of a liquid; the speed of an animate object as opposed to an inanimate one; the speed of matter as opposed to the speed of energy?[11] The entire cosmos is in motion, and it might at first seem appropriate to formulate a question about the speed of that "thing" designated by the noun *dark*. The incongruity is grasped with the recognition that *dark* is a noun that serves to label an absence rather than a presence. There is no "thing" to have speed.[12] The question is appropriately incongruous and is perceived as a joking question.

A second purported counterexample to incongruity theory that Hurley, Dennett, and Adams identify is a joke in Freud's *Jokes and Their Relation to the*

Unconscious about someone rubbing mayonnaise in his hair at a dinner party and then excusing himself by claiming he thought that it was spinach (Freud 1960, 8:138–39). It is a non sequitur only to the extent that it is a joke that contains a non sequitur. It has previously been discussed in terms of appropriate incongruity (Oring 2003, 16–18).[13]

There are some other questions to be raised about the adequacy of FBT, and the matter of epistemic commitment certainly is one place to start. Consider the Polack joke discussed in chapter 2. "How many Poles does it take to change a light bulb? Five. One to hold the light bulb and four to turn the table he's standing on." The joke depends on recognizing a stupidity script to make the incongruous number of people necessary for the job seem appropriate. A Polack is a figure who is so stupid that he never can perform a task directly and simply. In the late 1970s, a whole set of jokes seems to have been spun off from this archetype with the format "How many _____ does it take to change a light bulb?" with the blank being filled in by a variety of ethnic, occupational, gender, and other groupings. For example: "How many Californians does it take to change a light bulb? Ten. One to screw it in and nine to share the experience." For law students the answers is six: "One to change it and five to file an environmental impact report." For Republicans, three: "One to change it and two to see how good the old one was" (Dundes 1981, 263). After being exposed to a few such jokes, recipients would quickly learn (1) the question is the setup of a joke, (2) the answer would likely identify an incongruous number of people necessary to change the bulb, (3) the number would be justified in terms of some stereotypic trait of the group identified in the question, and (4) this characteristic would be spurious as it was not something that would genuinely affect the performance of the task.[14] It is hard to identify, however, what covert, committed beliefs would be falsified. The belief that a single person should be sufficient is no longer a covert or committed one. It has been made overt and subjected to scrutiny. What remains to be revealed—it is unlikely to be guessed—is the trait of a Californian, a law student, or a Republican that might justify the unusual number of people necessary for the job. The joke answer justifies the number of people necessary but falsifies no covert belief.

Hurley, Dennett, and Adams also try to show that certain forms of *unresolved* incongruity evoke a humorous response. They give the example of a magician who, holding up a long piece of rope with a loop dangling from the bottom of his hand and three ends poking out the top, says, "How can a rope have three ends?" The audience agrees that a second rope must be hidden inside his hand. He pulls the loop down until all three ends disappear into his hand and then continues pulling until two ends pop loose and hang toward the floor. The magician then opens his hand that held the three ends and it is empty (Hurley, Dennett, and Adams 2011, 201–2). This trick elicits both awe and laughter.[15]

What are the epistemic commitments involved in this trick? A strand of rope cannot have three ends. This is normally a covert epistemic commitment, but it is made overt in the context of the magic trick. There is the incongruity of only a single length of rope emerging from the magician's hand. There is a puzzle as to how this feat of transforming three rope ends into a single strand of rope is accomplished. But even though the majority of the audience cannot grasp how this transformation is accomplished, the audience nevertheless recognizes that a skilled magician is *performing a trick.* This is another overt epistemic commitment. There is no manipulation of the axioms of geometry or the laws of physics, only a manipulation of the perceptions of the audience. Consequently, there is a measure of appropriateness to the incongruity because audience members know they have been tricked even though they can't see how. (Hypotheses may be offered; for example, that the magician palmed the short piece of rope.) Of course, the mechanism will be known to other magicians who are watching the performance, and they will evaluate the trick in terms of the style of its presentation. Nevertheless, knowing that one has been tricked provides a measure of appropriateness for the incongruity. A magic trick can both astound *and* amuse.

In a joke, an audience is also tricked, but those tricked usually glimpse, at least in part, the mechanism responsible (e.g., the pun, the conjoining of the syllables of different words, the reversal, the displacement, the false logic, the allusion). So there is an appropriate incongruity in the magic trick as in the joke, although there are significant differences. All in all, the laughter that results from the performance of a magic trick might be accounted for in terms of appropriate incongruity (although we don't really know what *kind* of laughter such tricks provoke and whether it is identical to the laughter in response to a joke). Laughter in response to magic tricks should actually generate more problems for FBT than for the appropriate incongruity perspective since it is not clear that any of the epistemic commitments made during the performance of a trick are covert, and it is not clear that audience members' beliefs are committed rather than wary ones. I would think that audiences of magic shows actually expect there to be something other than what their everyday committed beliefs would assume. They expect that—somehow—the three ends will result in only a single strand of rope.

In a television interview with a sleight-of-hand magician some years ago, the interviewer inquired whether the magician ever did his magic outside a performance venue—just fooled around with it in everyday situations unbeknownst to those around him. The magician replied that in the past he had done some sleight of hand while shopping at the supermarket, but some people who observed him became so upset that he gave up doing it. They did not know he was doing tricks and were disturbed. They were not amused or even puzzled. An overt epistemic commitment to the belief that one is being tricked would seem to be essential for the appreciation of sleight-of-hand effects, and the belief that one is being tricked makes one wary of almost all other commitments.

There are at least two instances in which Hurley, Dennett, and Adams seem to equivocate about the nature of an overt epistemic commitment. They bravely reveal an incident in which Daniel Dennett was challenged at a conference by a member of the audience who asked what if he came to hear Dennett with the expectation that the scholar would be talking about consciousness (a central theme in Dennett's work) only to find him presenting on the topic of humor? Why, the audience member asked, wouldn't this be funny since it seemed to meet all the requirements of the theory? Dennett did not have a good answer at the time, but one was formulated in *Inside Jokes*. Essentially, Hurley, Dennett, and Adams argue that the audience member only had a "hunch," not a committed belief, that Dennett would be speaking on consciousness. A committed belief would be something like expecting Dennett to be wearing men's clothes and speaking in English (Hurley, Dennett, and Adams 2011, 199–200). Perhaps, but this sounds a bit too much like special pleading.[16]

A similar equivocation seems to arise when discussing this puzzle: "A man and his son are in a car accident. The man dies and his son is taken to the hospital. 'I can't operate on this boy,' the surgeon says, 'He's my son.'" The puzzle is well known, and the solution is that the surgeon is the boy's mother. The false-belief theorists claim that this puzzle (they call it a riddle) is not funny.[17] For those who do not immediately solve the puzzle, Hurley, Dennett, and Adams claim, there is a *noncommitted* belief that the surgeon is a male. There is a *prejudice*, but that is not a complete commitment. Consequently, there is no humor (Hurley, Dennett, and Adams 2011, 195). One might normally think a prejudice is a committed belief; one acts on the basis of prejudices just as Hurley, Dennett, and Adams suggest one acts on the basis of committed beliefs (Allport 1958, 187; Hurley, Dennett, and Adams 2011, 104). Assuming they are right that humor does not result from the revelation of the puzzle's answer, I think more concise and convincing explanations could be offered. First, the surgeon situation, which they characterize as a riddle, is really a puzzle. Puzzles generally require deliberation and thus do not have the same humorous consequences as jokes (Oring 1992, 6). Solutions are more of the "aha" sort than "ha-ha." Second, that the surgeon proves to be the patient's mother completely resolves the contradiction in the scenario. The appropriateness of the incongruity is legitimate in every respect. It is not rooted in some kind of spurious connection. Third, the expectation that the surgeon must somehow be male is a prejudice, and the revelation that one has been stymied in solving the puzzle by a sexist prejudice may be accompanied by negative emotion that inhibits both amusement and laughter.

One type of mistake to which Hurley, Dennett, and Adams give no credit as a basis for humor is forgetting. They go through a rather elaborate analysis of permutations of situations of forgetting and why they would not engender first-person humor—the kind of humor we experience based upon a mistake of our own as opposed to third-person humor, in which we recognize a mistake made by someone else (Hurley, Dennett, and Adams 2011, 188–91). Consider, however, the following—very long—joke, which is usually orally performed but must be presented here in print:

> There is a black American jazz saxophonist who has had a successful career and in his heyday performed throughout the United States and Europe. But as he got older, he found that his memory seemed to be diminishing, and although he could play a carefully rehearsed set, after the set, when people made requests, he couldn't seem to remember a single tune. He gets so frustrated with being unable to play encores that he gives up performing entirely and is eventually forgotten by the jazz scene. He plays at home and only to himself.
>
> After ten years in his self-imposed retirement, he receives an offer to play in a club in Paris that he had played in the past. He is thrilled that they still remember him, but he is very wary of performing and embarrassing himself again. Nevertheless, he so loves performing that he decides to accept. He prepares his set and diligently studies all the standards as well so that he can play an encore if one is requested. Thus prepared, he flies to Paris and goes to the club.
>
> The club is on the third floor of a building and he goes up and is warmly greeted by the manager. That evening, he performs and gets through his set to the acclamation of the large audience that has come to hear him. When his set is finished, he nervously takes requests. The first request is for "Somewhere over the Rainbow." Fortunately, he has prepared this tune and begins to play: "Dah-dah-dah-dah-dah-dah-dah" [tune of "Somewhere over the Rainbow"] and gets through it well enough, but when he comes to the bridge he can't remember it. So he plays the tune again, hoping it will come back to him. He gets through the tune, and once again can't come up with the bridge. Now he is getting really frustrated. He goes through the tune for the third time and once again can't remember the bridge. He is so exasperated, embarrassed, and infuriated that he throws his saxophone to the floor and rushes toward a window at the end of the stage and throws himself through it, falling three stories to the street below. Lying on the pavement—broken and bleeding—he hears the ambulance coming: "Ah-ah-Ah-ah-Ah-ah-Ah-ah."

To get this joke, one has to know what the siren of a French ambulance sounds like. One also has to recognize the close resemblance between that sound and the beginning of the bridge in "Somewhere over the Rainbow" (the tune that accompanies the lyric "Someday I'll wish upon a star and wake up where the clouds are far behind me"). In this joke, no contradictions arise in a mental space and no epistemic commitments are falsified. Everything would seem to be as it should be. But there is an appropriate incongruity: only at the moment of his dying, when it is too late, does the musician remember the tune, and he is reminded of the tune by the ambulance that is coming because of his actions arising from his frustration at not being able to remember it. The incongruity is appropriate because the sound of a French ambulance has the same melodic contour as the beginning of the bridge. But it is not only the mindset of the musician that is at the root of this joke. This joke works when listeners can't bring the tune of the bridge to mind either. In other words, the joke would seem to depend as well upon first-person forgetting and remembering.

THE EVOLUTION OF HUMOR

What we call humor is an evolutionary spandrel (Hurley, Dennett, and Adams 2011, 154). *Spandrel* is a term that originated in architecture to designate the roughly triangular surfaces at the top of a rectilinear surface that has been pierced by an arch. Spandrels are an almost necessary consequence of creating an arch. In evolutionary biology, the term refers to the byproduct of an evolutionary adaptation that may not itself be adaptive. The argument for the evolution of humor, in a nutshell, is as follows. In the course of its development, the human brain has had to engage in a time-pressured heuristic search in an effort to anticipate what will be experienced next. This search is necessary for survival. It occurs in real time, on the fly, and is not and cannot be rigorous. The brain must necessarily jump to conclusions. In other words, it is prone to error, and content may be introduced that corrupts the brain's store of world knowledge. Consequently, there has to be some error-checking mechanism to catch mistakes as they are made. When new elements cannot be easily incorporated into an established mental space, new spaces are generated in a search for coherence, and it is such a search for coherence that is responsible for humor. When new information allows for the disambiguation of earlier information, there is an adjustment to the mental model. The brain never has complete information and must make assumptions that are held until they are shown to be wrong. This constant error-checking activity is a crucial one, and consumes considerable energy. It competes with other activities in which the brain and the organism as a whole are engaged. Because it is such an important activity, rewards are necessary to promote it if it is to be maintained. Mirth is the reward. There are other epistemic or cognitive emotions—for example, curiosity, discovery, insight, dismay, boredom—that reward or punish acts of reasoning and epistemic certainties or the lack thereof (Hurley, Dennett, and Adams 2011, 12–13, 66–67, 76, 79, 97–101, 122).

Hurley, Dennett, and Adams are partial to the notion that laughter may have evolved from a *false-alarm* call. A number of species have a special call that cancels an alert that has been judged to be mistaken (Ramachandran 1998). These theorists wish to combine this notion with play theory, which asserts that play is necessary for the development of individual physical, mental, and social skills. As play often involves behaviors that are very similar to aggression—chasing, wrestling, and nipping—it has to be indicated that the behaviors are something other than they appear; Gregory Bateson's "This is play" frame (Bateson 1972, 177–93). The potentially belligerent aspects of play activities have to be cancelled so that they are regarded as benign. Chimpanzees, for example, use "play faces" and pants to communicate nonaggression. In play chases, there are moments in which the expectation of capturing or being captured fails to be realized. The animal may "laugh" as a result of its own faulty model.[18] "Laughing at all forms of humor may just be a vestige of this early behavior" (Hurley, Dennett, and Adams 2011, 260–63). These early forms of humor and laughter are later co-opted by evolution for other purposes, not the least of which is sexual selection, for laughter signals something about knowledge resources and cognitive abilities and, consequently, fitness for reproduction (264, 267–68).

I am supposing that whatever empirical evidence has been gathered to support a hypothesis that humor and laughter enhance sexual attractiveness has been collected in relatively recent times and from experiments in Western societies that primarily involve university undergraduates (e.g., Murstein and Brust 1985; Cann, Calhoun, and Banks 1997; Bressler and Balshine 2006; Greengross and Miller 2011). To my knowledge, the question has not been explored in the ethnographic literature describing non-Western peoples; nor would I expect that sufficient, comparable data could be found there to address the question. It is known, however, that the sense of humor is not as highly valued in some cultures as it presently is in Western societies (e.g., Yue 2011). The identification and positive evaluation of a "sense of humor" would seem to be a rather recent development even in the West (Wickberg 1998, 46–119). Do we really know whether humor and laughter are species-wide sexual attractors (see Weisfeld et al. 2011)?

There is something to like about false-alarm theory. Laughter can be spontaneous and involuntary, arising from the feeling of amusement (Duchenne laughter), or voluntary (non-Duchenne laughter) and used primarily as a means of social signaling (Provine 2000, 47; Hurley, Dennett, and Adams 2011, 19–24). Both kinds of laughter register a *discounting* of actions, messages, events, and even persons. Laughter at a joke discounts the legitimacy of the mechanisms and arguments of the joke. Laughter during play discounts the seriousness of the competition and the seeming aggressiveness of the behaviors employed. Likewise, laughter in social situations communicates friendliness and discounts any criticism or impoliteness that might inadvertently be conveyed. Derisive laughter discounts the value of the person at whom it is directed. Even the maniacal laughter that is sometimes engendered by tragedy may be a reaction that essays to deny and discount the reality of a terrible event. The only laughter that would seem to escape this characterization is the laughter of joy.[19]

The only problem with this account is that logically speaking, voluntary laughter would seem to be modeled on involuntary laughter. The original false-alarm signal, after all, would have to have been automatic and involuntary to be effective. Yet, the kinds of primate laughter available for comparison with human laughter seem really to be of the social signaling—"this is play"—sort. So from the point of view of the empirical evidence, and presuming the two kinds of laughter are necessarily related, the order of their development would actually seem to be the reverse of what logic would tell us.

According to FBT, humor develops from something that was originally a debugging routine meant to protect the integrity of human knowledge—knowledge that is necessary for human survival—and from signaling in the activity of play. The primeval humor mechanism was originally adaptive but no longer fulfills an adaptive role. Humor is like predilections for super-sweet substances (saccharine), enhanced smells (perfumes), or super-intense sexual stimuli (pornography), which are likewise grounded in genuinely adaptive biological mechanisms that no longer contribute to biological fitness and may even prove deleterious (Hurley, Dennett, and Adams 2011, 63, 159, 274). Built originally on an adaptive mechanism, humor becomes an end in itself.[20]

One cannot help but wonder about a debugging mechanism that depends upon mirth to enhance the probability of survival. After all, if one is rooting out errors, some potentially life threatening, on the spur of the moment, is it really a propitious time for a reward, let alone a reward that is potentially debilitating, as certain kinds of laughter can be? Furthermore, humor, as we know it, is linked with minor error corrections in generally unthreatening circumstances. For serious growth in the human ability to formulate successful responses to serious threats, other cognitive strategies would seem to be critical (Greengross and Mankoff 2012, 454). In any event, from an evolutionary perspective, the reward for effective data assessment and acquisition should not be amusement or laughter but survival itself.

I am somewhat uncertain what the status of the error-checking mechanism actually is. Is it to maintain data integrity, or is it to monitor and improve inferential integrity (Hurley, Dennett, and Adams 2011, 127, 266, 289)? I can't see how data maintenance is likely, since in most situations the recognition of a false belief is only locally false—for that specific time and situation—and it might prove problematic to install that recognition as a part of world knowledge to be called up from long-term memory. If my heuristic causes me to infer that a neighbor's contorted countenance indicates that he is angry and perhaps prone to attack, but then he vomits, indicating that he has eaten or drunk something nauseating, would it be wise to presume that future contorted countenances should be ascribed to alimentary difficulties? I might register my error in one situation, but would I be in a position to learn from it, particularly since the assumption that my neighbor is angry rather than ill is perhaps the safer default assumption? Might it not prove risky to replace a diagnosis of anger with one of nausea in my database? Increasing the range of interpretations in my database might not prove adaptive either, as too many possibilities could impede making an on-the-spot decision about the meaning of a behavior and the most appropriate response to it.

If inferential ability is what is being honed in the recognition of false beliefs, other questions arise. This whole evolutionary scenario is essentially a just-so story—a backward projection of current conceptions of how cognitive processes work in creating real-time situational meaning and predictive reliability. It is combined as well with a back-formation from the False-Belief Theory of humor, which is part and parcel of the same cognitive program. If humor is theorized as the recognition of mistaken covert beliefs, then it must arise from some mechanism of mistake diagnosis in humankind's evolutionary past. After all, humor is universal and must come from somewhere, and the proposition that it originates in some error-checking mechanism would seem as good a guess as any and probably better than some (e.g., Gruner 1978, 48–90). Nevertheless, if one looks at both contemporary and bygone engagements with jokes, riddles, comic tales, parodies, puppet shows, and numerous other forms of humorous stimuli, it would also seem that the human brain has not learned very much over the hundreds of thousands of years of hominid evolution. Humans continue to make the same errors over and over again. They are misled by the same joke mechanisms, taken in by the same plot devices, and fall for the same practical jokes. With such a long history of error checking, how is it that humans continue to be so easily duped? If the mechanism that is ultimately responsible for humor is intended to promote human learning, it seems sadly akin to our formal learning institutions in this country, for there are no creditable signs that much in the way of real education has taken place. It is a good thing too, because if the human brain corrected all its propensities to wrongly commit and learned to infer too well, humans might have to do without humor altogether.[21]

I think that the formulation of FBT may have been overly influenced by its evolutionary perspective. Evolutionists often find the question "What is it for?" more basic than "What is it?" Hurley, Dennett, and Adams offer the example of the mechanical apple peeler-corer, an instrument it would be difficult to understand but which becomes obvious once its purpose is known (Hurley, Dennett, and Adams 2011, 9–10). That is true. We can more easily grasp the significance of the parts, the relationship between the parts, and the operation of a machine once we are told what it is for. Nevertheless, in a scientific endeavor, one should be able to deduce the purpose of the machine from a close examination of its parts and their relationship. In nature, after all, there is no one to tell us what something is for. The designer is necessarily silent. Consequently, the parts must be identified and the operations grasped before questions of purpose can be properly addressed. There is no choice but to work backward from what humor is understood to be *now* to how and from what it might have developed. To bounce, however, between a phenomenon we can observe and its purported evolutionary origin, claiming each scenario illuminates the other, probably does not promote the suasiveness of either account.

Even if FBT has analyzed humor correctly—and there is no cause to think it has—and even if it did develop from a primitive debugging mechanism in processes of situational assessment, the fact of the matter is that what humor is now is a far more complex phenomenon. It cannot be apprehended simply as a "supernormal" variant of that mechanism, any more than love can be regarded simply as a supernormal variant of sex. Somewhere in the history of the species, culture arose. And although culture is necessarily built upon a natural foundation, it is an entirely new edifice and must be understood in its own terms. In love, the idealizations, the fixations, the renunciations, the suffering, the philosophies, the theologies, and poetry are not just the natural excrescences of sexual and reproductive drives. We love not only sexual partners but nations, saints, art, literature, nature, pets, jobs, sports teams, and ideas. We even love the idea of love. If humor arose from an aboriginal debugging mechanism, it has so evolved that it is no longer simply a matter of mistaken epistemic commitments proper.

We are in the process of disambiguating sentences, actions, and events all the time. In the course of both our solitary behaviors and our social interactions, we mishear, misread, misconstrue, and yet we effortlessly correct our first impressions (Hurley, Dennett, and Adams 2011, 97–100). Only some of this error discovery and correction results in humor. Were this not the case, we would probably be smiling, chuckling, and laughing all the time. But we smile, chuckle, and laugh

only some of the time (and much of that is social signaling rather than amusement) because it takes a special kind of error correction to produce humor. It is
the nature of what awakens our sense of an error that matters and the fact that
what awakens us to error is recognized as a kind of error in its own right. There
is the perception of a structure of ideas without which our jokes and witticisms
would be empty and meaningless.

There are several things, nevertheless, to like about FBT. Hurley, Dennett, and
Adams remind us that humor is a process in the mind and not an object in the
world. Psychology is ultimately essential to grasping this process. They are also
right that humorous stimuli trick us. They cause us to commit to particular con-
struals of words, sentences, actions, and events that are, in the course of a joke,
upended. Hurley, Dennett, and Adams give some recognition to incongruity theory even if they themselves misconstrue the notion of "resolution," or what I call
"appropriateness." They are certainly right to note that the sense of amusement
must have developed from something else, and are justified in speculating about
its evolutionary origin. They are also right to criticize incongruity theory for the
absence of an unambiguous definition of incongruity or, I might add, appropriateness. And they are right in their claim that even if appropriate incongruity were
a structure that underlies humorous stimuli, it only describes rather than explains
the phenomenon (Hurley, Dennett, and Adams 2011, 46, 51).

Nevertheless, if appropriate incongruity proves to be the correct description of
humor, that description is fundamental to what it is that has to be explained. It will
not do to supplant it with some other description (e.g., mistaken commitments)
and explain that. I would be happy to know why the discovery of the appropriate
incongruity of the judge taking equal bribes from the lawyers so that he can claim
to proceed impartially is funny, while the mere, even if sudden, discovery that the
judge is corrupt does not. It is also well to remember that if "incongruity" and
"appropriateness" escape precise definition, the notion of "false belief" may not
be well defined either. A joke makes us realize that our first commitments were
misplaced, but they are no more false than the beliefs that make one revise that
initial commitment. If we come to believe that the difference between 0 and 8 is
truly a matter of apparel, there is probably no joke to get. Rather, something closer
to a mystery of a Pythagorean sort would seem to be in play. So the initial commitment that 0 is *not* 8 all the while remains in force. What is gleaned is that the two
numerals on the page can be interpreted in at least two ways: as anthropomorphic
shapes and as symbols of quantity. To ignore these two interpretations is to ignore
something fundamental about this joke and all jokes.[22]

FBT predicates humor on the discovery of false beliefs, and it is true that humorous stimuli do abound with pathways to misattribution, misunderstanding, and

erroneous supposition. Incongruity theorists know that jokes mislead, even if they do not put the matter of false belief at the center of their understanding. Cognitive shifts occur in humor as well, and while most incongruity theorists do not discuss cognitive shifts either, they would acknowledge that such shifts take place in the registering of incongruity and its appropriateness (Latta 1999; Oring 1999, 460). That being said, I think the major oversight of FBT is its assumption that the epistemic conflicts that engender humor are resolved by discovering the falsehood of one of the conflicting beliefs.[23] FBT seems to overlook the possibility of the *cooperative option*: "A creative insight dissolves what is only an apparent conflict" (Hurley, Dennett, and Adams 2011, 112). There is a good reason that Arthur Koestler (1964) includes a section on humor along with sections on art and science in his work on human creativity, for humor is rooted in synthesis. Thus, a judge can be bribed and impartial; an armored vehicle can be substituted for an aquarium when the word *tank* is employed; "passing *a* bar" is sufficiently similar to "passing *the* bar" and may be substituted for it if it is understood that such substitutions have no real-world consequences. Jokes are not reconciliations of epistemic commitments in which only one side wins. Granted, such cooperative resolutions in humor depend upon allowing demonstrably spurious factors to operate in the equation. The cooperation is of a "faulty" sort. Perhaps this is akin to the admission of $\sqrt{-1}$ into algebra. There is, after all, no number that produces a negative when multiplied by itself. Nevertheless, tolerating its usage leads to some really tremendous results.

Framing Borat

For every ten jokes, thou hast got an hundred enemies.
—LAURENCE STERNE

Borat: Cultural Learnings of America for Make Benefit Glorious Nation of Kazakhstan (2007) was released in the United States on November 3, 2006.[1] The film garnered much attention, earned a considerable amount of money, won numerous awards, and accumulated a veritable archive of reviews, commentaries, and condemnations.[2] It is a comedy that pretends to be a documentary of the trip of journalist Borat Sagdiyev from his little village of Kuzcek to the United States in his quest to learn lessons that would benefit his native country of Kazakhstan. He is accompanied on his trip by Azamat Bagatov, who is purportedly directing the documentary. In the course of his tour, Borat sees actress Pamela Anderson on an episode of *Baywatch* and falls in love with her, so he sets off for California to woo and marry her. The movie is primarily constructed of Borat's interviews and encounters with a variety of real-life individuals and groups on his trip across the country. The comedy turns on the fact that the character Borat is a fabrication of the actor Sacha Baron Cohen, but his interlocutors take his sexist, racist, and totally clueless persona at face value and respond accordingly.

No verbal description of the film is likely to capture the nature of the comedy. It has to be seen in order to be appreciated. Part of the attraction—and repulsion—of the film is seeing how far Baron Cohen is willing to go in violating social conventions in carrying out the Borat role. For example, in an interview with Bob Barr, Borat offers the Georgia congressman some cheese, which he claims is a customary expression of hospitality in Kazakhstan. Only after the congressman has tasted some does Borat reveal that it is made with his wife's breast milk. When Borat appears on a local newscast in Colorado, he pretends that he does not know that the show is already on the air and asks the newscaster where he can "make a urine."

The film was banned in all Arab countries except Lebanon, and the Russian government refused to issue a distribution license for *Borat* because it might "humiliate different ethnic groups and religions" ("*Borat*" n.d.; "*Borat* Spoof" 2006). The Anti-Defamation League issued a press release registering its concern that some members of the film audience might not be sophisticated enough to "get the joke" in Borat's "boastful expressions of anti-Semitism and stereotyping" and that some might find it "reinforcing their bigotry" (ADL 2006). The European Center for Antiziganism filed a complaint with German prosecutors about the film's depiction of Gypsies ("*Borat*" n.d.). In addition, lawsuits were filed by individuals appearing in the film who claimed damage to their dignity and livelihoods.

Kazakhstan also banned the film and threatened to sue Baron Cohen. In an effort to counter images and ideas promoted in *Borat,* the government of Kazakhstan took out a four-page info-advertisement in the *New York Times* emphasizing the country's strong ties with the United States, its renunciation of nuclear weapons, its rich mineral resources, its business-friendly environment, its modern tourist accommodations, and its religious pluralism and tolerance ("Kazakhstan in the 21st Century" 2006). Despite the ban on the film, the DVD quickly became the most-ordered product by Kazakhs from Amazon UK. Eventually the government of Kazakhstan did an about-face and thanked Baron Cohen for his contribution to tourism: visa applications to the country increased tenfold in the wake of the film's success ("Kazakhstan Thanks Borat for 'Boosting Tourism'" 2012).

Two aspects of the film are addressed below: the way targets of the comedy are framed, and the knowledge resources available in interpreting the film, particularly in relation to these purported targets. It is possible to classify the film's targets into two general categories: (1) individuals and groups explicitly commented upon, and (2) those who are implicitly targeted by virtue of the situations into which they are put and the things they are induced by Borat to say or do.

The first category of targets includes (in approximate order of the salience of the invective) Jews, women, Uzbeks, Gypsies, and the mentally defective. All of these groups are referred to by the character Borat in some explicit way. The invective against these groups is not all of a type. First, the invective is framed by Borat, a simpleton who is portrayed as primitive, clueless, crude, brazen, incestuous, vindictive, and a bit of a social climber. Consequently, his comments on Jews,

women, Gypsies, Uzbeks, and "retards" are utterly discountable given the character of their source. Second, Borat's remarks are self-framing: they beggar belief on
the part of modern audiences. He claims that women's brains are the same size as
the brains of squirrels, that Jews can transform themselves into cockroaches, and
that Gypsies cast spells to shrink people to the size of Barbie dolls. Even without
the establishment of the character of Borat as a buffoon, these expressions would
serve to reframe audience perception of the character since they are utterly dissonant with conventional knowledge and understanding.

Finally, the film *Borat* is framed as comedy. The advertising and reviews all
proclaimed it as such. Audiences were under no misapprehension that they were
seeing a documentary. The comedy frame indicates that what is presented cannot
simply be taken at face value. The same holds true for Borat as a representative of
Kazakhstan and his depiction of Kazakh attributes—attributes that *he* takes to be
wholly positive. Again, while countries can be legitimately represented as techno-
logically backward and poor or generally anti-Semitic, no country is likely to have
"town rapist" as an official social position, have a state religion that "follows the
hawk," or celebrate a "running of the Jew" in Pamplona's style of the running of
the bulls. Consequently, Borat's positive promotion of his country's technical and
social progress—having "superior potassium" or the age of sexual consent being
raised to eight—cannot be taken at face value.

It is perhaps appropriate that the film is bracketed by Borat's attempts to learn
how to use "*not*" jokes.[3] He takes lessons from a humor coach toward the beginning of the film, but he never fully succeeds until he finally uses the formula
appropriately at the end of the film. As he is being forcibly subdued by security
personnel after attacking Pamela Anderson at her book signing, he says, "I am not
attracted to you anymore—*not*." All Borat's declarations about particular ethnic
groups in the movie are, in a sense, variations of one big *not* joke. And like the *not*
joke, they all undo themselves.

Curiously, African Americans have a fairly low profile in the film. It is true
that Borat refers to presidential candidate Alan Keyes as a "real chocolate face."
That epithet, however, may not signify an insult from someone who is as clueless as Borat about American racial politics.[4] Later in the film, after he meets a
group of young African Americans on an urban street and learns from them how
to use black street talk, he enters an upscale hotel and says to the man behind
the desk, "What's up with it, vanilla face? Me and my homie Azamat just parked
our slab outside. We're looking for somewhere to post up our black asses for the
night, so bang bang, skeet skeet, nigga. We just a couple of pimps, no hoes." So
the "chocolate face" he employs earlier is inverted in his reproduction of black
street lingo. Indeed, if there is a character in the film that could be said to be

portrayed sympathetically, it is Luenell, a black prostitute. At the conclusion of the film, Borat seeks her out, and she accompanies him back to his village of Kuzcek.

It is not difficult to surmise why Kazakhstan was chosen as the object of ridicule. Kazakhstan is a country in central Asia about which few people in the West have any knowledge beyond the fact that it was a former Soviet republic and consequently might still be suffering from the effects of a state-controlled economy. This near-complete hole in the geographical, political, and cultural knowledge of Westerners made it a superior choice. Uzbekistan, Tajikistan, Kyrgyzstan, or Turkmenistan might have worked as well, but only Kazakhstan—which is larger than western Europe—has the necessary geographical heft. I doubt that many people could name its capital or know much about it other than, *perhaps*, it has given up the nuclear weapons that were stationed there, and it is where Russia maintains its space-rocket launching facility. I would guess that there were some members of the film audience who did not know Kazakhstan is a real country. But those who did were likely to recognize that Borat's representation of that country bore no relation to reality.

Because viewers of the film would likely recognize that Kazakhstan had been part of the Union of Soviet Social Republics, and because the Soviet Union in the minds of many equals Russia, the film's characterization of Kazakhstan is largely an extension of stereotypes about Russia and eastern Europe more generally. Hence the enormous emphasis in the film on Kazakh anti-Semitism, even though there is little relation between the history, demographics, and status of the Jewish community in Kazakhstan and the Jewish community under the empire of the czars following the partitions of Poland at the end of the eighteenth century. The same might be said of Borat's anti-Gypsy rhetoric; it is more a reflection of attitudes toward the Roma in Europe than in Asia.

Would a mythical country have worked as well as Kazakhstan for comedic purposes? Probably not. Humor often benefits from some proximity to reality. That is what gives it its "edge." For those who may have bought the depiction of Kazakhstan as an accurate representation—the joke was on them. It seems doubtful, however, that there were many such people. The Polish jokes that circulated in the United States in the early 1960s would probably not have been as successful either had they targeted some ersatz group.[5] While there were historical and sociological reasons that served to make Polish Americans the targets of these jokes, most people who told such jokes did not believe that Poles were genuinely stupid or dirty (C. Davies 1990, 40–83). Polish Americans told the jokes as well.

The other targets in the film are people who are put in uncomfortable situations as a result of Borat's speech and behavior. Much of this humor might be described as practical joking, which is "a competitive play activity in which only one of the two opposing sides is consciously aware of the fact that a state of play is occurring . . . that is, until the unknowing side is made to seem foolish or is caused some physical and/or mental discomfort" (Tallman 1974, 260). In this regard, Baron Cohen spares no one: New York pedestrians, driving instructors, television news people, humor coaches, congressmen, rodeo managers, bed-and-breakfast owners, etiquette coaches, dining society members, gun salesmen, car salesmen, mortgage brokers, fraternity boys, or Pentecostals. Practical joking is often, but not always, an in-group activity. Even within an in-group, it can cause some pain and discomfiture. When it is perpetrated on strangers and made public to an audience of millions, it can prove particularly embarrassing.

This is the problem in Baron Cohen's work. He uses ordinary people who are unaware that they are being tricked, and who appear in a film whose purpose they do not understand. Audiences are likely to accept such tricks when they are played on public figures. They may be less accepting when they are played on ordinary folk. Nevertheless, a good number of Borat's victims seem to have behaved quite well—the driving instructor, the humor coach, the etiquette coach, the bed-and-breakfast owners, television newscasters, and Pentecostals—and did not support his racist or sexist gambits. The dining society members are extremely hospitable even if they seem too ready to believe that someone could be as backward as Borat and that all he needed was to be "Americanized" a bit. I remember once hearing the following statement attributed to anthropologist Margaret Mead: "It is precisely when they are behaving well that Americans think they are being taken for suckers." It is a proposition worth remembering, even if she never quite said it.[6]

Only some of the New Yorkers, the rodeo manager, the rodeo audience, and the frat boys betray their hostilities and prejudices and condemn themselves. The car and gun salesmen fail to respond to Borat's wanting to know how capable the weapon or vehicle in question might be for killing a Jew or Gypsy, but reflection suggests that they might have felt either that they did not properly understand him or that they were not about to get into a confrontation with him over his prejudices.[7] The practical joking is essentially directed at individuals—not social groups or types. (Southerners seem to be frequent targets, but this might be a result of Baron Cohen's itinerary. The rodeo manager looks as though he is from the West, but the rodeo took place in Virginia.)

People who sued the production claimed that they were personally humiliated or their livelihoods suffered.[8] This humiliation and damage arose from their behaving as themselves in their everyday personas. They were not acting parts. They were participants in a scenario about which they had not fully been advised. Curiously, the largest of the lawsuits—some $30 million—was filed by the residents of Glod, the Romanian village that was presented as Borat's Kazakh village of Kuzcek. Like the other "victims" of this film, the villagers claim they were lied to about the true nature of the work. They also claim that they were humiliated on "ethnic grounds." The village, it seems, is overwhelmingly Roma. In addition to monetary compensation, they wanted changes to the opening of the film and a formal apology. Their lawyer, Edward D. Fagan, stated that the film was funny only when it made Americans look like idiots, not "when it makes fun of under-privileged people and their misery and ethnic background" (Pancevski 2006).

It is doubtful that more than a very few people viewing the film recognized the real ethnic identity of Borat's mythical home village or even the country of origin of that village. The village would have remained totally anonymous were it not for a small acknowledgment in the film's final credits.[9] In fact, the suit has only called attention to the villagers' identity and exacerbated their supposed griev-ance. What is particularly interesting about this suit is that the villagers of Glod—unlike most other victims of Sacha Baron Cohen's joking—played *a part* in the film. They were playing Kazakh villagers, not themselves. It is as though the lead actor in Shakespeare's *Macbeth* sued the play's director because he was unfavor-ably portrayed as a serial killer.[10]

The villagers' lawyer Fagan complained, "Mr. Cohen makes a great point about anti-Semitism in his film. But as Jews do not have horns, Roma are not rapists and prostitutes" (Pancevski 2006). Exactly so! What member of the viewing audience would fail to grasp this basic point? Fagan's claim that it is the Roma who are demeaned in the film—rather than fictional Kazakh villagers—implies that Glod has to be defended from the charges that it has a town rapist, that the town welder is also an abortionist, that the oldest woman in the village is forty-three, that the village conducts an annual running of the Jew, and that the village is home to the "number four prostitute" in all Kazakhstan; or is it Romania?

An extensive body of commentary accompanies this film. Advertising, pro-motional events, deleted scenes, web postings, interviews, blogs, and newspaper articles all serve to expand the knowledge resources available to the viewer. There is at least one biography of Sacha Baron Cohen (Stowe and Stump 2007). Google responds with 15 million hits for "Borat." There is a twenty-page article about the film in Wikipedia, with some 114 footnotes. This commentary also serves to frame the film and shape the way in which it is received and interpreted. For example, Sacha Baron Cohen is regularly identified as an observant Jew who speaks Hebrew in the film, as having studied history at Cambridge University, and as having writ-ten his thesis on the American civil rights movement. Ken Davidian, who plays Azamat Bagatov, his director and companion, speaks Armenian throughout the film.[11] These bits of information serve to defuse any charges of anti-Semitism or racism that might be leveled against Baron Cohen, and suggest that neither of the principals knows much—if anything—about Kazakh language, Kazakh culture, or Kazakhstan.

There is a particular concern in these materials to assess what is real in the film: who are actors and who are dupes? What is documentary and what is staged scenario? What were the filmmakers up to, and how much is our response a response to what is "real"? Some of this enormous commentary may prove to be illuminating, or it may prove as misleading as the film itself. All that is clear from the film is that a camera—and thus one might infer a camera operator and perhaps a sound technician—was ever present. How did Borat and Azamat manage to stand naked in an elevator and then invade the "Mortgage Brokers Annual Banquet" without being arrested for indecent exposure? The scenes look real enough, but were they, and how were they carried out? The filmmakers don't seem to be willing to say. When asked to reveal how certain scenes were set, actors refused to answer, claiming to be "sworn to secrecy" (L. Carroll 2006). The only information comes from those who appeared in the film, did not realize they were being duped, and chose to talk to the press or pursued legal cases in court. So the knowledge resources used to interpret the humor in this film include: (1) the ordinary knowledge that the average person in the United States or any Western country brings to any comedy, (2) a knowledge that derives from the press and the World Wide Web that might be accessed both before and after seeing the film, and (3) an awareness of a body of knowledge that can resolve questions about the making of the film but that is not—at least at present—accessible. The eighty-four-minute film was reportedly edited down from more than 400 hours of footage (Strauss 2006, 59, 62). What scenes, actions, and behaviors were omitted; which scenes were carefully constructed through judicious editing; and which scenes were the product of acting can only be imagined, but such imaginings probably play some part in framing the comedic action in the film as well (Marchese and Paskin 2006).

Why should people care about what is staged and what is real in the film? Since it is all comedy, what difference should it make? Either it is funny or it is not. After all, it is quite unusual to ask whether a joke is true or not. The film, however, depends not only on the ludicrousness of the Borat character but on what people reveal about themselves in their encounters with him. These revelations would be meaningless if they were thought to be merely staged. Furthermore, part of the film's attraction lies in seeing how far Baron Cohen is willing to go to produce his comic effects. What risks is he willing to take? To answer such questions, one needs to be able to separate the real from the contrived. Accounts of practical joking—whether oral or cinematic—demand a verisimilitude that can only be established by reference outside the comedic frame. The opening scenes in the film set in Borat's village of Kuzcek are presented strictly as comedy. There is no reason to be concerned whether they are situated on a stage set rather than in a real village, or employ movie actors rather than real villagers. The humor is contained within the frame of the film. However, once the film moves into documentary mode and Borat engages known politicians, subway riders, and *Baywatch* stars, an evaluation of the reality of the scenes is demanded. Baron Cohen's audacity and his subjects' self-revelations are both meaningless if the practical joking is held to be performed for the viewer's benefit. Consequently, a good deal of the film's humor is not insulated within the frame. The viewer must break the film's frame and come to some sense—right or wrong—as to whether Borat's interactions are with real people who do not understand what is going on.[12]

The humorous frame of the film is challenged on other grounds as well. Humor is evaluated not only for its funniness but for its seemliness. There is always the possibility of challenging some statement, behavior, or image within the humorous frame on moral grounds. A moral claim might also be leveled against something associated with a humorous product (e.g., workers in a film comedy were underpaid; the revenues of a joke book are being directed to some malevolent end). A complaint might even be made that a comedy does not apportion its criticisms equitably to individuals and groups.[13] In the above circumstances the humor is no longer humor but is transformed into serious discourse (Emerson 1969). Statements within a comedy are assessed for their moral rectitude and are found wanting for the injury they cause or for their overall lack of sensitivity and compassion. George Saunders, writing in the *New Yorker*, invokes the images of the one-armed old man from the village of Glod weeping "in his room at the memory of being tricked into wearing a sex toy on his arm" and the woman at the dining society dinner—whom Borat did not think so attractive—"crying quietly so as not to alarm the kids" because she might have suffered from feelings of unattractiveness and inferiority all her life (Saunders 2006). This kind of moral objection will always be able to challenge a humorous frame, but it is difficult to tell who is manipulating the unsuspecting characters in the film more: the moviemaker or the morally outraged commentator. Somehow, someone is being framed.

CHAPTER SEVEN

Risky Business

Political Jokes under Repressive Regimes

The existing system constituted a separate world of the absurd, a realm of lies so funny you could die laughing.
—DAVID REMNICK

Although oftentimes sources of amusement and delight, jokes and witticisms can exact severe penalties. Sometimes these are merely the social censures that result from joking about a sensitive topic in an uncongenial environment to an unreceptive audience—telling "sex jokes" at a Coast Guard Academy dinner, for example, or appearing in blackface and telling race jokes at a Friar's Club banquet.[1] Other times, however, the costs of joking are more pointed, painful, and permanent. When Theocritus of Chios was told that he would be pardoned by King Antigonus I (382–301 BCE) if only he would "stand before the eyes of the king," Theocritus, knowing the king had only one eye, responded, "Well, then, reprieve is impossible." Theocritus was executed for this remark (Clement and Hoffleit 1969, 13). Sotades of Maroneia told King Ptolmey II Philadelphus (308–246 BCE) that by marrying his sister Arsinoë he had thrust "his prick into a hole unholy." The king had his general seal Sotades in a leaden jar and drop him in the sea (Athenaeus 1959, 345). The humorous invectives of Marcus Tullius Cicero against Marcus Antonius resulted in the nailing of the orator's head and hands to the speaker's rostrum in the Roman forum (Corbeill 1996, 216). After the Sung emperor Xingzong was defeated in battle by Li Yüanhao in 1044 CE, the emperor fled and barely escaped capture. Li Yüanhao cut off the noses of several of the emperor's men whom he captured. Later the emperor's jester remarked to the emperor, "Let's see whether your nose is there or not," alluding to the emperor's pusillanimous flight. The emperor became so enraged that he had the jester strangled behind a tent (Otto 2001, 143). Rulers have proven just as unreceptive to jokes made at their expense in modern times. A Nazi court condemned Josef Müller, a Catholic priest, to death for telling a joke about a dying German soldier requesting that a portrait of Hitler and Goering be placed on either side of him so that he could "die like Jesus"; that is, between two thieves (Lipman 1993, 34).[2] In 1984, Omar al-Hazza, a top Iraqi officer, made a joke about the identity of Saddam Hussein's mother. (Saddam Hussein and his four brothers each had different mothers.) Al-Hazza's tongue and the tongues of his sons were cut out as their wives looked on. Then, al-Hazza's male family members were killed before his eyes and his daughters were turned out of their homes. Finally al-Hazza himself was executed ("Periscope" 2003, 10). Over the centuries, other wiseacres have lost lives and limbs or—if they were lucky—only liberty and livelihoods for their joking remarks (Otto 2001, 139–42).[3]

Joking is a risky business: not merely socially hazardous but physically dangerous. I am interested in exploring the making of jokes under such risky conditions—that is, under conditions in which jokers and their audiences recognize the perilous circumstances of their humorous collaborations. Such joking is most predictably risky under totalitarian regimes—regimes with authoritarian rulers, press censorship, secret police, informers, and summary or extrajudicial trials, as found in Nazi Germany, the former Union of Soviet Socialist Republics and its socialist "allies," Franco's Spain, Ba'athist Iraq, and possibly, I would imagine, in Communist China, North Korea, Cuba, Hoxha's Albania and, perhaps, on occasion in Iran—imperial and Islamic. In these countries, there was not merely an effort to control what was printed in the press or broadcast through the electronic media but an attempt to control what was orally communicated by individuals face-to-face.[4] In other words, there was an effort to suppress folk humor—the humor of everyday conversation and everyday life.

The kinds of jokes I speak of are well known. They might be directed against leaders or against economic and political conditions. Three examples:

Hitler and Göring are standing atop the Berlin radio tower. Hitler says he wants to do something to put a smile on the Berliners' faces. So Göring says: "Why don't you jump?" (Herzog 2010, 167)[5]

Krupskaya [Lenin's widow] was giving a talk about Lenin at a school. "Lenin was a very kind man," she said. "One day he was shaving outside his dacha [country villa] with an old-fashioned razor. A little boy came to watch him and asked Lenin, "What are you doing?"

"I'm shaving, little boy," Lenin replied.

"Why does that make him a kind man?" asked one of the children.

"Can't you see," said Krupskaya, "he could have cut the little boy's throat but he didn't." (C. Davies 1998, 178; Adams 2005, 127–28)[6]

A lecturer on Political Science declares: "Our country has achieved tremendous gains in the production of meat."

[Chaimovich's voice in the audience]: "Where is the meat?"

"And of milk."

[Chaimovich's voice again]: "But where is the milk?"

"Well," the lecturer concludes, "are there any questions?"

[A voice from the audience]: "Yes, but where is Chaimovich?" (Draitser 1978, 46; Adams 2005, 47)

Indeed, versions of such suppressed jokes have been reported from various times and places and vary only in superficial details.

A man is running in panic down a Bucharest street. A friend stops him. "Why are you running like this?"

"Didn't you hear? They have decided to shoot all the camels."

"But for heaven's sake, you're not a camel."

"Yes, but these people shoot first, and then they realize you're not a camel."
(Banc and Dundes 1989, 33)

This joke was often told with an animal protagonist; instead of camels, the target animals might be dogs, cats, rabbits, bears, giraffes, buffaloes, or donkeys. In some versions, the person fleeing has heard they are castrating anyone with more than two testicles. When the friend protests that he has only two testicles, the man replies, "But these people cut them off first, and then they count them." The joke has been reported from Nazi Germany, Russia—Soviet and czarist—Romania, and the Middle East (Kishtainy 1985, 174; Banc and Dundes 1989, 33–34). It has been traced back to the works of eleventh- and twelfth-century Arab and Persian authors (Omidsalar 1987; Marzolph 1988).

In another joke, two Nazis meet in Berlin:

"How are things with you?" asks one.

"Very well thank you. I have a fine job," says the other.

"What sort of job?"

"I sit on top of a steeple all day and watch so I can report to the Führer when Germany has conquered the world."

"What is your salary?"

"Twenty marks a week."

"Well, that isn't much."

"That's true . . . but it's a lifetime job." (Lipman 1993, 94)

This joke was also told in the Soviet Union about the realization of world revolution (Larsen 1980, 1; Adams 2005, 12–13), by Tunisians about the coming of Arab unity (Kishtainy 1985, 133), and by Jews about the coming of the Messiah (Telushkin 1992, 147). This joke, however, could easily be adapted to any kind of political regime, as it merely depends on an opposition between the ideal and real. It could even be used to register the illusory nature of the American civic ideology of "one nation, under God, indivisible, with liberty and justice for all."

What characterizes joking in repressive regimes is less the nature of the joke texts than the circumstances of their telling.[7] In Franco's Spain and the shah's Iran, a joke about the head of state could be considered a lèse majesté that could be formally prosecuted (Pi-Sunyer 1977, 183) or less formally avenged by a group of policemen at a local station house. During Stalin's regime, a carelessly told *anekdot* could earn years of hard labor.[8] Leon (pseudonym) spoke of a friend who was invited to a cafe near Moscow State University where he was a student and encouraged to tell jokes. His host, however, worked for the KGB and this eighteen-year-old student was arrested and didn't return for six or seven years (Leon, personal communication, April 30, 2003).[9] A refugee in the United States after World War II told of an acquaintance sentenced to three years for jostling a Communist Party worker and explaining, "I have no time because I have to fulfill the 5 year plan" (Fitzpatrick 1999, 186). Even after Stalin, such jokes could be considered "anti-Soviet conversation" (3) or "propagation of known falsehoods denigrating the Soviet system," and tellers or listeners could wind up in a correctional labor facility, lose their jobs, or be denied promotions (Draitser 1978, 5; Graham 2009, 8).

Consequently, anti-regime humor was always told with the greatest circumspection—"with a keen eye as to who is within listening distance" (Brandes 1977, 335). "People were reluctant to tell jokes to strangers. Informants usually spoke in low tones after glancing around to see if there was anyone else listening" (Dundes 1971a, 51).[10] Therefore, such jokes have come to be labeled "underground humor" or "whispered anecdotes" (*Flüsterwitze*) (Draitser 1978; Lipman 1993, 18).[11]

The situation of telling such jokes is perhaps epitomized by the account of Klava, a Jewish woman from Odessa.[12] Klava, born in 1948, remembered growing up with political jokes: "It was a national pastime." Odessans prided themselves on their jokes and on being good jokers, and this reputation was recognized by people from other parts of the country as well (Harris and Rabinovich 1995, x). But Klava was always aware that jokes and other kinds of discussions could not be freely shared. "It was a given . . . You are not to repeat . . . Only to your family members and your friends" (personal communication, April 20, 2003). There were very strict—though unofficial—quotas for Jews at the university, but Klava, like many seeking education and advancement, obtained her degree in engineering. She was employed at a large firm, but she eventually quit her job and became a manicurist. She planned to apply for permission to emigrate, and she knew that once she applied, she would lose her engineering job. By obtaining a job as a manicurist before submitting her application, she could assure herself a source of income while awaiting permission. Nevertheless, she did not immediately apply because her family did not want her to leave.

One day in 1974, she had several clients in the shop waiting to have their nails done. One of her longtime customers came in without an appointment, needing a manicure because she was going on vacation. She agreed to wait until Klava had finished with her scheduled customers. The year 1974 was a celebratory one in the Communist calendar—a Lenin anniversary—and Klava and her customers exchanged jokes and witticisms, many about Lenin.[13] Several that she remembered were:

> When we say Lenin, we mean [Communist] Party. When we say Party, we mean Lenin. And this is how we deal with everything. We say one thing, we mean something else.
>
> And then they came out with a bed that sleeps three—"Lenin is always with us."
> (Klava, April 20, 2003; see also Adams 2005, 123–24)

Party slogans were a popular target of joking even in Stalin's time (Fitzpatrick 1999, 184). Here, familiar Communist slogans are turned into jokes about the inability to say anything honestly and straightforwardly or to be rid of the presence of Lenin and the society he orchestrated.

Klava remembered relating another joke about Lenin's anniversary:

> A young engineer [is] working in a big industrial plant. And he was a very exemplary man. He was coming to work very neatly dressed—always. And one day, all of a sudden, he shows up and he's all disheveled. His clothes are wrinkled. His tie is wrinkled. And the boss calls him in and says, "What happened? You always set an example. All of a sudden you come . . . look at yourself. Look how you look. What happened?"
>
> "You know, I got up in the morning. I turned on the TV set. And there they go. Celebrating Lenin's hundredth birthday. 'We promise . . .' I turned it off. I turn on the radio, and there they go again celebrating Lenin's hundredth birthday. 'We promise, we promise . . .' I turned it off again. I was afraid to turn on the iron."
> (Klava, April 20, 2003; see also Adams 2005, 124)

These were the kinds of jokes that Klava remembered sharing with her scheduled customers on that occasion. Her unscheduled customer sat and listened the whole time. The rest of the story is told in Klava's words:

> After the two girls left, and she was in the chair. And as I was working on her, she told me, "Klava, do you know who I am?"
>
> I said, "Of course, your name is Ludmilla Ivanovna."
>
> And she said, "Do you know where I work?"
>
> "Of course, it's in the municipal hall."
>
> She said, "Do you know what department I work in?"
>
> "I have no idea."
>
> "It's department number one," which was KGB . . . And the joke was said, it was Lenin's hundredth birthday, and so all the jokes were about it. "There was a competition for the best joke about Lenin. And the first prize is ten years to where Lenin used to go"—jail, exile.
>
> And she looked at me, and the smile disappeared from her face, and she told me, "If I did not value you as my manicurist, I would send you for ten years to where Lenin used to go."
>
> And that was a decisive moment, because I wanted to go [emigrate] like three years ago, and my family did not want me [to]. I was scared. I was very scared, more than in my whole life, before that or after that. (Klava, April 20, 2003)

That night Klava called her family together and told them what had happened and that she was going to submit her application to emigrate. It took her only three months to obtain permission, and then she had thirty days to leave the country. Her parents also applied to leave but they were refused, and she had to leave without them.

This account gives some sense of the danger that was understood to accompany the telling of jokes under a totalitarian regime. One could never be absolutely certain of the person one told jokes to, and if one heard a joke, unless it was from a family member or a close friend, one could never be sure whether one should report the incident. What is particularly interesting about Klava's experience is that the woman from the KGB threatens her with a joke—a joke that picks up on the topic of Lenin, which had characterized the previous joking, and the joke is itself about joking—that is to say, a *metajoke*.[14] The KGB officer asserts her power by means of the very same kind of expression that she is condemning. There is no system of rules that applies to all. Privileged persons may ignore the rules.[15] In fact, the KGB officer doubly ignores the rules: first she threatens Klava by means of a proscribed form of expression, and then she lets Klava off for personal reasons—because she is a good manicurist. The message is clear: the exercise of state power is arbitrary, unpredictable, and consequently the more terrifying.[16]

It is worth noting that sometimes jokes served to communicate the exact opposite message. In the first months of Robert Cochran's Fulbright scholarship in Romania in 1985, he was watching television in a friend's Bucharest apartment. As the familiar scene of Nicolae Ceaușescu waving his hand back and forth to his admiring and applauding audience appeared on the screen, the friend remarked, "It's the only way he serves us; almost every night he cleans the television" (Cochran 1989, 259). This friend turned out to be an "assigned friend" whose job it was to report on the conversations and interactions of foreigners—as probably all friends and acquaintances of Westerners did during the Ceaușescu era. But the telling of this joke was an indication that there was a real friendship developing between the two. The Romanian became Cochran's friend despite the fact that he was an informer. Cochran heard several good jokes from him during the period of his stay in Bucharest. In this case, it is the one who is reporting to the secret police who reaches out to establish a connection by means of a joke.[17]

Given the conditions under which jokes were told behind the Iron Curtain and in other totalitarian states, it seems worthwhile to revisit some of the hypotheses about political jokes that have appeared in the literature over the years to see how well they account for the kinds of joking that have been described. There are six hypotheses to be considered. A few are frequently conflated in the writing of scholars and journalists, but it will prove important to distinguish between them.

The first hypothesis has not, to my knowledge, ever been discussed. It might be called the null hypothesis of whispered political joking. It states that whispered jokes about authoritarian or totalitarian regimes are in nowise different from any other kind of jokes told about any aspect of life. They are not distinctive kinds of jokes but only one type in a series of types, and they are governed by the same motives—the same joke-making impulses that create sexual jokes, ethnic jokes, marriage jokes, mother-in-law jokes, absent-minded professor jokes, religious jokes, and so on. This hypothesis should not be summarily dismissed. There is something to the notion that jokes are aestheticizations of ideas and experience— an artistic manipulation of the content of everyday life. Jokes and other forms of humor are simply the most popular forms for such aesthetic expression in modern society. In another time, in another place, that expression might have been achieved in a tale, a dance, a song, or graphic art. Seth Graham probably comes closest to promoting this hypothesis when he characterizes Soviet jokes—especially those related in the 1960s through the mid-1980s—as "a form of popular expression and entertainment . . . a national pastime of an informed citizenry . . . a carnivalesque genre-laureate in the organic hierarchy of popular discursive forms that had developed concomitantly with the state-prescribed *ars poetica*." Graham's view stems from his emphasis on the literary qualities of the genre rather than its psychological functions. Nevertheless, he does suggest that jokes did make "the purported desert a more hospitable environment for the cultural consumer" (Graham 2009, 63–65).

However, there are some facts that speak against such a hypothesis. My informants spontaneously commented on the distinctiveness of these jokes. "We lived by political jokes," one said (Vira, personal communication, March 31, 2003). "That's what we survived on," said another (Klava, April 20, 2003). In other words, informants felt that these jokes were special and not to be lumped with other kinds of jokes they might tell. Some Norwegians kept and preserved joke diaries during the Nazi occupation between 1940 and 1945 (Stokker 1995, 9–10, 13–15). Of course, this sense that political jokes are special may simply have resulted from the danger that attended their telling. Things that are dangerous or forbidden are often more exciting and stand out against the backdrop of ordinary life.

Yet, if political jokes were of a piece with the rest of joking, one wonders why people would risk telling them. One could satisfy the aesthetic impulse by telling jokes about relatively safe topics: mothers-in-law, cramped apartments, the weather, alcoholism, or Western society and culture. Under Communist rule humor, at least certain kinds of humor, was allowed—even encouraged. After all, there were the numerous satirical magazines: the Czech *Dikobraz* (Porcupine), the Slovak *Rohac* (Stag Beetle), Poland's *Szpilki* (Needles), Bulgaria's *Sturshel* (Hornet), Romania's *Urzica* (Nettle), Hungary's *Ludas Matyi* (named after a peasant boy who outwits his landlord), East Germany's *Eulenspiegel* (a German folk trickster) and Russia's *Krokodil* (Crocodile) (A. Rose 2001–2002, 66–67; J. Sanders 1962a, 26). All of these magazines were approved organs and had very substantial numbers of subscribers. They contained a good deal of nonpolitical humor, but they also contained cartoons directed at the West as well as satire aimed at domestic low- and middle-level government functionaries and the operations of various institutions. Thus, humor concerning the ineptness of bureaucrats, the shirking of laborers, the stupidity of newspaper editors and administrators, the inefficiencies and shoddiness of agricultural and industrial production appeared in their pages. Of course, the boundary between acceptable and unacceptable humor was a fine one, and editorial staffs of these journals were sacked when they overstepped that boundary (J. Sanders 1962b; A. Rose 2001–2002, 66; Graham 2009, 11). Again, if whispered political humor was just one strain in the arts of everyday life, there was no compelling reason to hazard liberty or livelihood in purveying it. There were plenty of opportunities to create and appreciate humor that did not entail the risks that whispered anecdotes did. Yet, the topics of jokes—even during the

Stalin era in the Soviet Union—seem largely to lie in the forbidden political arena (Fitzpatrick 1999, 3).[18]

A second hypothesis to be considered is that jokes and other forms of humor are vehicles for speaking about what would otherwise be unspeakable. This somewhat oxymoronic perspective suggests that jokes convey messages that would be difficult or impossible to express directly. In discussing Romanian political jokes, Alan Dundes has written, "In political jokes in Iron Curtain countries, one frequently finds said what many individuals feel but dare not utter" (Dundes 1971a, 51). Dundes and his collaborator C. Banc elaborate, "Criticisms can be uttered only sotto voce and that is why political jokes play so important a role in Eastern Europe . . . One can speak in jokes when one cannot speak otherwise . . . In Eastern Europe, what one cannot talk about are the inadequacies of the government. Hence, there are far more political jokes in Eastern Europe than in the United States" (Banc and Dundes 1989, 10). Charles E. Schutz agrees: "Humor is the first and most natural form of secret speaking and writing . . . The comical form conceals messages that we could speak or write more directly or forthrightly . . . The greater the potential for conflict, the greater the comic veil . . . The indirectness or disguises of humor may be due to fear, propriety, perversity, or entertainment" (Schutz 1995, 52, 53–54, 62), and undoubtedly it would be fear that Schutz would see as the motivating factor in shaping the political joke under totalitarian regimes.[19] Anthropologist Don Handelman, although speaking of joking rather than jokes per se, saw it as permitting the expression of "discrepant messages that . . . do not overly disrupt official reality" and that can therefore be successfully communicated even though they may contain criticisms of serious issues in the real world (Handelman 1974, 67).

This view of the disguise function of joking was formulated by Sigmund Freud, largely in reference to the sexual joke: "Only when we rise to a society of a more refined education do the formal conditions for jokes play a part. The smut becomes a joke and is only tolerated when it has the character of a joke. The technical method which it usually employs is the allusion—that is, the replacement by something small, something remotely connected, which the hearer reconstructs in his imagination into a complete obscenity. The greater the discrepancy between what is given directly in the form of smut and what it necessarily calls up in the hearer, the more refined the joke becomes and the higher, too, it may venture to climb in good society" (Freud 1960, 8:100). In other words, something that could not be expressed directly in society could be expressed using the allusive techniques of the joke.

How well does this conjecture account for political jokes? In fact, it does not seem to explain political jokes very well—particularly the whispered anecdotes from behind the Iron Curtain. For the jokes are themselves dangerous communications. The indirection or allusion in jokes offers little or no protection. Under Stalin, telling political jokes could initiate a process that might well end in the gulag.[20] Even after Stalin, jail or a destroyed career could result. When I asked an émigré from the USSR whether she knew of people who got in trouble for telling jokes, she said, "We knew it left and right. People were telling on each other . . . That was the beauty of it [the system]." People did not tell jokes to just anyone. They told them only to close family or friends whose trustworthiness had been established over the course of years.[21]

Nor would they listen to jokes from just anyone. Again, Klava:

> If someone would tell jokes, and you didn't report, someone might report you that you were not one who reported . . .[22] [When I heard a joke from someone I didn't know], I would refrain from reacting at all. I just played the role of an idiot. I didn't get it. And it was a signal to them. Take it anyway you want, and try and repeat it and expose yourself more without knowing why I didn't react. Or just get that I don't want to hear it. (April 20, 2003)

But jokes were not the only way that people communicated. People also complained to one another and criticized conditions. They discussed the incompetence of leaders, shortages, the discrepancies between official pronouncements and reality, and the injustices and failures of the system. And to whom did they complain and with whom did they share their social and political views? The very same people to whom they told their political jokes.

In other words, people could and did speak rather directly about the very situations that were addressed in the jokes. There is no indication that jokes served as any kind of encrypted channel of communication that insulated the tellers and hearers from reprisals by the authorities. Both humorous discourse *and* serious discourse were dangerous. Both required extreme caution. One could not serve as a surrogate for the other.

Closely allied with the hypothesis of political jokes serving as a means of indirect and thus sanctioned expression is the hypothesis that political jokes give vent to frustrations with and aggressive feelings toward the political regime. This connection is natural. Because the jokes are seen as providing a sanctioned frame for the communication of otherwise dangerous ideas, they naturally come to be seen as the major or only outlet for the expression of such ideas and their associated emotions. Dundes accepts without question that Romanian jokes "provide a much needed vent for emotion," and that they succeed in doing so because they "provide a socially sanctioned frame which normally absolves individuals from any guilt which might otherwise result from conversational . . . articulations of the same content" (Dundes 1971a, 51). Stanley Brandes, commenting on political jokes in Franco's Spain, also sees them as "a safety valve for anti-regime sentiment" (Brandes 1977, 345; see also Harris and Rabinovich 1995, ix). Writes Brandes, "The mixture of rage and fear, hostility and self-defense, which is important in all humor, is nowhere more apparent than in the field of politics . . . When people live under politically repressive circumstances, they are likely to vent their anger and frustration through . . . jokes . . . or related genres, and thereby create for themselves a temporary escape from omnipresent and severe restrictions on freedom of expression" (Brandes 1977, 331). Oriol Pi-Sunyer, writing about the same tradition of Spanish jokes, agrees: "Humor in such circumstances . . . helps to alleviate anxiety, and there were periods during the long Franco rule when levels of anxiety were very high" (Pi-Sunyer 1977, 185). George Mikes sees laughter as "the only weapon the oppressed can use against the oppressor. It is an aggressive weapon and a safety-valve at the same time" (Mikes 1971, 109). Lee Townsend views the jokes and caricatures published in nineteenth-century Berlin as expressions that permitted Berliners to "vent their spleen about life and love's everyday irritations" (Townsend 1992, 196). Alleen and Don Nilsen concur: "Antiauthority humor illustrates the theory that people use humor to relieve stress by making fun of situations where they feel put upon" (Nilsen and Nilsen 2000, 36). Charles E. Schutz, although less focused on whispered anecdotes, sees political humor of all sorts as sublimating aggression. The creator of political and social satire, according to Schutz, is the "aggressor against a political personage or social institution. By his comic genius he has translated his anger or resentment into a satirical attack in which his target is made the butt of humor for an audience. The target becomes a victim and the aggressor's anger is expended peacefully" (Schutz 1977, 77). Christine Pelzer White sees peasant plays that mock the dominant classes as a safety valve (White 1986, 54), and James C. Scott feels that all hidden expressions of resistance are symbolic expressions of suppressed anger in the face of domination, although he is skeptical that anger is actually relieved through such expressions (Scott 1990, 186–87).

Again, all these views are emendations of Freud's view of tendentious jokes: "Jokes . . . make possible the satisfaction of an instinct (whether lustful or hostile) in the face of an obstacle that stands in its way. They circumvent the obstacle and in that way draw pleasure from a source which the obstacle had made inaccessible . . . The pleasure in the case of a tendentious joke arises from a purpose being satisfied whose satisfaction would otherwise not have taken place" (Freud 1960, 8:117). Although Freud was particularly concerned with the internal censorship of sexual instincts, he was quite aware that jokes could be employed when the constraint was external and the situation straightforwardly political.[23] Building on

Herbert Spencer's notions of laughter (Spencer 1860, 395), Freud saw such jokes as a means for the discharge of excess energy. A joke, in Freud's view, circumvents an inhibition and makes the energy employed in maintaining that inhibition superfluous. That energy is then discharged in laughter (Freud 1960, 8:146–49).[24] Ultimately, the whole view of the expressive and discharge function of jokes goes back to Aristotle's intimation that tragedy provides an outlet for the emotions (Aristotle 1970, 25).

Cathartic, discharge, or safety-valve theories of joking are as problematic as they are pervasive. The problem is that while it is easy to recognize the performance of a joke, it is far more difficult to register the catharsis or venting that is claimed to result. Too often, the jokes themselves become the indices of the anxieties, frustrations, or emotions discharged. To take an extreme example, one scholar concluded that people were coping with "fear of space travel" and "of the unknown" because he was able to collect large numbers of jokes involving Martians, moon men, and space explorers (Winick 1961, 48–49). Unfortunately, the only indicator of these fears and anxieties were the jokes themselves. There was only one variable, not two. In far too many cases, the mere existence of jokes about a particular topic is accepted as a demonstration that (1) fears and anxieties exist with reference to that topic, and (2) those anxieties are discharged or relieved in the act of telling and appreciating jokes about them. While it is easier to presume that many Soviet citizens strained under the political and economic conditions imposed by Communist rule, were critical of the party and its leaders, and truly feared the political regime, the cathartic explanation, nevertheless, leaves much to be desired. We are faced with the fact that such anxieties and frustrations were often expressed directly.[25]

In the Soviet Union in the 1930s, people wrote anonymous letters to the authorities expressing anger and heaping abuse on the regime. Leaders were sometimes threatened. Some authors of these letters even dared the police to try to identify them (Fitzpatrick 1999, 186). In other instances a more dangerous ploy was used. An anonymous note was passed up to the speaker at a party meeting and the speaker might as a matter of course read it out loud. At a party meeting in Moscow in 1929, Vyacheslav Molotov read out the following note that had been passed to him:

> Comrade Molotov! You shout about self-criticism, but . . . if someone would criticize the dictatorship of Stalin and his group, then tomorrow he will fly . . . to the devil, to prison, and further . . . Many are against you, but are afraid to lose a crust of bread and their privileges. Believe me, all the peasantry is against you. Long live Leninism! Down with the Stalinist dictatorship. (Fitzpatrick 1999, 187)

For those who were not so brave as to defy the authorities directly, other modes of expression were available. People engaged in "kitchen conversations"—that is, candid conversations with close relatives and friends often lasting late into the night.[26] What was discussed during these conversations was, as one informant put it, "everything that it was risky to say." People complained, people criticized, people expressed themselves without inhibition (Leon, June 18, 2003; Vladimir, April 23, 2003). They also discussed forbidden broadcasts on Voice of America and the BBC, which they regularly listened to, and talked about the underground *samizdat* literature they read.[27]

If the hypothesis that the circumvention of an inhibition in a joke results in a discharge of energy that produces a cathartic effect is accepted, it must be recognized that such inhibitions were regularly circumvented. What did the jokes accomplish that was not accomplished by these other means? What, exactly, did these jokes do?

A fourth hypothesis about whispered political jokes is that they are, in actuality, revolutionary acts. Most frequently cited is George Orwell's comment that "every joke is a tiny revolution" (Orwell and Angus 1969, 184).[28] Others have elaborated upon the theme. George Mikes: "Every joke whispered against a regime, every laughter at the expense of the Hitlers and the Stalins of this world is a nail in their coffin" (Mikes 1985, vii). Oriol Pi-Sunyer regarded political jokes told in Spain as "the oral equivalent of guerilla warfare" (Pi-Sunyer 1977, 187). Egon Larsen titled his history of the political joke *Wit as a Weapon*. Hans Speier stated that "ridicule is ... a weapon. Tyrants who do not permit jokes to be aimed at themselves use it against their enemies" (Speier 1969, 182).

Comics, writers, and journalists have been perhaps the greatest purveyors of such views. Mel Brooks stated that "if you ridicule [dictators], bring them down with laughter—they can't win. You show how crazy they are" (quoted in A. Rose 2001–2002, 68). Milan Kundera (1969, 226) has one of the characters in his novel *The Joke* opine that "no great movement designed to change the world can bear to be laughed at or belittled, because laughter is a rust that corrodes everything." In *National Review Online*, Andrew Stuttaford characterized Osama bin Laden as "someone to jeer and scoff at, a clown in a cave to be mocked, parodied, derided, lampooned, taunted, and ridiculed ... A loser" (quoted in A. Rose 2001–2002, 68), as if the threat that bin Laden and his organization posed were somehow diminished through ridicule.

The term *revolution* denotes a drastic change in social and political conditions. The idea of a joke as a political "weapon" suggests that it inflicts damage on a regime. Yet jokes, to my knowledge, have never been implicated in revolutionary change. Orwell's term was perhaps unfortunate, because he did not mean to suggest that social changes were initiated or accomplished by joking. He believed that the joke "upsets the established order" (Orwell and Angus 1969, 284), but not necessarily the order of the real world. The joke aims to destroy dignity, but whether that regime loses its sense of dignity—or whether any change comes about even if it does—is quite another matter.[29] Brandes (1977, 345) did not see any positive effect of Spanish jokes on political life in Franco's Spain. Hans Speier recognizes ridicule to be a weapon, but more in the hands of the strong than the weak. For the weak, jokes serve only to "help the victims of repression and persecution bear their suffering" (Speier 1969, 182).[30] Other scholars have also questioned the real-world efficacy of political joking. Khalid Kishtainy, writing of Arab political humor, notes, "People joke about their oppressors, not to overthrow them but to endure them" (Kishtainy 1985, 7). People who have guns have no need of jokes (179). Alexander Rose sees Russian political jokes as essays in endurance, "temporary pain relievers serving as a substitute for being allowed to participate in real politics" (Rose 2001–2002, 68). Political jokes, according to Robert Cochran, are "at once an assertion of defiance and admission of defeat . . . No public change is effected" (Cochran 1989, 272). Indeed, Hans Speier actually considers political jokes accommodations with repression. The telling of such jokes assuages guilt over the failure to act politically (Speier 1998, 1395–96).[31] Rudolph Herzog thinks that the whispered jokes told during the Nazi era were "a surrogate for, and not a manifestation of, social conscience and personal courage" (Herzog 2010, 3). Thus, jokes are not an instrument of political revolution but an index of political fecklessness and resignation.

And resignation was endemic. In the face of Soviet power, the people were mostly "fatalistic and passive" (Fitzpatrick 1999, 234). Linda Mizejewski, another Fulbright lecturer in Romania in the mid-1980s, was dismayed and then angered by the utter resignation of the Romanian people. "We were not prepared for the silent shrug, the lack of anger, the hopeless shaking of the head in the face of each absurd new shortage . . . How can they take it, how can they put up with it?" (Mizejewski 1987, 62). But as essays and books amply demonstrate, if the Romanians were passive and compliant, they had innumerable jokes.

Anthropologist Mary Douglas (1968, 369) characterized the joke as an "anti-rite." She regarded it as "anti" because the joke destroys harmony and overturns established order. She called it a "rite" because it is an expressive, symbolic formation devoid of impact on real-world affairs. It is not a technology. It does not *do* anything.[32] It is merely an exercise in cognition.

There is one place in the scholarly literature where it has been argued that whispered jokes might have had some positive political effect. Kathleen Stokker, who surveyed humor in Norway during the Nazi occupation, pointed out that resistance to the Nazis in the early years was sporadic and came largely from individuals. There was no organized opposition. The circulation of anti-Nazi humor, she argued, may have helped to educate, allay fear, reduce the sense of individual isolation, boost morale, and engender a sense of solidarity conducive to a more organized resistance. At the very least, the jokes may have, *after* the war, provided the Norwegians with a sense—most probably a false sense, she adds—that they had resisted as a nation and that they could return as one whole to the reestablishment of the state and the values that they had previously shared (Stokker 1995, 206–14; see also Herzog 2010, 13).

But the humor that Stokker documented in her work was not merely whispered anecdotes that were recorded and hidden away in personal diaries or published in collections after the war. Much anti-Nazi humor was published in underground newspapers, printed on publicly posted placards, rendered in graffiti, or circulated on postcards and even mock postage stamps. In other words, Norwegian humor was not all of the interpersonal variety. A good deal of the humor registered defiance *in public* and produced spectators who might be moved to action as they recognized the existence of an organized and active opposition.[33] Whispered anecdotes were not publicly defiant. Although they involved confidants, there was no spectatorship, and they established no public. Of course, whispered anecdotes proved important to individual Norwegians during the occupation, but that they were responsible for a change in political conditions either during the occupation or after remains to be demonstrated.[34]

A fifth, and recently proposed, hypothesis of political joking shifts the discussion from the relations of citizens to state power to their relationship to the symbols of that power. Alexei Yurchak (1997) argued that since the 1970s, the majority of Soviet citizens regarded the pervasiveness of official ideology as a given that was discounted in everyday consciousness. Life went on not by repudiating, validating, or even ridiculing the "hegemony of Soviet representations," but by ignoring it. The citizenry—both leaders and ordinary citizens—simply conducted their lives in parallel, shaping their everyday behaviors in and around these representations as one might accommodate the weather. Soviet ideology was regarded as false but it was not contested because no other public representations of reality were possible, even for those in power. For example, people participated in parades on May Day because they were inevitable. Participation did not evidence support for socialist definitions of reality, and various forms of carnivalesque behaviors engaged in during parades did not reflect either opposition or ridicule. Parades were simply a part of life, and people enjoyed themselves because crowds and parades were opportunities for enjoyment. They could carry signs without even knowing what was written on them. Official holidays, speeches, party meetings, and other occasions were simply scenes set for them and from which they sought to extract the maximum amount of personal satisfaction. Most leaders also acted as if the ideology were not recognized for what it was. They acknowledged the salutes of the people as they paraded past the reviewing stands, and secretaries at Komsomol meetings recorded the unanimous votes of the members even though they were aware that the attendees had been sleeping, reading, or playing cards throughout and could not have known what motion they were in fact approving.

A deeply cynical perspective was necessary to live in these circumstances. It required what Yurchak (1997) calls *pretense misrecognition*. People recognized the falsity of the official ideology but had to pretend that they did not. Political humor, Yurchak argued, proceeded from this cognitive dissonance.[35] It served to expose both the lie and the pretense that it was not a lie. In this context, political anecdotes were not signs of resistance against official ideology, nor were they ways of speaking surreptitiously, or efforts to recover a measure of self-respect in an oppressive environment (the next hypothesis to be considered). In essence, the humor was *self-mocking*, as it exposed the tellers' own contradictory and self-duplicitous behavior. The jokes "exposed the coexistence of two incongruous spheres, official and parallel, and the subject's simultaneous participation in both" (180).

To illustrate his point, Yurchak cites anecdotes that explicitly employ clichéd expressions (italicized below) or that deal with activities defined in terms of official claims: "What is the most constant element of the Soviet system?—*Temporary problems*." "In what aspect is socialism better than other systems?—In that *it successfully overcomes difficulties* which do not exist in other systems." "How will the problem of lines in shops be solved in communism? There will be nothing left to line up for" (Yurchak 1997, 179). In each case the lie of the system is revealed in the punchline and breaks through the suppression of that lie. The jokes highlight the discrepancy between the people's sense of the falsity of the system and their pretended blindness to it.

The pleasure audiences received from such jokes—beyond what they might receive from any joke—was the lifting of a repression, the repression of one's own pretense that no discrepancy existed between official and parallel practices.[36] The jokes allowed people to articulate their predicament *without having to analyze it*. That is, the jokes did not lead to reflection about the official lies or the pretense that the lies did not exist. The jokes served not to ridicule the official reality but to adapt the normal Soviet citizen to living with it (Yurchak 1997, 182).

Yurchak's thesis is original and ingenious, but it too raises questions. First, it depends upon a double division of the data. Soviet *anekdoty* are explicitly separated from political humor in other times and places. They cannot be conflated with political jokes in Nazi Germany or fascist Spain, let alone with anti-regime humor in postcolonial Togo (Yurchak 1997, 162–63). Furthermore, late-Soviet joking is split from earlier joking, and the description and theory apply only to the generation of late socialism—people born between the mid-1950s and the early 1970s (Yurchak 2006, 31). While such divisions may be justified, they do not contribute to theoretical economy.

Yurchak suggests that there was a change in the jokes between earlier and later periods and an increase in the number of anecdotes in the Brezhnev period. Certainly the jokes that centered on party slogans, which he highlights, were popular under Stalin and even Lenin. Also, it is almost impossible—in the absence of systematic collecting and archival storage—to ascertain the quantity of oral jokes in any particular period. There is no compelling reason to think that many of the jokes from earlier periods did not persist and remain popular later on.

Also, the hypothesis works only if there was an absence of serious commentary about the Soviet system. Yurchak admits that if ironic and critical commentary—such as is displayed in a letter he reproduces (Yurchak 1997, 181–82)—were common in late socialism, it might undermine his argument for it would belie the repression of the recognition of official lies. But were such commentaries rare? My own informants indicated that they were frequent. One would also need to assess the place of *samizdat*, *tamizdat* (foreign publication), and *magnitizdat* (home-recorded media), the BBC, and Voice of America in this later period. If adaptation to the hegemony of representations depended on pretense misrecognition, could people reading or listening to such productions have escaped an honest confrontation with their own pretenses?[37]

Finally, Yurchak ignores or plays down the element of risk in joke telling. Klava, whom I quoted earlier about her 1974 encounter with the KGB official, was born in 1948. She misses by only a few years the window for the late-socialist generation. But if what is called late socialism is in fact characterized by dramatic reductions in joke-telling risk, then this factor alone could alter the circumstances and significance of joke telling. There may have been no substantive difference between earlier and later periods with regard to pretense misrecognition, or this pretense may in itself have been a pretense.[38] If jokes were no longer a truly risky business in late socialism, then they would no longer constitute *Flüsterwitze*. Their significance would necessarily change.[39] Consequently, the failure of the Soviet regime would be less a function of the disintegration of the "spiritual substance" of the community, as Yurchak (1997, 188) suggests, than the breakdown of the panoptic and disciplinary technologies of the state (C. Davies 1998, 175; Graham 2009:103–4). Or, as my informant Leon put it, "The writing was on the wall. We just didn't see it. The executioners were tired. You can't run a terrorist regime when you're fat and lazy" (April 30, 2003).[40]

The last hypothesis of political joking is the one that Yurchak's own thesis was meant to challenge. It concerns identity and the maintenance of self. Political jokes, it is argued, offer their tellers and listeners a brief respite from the realities of everyday life, a moment when they feel that they—rather than the authorities—are in control. To complain about or criticize a political system is to take that system at face value. It is an admission that the system defines and regulates life. Perhaps one may vent anger and aggression through such complaint and criticism, but ultimately the terms of the encounter are established by a set of objective conditions—that is, the regime. To read samizdat or to listen to illegal radio broadcasts are likewise engagements with objective political conditions in their own sphere and on their own terms.[41] The jokes, however, are different.

Recall the joke about the "bed that sleeps three—'*Lenin is always with us.*'" The party's intrusion into personal life is carried to an absurd conclusion—the development of a piece of furniture designed to accommodate both Lenin and the conjugal couple. The joke about the disheveled man who was afraid to turn on his iron for fear that he would only be exposed to further propaganda again extends regime practice to an absurd conclusion. Soviet propaganda is so relentless and pervasive on radio and television that all electronic appliances are suspect as potential channels for its dissemination. In the joke "When we say Lenin, we mean Party. When we say Party, we mean Lenin," the proclamation of ideological unity becomes irrefutable evidence that the Party either cannot say what it means or, more insidiously, does not mean what it says.[42]

The political joke, with its incongruities and its mechanisms for making those incongruities appropriate, allows for a momentary revision of reality (Oring 2003, 13–26). The joke is a reductio ad absurdum by means of which the regime, the leaders, the rhetoric, the incompetence, the hardships, the duplicity, the surveillance, and even the terror are domesticated and discounted. In each of these jokes, a space is created—however small—that the Party cannot penetrate. The joke rejects conventional logic and with its own counter-logics affirms the independence and integrity of tellers and hearers.

These jokes do not merely express opinion. They objectify that opinion and crystallize it in aesthetic forms. And while no genuine public is created for this opinion, in some sense, the jokes stand as the oral artifacts of an "alternate moral universe," the monuments of a buried civilization (Scott 1976, 240). Of course, any victories that emerge from such an enterprise are fleeting and purely psychological. They are rather modes of "consolation," manifestations of "spirit" (Cochran 1991, 16, 20), exercises in the maintenance of "self-esteem" (Mikes 1971, 109), serving to maintain "good morale" (Obrdlik 1942, 712), and as sources of "liberation" (Limón 1997, 74). Perhaps Freud said it best. Humor allows an "exaltation of the ego" and reflects "man's tenacious hold on his customary self and his disregard of what might overthrow that self and drive it to despair" (Freud 1960, 8:229, 234).[43]

And there were those who "despaired." At least, there were those who simply subordinated themselves to the system without any visible signs of disturbance. The father of my informant Boris was arrested and accused of sabotage in the last year of World War II because he had refused to approve for flight an airplane that he believed was unsafe. Because of a curious set of circumstances, Boris's father was not shot. He managed to get released and returned to work. But he had been so "scared by his experience that he couldn't even afford to say something like that [jokes] at home. He would read the paper and he would say, 'It's written in the paper, therefore it's true. The matter is closed'" (Boris, personal communication, May 15, 2003).

None of my joke-telling informants entertained hopes that the Soviet regime would end or be substantially ameliorated in their lifetimes. None of them were actively trying to change conditions or the regime. "Most people would say," said Boris, "this is not my business. Leave me out of it. Let me live my life, do my menial little job, come home, drink a glass of vodka, and forget about the whole thing" (also see Nemzer in Graham 2009, 68). One might argue that they had also despaired. But that despair was political only. Boris, and many others like him, did tell jokes. Boris did not learn them from his father at home. He learned them in school and on the job. Through such jokes, Boris could deny consequence to a regime that tried to comprehensively describe and define his life and with which, in some way, he was forced—like every other Soviet citizen—to collaborate each and every day. The jokes created a world impervious to economic conditions, governmental demands, and ideological doctrines.

There is some evidence to support this hypothesis. Experimental data suggest humor and comedy engender hope (Vilaythong et al. 2003), although one must wonder what exactly in the Soviet Union there was to hope for. Moreover, Antonin Obrdlik observed that jokes told about the regime in Czechoslovakia after the Nazi takeover had the effect of immediately lifting the mood of their listeners (1942, 712).[44] Two of my informants who made plans to leave the USSR in the 1970s reported that once they began the process of applying to leave, their joke telling stopped. At least in their cases, programs of action may have made jokes superfluous. Therefore, it must be acknowledged that any enhancement of mood, any exaltation of self afforded by the jokes, may have been bought at the expense of real action. Perhaps no serious political action was possible. But if the jokes were a substitute for action, political joking might be characterized as more a technology of domination than resistance.[45]

Some sense of the self-defeating aspect of political humor is undoubtedly the reason that several informants suggested that the KGB actually created, or at least purveyed, political jokes. The jokes were circulated from time to time, they said, in order to relieve stress and defuse tense political or economic situations. This view has also been promoted in the scholarly literature, although no evidence has been presented to support it. Certainly members of the KGB knew and told political jokes. There is no indication, however, that they were responsible for either their creation or their dissemination.[46]

A problem remains. If the jokes were merely symbolic and joke telling did not have any real-world consequences, what, ultimately, distinguished Boris from his father?[47] Both worked, both endured, both survived. How did Boris and his father differ except that Boris told jokes? But jokes are the phenomena that we are attempting to understand and explain; they cannot be invoked to explain themselves. We are left with the real possibility that political joke telling contributes nothing at all to survival, adaptation, endurance, or even equanimity in a repressive society. Political joking, in other words, may have no discernible functions at all.[48]

So why tell political jokes under repressive regimes? Why engage in such risky business for something that is of so little consequence in the real world? An answer would not seem to emerge from theory, but a glimpse may perhaps be had from an old joke:

A man complains to a friend that his home life has become unbearable. His brother-in-law has moved into his house and thinks he's a chicken. From morning till night the brother-in-law goes about scratching, pecking, and clucking. It is driving him and his wife to distraction.

"Why don't you have your brother-in-law committed?" asks the friend.

"We would," he replies, "but to tell you the truth, we need the eggs."[49]

CHAPTER EIGHT

Listing toward Lists

Jokes on the Internet

The human animal differs from lesser primates in his passion for lists.
—H. ALLEN SMITH

When confronting the issue of humorous folklore on the Internet, certain questions necessarily arise. What part of humor is folklore? What constitutes folklore on the Internet? When does humor on the Internet become the concern of the folklorist? After all, not all humor is considered folklore. Most folklorists would not regard a spontaneous witticism made in the course of a social encounter as folklore. Innumerable witticisms are generated in conversation each and every day, and no folklorist has ever set out to document them. Nor would many folklorists regard television situation comedies as falling within their province. Although some blurring of boundaries between folklore and popular culture has occurred over the years, television sitcoms, whether broadcast on television or streamed from an Internet site, remain firmly in the popular culture camp. This essay entertains the question of what constitutes folk humor in cyberspace, and it is explored with reference to a humorous genre that in some ways seems emblematic of the Internet as a whole.

If humorous folklore is considered to consist of specific genres—jokes, riddles, bawdy songs, pranks, witty proverbs, comic tales, and the like—there will be an inclination to see these genres as folklore on the Internet as well. Once something has been labeled *folklore*, there is a tendency for that label to stick. No one defines folklore as an invariable list of genres, however.[1] Expressions, behaviors, ideas, and objects are regarded as folklore because they are the results of some process. The key processes that have served to define folklore are "tradition" and "art" (Leach 1949, 403). Contemporary formulations of folklore as tradition see it as forms and practices from the past passed on by means of oral communication or customary example (Brunvand 1998, 11). Those who focus on the aesthetic character of folklore regard it as "verbal art" (Bascom 1955) or "artistic communication in small groups" (Ben-Amos 1971, 13). Some have also held folklore to be the culture of certain social groups and classes: peasants, farmers, the urban poor (Leach 1949, 401). Such groups and classes were singled out because they were held to preserve traditional knowledge and maintain traditional practices. The association of folklore with these groups divorced from, or at the margins of, mainstream society gave rise to the idea that folklore constitutes the "unofficial" or "vernacular" culture in modern society, as opposed to the culture of those at the centers of social, political, and economic power: the corporation, the government agency, the university, the museum (Dorson 1968; Howard 2005).[2] Thus, there are three potential ways to conceptualize folklore on the Internet:

1. Folklore is the product of traditional or artistic communications that emerge in oral, face-to-face interactions in society which then move onto the Internet.

2. Folklore is created by processes not unique to face-to-face social interaction. It is created on the Web through means analogous to those processes. This presumes that there are Web-based traditions or artistic communications wrought in Web-situated groups.

3. Folklore is the "unofficial" or "vernacular" culture of the World Wide Web. It is a culture distinct from the corporate, bureaucratic, governmental or other institutional cultures that inhabit cyberspace. (Bronner 2009, 23; Howard 2005, 324–25)[3]

To date, it would seem that references to traditions on the Web have been mainly directed at materials that first circulated through oral channels before migrating to a digital environment. To some extent, all culture is traditional since everything depends on models from the past. Even corporate web pages, for example, depend on layouts and designs derived from other media or other sites. Nothing is ever completely new. Consequently, the concept of folk traditions born and bred on the Web remains somewhat hazy, although it may not be difficult to identify certain specific Web-based traditions.

Emoticons are one example. The term is a portmanteau word composed of *emotion* and *icon* and originally consisted of ASCII characters employed to serve paralinguistic functions in textual communication ("Emoticons" n.d.; Kirshenblatt-Gimblett 1995, 74–76). Thus :-), when rotated ninety degrees clockwise, resembles a smiling face, and :-(resembles a frowning one, and each can be employed to indicate the emotional tone of a statement. Etymology notwithstanding, however, emoticons are less concerned with registering emotion than marking the intent of the statements in which they are embedded. Emoticons are largely concerned with pragmatics (Dresner and Herring 2010). But even emoticons, which seem unique to computer-mediated communication, have antecedents in telegraphy and teletype, and a short list of these was published in the magazine *Puck* in 1881 ("Emoticons" n.d.).

Transporting "artistic communication in small groups" into an Internet context raises the question of what constitutes a small group, and how one assesses the nature of Web-based interaction. Certainly, some videos displayed on YouTube have attracted thousands, even millions, of viewers. The audiences for them cannot in any sense be considered "small." And although there are mechanisms for submitting feedback to content providers as well as responding to other viewers, these communications are asynchronous and differ from what goes on in the joke-telling or song-singing environments of small, face-to-face groupings. A YouTube video seems more akin to a television broadcast, although it is produced by individuals rather than corporations. The producers of the content—unless they are actually in the video—are likely to be anonymous.[4] Yet there are also chat groups, discussion lists, or even interactive games in which aesthetic expressions may be created or deployed much as they are in face-to-face groups. All in all, the question of what constitutes folklore—or, more specifically, folk humor—on the Internet would not seem to be entirely a straightforward one.

Because of the range of humorous materials that need to be considered and the variety of ways that humor can appear online, the discussion that follows will be limited to examining a certain type of verbal joke in a digital environment. A "joke" is a brief communication whose humor is abruptly apprehended only at its conclusion (Oring 1992, 81–93).[5] Furthermore, only "canned" jokes are considered—those that can be shown to exist as relatively fixed forms in space and through time. Jokes can be verbal and/or visual, although identifying the conclusion of a purely visual joke—a cartoon, for example—may prove a matter of some difficulty.[6] There are several potential environments for the appearance of verbal jokes on the Internet: e-mails, listservs, forums, chat rooms, archives, and streaming video performances. Unfortunately, all these venues cannot be addressed in the space of a single essay.

Even if one does not go looking for jokes on the Internet, they can hardly be avoided. Jokes are regularly included in e-mails; in fact, the communication of jokes is the sole point of a good number of e-mail messages that people receive. Jokes received via e-mail can then be forwarded to other individuals. There is no

need to retype the joke or transform the text of the e-mail in any way. The forward can remain completely faithful to the text, which was received and passed
on without any alteration whatsoever.[7] If the notion of tradition is rooted in the
replication of past ideas, behaviors, and expressions, then the Internet allows for
the faithful reproduction of the form and substance of a message. The modern
era, in fact, has produced all the great replicative technologies: printing, machine
manufacture, photography, broadcasting, analog and digital audio and video
recording. It is a wonder, then, that modernity has not been designated the "Age
of Tradition."

The theoretical stability of jokes in e-mail forwards distinguishes them from
jokes communicated via oral, face-to-face channels. While e-mail jokes may
be disseminated in a manner that parallels oral joke dissemination—to sets
of friends and acquaintances known to appreciate jokes—there are some very
noticeable differences. E-mailed humor lacks the texture of "actors, scene, and
setting" (Frank 2009, 100). It does not demand a reaction, and a purveyor of
e-mail humor usually cannot be sure that the humor is read, let alone appreciated. Consequently, purveyors often preface their e-mails with some affirmation
of the humor's quality to persuade the receiver that the humor is worthy of scrutiny (101). While such attestations can occur in oral communication ("I heard
this great joke"), the oral teller must take responsibility for the quality of the presented material at the moment of its performance. Testimonials in these situations are optional. "Have you heard this one?" or "That reminds me of a joke," or
even breaking directly into performance with "A guy walks into a bar" can serve
as sufficient attestation to the joke's quality since the performance is subject to
immediate communal evaluation. In the face-to-face communication of humor,
even a nonreaction is registered as a reaction (101). Given the great volume of
e-mail communication, users must rapidly develop a small list of people whose
joke forwards they come to trust to be worth their while. When a joke forward is
received, what is assessed is not the materials, as they remain to be viewed; and
not the performance, as there is none; but the source (102). Receiving jokes from
an unknown or dubious source is likely to result in communicative failure. The
e-mail may be deleted without being opened.[8]

It seems obvious, but worth noting nevertheless, that verbal jokes that regularly
appear in e-mails (unlike some other humorous forms) have no analogies in the
paperwork lore circulated in written, hand-drawn or, more often, photocopied
form. There are virtually no photocopied verbal jokes. When people want to communicate a joke in person, they do not hand over a piece of paper with a text on it.
Nor do they send someone to consult a book of jokes ("There's this great joke on
page twenty-five of Isaac Asimov's *Treasury*"). One communicates the joke orally

or not at all. Only when such communication is not possible—usually because distance makes oral delivery difficult or secrecy is required—does a verbal joke get encoded as text.[9]

Visual humor does not operate under the same constraints. Photocopy lore was used in face-to-face communications (Dundes and Pagter 1975, 1987, 1991, 1996, 2000). Visual jokes (such as cartoons) are difficult or impossible to transmit verbally without undercutting their humorous qualities. A verbal description of a cartoon, for example, may sacrifice its economy of expression or reduce the interpretive challenge to the receiver. Consequently, a cartoon might be handed over to a recipient, but a written copy of a verbal joke will not be. Obviously, cartoons can also be mailed, faxed, or otherwise digitized for communication at a distance. There are types of verbal jokes, however, that can be transmitted in document form: jokes organized as *lists*. The best way to grasp the nature of the form is to look at an oral narrative joke that was reformulated as a list in the Internet environment. First, the oral narrative:

> There was a young priest who was just starting to preach and stuff. And one day, it was the first time for him to lead the Sunday Mass, and the head priest was giving him some little hints to follow and told him to come back to his office when Mass was over and he would tell him what he did wrong. So the young priest goes into the church and leads the Mass and makes announcements and everything, and when it was over he went back to the head priest's office, and the head priest told him what he did wrong. The head priest says, "You did three things wrong, but other than that you did fine. First of all, we do not refer to Our Lord and Savior Jesus Christ as the late J.C. Second, Daniel slew the lion; he did not stone the bastard to death. And worst of all, the Ladies' Circle is having a taffy pull at St. Peter's and not a peter pull at St. Taffy's." (Mitchell 1977, 327)

Oral narratives that become lists generally end with a brief set of—usually three—statements (Olrik 1965, 133–34). On the Internet, however, the number of statements may be greatly extended. A forwarded e-mail joke sent in 1996 had a setup similar to the above text, but the list of the older priest's corrections grew substantially:

> A new priest at his first Mass was so nervous that he could hardly speak. After Mass, he asked the monsignor how he had done. The monsignor replied, "When I am worried about getting nervous on the pulpit, I put a glass of vodka next to the water glass.[10] If I start to get nervous, I take a sip." So the next Sunday he took the monsignor's advice. At the beginning of the sermon he got nervous and took a drink. He proceeded to talk up a storm. Upon return to his office after Mass, he found the following note on the door:[11]

1. Sip the vodka, don't gulp;

2. There are 10 commandments, not 12;

3. There are 12 disciples, not 10;

4. Jesus was consecrated, not constipated;

5. Jacob wagered his donkey, not bet his ass;

6. We do not refer to Jesus Christ as the late J.C.;

7. The Father, Son, and Holy Ghost are not referred to as Daddy, Junior, and the Spook;

8. David slew Goliath, he did not kick the shit out of him;

9. When David was hit by a rock and fell off his donkey, don't say he was stoned off his ass;

10. We do not refer to the cross as the Big T;

11. When Jesus broke the bread at the Last Supper he said, "Take this and eat it for it is my body." He did not say, "Eat me";

12. The Virgin Mary is not referred to as Mary with the cherry;

13. The recommended grace before a meal is not: "Rub-a-dub-dub, thanks for the grub, yeah God";

14. Next Sunday, there will be a taffy pulling contest at St. Peter's, not a peter pulling contest at St. Taffy's.

Two of the three lines in the oral joke are found in this e-mail version. Another e-mail received a year earlier contains the same list, word-for-word in the same order, except there was a fifteenth entry: "And finally, the names of the four apostles are not Leonardo, Michelangelo, Donatello, and Raphael."[12]

Fifty websites that contain versions of this joke list between six and fifteen statements by the priest. Most contain between ten and fourteen. Unlike the oral version, all employ a setup in which a priest—it is invariably a priest—is drinking during his sermon. It is clear that some of the versions of the joke on different websites are identical. One website provides a word-for-word version of the 1996 e-mail joke quoted above, although the list is not numbered; dashes substitute for numbers ("HK Expats" n.d.). Another list is also a word-for-word duplicate of the 1996 e-mail joke, but contains some typographical errors ("Fortune City" n.d.). Perhaps in formatting a joke for a new environment some words are deleted and need to be retyped and are retyped incorrectly. So it is not entirely a matter of copying and pasting. Something analogous to scribal error seems to be taking place online as well.

More than scribal error is involved, however. Often, the list is reworked so that it exists in different versions on different websites. There is, for example, considerable variation in the specific items included and the order of their presentation. Yet this variation is not entirely random. It is, to some extent, rule governed. If, for example, item 1 about sipping rather gulping the alcoholic beverage is present, it is always item 1, probably because it is directly related to the setup and grounds all the other mistakes. Items 2 and 3 ("there are 10 commandments, not 12; there are 12 disciples, not 10") always appear as items 2 and 3 unless item 1 (about sipping rather than gulping the alcohol) is absent. In that case, they become items 1 and 2; they never appear in any other positions. This is probably because they are metrically balanced in a chiasmic structure and establish a rhythm for the unfolding of the list. Furthermore, they represent only minimal speech errors. In any other position these entries might undercut a sense of the increasing outrageousness of the priest's blunders. It would seem that later entries must be as or more outrageous than previous entries, and that the list is meant to be perused in the order of its entries and not haphazardly skimmed.

Most of the lines in the fifty other versions collected were contained in the e-mail joke as well, although there might be some variations in their formulation (for example, "And you should refer to the mother of Christ as the blessed Virgin and not Mary with the cherry"). Occasionally there are lines in some versions that are not found in the 1996 e-mail text: "Jesus' parents were not Peter, Paul, and Mary"; "Moses parted the waters of the Red Sea, he did not pass water"; "The Pope is consecrated, not constipated [related to item 4] and we do not refer to him as 'The Godfather'"; "We do not refer to Judas as 'El Finko' [or 'El Bastardo']"; "Do not refer to Jesus and the Twelve Apostles as 'J.C. and the Boys'" (related to item 6); "When the multitude were fed with loaves and fishes, Jesus did not mention chips"; "Lastly walk down from the pulpit; don't slide down the banister"; "'It's hallowed be your name'; his name's not Howard"; "Last but not least in marriage we say, 'Till death do us part,' not 'dying because of fart.'" These lines, however, are dispersed throughout the fifty lists. Only on one website do as many as three of these anomalous entries appear together in a single list ("Tristan Café" n.d.).

In jokes, the final position is critical. In the above list, it also seems to be important. Theoretically, any item might conclude the list. However, as items 1 through 3 of the e-mail version invariably occupy the opening positions, they are necessarily eliminated as choices for the final slot. Even so, the remaining choices are not equal candidates. On the fifty websites I visited, nine items were found in the final position, but there was a considerable discrepancy in their distribution: "Peter pull at St. Taffy's" (60 percent); "Mary with the cherry" (24 percent); "Rub-a-dub-dub" (4 percent); "The Godfather" (4 percent); "Consecrated, not constipated" (2 percent); "Holy Spook" (2 percent); "Eat me" (2 percent) "Dying because of fart"

(2 percent); "Don't slide down the banister" (2 percent). In other words, 84 percent of the lists used only two items in the final position.

To a great extent, the final position in a joke is governed by aesthetic criteria. Even though it is presented as a list, the text remains a joke. The final line is a punchline and must, to some extent, break the pattern set by previous entries. Since only two items dominate the final position on the list, it suggests considerable agreement as to what constitutes the "best" line to fulfill this function.[13]

Not only can certain narrative jokes be elaborated as lists on the Web, but lists can serve as the underlying structure of humor. A great deal of humor in e-mails, social networking sites, forums, and Internet archives appears in the form of lists. For example, the following list was received in an e-mail in 2006 and variants can be found on numerous websites:

We all know that:

> 666 is the Number of the Beast

But did you know:

> 668 The Neighbor of the Beast
>
> 606 The area code of the Beast
>
> 1-800-666-HELL The Toll-Free Number of the Beast
>
> 666.6667 The Wrong Number of the Beast
>
> 666. . .999 The Quotation Mark of the Beast
>
> 2 × 4 × 666 The Lumber of the Beast
>
> 666A The Tenant of the Beast
>
> 555 The Number of the Wannabeast
>
> $665.95 Retail price of the Beast
>
> $699.25 Price of the Beast plus 5% Sales Tax
>
> $769.95 Price of the Beast with all accessories and replacement soul
>
> $656.66 Walmart Price of the Beast
>
> 00666 The Zip code of the Beast
>
> 1-900-666-0666 Live Beasts! One-on-one Pacts! Call Now! Only $6.66/minute.
> Over 19 only please.
>
> Route 666 Highway of the Beast
>
> 666 F Oven temperature for roast Beast
>
> 666k Retirement plan of the Beast
>
> 6.66% 5-year CD interest rate at First Beast National Bank, $666 minimum deposit
>
> i66686 CPU of the Beast

666i BMW of the Beast

DSM666 Diagnostic and Statistical Manual of the Beast

333 The Beast's Better Half.

The list plays off a single theme: in this case, the number of the Beast mentioned in the book of Revelations (13:18). Each item in the list (except for the first) constitutes a joke. Most of the lines are relatively independent of one another and individual entries could be dropped or reordered without any significant effect on the list as a whole. Certain lines, however, can generate subthemes. An example is the series of items that deal with dollar prices associated with the Beast. The first example—"$665.95 Retail Price of the Beast"—can stand alone, but some of the other prices would not work well in the absence of that one. In other words, sublists with subthemes may be generated within lists, although they still adhere to the theme of the list as a whole.

Although each item in the list is humorous, there is no narrative setup, no necessary denouement, and consequently no entries with greater claim to the final position. In fact, there is no concluding position, and websites reveal considerable variability in the order and final entries on their lists. It may be convenient to regard this type of humor as a *joke list*, as each item in the list is humorous, but the items do not add up to an integrated joke with a punchline, and to regard the example of the misspeaking priest as a *list joke*, since the whole must still add up as a joke where the final position remains critical (Oring 1992, 81–93). Joke lists can vary considerably:

Okay, we all know that 666 is the Number of the Beast. But did you know that:

660: Approximate number of the Beast

DCLXVI: Roman numeral of the Beast

666.0000: Number of the High Precision Beast

0.666: Number of the Millibeast

/666: Beast Common Denominator

666^{-1}: Imaginary number of the Beast

1010011010: Binary of the Beast

0000001010011010: Bitmap of the Beast

6, uh . . . what?: Number of the Blonde Beast

1-666: Area code of the Beast

00666: Zip code of the Beast

1-900-666-0666: Live Beasts! One-on-one pacts! Call Now! Only $6.66/minute. Over 18 only please.

$665.95: Retail price of the Beast

$699.25: Price of the Beast plus 5% state sales tax

$769.95: Price of the Beast with all accessories and replacement soul

$656.66: Wal-Mart price of the Beast

$646.66: Next week's Wal-Mart price of the Beast

Phillips 666: Gasoline of the Beast

Route 666: Way of the Beast

666 F: Oven temperature for roast Beast

666k: Retirement plan of the Beast

666 mg: Recommended Minimum Daily Requirement of Beast

6.66%: 5-year CD interest rate at First Beast of Hell National Bank, $666 minimum deposit.

Lotus 6-6-6: Spreadsheet of the Beast

Word 6.66: Word Processor of the Beast

i66686: CPU of the Beast

666i: BMW of the Beast

DSM-666 (revised): Diagnostic and Statistical Manual of the Beast

668: Next door neighbor of the Beast

667: Prime Beast

999: Australian Beast

Win666: Operating system of the Beast. ("Laugh Break" n.d.)

While numerous items from the previous "Numbers of the Beast" list can be found on this one, there are many items that are different (for example, many of the mathematical and computer-inflected items). Items that appear in the previous list are absent in this one (such as "666A The Tenant of the Beast"; "666. . .999 The Quotation Mark of the Beast"), and some items are expressed differently ("Route 666: Way of the Beast" versus "Route 666 Highway of the Beast"). The positions on the list also vary ("668 The Neighbor of the Beast" comes at the top of the previous list but is fourth from last in this one). What seems clear is that there is great variation in joke lists, despite the ease of digitally copying and pasting materials into new online environments. Joke lists on the Internet manifest "multiple existence in space and time, and they exist in variant forms," as had previously been found to be true of photocopy lore (Dundes and Pagter 1975, xvii). Despite the theoretical possibility of the exact reproduction of humor in cyberspace, it is not what happens. Versions and variants are inevitably generated (Shifman and Thelwall 2009, 2571).

Oral narrative jokes seem to grow by slow transformation over time. Modifying a narrative joke requires constant attention to the whole text. A single word change can destroy the joke (Clements 1973). Such jokes develop by means of small and subtle changes. As jokes undergo these changes, the whole must remain a joke if it is to continue to exist. Consequently, the alteration of a narrative joke is never just a matter of addition. A narrative joke, for example, cannot be filled with irrelevant details that may distract notice from the elements necessary to grasp the punchline. Nor can matter simply be appended after a punchline (Oring 1992, 81–93). Joke lists or list jokes, however, only require the generation of new entries that conform to its structural, metrical, and thematic pattern. Appropriate materials from other sources can be included, and new material can be invented. In other words, joke lists and list jokes are *compiled*; they do not organically *evolve*.[14]

Although all kinds of jokes and humor inhabit the World Wide Web, lists especially seem to have proliferated. They can appear as a series of test or application questions and answers, formulas, rules, proverbs, aphorisms, greetings, quotes and misquotes, bumper stickers, signs, instructions, laws, translations, glossaries, product names, menu items, letters, excuses, calendar entries, haiku, photographs, and telephone answering-machine messages. The question is why has the Web been so hospitable to humor in list form?

Of course, lists have been staples of American popular culture for some time: the top 10 or 100 most popular songs, albums, books, films; the richest, most influential, best- and worst-dressed people; the poorest, most robust, and most corrupt economies; the top news, science, and sports stories of the year. There are books of lists and lists of lists. Many of these invoke a spirit of play, but the list does not seem to have been a major template for humorous production. There are, however, exceptions. Looking back, there is Pooh-Bah's inventory of potential victims in Gilbert and Sullivan's *The Mikado* (act 1); the remarks that Cyrano de Bergerac contends could be made about his nose (act I, scene 4); chapters in François Rabelais's *Gargantua and Pantagruel;* and perhaps the proverb paintings of the Elder and Younger Brueghels.[15] But it is hard to retrieve a plethora of examples. As a humorous genre, the list seems new.

Oral, face-to-face communication does not seem conducive to the performance of humorous lists, although lists are performed on late-night television talk shows. Johnny Carson, Jay Leno, and David Letterman, among others, have all performed comic routines based on lists. Internet lists do have their predecessors. Some entries in the mid-nineteenth-century humor collection *The American Joe Miller* are lists (e.g., Kempt 1865, 40, 47–48, 55–56, 66–67, 73–74, 187, 207–8), and lists regularly showed up in photocopy lore before the Internet came into being (e.g., Dundes and Pagter 1975, 39, 50, 51–56, 59, 60–63, 73–75, 200). The list form also characterizes certain kinds of graffiti (Longenecker 1977). The Internet, however, seems to have greatly accelerated the growth of the format.

To begin to grasp the significance of lists on the Internet, it is necessary to note their specific qualities. Lists are essentially *visual*. They are an outgrowth of writing. And while oral lists exist—genealogies, rosters of kings, ritual recitations of objects or names, cumulative and chain tales, catalog songs (Renwick 2001:59–91; Uther 2011, 3:510–31;)—they are relatively rare. When writing was first developed in ancient Mesopotamia, the bulk of the output from this new medium was not literature but inventory: administrative and economic lists documenting production, expenses, receipts, accounts receivable (Goody 1977, 78–79, 105). In any event, humorous lists are predominantly textual. Even the lists performed by television comedians are written and read rather than orally re-created. The "Numbers of the Beast" list is particularly visual since most people have difficulty processing numbers aurally. From the beginning, computers pushed users toward visual imagery. Emoticons and signatures often involved the creative use of ASCII characters (Kirshenblatt-Gimblett 1995, 82–86; Bronner 2009, 27), and cartoons and other elaborate images were created as well. Programs were even written in BASIC to animate those primitive computer images.

Lists, theoretically, are open-ended. They have no natural boundaries. They can be added to or subtracted from without any violation to the sense of a whole.[16] Such changes, however, depend on the medium in which the list has been textualized. In cuneiform, a list with additions and subtractions might require laborious recopying. A handwritten list also needs to be recopied. Additions and crossings-out are possible, but evidence of the changes remains. Typewritten and printed lists also have to be retyped or reset and reprinted. Digitization, however, leaves no traces behind. Consequently, computers make lists into creative structures amenable to easy revision and elaboration.

Lists can speed one up or slow one down (Belknap 2004, xiii). Some lists can be skimmed and sampled as well as perused. This is true for humorous lists. One can skip through the entries in the "Numbers of the Beast" list, grasp its overall sense, and appreciate those particular entries that one happens to light upon without dwelling on each and every item. Narrative jokes cannot be so easily skimmed and sampled, however. Every word is potentially important. Some lists can impose an order—an order that it may be perilous to ignore. Skipping over entries in an itinerary, a recipe, or a flight-check can prove disastrous. List jokes share something of this order. While it is possible to skip through the "Sip, don't gulp" list, it is still important to register the final entry. Thus, joke lists, unlike narrative jokes, do not have to be accessed serially; they can be randomly accessed.

Individuals can make their own contributions to humorous lists. If people think they have come up with a suitable entry, it can be inserted; the new edition may be posted or otherwise passed on. Since the "Numbers of the Beast" list centers on a particular number, it is not surprising that those with a penchant for mathematics and computing seem to have made more than a fair share of the contributions. The list, consequently, is a collaborative effort, although the collaboration—as in oral folklore—remains invisible.[17] In theory lists can go on forever; in practice they cannot. They have a "load limit" (Belknap 2004, 31).

Lists also tend to replace quality with quantity (Goody 1977, 88). Items of very different qualities can be added to a list, and this seems particularly true of humor lists. It may never be known how the oral joke about the misspeaking priest came into being, but it is not difficult to imagine what happened to the joke once it began to circulate in its Internet form and establish itself on web pages.[18] Individuals felt they were capable of adding to the three-part mini-list of the oral joke with their own creations or by the addition of extant linguistic formulas that they felt suited the joke's structure and theme. For example, "Dying because of fart" seems to be an addition with limited circulation since it appears only in texts on a single website.[19] "Rub-a-dub-dub, thanks for the grub, yeah God," however, is a mock grace that exists independently of its inclusion in the joke ("Grace before Meals" n.d.).[20] "Howard be thy name" is known independently as a line from the Lord's Prayer as understood by children ("Children's Answers" n.d.). Unlike the epic poet working with a set of memorized formulas that are stitched together in the act of oral composition, the Internet bard generates new formulas on the basis of previous models that are compiled in a register (Ong 1982, 22). It has been claimed that orally based thought is *additive* (37–38), but it would seem to be true of these Web-based forms as well. The list is predicated on the conjunction *and*, even if that word never appears in the surface of the text.

Lists can be reviewed and reordered (Goody 1977, 89). Thus, the "Numbers of the Beast," as has been noted, can be found with different entries and in different orders. But a list can also be broken down and scavenged for its constituent elements. Hence individual entries from the "Numbers of the Beast" list have been used to adorn T-shirts, bumper stickers, and coffee mugs ("Sick, Sick, Sick" n.d.). There is a rock album called *668 Neighbor of the Beast* and an album track with the same title (Shredd 2000). There is also a beer of the same name ("New England Brewing" n.d.). One website offers a video made up of bits of *Star Wars* footage cobbled together. The video, which pretends to be the opening credits of a television show entitled *Han Solo P.I.,* closely adheres to the format of many of the opening credits of detective and police dramas from the 1960s and 1970s ("666A The Tenant of the Beast" n.d.). The video, like the website's name, consists of the cannibalized parts of greater wholes. In some sense, the list is the quintessential mode of aesthetic humor production on the Web; it is bricolage: compilation, recombination, and cannibalization for parts.[21]

It is interesting in this light to reconsider the use of emoticons in computer-mediated discourse. Lists of emoticons were published early on, but only a few emoticons really had pragmatic functions. Most were simply the result of playing with the set of 128 ASCII characters to produce representational images. In other words, lists of emoticons often were joke lists rather than dictionaries. For example:

> :-{ "Count Dracula" and
>
> :_) "I used to be a boxer, but it really got my nose out of joint"

were of limited paralinguistic utility and were created as jokes to reflect the ingenuity of their creators (Kirshenblatt-Gimblett 1995, 75–76; Raymond 1996, 173). In this vein, //:^ =) was fabricated as an Adolf Hitler emoticon, and there are web pages with variants of this type (see "Hitler Emoticons" n.d.). But again, these lists can be scavenged for parts, and artist Dan Piraro published a cartoon in which a German soldier presents a piece of paper with the Hitler emoticon on it to his senior officer and asks, "What is, 'backslash, backslash, colon, caret, equals sign, right parenthesis?' Is the Fuhrer using a new code?" ("Bizarro" 2011).[22]

A question naturally arises with respect to the relation of joke lists and list jokes to joke cycles that have been circulating for more than half a century, beginning with Little Moron jokes, sick jokes (for example, "Mommy Mommy" jokes), knock-knock jokes, Polack jokes, Italian jokes, elephant jokes, light-bulb jokes, dead-baby jokes, Jewish American princess jokes, space shuttle jokes, dumb-blonde jokes, Diana jokes, lawyer jokes, and the like. These cycles of jokes were invariably constructed in a riddle (question-and-answer) format. Riddle jokes were rarely performed singly. They were reeled off orally in a series, although there was no necessary order to the sequence except when subsets of jokes played off one another (Oring 1992, 16–28). Unlike lists, however, these joke sequences were *exchanged*, so that when tellers paused, other jokes in the cycle would be forthcoming from members of the audience. Nor did they come together as fixed lists since the jokes in the cycle and the sequence of their presentation substantially changed in subsequent performances. In other words, if the jokes in an orally performed cycle could be considered a list, it was a completely ephemeral one. It would never survive except perhaps in the documentary recording of an observing folklorist.

Online, cycle jokes appear as posts, as lists, and in archives where large numbers of jokes are sorted by category (see "Blonde Jokes" n.d.). Posting jokes in a forum seems closest to face-to-face exchange.[23] In a forum devoted to scale modeling, there was a posting of blonde jokes—some in narrative form. Responses acknowledging the success of jokes were forthcoming as they might be in a small face-to-face group: "ha thats billiant kiwi!!! deffinatly got some chuckles out of me!!" and "lol, very good duncan!" ("Scale Models 1" n.d.). One individual offered a blonde joke, indicating that it was her "first post ever," so the joke was used as an introduction and to break the ice as one might do when joining a face-to-face group of people in the midst of telling jokes. The forum moderator welcomed this new member, thanked her for her joke, asked her to tell about her own scale modeling experiences, and invited the newcomer to make the most of the website's resources ("Scale Models 2" n.d.).

In another forum where people post questions for which they want answers, a blonde joke was posted with a request: "Can someone please explain to me what this means? I don't get it. I saw it on Facebook and I got confused." The joke was:

> Okay, so a brunette was jumping over railroad tracks and chanting "22" over and over again. A blonde comes by and thinks it looks fun, so she copies the brunette. When a train comes by, the brunette jumps out of the way at the last second and the blonde doesn't. The brunette starts jumping over the tracks again chanting "23."

A number of respondents helpfully explained, "It's the 23rd blond she killed"; that is, the brunette had lured a total of twenty-three dumb blondes into the path of oncoming trains with her antics. Another person offered a nonblonde version of the joke. One respondent, however, was less charitable: "You're 24" ("Yahoo Answers" n.d.). These kinds of responses might occur in face-to-face interaction as well, as people variously offer to explain a joke, allude to or perform other versions, or ridicule a friend's inability to understand.

Similar responses to blonde jokes were forthcoming in the forums of *eBaum's World*: "pur good. my favs would be . . ."; "Hahah, those were great. Another"; "haha i like that last one, but chekc this"; "Nice"; "Those are pretty good!" As laughter signals appreciation in oral joke-telling situations, textual laughter or statements of approval are employed to register appreciation in forums and chats. There is a difference, however, between the two. Laughter can be, and often is, an involuntary response to humor. Textual laughter or expressions of appreciation are always delayed and deliberate and may be offered even when a joke was not genuinely appreciated. While laughter in face-to-face situations can be feigned, it can also be real. In computer-mediated communication, appreciation is not an automatic response but the report of a response. Nevertheless, such responses may be necessary for cooperative expression and to ensure, as much as possible, appreciation for one's own joke contributions. All those in this forum who reported laughter or commented favorably on a previous joke immediately contributed a joke of their own.

Even though jokes posted in a forum can resemble aspects of face-to-face communication, those joke exchanges do not evaporate. They remain on the forum web page as a series of posts. In other words, the exchanges look a lot like lists as they accumulate, and they can be scanned, perused, and copied whole or in part. Contributors to the blonde joke thread on the scale modeling website initially offered only one or two jokes until one poster offered twelve:

Blonde year in Review

January—Took new scarf back to store because it was too tight.

February—Fired from pharmacy job for failing to print labels . . . "duh" . . . bottles won't fit in typewriter!!!

March—Got excited . . . finished jigsaw puzzle in 6 months . . . box said "2–4 years!"

April—Trapped on escalator for hours . . . power went out!!!

May—Tried to make Kool-Aid. . . . 8 cups of water won't fit into those little packets!!!

June—Tried to go water skiing . . . couldn't find a lake with a slope.

July—Lost breast stroke swimming competition . . . learned later, other swimmers cheated, they used their arms!!!

August—Got locked out of car in rain storm . . . car swamped, because top was down.

September—The capital of California is "C" . . . isn't it??

October—Hate M &M's . . . they are so hard to peel.

November—Baked turkey for 4½ days . . . instructions said 1 hour per pound and I weigh 108!!!

December—Couldn't call 911 . . . "duh" . . . there's no "eleven" button on the phone!!!

What a year!! ("Scale Models 1" n.d.)

A series of blonde jokes has been assembled into a list organized by calendar month. In addition, the jokes have been stripped of their question-and-answer format and reduced to one-liners. This listing and reduction would be unlikely ever to happen in oral performance. It is unlikely that the poster composed this list as it can be found word for word on other websites (e.g., "Flowgo" n.d.). There seems to be a compulsion to produce lists online even in the midst of the most amiable single-joke exchanges.

It has been suggested that the serialized nature of folk creation—graffiti tags, joke cycles—is to be understood as the dominant culture's "ultimate penetration of the vernacular" (Dorst 1990, 187–89). In style and the speed of their spread, graffiti tagging and joke cycles have the quality of mechanically automatic—that is, industrial—production (186; Eco 2009, 353). In the case of graffiti tagging, it is perhaps easier to see why the folk would mimic the modes of production of the dominant order. Graffiti tags are a folk version of advertising. Taggers seek to compete with the dominant order on its own turf—public space (Sahlins and Service 1960, 88). Taggers can achieve their goals only by means of a rapid, if hand-wrought, reproduction of a message over a broad landscape. Joke cycles and Internet joke lists are different, however. While graffiti tags are broadcast by individuals to be recognized as nearly identical items, joke cycles and joke lists are purveyed as a differentiated series of entries. Unlike industrial commodities, the jokes in a list are not meant to be facsimiles but distinct items. Furthermore, the joking is a cooperative venture and rarely the product of a single source. All in all, the analogy between serialization and capitalistic production seems strained.

The relationship between lists and the Internet would seem to lie in the strong analogies between them. The conspicuousness of the list on the Internet owes largely to the fact that the Internet is more a visual than a verbal medium. The list is also a visual creation, visually processed. To be grasped, it needs to be *seen* as a whole and in its parts. The list is also an open structure. It invites modification—slight and significant—and therefore participation. A large part of what makes the Internet attractive is that it is not a passive medium. It is interactive and that interaction can be immediate, unedited, and uncensored. The Internet is democratic and common, although sometimes at the lowest of denominators. The list, consequently, is a structure that captures the virtues and vices of the medium itself as it allows the easy incorporation of contributions from disparate sources.

Lists also seem to dwell comfortably on the Internet for another reason. Although the list must be grasped as a whole and in its parts, it is not necessary to grasp each and every part. Often it is sufficient to grasp a sense of the whole and a few representative parts. In other words, a list may be perused, but it can be and often is skimmed or—in the language of the Internet—*surfed.* "Surfing" connotes moving from place to place by gliding over the surface of things.[24] One does not need to read each and every entry of the "Numbers of the Beast" list in order to grasp its overall sense and how individual parts contribute to that sense. A list is open to surfing much as are the pages of the World Wide Web itself.

A final relationship between lists and the Internet seems more than analogy. Internet users are confronted at every turn with lists: lists of folders, files, e-mails, and bookmarks; lists of "hits" produced by search engines; menus that guide access to its numerous sites. Although not visible, the whole of the Internet is directed by programs that are nothing more than lists of instructions that are executed serially. The World Wide Web is itself a list, as every entry leads to yet some other entry. In the words of Umberto Eco, it is "The Mother of All Lists" (2009, 360).[25]

What can one conclude about the joke lists and list jokes as folklore in the Internet environment? While there are lists that underlie oral rhymes, songs, and even tales (e.g., Hunt 1884, 2, 208–9; Hugill 1969, 171–73; Bronner 1988, 68), the structure holds a relatively minor place in the inventory of oral creations. If joke lists and list jokes are folklore, it is not because they are genres imported from the oral to the digital world. While they certainly could qualify as forms of "unofficial" or "vernacular" culture, these terms are so broad that they cannot easily serve to ground a term like *folklore*.[26] Joke lists and list jokes, however, are creations fashioned and purveyed *in a manner analogous to orally communicated artistic forms*. Although certain texts can, and sometimes do, replicate others exactly, they are not eternally fixed. Joke lists and list jokes are used, and in that usage they undergo the communal re-creation characteristic of oral folklore in the real world. Like folktales and folk songs, the lists are collaborative productions that can be and are reshaped in the acts of their conveyance. They are transmitted person to person in e-mails much as jokes are conveyed to friends in one-to-one conversations. They are posted in special-interest forums as a joke might be performed for a small group of people assembled for some specific purpose. Like oral folklore, these lists escape the confines of local groups and find their way across social boundaries and persist over stretches of time. These artistic forms become traditional, even if that tradition is situated only in a virtual world. Joke lists and list jokes are examples of humor that not only inhabit the Internet environment but are wrought by that environment. That is why they are central to any discussion of folklore on the Internet.

What Is a Narrative Joke?

And every joke that's possible has long ago been made.
— W. S. GILBERT

Narrative Strategy is one of the six Knowledge Resources (KRs) identified by semantic linguists in the General Theory of Verbal Humor (GTVH). The term is meant to refer to the genres or subgenres of verbal humor. Narrative Strategy has not received much attention in humor studies, and Salvatore Attardo and Victor Raskin, the proponents of GTVH, only casually illustrate what they mean by characterizing certain short, humorous texts as either expository, riddle, pseudo-riddle, question-answer sequence, and so on (Attardo and Raskin 1991, 300). These linguists have no real interest in this Knowledge Resource since its delineation could only result in taxonomy with no theoretical import. "Narrative Strategy" as used by GTVH is merely employed to refer to the "organization" of a joke (Attardo 2001, 23). This usage is somewhat unfortunate since a great many of the humorous texts GTVH proponents consider are not narratives in any literary sense of the term. In other words, the "Narrative Strategy" of a great many jokes is really not narrative at all.

Folklorists have felt comfortable referring to "narrative jokes" and "joke narratives" (Leary 1984, 39; Stein 1989, 103; Thursby 2006, 50–51; Bronner 2012, 123; Oring 2012a, 102), but they have never tried to define or even characterize the form. The time and energy they have devoted to the analysis of jokes has been largely directed to their contents. Consequently, folklorists have written about "elephant jokes" (Abrahams and Dundes 1969), "Polish jokes" (Clements 1969; Dundes

1971b), "viola jokes" (Dundes and Brown 2002), or "disaster jokes" (Bronner 1985; Smyth 1986; Oring 1992) in an effort to discern the meanings, motivations, and effects of these jokes. They have attended less to the literary analysis of jokes: to the structure, style, diction, and prosody of joke texts and performances. "Narrative joke," for folklorists, seems largely a residual category; it refers to jokes that merely differ from and are longer than "riddle jokes," "question-and-answer jokes," or "one-liners."[1]

A few humor scholars take the term *narrative* in a more restricted sense. In *The Humor of Humor*, Evan Esar (1952) describes, categorizes, and provides examples of a range of humorous genres, subgenres, and techniques. While these categorizations are anything but precise, Esar recognizes *joke* as a term that is often applied to a variety of forms, especially to what he calls the *gag* and *anecdote*. The gag he identifies, however, as a shorter form that is fundamentally dialogic (for example, "Why do you drink liquor?" "What do you suggest I do with it?" [25]), while the anecdote is a longer form. According to Esar, the joke and the anecdote are both *stories*. The joke relates a brief single-incident tale that "begins with a situation, has no middle, and ends with a surprising or unexpected outcome." The term *joke*, in other words, is meant to characterize a narrative joke, although it is to be distinguished from the anecdote since, unlike the anecdote, it does not focus on a celebrity or illustrate a moral point (28–29, 31–33).

Joel Sherzer (2002), an anthropological linguist, has also catalogued various forms and techniques of verbal humor. Sherzer defines *narrative joke* somewhat as Esar defines *joke*: "a short narrative that ends in a surprising punchline." Narrative jokes unfold in "a series of actions and often include directly quoted, dramatized dialogue" (38).

Esar and Sherzer agree that there is a type of joke that is expressed as a narrative—some sort of brief story with a surprising conclusion. Although the definition of "narrative" is not an entirely straightforward affair (Leitch 1986, 3–41), one common proposition is that a narrative presents a series of consequential events. It is a *"chain of events in cause-effect relationship occurring in time and space."* It begins with an initial situation that changes as a result of causes and their effects until a new situation comes into being, marking the conclusion (Leitch 1986, 7–8; Bordwell and Thompson 2004, 69). "The king died, and then the queen died" would not be a narrative because there is no necessary connection between the events (Forster 2005, 87). "The king died, and then the queen died of grief," however, might qualify as a narrative, although of such minimal stature that it would not prove particularly "tellable" (Leitch 1986, 10–12, 23–24).[2]

A narrative joke, consequently, would have the basic characteristics of a story: it would unfold as a succession of actions or events, and it would conclude with the characters in a new status or affairs in a new state. What constitutes an action or event? Having an initial situation with no middle and a surprising conclusion, as Esar characterizes the joke, does not seem sufficient. "Two guys walk into a bar" establishes an initial situation, but what follows could be a sequence of actions, a conversational exchange, or just a situation concluding with a punchline—for example, "Two guys walk into a bar; the other one ducked."[3]

Sherzer offers four examples of narrative jokes. The first two would seem to involve genuine narratives:

> A man was walking through Central Park, and he was stopped by a mugger. And he resisted. The mugger wanted to go through his pockets and he wouldn't let him. He resisted and the mugger beat him up badly. And finally he subdued him, went through his pockets and found fifty-seven cents. So he said, "For fifty-seven cents you put up such a fight? You could have been killed." "Oh," the man said, "I didn't know you wanted the fifty-seven cents in my pocket. I thought you were after the two hundred dollars in my shoe." (Sherzer 2002, 38)

> A priest was shipwrecked on a rock at low tide. Soon the water began rising, but luckily a rowboat appeared. The priest did not want to be taken on board, convinced that the Lord would help him. Soon the water rose to his hips, when a yacht approached. But the priest waved it off. When the water reached the priest's neck, a Coast Guard helicopter appeared. But he refused again still counting on the Lord. When the priest drowned he reproachfully confronted the Lord, asking why he had not been saved. "What do you mean?" the Lord answered, "Did I not send a rowboat, a yacht, and a helicopter?" (39)

These two jokes do outline a series of events. In the first, a man is confronted by a mugger who wants his money. He resists and is badly beaten. The mugger finds some coins in his pocket and questions the man as to why he resisted when there was so little money to be taken. The man reveals he was protecting a far greater sum of money in his shoe. In the second joke, a priest stands on a rock in rising water and is offered rescue by a rowboat, a yacht, and a helicopter. The priest refuses each in turn, trusting in God's salvation. Finally, he drowns and he is translated to heaven, where he confronts God, who informs him that he sent the rowboat, yacht, and helicopter.

Esar offers his own illustration of what constitutes a narrative joke:

> A famous author was traveling in a train with two talkative women. Having recognized him from his published portraits, they started to bore him at once, telling him in elaborate detail how much they enjoyed his novels, etc. He suffered their comment and praise as best as he could, and wondered how he could silence them.

Soon the train entered a tunnel, and in the darkness the novelist raised the back of his hand to his lips and kissed it with a loud smack. When light returned he found the two women regarding one another in icy silence. Addressing them with great suavity, he said: "Ladies, the one great regret of my life will be that I shall never know which of you it was that kissed me." (Esar 1952, 29)

As with the two jokes employed by Sherzer, this joke describes a series of consequential events: an author riding on a train is besieged by two admiring but talkative women. In the darkness of a tunnel, the author loudly kisses the back of his hand. After the train emerges from the tunnel, the women are reduced to silence. The author says that he regrets not knowing which of the two women kissed him.

The other two examples Sherzer employs to illustrate the narrative joke seem different from the first two:

A guy is begging on the street and asks a man walking by for spare change. The man replies, "'Neither a borrower nor a lender be'—Shakespeare." To which the beggar replies, "'Fuck you'—Norman Mailer."

A distinguished linguistics professor was lecturing on the phenomenon of double negatives. As he neared the end of his talk, he drew himself up and declared solemnly: "In conclusion, let me observe that while there are numerous cases where a double negative conveys a positive, there is no case where a double positive conveys a negative." Whereupon, from the back of the room, arose a small voice dripping with disdainful condescension: "Yeah, yeah." (Sherzer 2002, 38)

These two jokes would not seem to be narratives in the sense of the previous jokes about the mugging in Central Park and the priest who drowns in the tide. There is no causal sequence of events. A scene is set, and there is a spoken exchange—a "verbal duel" as Sherzer calls it (2002, 38). Certainly what the passerby says to the beggar provokes the beggar's surly response, as the self-satisfied lecturer's linguistic generalization provokes a response from the audience member. But there is no series of consequential actions with a new situation marking its conclusion.

Thomas M. Leitch also considers such jokes to be narratives:

A gorilla sat in a bar drinking a double scotch. The bartender said, "We don't get many gorillas here." "At these prices," said the gorilla, "you won't get many more." (Leitch 1986, 114)

As in Sherzer's jokes about the beggar and the linguist, a scene is set and a verbal exchange is recorded. But does this qualify as narrative? Can a conversational exchange constitute a sequence that can properly be labeled *narrative*?

Two friends are talking on the telephone:

Hello.

Hello.

How are you doing?

Pretty well. And you?

Not bad.

Have you gotten over your cold?

It's in its last stages.

In this ersatz, ordinary telephone conversation, each statement certainly conditions the response that follows. Although a situation is initially set—two friends are talking on the telephone—and although their statements are causally connected, few people would consider the whole to be a narrative. There is no series of connected *actions*, only one person speaking and another responding. If it can be agreed that this phone conversation does not constitute a narrative, should not the jokes about the exchange between the passerby and the beggar, the lecturer and the audience member, and the gorilla and the bartender be denied narrative status as well?

It still might be maintained that these three jokes are, in fact, narratives because each statement by a joke character engenders a change of state and thus constitutes an event (Bal 1985, 13). The skinflint belittles the beggar; the beggar retaliates and belittles the skinflint, thus restoring some kind of equilibrium. The linguist pontificates, and a voice from the back of the auditorium reverses the imbalance. Consider, however, a telephone conversation in which one party says to the other, "I think I know much more than you," to which that party either responds, "You do," *or* "I am sure you think you do." A claim to superiority is made by one party, which is accepted in the first case and wittily challenged in the second. There is a change of state, with or without reversal. But do such bits of conversation constitute narratives? Even casual exchanges of greetings between acquaintances passing on the street create and redress social imbalances. An unacknowledged greeting creates a severe social imbalance. A simple acknowledgment of the greeting restores balance. Yet I doubt that anyone would consider the exchange "Hello—Hi," or even the report of such an exchange to be an instance of narrative.

It is even harder to discover a change of state in the joke about the gorilla. The bartender makes a statement that is meant to operate as a question: what is a gorilla doing in a bar drinking a double scotch? The gorilla responds to the literal statement rather than the implied question (Oring 1992, 6–7). Unlike the skinflint or the linguist, there is no claim in the bartender's statement to superiority, so there may not even be a change of state. Should the gorilla joke be considered a narrative?[4] Should it be considered any more a narrative than an exchange of greetings? Leitch may hold "The king died, and the queen died of grief" to be a narrative (Leitch 1986, 13). How might he categorize "The king died, and the queen said, 'I guess I will have the dark wine with dinner'"?[5]

The three joke examples from Sherzer and Leitch, in fact, look very much like exchanges that Esar terms *repartee*. Repartee, in Esar's view, is a category of *gag*—a statement followed by a retort (Esar 1952, 166). It is not technically a story, and thus, in Esar's categorization, not a joke. Although Sherzer is an anthropological linguist and Leitch is a narratologist, the untrained Esar seems closer to the truth than either of the academics. While I am not that fond of Esar's term *gag*, the term *repartee* seems right on the mark and might constitute a subdivision of what might be called *dialogue jokes*.

Speech is not coextensive with action, nor is conversational exchange coextensive with narrative. Yet speech, at times, may constitute action. First, a series of consequential actions—a narrative—is often constructed from words. Second, a verbal exchange can engender the recounting of actions, as when, at Unferth's instigation, Beowulf recounts his swimming contest with Breca (*Beowulf*, ll. 532–89). Third, narrative may be recoverable from conversational exchange. In the series of questions and answers between a sickly Lord Randall and his mother in the famous ballad (Child 1965, 1:157–58), it becomes clear that Lord Randall has gone hunting in the woods, met his true love, and was given a meal to eat, the scraps of which were given to his hawks and hounds, which subsequently died. Lord Randall, his mother, and the ballad audience come to realize that he has been poisoned and is dying. Accordingly, he bequeaths to the members of his family his cattle, gold, and lands. To his true love he bequeaths the fires of hell. This narrative is not told by either Lord Randall or his mother, but it is recoverable from their verbal exchange.

Fourth, there are also the numerous cases in which speech constitutes an action and gives rise to other actions. A promise, a lie, a warning, a curse, a revelation, a challenge, an insult, or a proposal can condition subsequent events. When, for example, a wolf suggests to a little girl walking through the woods that she stop to admire the birds and look at the flowers, that speech has consequences. It persuades the child to delay her progress to her grandmother's house and gives the wolf time to arrive there before her (Hunt 1884, 1:110–14).

Although narratives are constructed from spoken words and may be recovered from conversational exchanges, and although certain forms of speech may, in fact, constitute actions, it would seem that direct discourse and verbal exchange do not in many—even most—jokes constitute that series of causes and effects recognizable as narrative. At the very least, they do not resemble the sequences of events familiar from other folk narratives: myths, legends, ballads, tales, and epics.

The ending of a joke also seems worlds away from the ending of other types of folk narrative. The conclusion of a folk narrative is not just a final element in a series of causes and effects. The concluding event in a narrative brings about some sort of closure that makes the course of the narrative a conceptual whole. Without such closure a narrative is likely to be regarded as unfinished. In the world of the folktale a fortune is gained; a kingdom is won; a family member is restored to health and safety; an escape is effected; an antagonist is defeated; a husband or bride is acquired; or one's original equilibrium, following its disturbance, is regained. A folktale is unlikely to have a hero leave home only to become stuck on top of a mountain shortly after departure. A story may be broken off at such a point because of some particular circumstance in the situation of telling, but there would be no sense that the story had concluded. It would not be amiss at some later time for someone to ask the narrator to continue the story that was suspended at the point the hero became stranded.[6] Folktales end in a new state for the protagonist in the narrative world.

In the jokes about the beggar, the linguist, and the gorilla in a bar, a scene is set and there is talk. The presumptions of the Shakespeare-quoting skinflint, linguistics professor, and bartender are undermined. But no one in the joke *does* anything. There is no chain of events. These jokes are unlike comic tales where, for example, a woman convinces her husband that he is being pursued and makes him hide in the chicken house while her lover escapes (Uther 2011, type 1419A); a boy steals a thief's clothing after convincing the thief to strip and climb down a well to retrieve a silver chalice (type 1525J); or a tailor pretends to make clothes for the king that can be seen only by those of legitimate birth, and everyone is afraid to admit they cannot see the clothes until a child reveals the tailor's imposture (type 1620).

The punchline of a joke is also a different kind of ending than that found in a tale. A joke concludes with something said, not with something done. This is certainly the case for an overwhelming majority of oral and printed jokes. The punchline of a joke is—almost invariably—a quoted "line." It is not a logical outcome of what came before. The punchline, rather, triggers a reassessment and reinterpretation of what came before. Contrary to the definition of a narrative offered above, jokes generally do not conclude with a new situation but with a new awareness on the part of the audience. A punchline brings closure to a text, but it does not ordinarily bring *narrative* closure. Rather, a punchline conditions the apprehension of an *appropriate incongruity*. It serves to create the awareness that some relation appears at once incongruous and appropriate (Oring 1992, 10–15; 2003, 1–12).

It is incongruous that the linguist's pronouncement that there is no case in which a double positive conveys a negative is greeted by the audience member with an expression of skepticism in the absence of evidence. But the skeptical expression—"Yeah, yeah"—in fact, constitutes that very evidence. It is precisely an example of a double positive that signifies a negative. What, at first, seemed an unsupported and incongruous challenge to the linguist's claim can be reconceived as utterly appropriate.[7]

Likewise, the joke about the beggar and the skinflint depends upon no series of events. A scene is set in which a verbal exchange occurs. The skinflint who justifies his tightfistedness with a quote from Shakespeare is responded to by the beggar. Had the beggar responded merely with "Fuck you," there would have been no joke. The joke comes about because the beggar attributes his expletive to a famous author, exactly as the arrogant skinflint had done. It is incongruous that the beggar's vulgar expression of contempt is cast in the form of a literary citation, but it is also appropriate because the beggar responds in the same haughty style as the skinflint, *and* "Fuck you" is a phrase likely to be found in a Norman Mailer novel.

It is incongruous that the gorilla responds to the bartender's implied question about how a gorilla comes to be drinking double scotches in a bar with a response about the price of drinks. But the response is appropriate because that question is only implied. Instead, the bartender frames the question as a statement about the infrequency of gorilla patrons. In that form, the reference to the price of drinks is a perfectly appropriate response. All in all, I would argue these three jokes are not narrative jokes. They set a scene but there is no sequence of actions or events. So, what is a narrative joke? Is there such a thing?

There are various ways that a narrative articulates with a joke. For example, a joke can unfold as a narrative—a chain of consequential events in time—with the punchline commenting on or responding to that chain of events.

A gangster and his moll[8] were walking down the street when she spotted a beautiful fur coat in a store window.

"Oooooo, I'd love that coat!" purred the young lady to her companion.

Without batting an eye, he picked up a brick, smashed the display window, retrieved the mink and draped it over her shoulders as they walked on. A short time later they passed a jewelry store.

"Oooooo, I'd love that diamond ring," she cooed, admiring a rock not too terribly much smaller than Gibraltar. Without saying a word, her Galahad picked up a brick, smashed the window, plucked the precious stone from the debris and placed it on her dainty finger.

They walked a short distance and as they turned a corner, she caught sight of a brand new Jaguar gleaming in a showroom window.

> Putting on her sexiest voice, the glamour girl whispered, "Oooooo, I'd love that beautiful Jaguar." Her boyfriend stopped, turned around and snapped, "Hey, whaddaya think I'm made of, bricks?" (R. Edwards 1993, 46)[9]

A woman expresses a desire for a succession of objects that her boyfriend then proceeds to steal by breaking the showcases in which they are displayed. The narrative series is terminated not through obtaining the most expensive and desirable object or even by an attempt and failure to acquire that object, as might occur in a tale. It is terminated by a punchline: "Whaddaya think I'm made of, bricks?" This line creates an appropriate incongruity. On the one hand, the line is incongruous because it resembles the phrase "Whaddaya think I'm made of, money?" an expression employed to indicate that there are necessarily financial constraints on one's largess. But as the gangster boyfriend has stolen everything and expended none of his own resources in acquiring the coat and ring for his girlfriend, his claim to constraints seems absurd. On the other hand, the line is appropriate because the boyfriend has been using bricks to break the display cases to steal the items and, in this sense, his means are, in fact, limited. In this type of narrative joke, there is no outcome, no achievement of a new state, no narrative closure. There is only the abrupt awareness of the appropriate incongruity to which the narrative has led.

A second way that a narrative structure may be articulated in a joke is by embedding. The joke unfolds in a conversational exchange in which a narrative is embedded.

> At a testimonial honoring a millionaire for his contributions to the Atlantic City community, the guest of honor wound up a speech by saying, "There was a time when I had sunk so low, I had to borrow a dime from a kind soul to use the men's room. When I went in, however, I discovered that someone had left the stall door ajar and so afterwards, I had a dime to drop in the progressive slot machine and win the jackpot. That win provided me with the capital to build my empire. I always say that if I ever encounter that kind person again, I'll share my vast fortune with him."
>
> From the back of the auditorium came a voice, "It's me! It's me! I'm the man who lent you that dime!"
>
> "Sorry Pal," said the quick-thinking millionaire. "The guy I'm looking for is the one who left the stall open." (R. Edwards 1993, 3)

The joke does not begin with a series of actions but with a millionaire speaking at his testimonial dinner. In that speech, he recounts how he acquired his fortune. Unlike the narrative in the previous joke about the gangster and his moll, this narrative is uninterrupted and complete. It begins with his being down and out, acquiring a dime, winning a jackpot, investing his winnings, and finally ends with his becoming rich. The millionaire then declares his willingness to share his fortune with the person who gave him his big break. This statement is not part of the embedded narrative but is rather a comment on certain events in that narrative. As in the previous joke, the punchline creates an appropriate incongruity. It is incongruous that the millionaire should repudiate the man who lent him the dime so many years before just after promising to reward him. It is appropriate, however, because of an ambiguity in his reference to those past events. It is true that had someone not lent him the dime, he would have had no money to drop in the slot machine. It is also true that had someone not left the stall open, he would have had no dime for the slot machine. In both this and the previous joke example, narrative constitutes part of what has traditionally been called the "setup" of the joke. The punchline responds to this setup, but it does not advance the narrative in any way.

A third articulation of narrative structure in a joke is illustrated by the following example:

A loving and devoted couple were looking forward to the big Halloween costume ball for months and even went so far as to rent matching gorilla suits. When the time came to leave, however, Louise was stricken with one of her killer migraines but insisted that her husband go ahead without her.

After an hour nap, Louise was feeling better and so she put on her new costume and went to the party, excited about how surprised her husband would be.

Spotting the other gorilla, Louise walked up and motioned him onto the terrace. The two gorillas danced together and then Louise gave a few fetching gorilla grunts, took his hand and led him out onto the deserted beach. Soon, with the moonlight working its magic, they were locked in a passionate embrace gorilla suits and all—and engaging in monkey business of the highest order.

After their tryst, the two gorillas walked hand in hand back to the party, but Louise, exhausted from her workout, took the opportunity to slip away and return home.

Later, when her husband came home from the party, he found her propped up in bed reading. Deciding to play it coy, Louise purred, "How was the party, Dear?"

"Okay, I guess" came his rather noncommittal reply.

"OKAY YOU GUESS?" She was highly insulted. "What do you mean by that?"

"Well, I couldn't get into it without you, Honey, so I spent the evening playing poker in the back room. Then he brightened and added, "But wait till you hear what happened to the guy I loaned the costume to!" (R. Edwards 1993, 34)

While this is a complex narrative recounting a series of events about going to a Halloween party, the punchline articulates with the narrative in a different way than in the two previous examples. In those jokes, as was pointed out, the punch-line commented on or responded to events in an unfolding narrative or in embedded narrative material. In this joke, the punchline *completes* the narrative line. The punchline reveals a *narrative function* that was hitherto hidden from view: the husband was not wearing the gorilla suit but had loaned it to someone else. In other words, the punchline does not merely comment on narrative material or respond to narrative material but is an essential part of the narrative structure.[10] To put this narrative in its chronological order: a couple plans to go to a costume party in gorilla suits; the wife gets a headache and so the husband goes alone. Because he is by himself, the husband takes off the gorilla suit and loans it to another man and goes to play poker in a back room. His wife, recovering from her headache, goes to the party and has sex with a guy in the gorilla costume, thinking it is her husband. This could almost be the scenario of a comic opera.[11]

I am tempted to call this third articulation of narrative and joke the "*true* narrative joke," following Archer Taylor's characterization of the "*true* riddle" (Taylor 1943, 129–30, my emphasis).[12] The problem with the word *true,* of course, is that it implies the existence of a Platonic form, which some folklore expressions resemble more faithfully than others. While there is nothing inherently "truer" about this third articulation of narrative and joke than any of the other articulations—in terms of its popularity, aesthetics, or entertainment value—I confess a predilection for the term because the punchline is essential to the narrative structure. The punchline reveals a missing narrative event.

The first two jokes cited by Sherzer—about the priest who refuses the rowboat, yacht, and helicopter and consequently drowns, and the guy who takes a severe beating rather than surrender the 57¢ in his pocket—would also seem to be true narrative jokes in the sense just defined. For only in the punchline is a hidden narrative function revealed: that the rowboat, yacht, and helicopter were sent by God, and that the mugging victim had previously secreted $200 in his shoe. This, however, is not the case for the jokes about the gangster stealing baubles for his girlfriend or the millionaire promising to reward the person who helped him acquire his fortune. In these jokes, no hidden narrative functions are revealed.

These three articulations of narrative and joke—the punchline reinterpreting some element of the narrative, an embedded narrative, and a revealed narrative function—are independent of one another, but that does not mean they cannot collaborate within a single text.

One sunny day about 40 years ago, a farmer confronted his son out behind the barn.

"Elwood, was it you who pushed the outhouse down the hill?"

"No sir, it sure 'nuff wasn't," replied the fresh-faced lad.

"Now, Son, let me tell you a little story. Back when George Washington was a
lad about your age, his father asked him if he chopped down the cherry tree and
George answered, 'I cannot tell a lie. It was I who chopped down the cherry tree.'
Well, Son, his pa was so impressed with his honesty that he didn't punish him at all.
So let me ask you again. Was it you who rolled the outhouse down the hill?"

"I cannot tell a lie," replied Elwood. "I rolled the outhouse down the hill."

With that his father produced a hickory switch and gave the boy a first class
wailing.

"But Pa," Elwood cried. "George Washington didn't get no beating when he
'fessed up to chopping down the cherry tree!"

"That's right, Son, but George Washington's pa wasn't in the tree at the time."

(R. Edwards 1993, 47)

In this joke, the farmer interrogates his son about the outhouse. He suggests that
Elwood won't be punished if he tells the truth. Elwood confesses to pushing the
outhouse down the hill. Elwood is beaten by his father for the act. Elwood challenges his father about his implied promise not to punish him for telling the truth.
There is a chain of actions and consequences. It is important to note that this
narrative completely unfolds before the punchline is revealed.

There is also a narrative embedded in the joke: a narrative about George
Washington confessing to chopping down the cherry tree and being spared
a whipping for his honesty.[13] The punchline of the joke, while it refers to those
events, is not about those events. It is about the events concerning the pushing
of the outhouse down the hill. One could imagine a joke in which the father did
not relate the story of George Washington and the cherry tree at all, but merely
assures Elwood that he would not be beaten for telling the truth. Nevertheless,
when Elwood does tell the truth, he is beaten. When Elwood challenges his father
about his beating, his father tells Elwood that he wasn't being beaten for telling
the truth or for pushing the outhouse down the hill, but for pushing the outhouse
down the hill while his father was in it. In this imagined version, there would be
no embedded narrative.

Finally, the punchline of this joke reveals a hidden narrative function: that the
father was in the outhouse when it careened down the hill. While punchlines are
always surprising, they are not always, or even usually, surprising in this fashion. Only sometimes do they reveal a narrative function that has been hidden or
obscured. So this joke involves narrative in three ways. First, it unfolds as a chain
of events. Second, the narrative of George Washington chopping down the cherry
tree is embedded in the unfolding narrative. Third, the punchline reveals a hitherto
hidden narrative function—that the father was using the outhouse that Elwood
pushed down the hill. The overlaying of these three dimensions of narrative in

this joke is, in fact, unusual. While these narrative dimensions can regularly be found in other jokes independently, only rarely do they appear together.

It is important to note that the narrative about Elwood pushing the outhouse down the hill and his father being in it at the time has to be *recovered*. It does not unfold directly. As with the ballad of Lord Randall, the narrative is reconstructed from conversation.

Another example:

> There was a young Scottish boy called Angus who decided to try life in Australia.
> He found an apartment in a small block and settled in. After a week or two, his
> mother called from Aberdeen to find out how her son was doing in his new life.
> "I'm fine," Angus said, "but there are really strange people living in these apart-
> ments. The woman next door cries all night long, and the guy upstairs bangs his
> foot on the floor all the time."
>
> "Well, ma laddie," says his mother, "I suggest you don't associate with people like
> that."
>
> "Oh," says Angus, "I don't Mam, I stay inside my apartment all day and night
> playing the bagpipes." (Keillor 2005, 213)

A telephone conversation is presented from which a narrative can be recovered. The narrative told straight is: Angus moves to Australia and takes up residence in a small apartment. He plays the bagpipes day and night and his neighbors cry and stamp on the floor. He find this strange and tells his mother about it when she calls. She tells him to avoid his neighbors. But the bagpipe playing is the hidden function that explains the behavior of the neighbors, which is only revealed in the punchline.

What is to be made of these three articulations of narrative with jokes? Do they simply characterize a distinction without a difference, or do they point to something fundamental and important? A clue comes from two pieces of research. In the first, Paull Franklin Baum followed the vicissitudes of a tale often known as "Dream Bread" (Uther 2011, type 1626; S. Thompson 1955, motif K444) since its appearance in the *Disciplina Clericalis* of Petrus Alphonsi in 1106 and the *Gesta Romanorum* in the thirteenth century (Baum 1917). In the second, W. Norman Brown traced a story that has come to be known as "The Silence Wager" (Uther 2011, type 1351) from a fifth-century CE Buddhist text to its peregrinations and transformations through India, Persia, Asia, and Europe (Brown 1922). Petrus Alphonsi's text of "Dream Bread" follows:

> Two burghers and a simple peasant, on their way to Mecca, found themselves
> with no food except enough flour to make a single small loaf of bread. The two

burghers took counsel together how they might cheat their companion of his
share, and proposed that whichever of the three should have the most wonderful
dream while the bread was baking should have the loaf all to himself. Thinking
thus to deceive the peasant, they placed the dough in the ashes and lay down to
sleep. But the peasant saw through their trick, arose and ate the loaf when it was
half baked, and lay down again. Then one of the burghers, as though frightened by
his dream, awoke and called the other. "What's the matter?" "I've had a wonderful
dream. Two angels opened the gates of heaven and brought me before the Lord."
"That is a splendid dream," replied the other; "but I dreamed that two angels
came, clove the earth asunder, and took me into hell." The peasant heard all this,
but nevertheless pretended to be asleep. The burghers, however, who were taken
in by their own trick (*decepti et decipere volentes*), called him to wake up. "Who is
calling me?" he cried in great terror. "Have you come back?" "Where should we
come back from?" "Why, I just had a dream in which I saw two angels take one of
you and open the gates of heaven and lead him before the Lord; then two angels
took the other of you, opened the earth, and led him into hell. And when I saw
this, I realized that neither of you would return, so I got up and ate the bread."
(Baum 1917, 278)

This is certainly a humorous narrative, but it is not a joke. The direct discourse in
the final line that announces that the peasant had eaten the bread is a revelation
for the tale characters only, not for the tale audience. The audience has been aware
that the bread had been eaten since the middle of the narrative. Consequently, the
final line is a not a punchline since it requires no "abrupt cognitive reorganization
in the listener" of previous narrative material. And if there is no punchline, the
text is not a joke but a form of comic tale (Oring 1992, 83).

Most earlier variants of this tale that Baum examines do not employ the technique of suppressing the fact that the third traveler ate the bread. This changes,
however, when he considers certain tales that were collected in the nineteenth
century (Baum 1917, 400ff). Only then do texts appear in which the action of eating the bread (or whatever the particular foodstuff happens to be) is revealed in
the final spoken line.[14] Before then, in example after example, the text discloses
that the third traveler—the peasant in the version given above—got up in the
middle of the night and ate the bread.[15]

A contemporary joke version of "Dream Bread" involving three Jewish tailor
apprentices—a Polish Jew, a Galician Jew, and a Lithuanian Jew (the third traveler)—is found in Naftoli Gross's *Ma'aselach un Mesholim* [Tales and Parables]
(Gross 1955, 215), and versions focusing on different ethnic groups (Irishmen,
African Americans, Latinos) can be found on the Internet.[16] For example,

There were three Irishmen, and they only had one pound of baloney between them. So one said, "Let's all go to bed, and in the morning the one who has the biggest dream gets the baloney." So when they got up in the morning, the first one said, "I dreamed I went to a banquet, and the table was spread with every kind of food imaginable." The second one said, "Well, I had a bigger dream. I dreamed that I died and went to heaven." Then they asked the third one what he had dreamed. And the third one said, "I dreamed that you went to a banquet, and that you died and went to heaven. And I figured that neither one of you was coming back, so I ate the baloney." (Baker 1986, 129)

In this text, the audience is made aware of the consumption of the baloney only in the final line. It reveals an action that had been concealed until that point from both the audience and the other tale characters. The line is a genuine punchline: the audience is made to reappraise what has transpired in the narrative. It is the revelation of a hidden narrative function in the final line that turns the twelfth-century comic tale of Petrus Alphonsi into a *true narrative joke*.

"The Silence Wager" is a story that is usually about a married couple—although it is also told about a group of men—who quarrel over who is to eat a last morsel of food or perform some menial task. They agree that whoever speaks first should lose the wager and the other will get the food or be absolved from the task. They maintain their silence despite all kinds of provocations from third parties until some imminent or actual violence provokes one of them to speak. The other then declares himself or herself to be the winner of the wager. While the tale often ends with a spoken line, like a joke—in a Scottish ballad version, "Goodman, you've spoken the foremost word, Get up and bar the door"—the narrative is a comic tale and not a joke (Child 1965, 5:91–92). Although it is not known until the very end who will speak first, there is nothing that requires reconceptualization when the final line is uttered. There is no misapprehension on the part of the audience as the narrative unfolds. No previous hidden action is revealed. What the characters know, the audience knows, and vice versa. Brown does not produce any joke versions of "The Silence Wager," but recent texts show how the tale seems to have been reframed as a joke:

Morris and his wife Esther went to the state fair every year, and every year Morris would say, "Esther, I'd like to ride in that helicopter." Esther always replied, "I know Morris, but that helicopter ride is fifty dollars, and fifty dollars is fifty dollars." One year Esther and Morris went to the fair, and Morris said, "Esther, I'm 85 years old. If I don't ride that helicopter, I might never get another chance." To this, Esther replied, "Morris that helicopter ride is fifty dollars, and fifty dollars is fifty dollars." The pilot overheard the couple and said, "Folks I'll make you a deal. I'll take the both of you for a ride. If you can stay quiet for the entire ride and not say a word, I won't charge you! But if you say one word, it's fifty dollars." Morris and Esther agreed and up they went. The pilot did all kinds of fancy maneuvers, but not a word was heard. He did his daredevil tricks over and over again, but still not a word. When they landed, the pilot turned to Morris and said, "By golly, I did everything I could to get you to yell out, but you didn't. I'm impressed!" Morris replied, "Well, to tell you the truth, I almost said something when Esther fell out, but you know, fifty dollars is fifty dollars!" ("Fifty Dollars" 2014)

In this version, an event is hidden from view. Esther has fallen out of the helicopter during the ride, but the action becomes apparent only in the punchline. This is a joke and not simply a comic tale. Furthermore, it is a true narrative joke as defined by its hidden narrative function.[17]

Although jokes are old, and even narrative jokes may be old, is it possible that true narrative jokes are a late development? Do hidden narrative functions in jokes begin to appear only in the nineteenth century? I have examined seven volumes of humorous texts—comprising almost 1,900 different jokes—assembled over a thousand years in China, Iran, Europe, England, and North America. The books include *The Philogelos,* whose earliest manuscript dates from the tenth century (but is believed to be several centuries older [Baldwin 1983, iv; Bremmer 1997, 17; Beard 2014, 185]); *Wit and Humor from Old Cathay,* which includes jokes from tenth- through nineteenth-century China (Kowallis 1986); *Resaleh-ye Delgosha,* from early fourteenth-century Persia (Zakani 2008, 89–150); *A Hundred Merry Tales,* believed to be compiled by John Rastell in 1526 (Klaf and Hurwood 1964; Brewer 1997, 97); *Joe Miller's Jests; or, The Wit's Vade-Mecum* (Jenkins 1963), published in England in the first half of the eighteenth century; *The American Joe Miller,* published in London at the close of the American Civil War (Kempt 1865); and *The Bathroom Joke Book,* from the twentieth-century United States (R. Edwards 1993).[18] The question is: are the three types of narrative joke equally distributed through time and across space?

An answer to this question is contained, to some extent, in table 9.1. In the first column, the seven sources are identified. In the second column, the number of analyzed texts in each book is indicated. In the third column, the number of texts whose final line is expressed in direct discourse (DD), indirect discourse (ID), action (Act), or some other manner (an explanation, report, comment, statement, or realization)—is listed, together with the percentage of each of the whole. In the fourth column, the number of narrative texts in the volume is specified. In the fifth and sixth columns, the number of embedded narrative texts and narrative texts with hidden functions is indicated as well as their percentage *of the total narratives* in that collection.

TABLE 9.1. A comparison of seven humor books from different centuries

Source	Number of texts	Final lines*				Number of narratives	Embedded narratives	Hidden function
		DD	ID	Act	Other			
Philogelos (<10th century)	252	193 (76%)	20 (8%)	34 (14%)	5 (2%)	19 (8%)	0	0
Resaleh-ye Delgosha (14th century)	142	139 (98%)	0 (0%)	2 (1%)	1 (1%)	23 (16%)	0	0
A Hundred Merry Tales (16th century)	100	82 (82%)	3 (3%)	13 (13%)	2 (2%)	50 (50%)	2 (4%)	0
Joe Miller's Jests (1739)	247	234 (94.8%)	10 (4.0%)	1 (0.4%)	2 (0.8%)	19 (8%)	0	1 (5.2%)
Wit and Humor from Old Cathay (10th–19th centuries)	291	272 (93%)	3 (1%)	8 (3%)	8 (3%)	102 (35%)	1 (1%)	1 (1%)
American Joe Miller (1865)	671	525 (78%)	68 (10%)	26 (4%)	52 (8%)	49 (7.3%)	2 (4%)	8 (16%)
Bathroom Joke Book (1993)	184	162 (88%)	3 (2%)	0 (0%)	19 (10%)	63 (34%)	8 (12.7%)	18 (28.5%)
Totals	1,887 (100%)	1,607 (85.1%)	107 (5.7%)	84 (4.5%)	89 (4.7%)	325 (17%)	13 (4%)	28 (8.6%)

* DD = direct discourse; ID = indirect discourse; Act = action

Of this mass of numbers, three seem significant. First, the total of the third column indicates the percentage of final lines that are delivered in direct discourse or indirect discourse. They constitute more than 90 percent of all texts. In other words, humorous texts are fundamentally about something said rather than something done.[19] Second, narratives constitute a minority—usually a significant minority—of joke texts. Most jokes are dialogic, and the humor is often rooted in a verbal comment or verbal exchange—Esar's repartee—rather than in an unfolding chain of events. Third, looking at the number of embedded narratives and narratives with hidden functions, there is a genuine paucity of examples in the compilations from before the twentieth century. Only in the collection published in 1993 does there seem to be any significant number of these kinds of narratives. Specifically, 12.7 percent of the narrative jokes in this book have embedded narratives, and 28.5 percent of the narratives in the book have a punchline that reveals a hidden narrative function. It is this second figure of 28.5 percent concerning hidden functions that I think may be important. It suggests that jokes with hidden narrative functions may be a late development in the history of humorous narrative. To put it more formally and more directly: *before the nineteenth century, humorous narratives in which a hidden narrative function is revealed in the punch-line are almost absent.* When a narrative function is hidden in humorous narrative texts from earlier centuries, it is hidden only from the characters in the narrative itself—not from the listening or reading audience. In the twentieth-century joke, however, the joke audience is apprised of the hidden function at the very same time as the joke characters and only at the very end of the narrative.

I am *not* suggesting that a hidden narrative function *never* appears before the nineteenth century. One need only look at Odysseus's telling Polyphemus that his name is "Nobody": this has a function that is revealed only later in the narrative (book 9, ll. 404–85). The lie that Odysseus tells Polyphemus is obvious at the instant of its telling. Its narrative function becomes clear, however, only after Polyphemus has been blinded and calls for aid from his fellow Cyclopes. The Polyphemus adventure is meant to be comic, and certainly Odysseus laughs at his own cunning (ll. 461–63), but the episode is a tale and not a joke. In fact, in the oldest manuscripts of the *Masnavi* (*Mathnawí*) of Jalálu'din Rúmí (1207–73), the "Tale of the Three Travelers" discussed above has a hidden function, and the eating of the morsel during the night is not revealed to the reader until the end of the tale. At various points, Rúmí injects philosophical discourses into his tale, so the story never proceeds in an uninterrupted fashion. The text, in other words, because of its length and discursive style, could not really be said to be a joke in any usual sense of the word. The would-be joke is merely a platform for more important religious ruminations. Nevertheless, Rúmí presents a version of the story in which a hidden function is revealed only at the story's conclusion (Nicholson 1977, 390–96). It would seem that Rúmí based his tale on a true narrative joke.[20]

If the preliminary results that I have obtained are confirmed, however, it might be said that the *true narrative joke* is a late development that arose from comic tales. This hypothesis may seem overly bold, and it may ultimately prove to be untrue. However, the hypothesis should be clear enough so that it might be invalidated with appropriately marshaled evidence. Consequently, the hypothesis can provide a focus for those who wish to explore the question of whether the different articulations of narrative and joke that have been delineated here constitute meaningful distinctions—distinctions *with* a difference—and it can draw attention to much-neglected topics: the literary aspects of jokes and the evolution of contemporary folklore forms.[21]

Demythologizing the Jewish Joke

Beneath every history, another history.
—HILARY MANTEL

More than a century has elapsed since the beginnings of a serious intellectual discourse on the subject of Jewish jokes. I would date that beginning with Sigmund
Freud's *Jokes and Their Relation to the Unconscious* in 1905. While there had been
some previous writing on the humor of Jews, his use of Jewish examples in a book
informed by a comprehensive psychological theory directed scholarly attention
to Jewish jokes as psychological and social phenomena.[1] These past hundred-plus
years have yielded something of a consensus on the origins, character, motivations, functions, performance, and quality of Jewish jokes and Jewish humor
more generally. There are some contrary opinions of course, but for the most part
the consensus view is presented below.

Definition. Jewish humor stresses the uniqueness of Jewish society and culture" (Nevo and Levine 1994, 126). It is "created by Jews, intended mainly for Jews,
and . . . reflects special aspects of Jewish life" (Ziv 1986a, 11). A Jewish joke is a
"humorous narrative whose dramatis personae are Jewish and act according to
stereotypic images" (Fischman 2011, 48). It is one "which would be pointless if
the Jewishness of a character were removed" (Cray 1964, 344). A Jewish joke is
one that could not be easily told about many other groups (C. Davies 1986, 76).
It makes "extensive use . . . of biblical verses, religious law, legends, prayers, and
rabbinical sayings" (Druyanow 2010, 120). A Jewish joke "must express a Jewish
sensibility. Merely giving individuals in a joke Jewish names, or ascribing the joke

to Jewish characters, does not a Jewish joke make" (Telushkin 1992, 16). Without the Jewish joke, Jewish culture cannot be understood (Nador 1975, 3).

Quality. Jewish humor is held to be of higher quality than other national humors (Druyanow 2010, 119). Not only are "Jews skilled at joke-making" (Ausubel 1948, 264), but the humor of Jews is regarded as "more acute, more profound, and richer in expression than that of any other people" (Landmann 1962, 194). "The Jewish joke is probably the best of all jokes" (Mikes 1971, 111). "Jewish wit is the foundation and pinnacle of all wit in general (Alexander Moszkowski, quoted in Revel 1943, 545). There is a "Jewish pre-eminence" in the field of humor (Bermant 1986, 4).

Origins. The Jewish joke and Jewish humor more generally spring from the soil of eastern Europe. They are an outgrowth of the society and circumstances of Jews in the Pale of Settlement, the area that today would comprise parts of Russia, Lithuania, Belarus, Poland, and Ukraine. "Jewish humor is Yiddish humor" (Kristol 1951, 433; Learsi 1961, 13; Spalding 1969, xv; Golden 1972, 12–13; Novak and Waldoks 1981, xiii; Bermant 1986, 60; Alter 1987, 25; Eilbirt 1993, 61; Hoffman 1997, 104), "born in the Empire of the Czars" (Mikes 1971, 102). The Yiddish language and the humor later spread throughout Europe and eventually moved to the United States (S. Cohen 1987, 2; Ziv 1986a, 11).[2]

If the Jewish joke is said to have originated in the Pale geographically, for some its true origins stem from sources outside the area. While some writers mined the ancient sources for examples of humor in an effort to demonstrate merely that the Jewish people were not without humor even in the earliest stages of their history and that the rabbis laughed like other people (Chotzner 1905; Isaacs 1911, 7), other writers saw in these examples more than a proof for the early existence of Jewish humor.[3] They maintained that there was a tradition of humor from which modern Jewish humor developed. Jewish humor, in other words, *evolved* into its modern form, and it retained some of the qualities present in the ancient sources (Bermant 1986, 4; Brodsky 2011, 25; Wisse 2013, 22). As one commentator asserted, Jewish humor is a "humor of irony," and it has been a "constant element from Elijah the prophet to Sholem Aleichem's Tevye" (Knox 1969, 153, 156; see also Ausubel 1948, 265–66; Ziv 1986b, 54; Yeshaye Zlotnik, in Gottesman 2003, 70; Wex 2006, 104).[4]

Characteristics. Beyond the simple reflection of Jewish names, roles, institutions, and social conditions, more specific characteristics of Jewish jokes have been identified. Jewish jokes are held to be especially self-critical. The targets of Jewish jokes are most often the Jews themselves. Sigmund Freud made this point in *Jokes and Their Relation to the Unconscious* (Freud 1960, 8:111–12) in 1905 and thus established a principle that seemed to distinguish the Jewish joke from jokes found in other nations. Although Freud was not the first to note the self-criticism in Jewish humor (see Adler 1893, 468), his use of Jewish examples in a psychological monograph gave his observation a special resonance. Hence the idea developed that Jews were self-hating and their humor was masochistic.

What is often overlooked is that Freud does not characterize Jewish jokes as masochistic. He offers no psychological interpretation of Jewish joking whatsoever. He merely notes that Jews were well aware of their real faults and the connection of these faults to their virtues.[5] Furthermore, he distinguishes the self-critical jokes of Jews from the "brutal comic stories" (*brutale Schwänke*) told by outsiders (Freud 1960, 8:111). It was Freud's disciples who set Jewish joking explicitly within a framework of psychopathology. Martin Grotjahn, however, characterizes the masochism of the Jewish joke as only a *mask* and not a real perversion. The Jew deflects his hostility away from his oppressor and onto himself. The self-critical joke demonstrates that the Jew can attack himself even more cleverly than his persecutors and thus achieve a victory over them (Grotjahn 1966, 22–23). Psychoanalyst Edmund Bergler (1956, 111) agrees. Theodor Reik admires Grotjahn's analysis, but he suggests that the masochism was real, and in his jokes, the Jew is trying to make himself an abject figure worthy of forgiveness and love (Reik 1962, 220–21). Few commentators on the Jewish joke have been able to avoid identifying Jewish jokes as Jewish creations that are uniquely self-mocking, self-deprecatory, or even self-hating (e.g., Kreppel 1933, v–vi; Simon 1948, 46; Ausubel 1948, 265; Mikes 1971, 102–4; Eilbirt 1993, 141–46; Novak and Waldoks 1981, xvi; Bermant 1986, 242–43; Telushkin 1992, 77–82; Wisse 2013, 7–11, 34, 106; but see Ben-Amos 1973; Oring 1992, 122–34; C. Davies 2002, 17–49).

The aggression of the Jewish joke is directed not only against the self but against Gentile oppressors (Simon 1948, 46; Learsi 1961, 12; C. Davies 2002, 51–75; Druyanow 2010, 136) as well as other members of Jewish society. The jokes are regarded as a way that Jews could safely react to external threats and deal with some of their internal divisions and problems (Ben-Amos 1973; Ziv 1986b, 50–51; Wisse 2013, 68).

Jewish jokes are also said to emerge from and to employ a particular language and logic. Jewish humor "consists above all in the pun" because the three-consonant roots in the Hebrew language can be read with different vowels and are thus open to different interpretations (Simon 1948, 42–43; Wex 2006, 82; Brodsky 2011, 13; Wisse 2013, 80–81; Friedman and Friedman 2014, 105). The absence of punctuation in traditional Jewish texts only increases the number of possible readings.[6] The well-known Soviet-era joke about Stalin reading a contrite telegram from Trotsky has been related to the ambiguities in reading Hebrew texts (Rosten 1970:xiv–xv; Brodsky 2011, 16–17).[7]

It has also been argued that Jewish humor engages in a certain kind of logic that is derived from the style and methods of Talmudic interpretation, which it both emulates and parodies. Jewish jokes have a "crazy logic," "insane rationality," "a logical rigor gone over the edge," the "humor of an intelligence running amok" (T. Cohen 1999, 45–68). It is a humor of "rebellious rationalism" (Kristol 1951, 433) or "logic—in despair" (Rosten 1970, xxiii). Many others have commented on the Jewish joke's penchant for impossible argument, elaborate reasoning, and hair-splitting (Untermeyer 1946, 521–26; Simon 1948, 43–45; Reik 1962, 114–16; Altman 1971, 141; Nador 1975, 5; Bermant 1986, 240–41; C. Davies 1986, 76; R. Raskin 1992, 30–32; Telushkin 1992, 41–61; Shloyme Bastomski, in Gottesman 2003, 88; Druyanow 2010, 130, 132; Finkin 2011, 91–94).

Impetus. "Impetus" refers to the conditions that would have given rise to the Jewish joke and promoted its dissemination. Two are regularly identified and they are not independent factors. First, there are the economic, political, and social conditions that defined the life of Jews in the Pale. Jews were mostly poor, ill housed, and ill nourished. They were subjected to edicts that restricted their occu-pations, movement, and freedom of action. They were also the targets of periodic violence that erupted spontaneously or was planned in collaboration with govern-ment authorities. Under these conditions, a Jewish humor develops that is steeped in tragedy (Howe 1987, 19). Jokes are meant to overcome an otherwise unbearable reality (Rohatyn 1911; Ziv 1986b, 53; Telushkin 1992, 17, 26; Goldsmith 1993, 15). They serve to corral the paradox of a Chosen People who are not shielded from the cruel forces of history (Wisse 2013, 28, 33, 153). "God-forsaken religiosity" brought forth a humor of "pious blasphemy" (Kristol 1951, 434). Or as Tevye says in *Fiddler on the Roof:* "I know we are Your Chosen People, but once in a while couldn't you choose someone else?"

Second, Jewish humor is also impelled by the Haskalah, the Jewish Enlight-enment. Before the Enlightenment, it is claimed, Jews were not a particularly humorous people (Altman 1971, 135). Despite a few "shafts of light" in the Bible and Talmud, humor is an anomaly rather than a hallmark of ancient Jewish liter-ature (Landmann 1962, 194). With the Enlightenment, Jewry became conscious of itself and its anachronisms (Simon 1948, 45), which engendered a "radical self-questioning" (Altman 1971, 134). "Humor needs to breathe the air of skepti-cism"—a skepticism that did not exist before the modern era. The Jewish jokester knows that he is one of the Chosen People, an idea that is "an outrage to enlight-ened intelligence." "The joke comes about if one ardently believes in a God who does not . . . exist" (Kristol 1951, 432, 435; see also Halkin 2006, 51).

Performance. There has not been much in the way of commentary on the ways in which Jewish humor is performed, but at least two properties have been noted. One is that what makes Jewish humor distinct is not its content but the tendency of Jews to rely on humor more than other peoples. Humor is simply a preferred method of expression in interpersonal communication (Loewe 1922, 6; Druyanow 2010, 119; Wisse 2013, 227–28).[8] The second is that Jews more frequently use jokes in conversation to illustrate a conversational point. These are not told for their own sake but are employed as metaphors—as glosses on conversation (Kirshenblatt-Gimblett 1974, 287–88).[9]

Functions. Jewish humor is aggressive, ascerbic, and retaliatory (C. Davies 2002, 17–49; Wex 2006, 132; Druyanow 2010, 133–34). It is also defensive and serves to deflect aggression directed at Jews from a hostile Gentile world (Grotjahn 1966, 10–12). Consequently, it provides the Jews with a sense of liberation and mastery (Druyanow 1963, 1:x). Perhaps the most frequently identified function, however, is that the humor alleviates pain and permits survival under difficult conditions (Adler 1893, 458; Rohatyn 1911, 11; Rosten 1970, xxiii; Mikes 1971, 104; Samuel 1971, 210–11; Ziv 1986a, 11; Alter 1987, 25; Druyanow 2010, 134). It allows for the transcendence of the unjust conditions of life (Niger 1972, 43). In other words, Jewish jokes and Jewish humor more generally constitute a consolation literature. This view is often identified with Sholem Aleichem's prescription: "Laughter is healthy; doctors prescribe laughter," although Sholem Aleichem's laughter was often spiteful rather than reparative (Howe and Wisse 1979, 36).

While there seems to be something of a consensus on the Jewish joke, the view is not unanimous. Sig Altman does not regard the Jews as a "'naturally' comic people" (Altman 1971, 123). Dan Ben-Amos challenges the notion that Jewish humor is self-critical. He argues that Jewish jokes are usually at the expense of others in Jewish society: rabbis, matchmakers, mothers-in-law, or *mohels* (circumcisers). There is no self-criticism if "there is no social identification between the ridiculer and ridiculed" (Ben-Amos 1973, 122–23). William Novak and Moshe Waldoks note in passing that suffering may not be Jewish humor's dominant theme (81, xiv). Alter Druyanow believed that language play was more characteristic of Gentile than Jewish humor and that irony in Jewish humor was rare (Druyanow 2010, 124–28, 130), and Nathan Ausubel also registered Jewish humor's "relative unconcern with mechanical word-play" (Ausubel 1948, 263). Dov Noy narrowly restricted Jewish jokes only to those that are based on verses in and interpretive styles of biblical, Talmudic, and midrashic study (Noy 1962). Perhaps more than two deviations from the mean is Hillel Halkin's suggestion that the medieval Arabic *maqama*—a rhymed prose narrative—was borrowed by Hebrew writers and used to parody sacred traditions (Halkin 2006, 50–51). In other words, Halkin, like some others, sees Jewish humor as an outgrowth of premodernity, although he does not trace it back to rabbinical sources.

Such is my compressed characterization of the characterizations of the Jewish joke and Jewish humor. The above reflects not what is known about the Jewish joke but rather what has been claimed. I do not mean to pronounce that these characterizations of origins, character, function, and so forth are necessarily wrong; I would merely suggest that all these characterizations of the Jewish joke should be regarded only as possibilities.

Whatever is true or not true of the "Jewish joke" and of "Jewish humor," it must be recognized that these terms are not congruent with the jokes or the humor of Jews. They are reifications and do not apply to the joking of all Jews but to humor of a certain kind that is said to be characteristic of the Jewish experience in Europe. Sephardic and Middle Eastern Jewish humor is left out the Jewish humor category because this humor is held to be more characteristic of the Arab, Turkish, and Persian cultures in which these Jewish communities were submerged (Ben-Amos 1991, 36; Wisse 2013, 20). The Jews of Israel are often left out of the Jewish humor calculation as well. Even Theodor Herzl believed that Jewish humor would disappear in a Jewish state (Wisse 2013, 30–31). The Jews of Israel, after all, are not cut off from nature. They engage in a full range of occupations, have considerable freedom of action, are not an oppressed minority, and are in harmony with themselves. According to several commentators, Israelis are not particularly funny (Landmann, 1962, 198; Mikes 1971, 114; Bermant 1986, 152; Telushkin 1992, 173). Unlike the humor of the Sephardic and Middle Eastern communities, however, Jewish jokes and Jewish humor in Europe are felt to be *distinctive* of the Jews. In other words, Jewish jokes are regarded as *un*characteristic of the cultures in which eastern European Jewry was situated.

The questions that must be addressed are not whether the Jews had humor and when they first acquired it. Instances of humor in the Bible, the Talmud, and Midrash are well known (although hardly abundant). All peoples, as far as we know, have humor—that is, they deliberately craft expressions intended to provoke amusement and laughter. The questions that must be addressed about "the Jewish joke" and Jewish humor" are: (1) how and when did these terms come into existence? (2) how and when did European Jews come to regard themselves, and to be regarded by others, as a people with a distinctive body and style of humor? and (3) how accurately do the printed and orally collected texts support the characterizations of the Jewish joke that have been described above?

FIRST OBSERVATION: JEWISH (ADJECTIVE) + JOKE (NOUN)

The connection of Jews with humorous matters was already recognized in Germany by the earliest decades of the nineteenth century. The term *Judenwitz* connoted a style of speech that was regarded as clever, pointed, caustic, mercenary, and destructive. *Witz* was opposed to, not a subcategory of, *Humor. Humor* was a term with entirely positive connotations and suggested the "benevolent appreciation of life's general absurdity." *Humor* was characteristic of German *Kultur* and refined sensibilities. It was a term applied to autonomous national cultures like those of Germany and England, while *Witz* referred to something submerged in and antithetical to the cultural mainstream. Jews were capable of *Witz* but not *Humor*. Consequently the terms *Witz* and *Humor* characterized fundamental differences in discourse styles and came to represent an opposition between Germans and Jews more generally (Chase 2000, 5–17).

In 1834, critic and feuilletonist Moritz Gottlieb Saphir (1795–1858) reacted against criticisms directed at the Jewish authors Ludwig Börne and Heinrich Heine:

> The thunderbolts hurled by Berlin criticism upon the heads of Börne and Heine always echoed with the word Judenwitz . . . It is indeed striking that Jews have appropriated wit almost exclusively as they have trade. The why and wherefore is not as obscure as one might think. From the mere fact that censorship circumcises humor almost everywhere it appears, humor considers itself a Jew and sticks by its brothers in faith. Yet there is more to it than that. The consummately tragic destiny of this nation, too, is the mother of its wit. The sheer duration of its distress left behind a sarcastic residue on the walls of its collective brain . . . The Jews have availed themselves of wit because it is the only branch of the military where they can in time make officer without an official order coming down that birth certificates are to outweigh service records . . . Learning may unlock doors to this or that official stall seat, but it is prohibited from wearing a Jewish beard! Wit, however, is a master key. It unlocks everything. It sits in the middle of Germany . . . and slips through the keyhole even as the police lock the door. (Saphir, quoted in Chase 2000, 242)

Here Saphir challenges those Berlin critics who attribute all that is witty and transgressive in Börne and Heine to their being Jews rather than to their being gifted writers. On the one hand, Saphir rejects Judenwitz as a canard, but on the other he accepts it because: (1) wit is born of the tragedies of his people, (2) wit is a great leveler as it is a matter of ability, not privilege, and (3) wit can elude the censors and be directed at all.[10]

Jefferson S. Chase (2000), who delineated this distinction in nineteenth-century German rhetorical styles, did not identify the earliest usage of the term *Judenwitz*. As he was concerned with literary history, he did not explore whether the term was also applied to Jewish oral styles before it entered the literary and cultural debates of the early nineteenth century. Nor did he investigate whether the term was first used by Jews to characterize their own communicative style and was only then appropriated by outsiders.[11] But what Chase registers is an early

association between Jews and *what we would today call humor,* the negative connotations of that association, and that this association was a term of opprobrium
directed by Gentiles at Jews.[12]

The earliest joke book about Jews published by a Jew that I am aware of is
Lippmann Moses Büschenthal's (1784–1818) *Sammlung witziger Einfälle von Juden,*
als Beyträge zur characteristik der jüdischen Nation (Collection of Comic Thoughts
about Jews, as a Contribution to the Characterization of the Jewish Nation), published in 1812. There are a few important things to note about this book. First is
its early date—1812. Second, Büschenthal was born in Strasbourg in Alsace, not
in eastern Europe. Third, the book is in good German and devoid of Yiddish
expressions. Fourth, it is published in Germany.[13] Fifth, Jews are identified as a
quick-witted and funny people. Sixth, jokes are held to reflect the characteristics of
the Jewish people. Seventh, Büschenthal maintains that he is trying to be objective
and includes materials that reflect both positively and negatively on the Jewish
people. Finally, Büschenthal argues that humor is rooted in cunning and Jews, like
women, have had to resort to cunning because of their helplessness (Büschenthal
1812, iii–iv; Gilman 1984, 597–98). Thus, the book seems both to take pride in and
to apologize for the Jews and the humor for which they have been castigated.

What about the status of jokes in the Pale of Settlement? I do not know the
earliest date for a book of Jewish jokes in Yiddish.[14] As yet, I have not come across
one that predates Büschenthal's collection. I would note that the early accounts
written about Jewish life in the Pale—at least the ones that I have read—hardly
mention humor at all. At most, there is a mention of pranking in connection with
the holidays of Simchas Torah (Rejoicing in the Law), Chanukah, and Purim
(Miller 1980, 23–25; Wengeroff 2010, 117, 157).[15] Early accounts also mention
the witty rhymes of the *badkhonim* (wedding jesters) (Lifschutz 1952; Bisberg-
Youkelson and Youkelson 2000, 114) and *Purim-shpiln* (Purim plays) (Roskies and
Roskies 1975, 232–34), but verbal jokes exchanged as part of social conversation
are hardly mentioned at all.[16] More prominent in the memoirs, autobiographies,
and memory books is the lack of food, the poor living conditions, the insulting
nicknames, fights, pranks, divorces, abandonments, and the abuse of children by
their teachers in *kheder* (elementary Hebrew school) (Roskies and Roskies 1975,
45–49, 125–27; Marsden 1983, 112, 164; Hoffman 1997, 97–98, 131–32; Kotik 2002,
145–46, 225–26; Wengeroff 2010, 122; see also Wex 2006, 141–58, 197–220). I do
not mean to suggest that this was what Jewish life in the Pale of Settlement was
all about, but such instances seem to hold a more central place in the autobiographies and memoirs than recollections of jokes or witty exchanges.

It is also instructive to peruse the *Ethnographic Program* for the study of Jewish
folklore and folklife published by S. An-ski in 1914 (translated by Nathaniel

Deutsch [2011]). Of the 2,087 questions in the survey, only 10 specifically ask about jokes (#456, #499, #730, #821, #831, #903, #982, #1,016, #1,136, #1,326), while another refers to pranks (#484), another to practical jokes (#603), and two to witticisms (#1,030, #1,032). What is interesting is that of these few questions, the great majority have some connection to the topic of marriage: old maids, dowries, matchmakers, wedding jesters, taking Yeshiva students home on the holidays (ostensibly to see whether they would make suitable matches for daughters), interviews with potential in-laws, and conversations between the prospective bride and groom. One question deals with jokes told to children, and three have something to do with the relationships between students and teachers. An-ski does not seem to imagine jokes as related to all aspects of life but only to a very few of them—that is, marriage and the relationship between students and teachers. In other words, in 1914 An-ski did not seem to regard jokes as something characteristic of Jewish life in the Pale but something circumscribed, occasional, and incidental. Or to put it another way, An-ski did not seem to put jokes at the center of eastern European Jewish folklore and culture and did not regard them as a touchstone of Jewish communal life.

A few years before the publication of An-ski's *Program*, Noyekh Prilutski's call to collect all manner of folklore did not include a mention of jokes. For Prilutski, Pinkhes Graubard, Yehudah Leib Cahan, and other Jewish folklorists, it seems *songs* were the true expression of the Jewish soul, not jokes (Gottesman 2003, 31–49). In this respect, they were faithful to the original call by Johann Gottfried von Herder to collect folk poetry as the authentic expression of national identity (Oring 2012b, 6–15). And in this respect as well, Jewish folkloristics was very much in tune with the concerns of folkloristics in western Europe, Scandinavia, and the United States.[17] Within a short time, however, jokes would be recognized as providing a unique "key to some of the spiritual recesses of the people" (Bar-Itzhak 2010, 116), and in the 1920s and 1930s, Alter Druyanow, Yehoshu'a Ḥana Ravnitskii, Immanuel Olsvanger, Yeshaye Zlotnik, and Nekhame Epsteyn all collected and published corpuses of Jewish jokes.[18]

SECOND OBSERVATION: COMPARATIVE METHODS

Although a few commentators on Jewish jokes have casually noted that a number of them might owe something to the jokes of other peoples in other languages (e.g., Kristol 1951, 433; Noy 1962, 48; Druyanow 2010, 125), only Richard Raskin seems to have taken this possibility seriously. Raskin sees the Jewish joke as evolving from a European body of jokelore and acquiring Jewish characteristics. Indeed, he believes that Jewish jokes may have developed from anti-Semitic jokes told about Jews by Gentiles (Raskin 1992, 167–76). While Raskin has identified some Elizabethan and other examples of jokes that later appear in Jewish guise, at present the evidence for the development of Jewish jokes from anti-Semitic ancestors is woefully thin. There is a substantial subliterature of German jokes about Jews. There is probably a parallel literature in Polish, Russian, Romanian, Lithuanian, and Latvian. How do these jokes relate to the numerous collections that were published by Jews themselves in the nineteenth—but mostly in the twentieth—century? Is there significant overlap between the materials? Have Gentiles borrowed jokes from previous Jewish collections or have the Jews incorporated Gentile jokes about Jews into their own collections and anthologies?

And how should the characterization of the Jewish joke that was synopsized at the beginning of this essay be evaluated? More specifically, is the Jewish joke more self-critical, more open to multiple interpretations, and does it employ a different kind of logic than jokes told by other groups?[19] The characteristics claimed for the Jewish joke are usually evidenced by only a few selected examples. In order to ascertain the relation between those jokes that have been characterized as Jewish and the jokes of other nations, more than the occasional parallel with the international joke literature needs to be identified (e.g., Druyanow 1963, 3:331–50). A method is required that will allow for a sampling of joke literatures whose characteristics can be analyzed, categorized, and compared. For example, if one is to determine whether Jewish jokes are indeed more self-critical than those of other peoples, or rely on different forms of logic, the notion of the self-critical joke or the nature of that logic first needs to be *operationalized*. I have yet to see an unambiguous definition of the "self-critical joke" or of "Jewish joke logic." It seems that these concepts are to be regarded as self-evident. Even if these concepts are successfully defined, representative bodies of Jewish jokes need to be compared with representative bodies of jokes from other ethnic or national groups (Juni et al. 1996, 324).[20] The task of creating corpuses of jokes for comparative and even statistical purposes is a major task. When it is accomplished, it will, no doubt, be endlessly criticized. Yet the task is a worthwhile one, and it will be interesting to see the first results of such deliberate and organized comparisons. We should recall that folkloristics began as a comparative enterprise, and it may be time for the field to return—at least in part—to its comparatist roots.[21]

Of course, we will never know entirely how representative those popular and scholarly compilations were in the first place. Popular joke books are likely to include jokes that the compiler believes to be the funniest and most likely to sell. Scholarly collections also have their biases. Despite the admonition of S. An-ski to his collectors to collect even obscene folklore, the fact is that, for the most part, they did not (Gottesman 2003, 102). How, for example, is *Sefer ha-Bediḥah ve-ha-Ḥidud* (The Book of the Joke and the Witticism) of Alter Druyanow (1963) transformed in its representation of the Jewish joke when the less seemly materials that he suppressed are integrated into the collection and accorded equal citizenship (Sebba-Elran, forthcoming)? Of course, the published collections of Jewish jokes are not likely to have been completely representative of Jewish oral jokelore, and while it is not possible to entirely rectify this situation, it is certainly something that needs to be taken into account when joke collections are employed as the basis for claims about the nature of Jewish humor and the Jewish psyche. Fortunately or unfortunately, the same might be said about collections of other ethnic and national humors: English humor, Irish humor, Scottish humor, German humor, French humor, or Russian humor. All the published collections are necessarily biased.

It will be rightly argued that a joke literature is largely an oral literature and should not be characterized in terms of collections of jokes published primarily for entertainment. This is true—to a degree.[22] It is also true, however, that to know anything of the oral literature of past times, even of the relatively recent past, one must rely on artifacts from that past, and in the case of jokes, these are the popular joke collections that have been published as well as the texts written down—usually much later—by folklorists in their field collections.

THIRD OBSERVATION: HUMOR IN USE

If Jews were prone to use humor in their discourse more than other peoples, some judicious comparisons should be possible. A sociolinguistic study of speech practices could be undertaken. The speech events under scrutiny would have to be comparable: for example, dinner conversations of families in restaurants or the language behavior of children in school classrooms. Some control for social class would also be in order. Of course, such studies might only contribute to deciding the question of the frequency of humor usage in contemporary times. When it comes to deciding whether the Jews of Europe in the nineteenth or early twentieth century made more use of humor than the groups around them, one would have to turn to written materials. Did Jews incorporate more humor in their letters to family, friends, and business associates than the members of other groups? Again, there would have to be some controls in place. One would not want to compare the letters of barely literate peasants with those of educated people in towns or cities. Some assessment of the frequency of canned jokes in written communications would also emerge, and a determination could be made whether Jews tended to employ such jokes as glosses more frequently than other groups.

FOURTH OBSERVATION: ENLIGHTENMENT

There are a number of points to recommend the notion that the humorous products and processes that Jews identified with and saw as distinctive were an outgrowth of the Jewish Enlightenment. At present, there is no evidence of a sense of identification of Jews with humor in the Talmudic or medieval periods, either by others or by the Jews themselves. What little humor was produced seems to have been employed for entertainment or as satire rather than a marker of Jewish difference. The humor may have turned on Jewish knowledge and behavior, but it was not a self-conscious form of expression. Lippmann Moses Büschenthal's book of jokes published in 1812 in Germany was one of the earliest to explicitly regard jokes as an expression of a Jewish character.[23] It would seem that Jewish joke books compiled by Jews in eastern Europe emerge only much later. The Haskalah began in the German states in the 1770s and then spread to Galicia, which the Hapsburg Empire acquired with the first partition of Poland in 1772.[24] Hapsburg control was extended after the third partition in 1795. The Haskalah then moved north into Poland and Lithuania in the latter parts of the nineteenth century (C. Roth 1972, 7:1433–52; Eliach 1998, 451–81). As the desire of Jews to participate in the larger society and culture spread—and that desire was almost exclusively that of the *maskilim*, the proponents of the Jewish Enlightenment— the concern to demonstrate the civilized status of the Jews also spread. The possession of a distinct humor, as even Moses Mendelssohn recognized, was one of the markers of that status (Mendelssohn 1997, 219). Consequently, the humor of Jews was collected, published, and reinterpreted as part and parcel of the Enlightenment program.

FIFTH OBSERVATION: CONTEXTUAL MATTERS

Lippmann Moses Büschenthal apologized for Jewish jokes being deceitful—a deformity of Jewish character that was a result of oppression. Moritz Gottleib Saphir also saw Jewish wit as a response to oppression. Later commentators have seen the Jewish joke as a means of consolation and a strategy for survival under very difficult circumstances.

Yet Jews are certainly not the only people to have suffered. Is there some indication that suffering generates jokes that are similar in their natures? Have the Armenians, the Poles, or the Irish produced a repertoire of jokes commensurate in some ways with that of the Jews? And what of those peoples who might be said to have been spared such a history—the English, the Spanish, or the Danes, perhaps? (The examples are open to discussion.) Can it be shown that the jokelore of these nations varies in significant and uniform ways from those nations that might be said to have a history of subjugation and oppression? And why have what are called "Jewish jokes" thrived in the United States, a land in which the social conditions of Jews scarcely resemble those of the communities in the Pale of Settlement?[25]

Even more to the point, if the history of Jewish suffering is long, why is the history of the Jewish joke not equally long? Unlike the Arabs and Persians, for whom substantial joke books existed in the Middle Ages (Omar 2004, 319–22), there is nothing to suggest an old tradition of jokes for Jews. Of course an absence of proof is not proof of absence, and there may have been joke books compiled by Jews describing Jewish characters, situations, and events that have not survived— especially since such books would likely have been frowned upon as frivolous and contrary to injunctions to serious Torah study. There was, however, opposition to frivolity in Muslim societies as well; nevertheless, such books were compiled and have survived.

And what of the claims that jokes or humor more generally have contributed to Jewish survival? Freud observed in the very last part of *Jokes and Their Relation to the Unconscious* that a joke in the face of impending disaster might evidence "man's tenacious hold upon his customary self and his disregard of what might overthrow that self and drive it to despair" (Freud 1960, 8:229). In other words, jokes made in the face of peril, or even imminent death, reflect a triumph of the ego. Such jokes deserve, according to Freud, the utmost admiration. But he does not suggest that they are an aid to survival; nor does there seem to be more than anecdotal evidence to support such a hypothesis (e.g., Obrdlik 1942; Lipman 1993, 8–22).[26]

Although the Jews have recognized their history as a history of suffering—and others have so recognized it as well ("Review of Life and Opinions of Heinrich Heine" 1876, 82; Hoffman 1997, 130)—this conception of suffering is not entirely historical. This is not to say that it is imagined or untrue. The Jews of Europe were repeatedly denied the right to own certain kinds or property or engage in particular occupations. They were shunned, tortured, driven from their homes, and murdered. But specific incidents or periods of suffering—the Crusades, blood libel accusations, the Spanish Inquisition, the Chmielnicki massacres in mid-seventeenth-century Ukraine, or the pogroms during the reign of the czars— were accumulated and compressed into an unvarying account along with the bondage in Egypt, the tyranny of Antiochus IV, the attempt by Haman to destroy the Jews of Persia as described in the book of Esther, and the destruction of the first and second temples. As is read at every seder in the Passover Haggadah: *Elah be-khol dor va-dor omdim aleinu le-chaloteinu veha-kodesh-barukh-hu matzileinu me-yadom* ("But in every generation some have arisen against us to annihilate us, but the Holy One, blessed be His name, always delivers us from their hands"). This is not history as we understand it today. It is theology, the theology of exile (Kriwaczek 2006, 24). Jewish jokes and Jewish humor are never regarded as reflecting the vicissitudes of Jewish history. There is, of course, the occasional reference to a particular historical event or personage in the content of a joke. But the Jewish joke is never imagined as something that changes in its sensibilities or characteristics in response to changes in time and circumstance. The Jewish joke remains what it is during times of banishment *and* return, subjugation *and* autonomy, privation *and* prosperity, war *and* peace.

Suffering, in other words, is a kind of cosmological constant in the reckoning of Jewish experience and expression. A tragic history becomes the context for the interpretation of almost everything. Yet when Jewish history is perceived as unending tragedy, and the Jewish joke is read in relation to that history, Jewish joking should seem totally anomalous. After all, why should a people who suffer so unremittingly and so deeply joke about anything at all (Richman 1954, xi)? The jokes cannot be regarded as a normal expression of pleasure and elevated spirits. The conclusion, then, is that there must be something special about Jewish jokes. In other words, an observation about Jewish jokes in relation to a tragic Jewish history marks the jokes as somehow special; and then the specialness of Jewish jokes is attributed to that tragic history.[27] The understanding of the Jewish joke in the context of Jewish history seems suspiciously circular.

In the 1950s and 1960s, William Bascom (1954, 333–36) and Alan Dundes (1964) urged folklorists not merely to collect folklore but to understand it. Texts were to be understood in relation to their social contexts. Performance perspectives that emerged in the 1970s only furthered this social-contextual orientation. The contextual perspective, which informs much of the folklore work done by folklorists today, nevertheless has its limitations. It directs the researcher to focus on a text and to discover its raison d'être in relation to a set of conditions in which it is communicated. When a folklorist says "context," the default understanding of the term is social context—the immediate conditions of the material's communication—but there clearly are others (Oring 1986, 135–42).[28] The ideas expressed about the functions of the Jewish joke in the Pale do not come from reading them in relation to their social contexts—contexts that have never been recorded and are no longer obtainable. So in what context should a Jewish joke—or any folklore text—be read? This question actually is deceptive. There is no proper context for the reading of a folklore text. Rather, what is meant by context is *whatever extra-textual materials are employed in making sense of a text.* Consequently, there can be no de jure privileging of one context over any other context. What folklorists call *context* is simply an attribute of the sense-making process. What context one chooses to closely examine depends upon the specific question one is asking.

Contextual studies invariably harbor hidden problems. Where does one look for the meaning of a text and why? A fitting connection between text and context will always be found because were a relationship not found, the context would probably never have been resorted to in the first place. In any event, once one decides to look for a relationship between a text and a particular context, some connection will make itself apparent. The principle seems to be: "Seek and ye shall find" (Matthew 7:7). If Jewish suffering is the context in which one looks to understand the Jewish joke, the Jewish joke will make sense in the context of Jewish suffering. A textual/contextual problem is like a quadratic, cubic, or quartic equation: there is always more than one solution and some of these solutions will be imaginary.

Contextual approaches provide readings of folklore texts—sometimes rich and imaginative readings. But folklore studies has laid claim to being more than an ability to read folklore texts in rich and imaginative ways. Folklore studies has claimed a concern with more general understandings of how texts—whether jokes, songs, or *Märchens*—come into being and the processes that shape their production, condition their reception, and promote or inhibit their transmission. Folklorists have wanted not only to *interpret* folklore but to *explain* it (Oring 1976, 77–79). I am certainly not suggesting that contextual studies be abandoned. I am not against rich readings of interesting texts. But if they continue to be the only method by which folklore studies proceeds, folklore studies is doomed to enter what has been called an "inductive cycle," from which it can never emerge (Zan 1982, 24). The only way to break such a cycle is to move from induction to deduction—that is, to generate hypotheses about folklore that can be *tested*.[29]

What follow are five hypotheses about Jewish jokes. The point must be stressed that these are *hypotheses*—not conclusions. The object of formulating them is that they might be *falsified* using appropriate data and argument. They are meant to provide a focus for research and to move the study of Jewish jokes beyond the comfortable suppositions that have been regularly repeated over the past century. I hold neither the desire nor expectation that these will prove unassailable.

HYPOTHESES

Hypothesis 1. Jewish joke and *Jewish humor* as terms and as concepts do not originate in the Yiddish-speaking areas of the Pale but develop in Germany by those who are critical of the pointed and caustic wittiness of Jews and wish to distinguish it from things German. As Jews pressed their claims to be recognized as part of Western civilized society—for which the possession of humor was deemed necessary—their humor was characterized as distinctly "Jewish" and not really humor at all. This rejection lasted from the end of the eighteenth century, when their claims were first made, into the twentieth, right through the Nazi period (Weininger 1906, 318–19; Gordon 2012). The designations "Jewish joke" and "Jewish humor" in other words, are thrust upon the Jews, but they accept them as a mark of their distinction and use them to claim a place in civilized society. Only later do these terms come to be identified with the jokes and humor of the Jewish communities in eastern Europe and become positive cultural representations.

Hypothesis 2. Jewish humor is not a distinct humor. It develops out of a common fund of jokes and stories that is shared across national and ethnic boundaries. Jews tend to Judaize jokes, using Jewish names, roles, behaviors, languages, settings, artifacts, and events to give them a quality that people regard as Jewish (Nevo 1991). But if a sufficiently large "randomly" selected sample of Jewish jokes is compared with an equal sample from other nations (Irish, Poles, English), they will be found to be similar in their natures and distributions. The jokes in both samples will be concerned with marriage; husbands, wives, and children; clergy; sex; language; politics; occupations; the rich and poor, hicks and city folk; the clever and stupid (see Jason 1967, 54; Ben-Amos 1991, 36). Jewish jokes will have no distinct logic, prove no more self-critical, or use language differently than the jokes of others nations in Europe. What will vary are the characters, roles, scenarios, and behaviors—that is, the cultural content of the jokes (Nevo 1991).

Hypothesis 3. Jews will not be any more prone to use humor than other ethnic or national groups. They might exceed some other groups in their frequency of humor use, but there will be other groups that are equally and perhaps even more active in the use of humor than Jews. There will be no more use of jokes as glosses by Jews than by other groups.

Hypothesis 4. The humor of Jews only becomes "Jewish humor" in the context of the Haskalah, the Jewish Enlightenment. Consequently, any pre-Enlightenment printed or manuscript collections of jokes or other forms of humor produced by Jews will not highlight that humor as distinctive, regard it as an expression of Jewish character, or conceptualize it in relation to a Jewish sense of self. A historical-geographical study of joke books compiled by Jews that does identify the humor as characteristic of Jews will show that they begin only with the Haskalah, spreading through Europe with that movement from west to east.[30]

Hypothesis 5. If situations of suffering or perceptions of suffering engender the creation of jokes, Jewish suffering does not engender jokes of a different kind than those produced by any other suffering people. This hypothesis is not easily testable, but as there are reminiscences of jokes and joking even from the death camps (e.g., Lipman 1993; Ostrower 2014), there might be enough in the way of materials to initiate a small comparison. Poles, Russians, and German Communists also found themselves in camps during the Second World War. In the Soviet era, those sent to the gulag often organized themselves by ethnicity in the various camps (Applebaum 2003, 295–306). I don't know whether there is a sufficient literature to be useful for any kind of comparison in the Soviet case. It may be that there was only a generalized "camp humor" that was common to all prisoners, whatever their origin or ethnicity. If that were so, such data could not be used to invalidate this hypothesis. One would have to craft an alternative means of falsifying it.

CONCLUSION

The distinctiveness and centrality that have been claimed for the Jewish joke in the Jewish imagination seem at present mythological ideas. A type of folk expression has been elevated to the status of a cultural symbol, becoming so infused with value and emotion that its authenticity seems unchallengeable.[31] Jewish humor is claimed to define a community and to display its unique qualities.[32] What the *Kalevala* is for the Finns, the joke would seem to be for the Jews. While I believe that there is a place for mythological ideas in society, I also believe that folklore scholars are duty bound to study them. Scholars of religion have argued that what distinguished Judaism from other religious systems in the ancient Near East was that Judaism was the first to bring God into history (Kirsch 2001, 12–14). It is time to demythologize the Jewish joke and bring it firmly into the realm of history as well.

From the Ridiculous to the Sublime

Jokes and Art

When we separate music from life we get art.
—JOHN CAGE

JOKES AND PHILOSOPHERS OF ART

Humor and laughter are human—some would say distinctively human—propensities. As such they have attracted philosophical reflection. Plato, Aristotle, Thomas Hobbes, Immanuel Kant, Arthur Schopenhauer, and Herbert Spencer all had something to say about the subject, but this commentary has been intermittent and usually brief.[1] In the past century, Henri Bergson (1956) wrote a substantial treatise on the subject, and Sigmund Freud, who wrote perhaps the single most important work on jokes and humor (Freud 1960), is sometimes claimed by philosophers as one of their own. Handbooks and encyclopedias of philosophy often include an entry on humor or jokes (Levinson 1998; T. Cohen 1998; Monro 2006; Morreall 2006), but the treatments are something of a piece. There is a review of theories of humor followed by a discussion of humor and ethics.[2] Noël Carroll's (2003) essay "Humour" in *The Oxford Handbook of Aesthetics* is a somewhat recent example. The longest section of this essay surveys and critiques various humor theories—superiority, incongruity, release, and what he calls "dispositional." The second-longest section deals with questions of morality and humor. The shortest section of the essay addresses the relation of humor and comedy to art. In this section, Carroll bravely suggests that certain comedies, like Shakespeare's *A Midsummer Night's Dream*, are undoubtedly art, but he goes on to state that "not all comedy or invented humor falls into the category of art." Jokes, for example, do not fall into this category because they are "one-shot affairs"; they do not "invite sustained contemplation"; and "one is not seized by their structural complexity and ingenuity, or intrigued by their perspective on the human condition." Some jokes may prove to be exceptions to this negative characterization, Carroll admits, "but the vast majority are not" (358).[3]

ART IN THE TWENTY-FIRST CENTURY

Carroll's own theory of art is well known. He does not trust that some essence of art will be identified, nor does he think that a satisfactory definition of art will be given in terms of necessary and sufficient conditions.[4] He believes, however, that even if the essence of art or the conditions for something being art are undecidable, it is still possible to identify particular objects as works of art. Works of art, he claims, are identified through narration: by telling tales that relate a particular work to historical antecedents whose status as art has already been established.[5] Carroll's theory is a consequence of the emergence of the avant-garde. The relations of avant-garde productions to previous artworks were problematic. Indeed, avant-garde works were revolutionary and subverted artistic traditions. They became art, according to Carroll, only when compelling historical narratives (Carroll [1994, 22] holds for "truthful" historical narratives) of their relation to previous works of art could be recounted (16).[6] In other words, art is created through discourse. Artworks are created in the act of being spoken of in a certain manner.

Carroll is only one of a number of philosophers (e.g., Danto 1964; Dickie 1974; Bailey 2000) who have advanced theories and definitions of art without reference to the aesthetic features of particular works. Aesthetic definitions of art were generally repudiated in the later part of the twentieth century for a number of reasons. First, no aesthetic criteria essential to art—and only art—could be identified (Weitz 1956, 28–30; Kennick 1958, 319–24). What had been considered aesthetic attitudes, concepts, and experiences were not restricted to art but were applicable to nonart as well—to nature, for example (Shusterman 1997, 34). Second, ideas essential to art in the eighteenth and nineteenth centuries—beauty, sublimity—that conditioned certain kinds of responses could no longer serve in the twentieth and twenty-first. Art could be ugly, repulsive, disturbing, or boring and thus effect responses that were far removed from the pleasure and delight associated with artworks in earlier times (N. Carroll 2002, 148–49). Third, aesthetic theories decontextualized art. Divorced from historical and social contexts, conditions of production and consumption were concealed (Danto 1964, 580; N. Carroll 2000b, 14). Fourth, aesthetic definitions, particularly those that depended on aesthetic experience, were not restrictive enough. There was a fear that *art* could wind up including everything under the sun (Beardsley 1982, 33; N. Carroll 2000b, 11; Dickie 2000, 139; J. Anderson 2000, 83–84).

Carroll's theory was in tune with theoretical moves in a number of disciplines in which discourse and practice became the objects of attention. The phenomenal world was of less concern than the ways in which that world was talked about or acted upon. The identification of works of art was a matter of identifying those works that had been the subject of certain kinds of treatment. Artworks were established socially and discursively. What art actually *was* was another matter entirely; something likely to remain beyond definition or perhaps even useful characterization.

Jokes, however, were not art according to Carroll, because they were not ingenious or complex, were unworthy of sustained contemplation, and had no intriguing perspectives on the human condition (Carroll 2003, 358). This assessment, it must be noted, does not square with his own narrational theory of art.[7] In his discussion of jokes, there is no reference to the presence or absence of historical narratives, only to what might be regarded as traditional criteria employed in the definition of art: complexity, ingenuity, worthiness of contemplation, and the expression of a valuable perspective on the human condition. Thus, art is regarded strictly in terms of the aesthetic properties of the object, aesthetic attitude, and truth. Carroll's objection to jokes, in other words, is framed in terms of necessary and sufficient conditions, conditions that Carroll had previously rejected as likely bases for definition.[8]

It would not be difficult to show that jokes can be ingenious and complex, merit contemplation, and offer insights into the human condition. Carroll, in any event, admits that *some* jokes *might* be art, so it does not seem worthwhile to review examples merely to confirm his suspicion.[9] I propose instead to look at jokes particularly—sometimes humor more generally—and their similarities to and differences from art. *My point is not to argue that jokes are art*, although I believe they are. My definition of art—which is exceedingly broad—would include jokes and much else.[10] What constitutes art is less a matter of evidence-based argument than a priori definitions or definitions based on a priori commitments to certain objects and expressions. I discuss the construction of jokes, their operation, and their effects because I sense that thinking about jokes might contribute to thinking about art.[11]

In this effort, one is left largely to the examination of jokes from an aesthetic point of view. Discursive and institutional approaches are for the most part beside the point. There are no narratives that attempt to link particular jokes to previous artworks. The historical narratives that do exist for jokes are concerned rather in demonstrating their traditionality, not their artistic status.[12] Even if we could frame discursive or institutional theories that might allow us to call jokes "art," we would have learned little about either jokes or art. Fortunately, aesthetics has made something of a comeback in philosophical circles in recent years, so it is possible that an aesthetic discussion of jokes might once again prove relevant to matters of art (N. Carroll 2000a, 2002).

SIMILARITIES AND DIFFERENCES BETWEEN JOKES AND ART

Intention. Philosophers have been troubled with aesthetic definitions of art in part because there are many objects that can command attention and evoke an aesthetic response: a sunset, a mountain, a storm, a piece of driftwood, or the accidental result of some human activity. The objects of an aesthetic attitude and response do not themselves depend upon intention. Many philosophers restrict the term *art* to artifacts and then often to artifacts intentionally produced (e.g., Tolhurst 1984, 265; Stecker 2000, 47; J. Anderson 2000, 78). A piece of found driftwood is not usually regarded as art, but some allow that if a piece of driftwood were displayed in a museum or gallery, it would have been artifactualized through the process of its display (S. Davies 1991, 119–41).

Thus, there are those who believe that art is made but never found. Humor is both made and found. It can be found in nature—for example, a passing cloud may resemble a person one knows. Circulating on the Internet are English signs from non-English-speaking countries. One, purportedly from a restaurant in Nairobi, read: "Customers Who Find Our Waitresses Rude Ought to See the Manager" ("Mistranslations" n.d.).[13]

Sigmund Freud related the following story:

> A brother and sister—a twelve-year-old girl and a ten-year-old boy—were performing a drama composed by themselves before an audience of uncles and aunts. The scene represented a hut by the sea-shore. In the first act the two author-actors, a poor fisherman and his honest wife, are complaining about the hard times and their small earnings. The husband decides to cross the wide seas in his boat to seek his fortune elsewhere, and, after tender farewells between the two of them, the curtain falls. The second act takes place a few years later. The fisherman has returned a wealthy man with a big bag of money; and he tells his wife, who awaits his arrival outside the hut, what good fortune he has met in foreign lands. His wife interrupts him proudly: "I too have not been idle." And thereupon she opens the door of the hut and reveals to his eyes twelve large dolls lying asleep on the floor. (Freud 1960, 8:183–84)

The children who performed the play were nonplussed by the uproarious laughter of their relatives. They could not fathom what provoked the response. Yet no one would argue that humor did not occur or that the laughter was an unfitting response simply because the children had not intended it.[14] No one would call the occurrence by any term other than "humor," even though that noun might be modified with the adjective "unintended" or "accidental." For "humor" there is terminological continuity between what is found and what is made, what is intended and what is unintended. Not so, it would seem, for "art." For a goodly number of philosophers, art must be intended.

Of course, unintended humor cannot be analyzed for its creativity, expressiveness, or as a form of communication since there is no possibility of creativity, expression, or communication without conscious or unconscious intention. Consequently, creativity, expression, and communication cannot be made part of a definition of humor because humor need not be intentional. Similarly, it would be problematic to define humor in terms of its design, if what is meant by "design" is an intentionally wrought pattern (Beardsley 1958, 191). This shows that interesting and important questions can be asked about objects without the necessity of defining those objects in terms of those questions. Questions about intention, expression, and communication will get asked about humor whether or not they serve as part of a definition of the concept itself. To define humor in terms of expressive or communicative factors would beg the question. Such a definition would establish the expressive and communicative qualities of humor a priori without a need for analysis of its actual properties.

If humor can be apprehended without being intended, it may also be intended without being apprehended. What is meant to be a funny aside in the midst of a conversation registers as error, rudeness, or non sequitur rather than humor. It is incumbent on a producer of a joke or witticism to judge the ability of a particular audience to recognize that humor. This is particularly true of humor on the fly—humor attempted in the course of social interaction—where there is a known audience. If an audience fails to apprehend intended humor, it is usually the fault of the humorist, either in producing an adequate piece of humor or in accurately assessing the capabilities of the audience to apprehend it.

Outside face-to-face social interaction, the situation is more complicated. The author of a joke book cannot be held responsible for the reception of that humor in different locales or historical periods. Consequently, what is intended as humor, and what may have been apprehended as humor in the author's own time and place, can lose its status as humor. There are books and articles that have expounded on the humor contained in ancient texts. But unless an ancient author explicitly states in the text that something was meant to be humorous, or that someone laughed in response, the bases for such identifications may be tenuous. One may note a pun in the Hebrew of Genesis (3:1)—"the serpent was shrewd" or "the serpent was naked"—but not whether that double meaning was humorously intended or humorously apprehended at the time the text was written. There are statements and actions in the Icelandic sagas that strike us a funny today but were probably not meant to be humorous. An intentionalist definition of humor is not workable since intentions are often unknown, and nonhumorously intended statements and actions often provoke great hilarity.

Much of this discussion of humor seems relevant to the discussion of art as well. Art may be intentional or accidental. Its existence, like that of humor, might depend upon either intention or apprehension. And the failure of an audience to "understand the object presented to them" (Dickie 2000, 96) might also be charged as a failure of the producer to make an effective work or gauge the abilities of an audience to discern it. Should an ancient figurine of a deity be considered art if it was intended only for prophylactic or propitiatory purposes? Is it not the contemporary reception of such a piece that subsumes it in the category of art? While it is important to know when art is intended, that knowledge need not, and probably should not, be part of the definition of *art*.

Significant form. Humor possesses a distinct structure characterized as "appropriate incongruity." Two conceptual domains that would normally seem incompatible from some theoretical, practical, or customary point of view are appropriately, if spuriously, linked (Oring 1992, 1–15; 2003, 1–12).[15] The joke is one particular form of humor. It is distinguished by a concluding section known as the "punchline" in which an incongruity is made appropriate or something seemingly appropriate is made incongruous in a sudden and surprising way (Oring 1992, 81–93). The means by which this transformation is effected has been referred to as the joke's "technique" (Freud 1960, 8:18), "trigger" (V. Raskin 1985b, 114), or "logical mechanism" (Attardo and Raskin 1991, 303–7). Thus humor in general, and the joke in particular, has a structure that must be discerned if it is to be recognized and appreciated. If the structure is not apprehended, humor will not be perceived. If an appropriate incongruity is not perceived with the final line of a joke, one would be in the presence not of a "bad" joke but of no joke at all (even if the intention to make a joke were recognized). A joke depends upon what Clive Bell calls "significant form," although he is speaking primarily of the relations of lines, colors, shapes, and volumes in paintings (Bell 1958, 17–20). To apprehend a joke is to apprehend the significant form of appropriate incongruity. But in the joke, this form is a structure of meanings, not a structure of words, actions, or images per se. In fact, this structure is not to be confounded with other structures that govern the joke. A joke may unfold as a narrative, for example, but the structure of the joke is not the structure of the narrative (see chapter 9).

Jokes are semantic affairs.[16] Words and images in jokes always depend on their semantic import. In Freud's anecdote, the dolls represent children (in both the play and the anecdote); the wife's display of the dolls signifies pride in productive achievement—akin to the fisherman's display of his bag of money; the numerous children signify repeated sexual encounters that could only have taken place outside the bond of marriage. Characters, actions, and scenes in jokes are elements of signification. They are not pure visual or oral forms. The perception and appreciation of a joke depends first and foremost upon an intellectual assessment of the elements of the joke and their relation to one another. A joke is not a sensuous affair, although it may be apperceived through sensuous words and images. The first experience of a joke is "complexly cognitive" (S. Davies 1991, 59). The cognitive, however, does not stand in opposition to the aesthetic (Zink 1954, 193; Scheffler 1991, 3; Nuñez-Ramos and Lorenzo 1997, 109; N. Carroll 2000a, 194; Butler 2004, 1–29).[17]

Nevertheless, the structure of a joke cannot be reduced to a logical or mathematical formula and still function as a joke. Whether printed on a page or orally delivered, jokes depend upon the use of particular words, phrases, tempos, intonations, and actions. In other words, each joke is a performance, and while there is no joke if the structure of appropriate incongruity is not apprehended, a joke also depends on the manner in which that structure is achieved in word, image, and action (Bauman 1992). Consequently, jokes may depend upon poetic, visual, and theatrical qualities.[18] These are properties of the medium of the joke. They enhance a joke's effects and can make it succeed or fail.[19] But they cannot create the joke in the absence of the basic conceptual structure. In the absence of a perceived appropriate incongruity, a poetic performance of a would-be joke is poetry, not a joke.

A joke works through misdirection. It sets up a pattern of expectations until an incongruity is recognized. That incongruity is made "appropriate" through the reconceptualization of previous information.[20] The means by which this reconceptualization is accomplished are spurious. The joke is a form of play, and it is recognized that the joke plays with sound, grammar, meaning, imagery, category relations, and logic in realizing its underlying structure. Jokes exploit a wide range of semantic valences for words, actions, and images. An audience recognizes that the joke does not employ legitimate, routine, or reasoned connections in establishing appropriate relations between incongruous categories. A joke resembles certain forms of illusionary painting. The techniques of such painting manipulate the conventions of representing three-dimensional space on a two-dimensional surface. The means by which the effects are achieved may not be instantaneously grasped, however. Sometimes such paintings can seem more like puzzles and may prove more disturbing than amusing (e.g., Seckel 2004, 72, 123).[21]

Apprehension and appreciation. Someone may realize that she is confronted with a joke, hold clearly in mind the appropriate incongruity that has been created, and even grasp the techniques employed and the manner in which they operate. This does not ensure that she will enjoy the joke. There is a difference between *apprehending* a joke and *appreciating* it. I would imagine that this relates to the distinction between epistemic and phenomenological experience. Those who can perceive the joke structure experience it as a conceptual form, but that form may not register emotionally (Ismenger 2003, 100). Ted Cohen speaks of the difference between "finding the funniness" and "feeling the funniness" of a joke (Cohen 1983, 121). He further claims that this is analogous to responses to artworks that one sees as good without liking them (121n2). One may see that something is a joke, see why it is a joke, and grasp how it operates without necessarily liking it. Appreciation depends upon a sense of value: the value of the joke's structure, technique, content, setting, and style.

I have trouble, however, imagining how someone might apprehend the joke, regard it as a *good* one, and yet not appreciate it. There are only two hypotheses that I can propose that might account for such an occurrence. One is that there is something in the individual that blocks appreciation: some negative disposition toward the contents of the joke, the performer of the joke, the situation in which it is performed, or the genre itself.[22] Such a person can only imagine how someone *else* might see the joke as a good one even though she cannot. Analogously, I can imagine that someone can see the positive qualities of a marine painting but be negatively disposed toward the painter or the genre. The other hypothesis is that there is a disjunction between what an individual says constitutes a good joke or work of art and what she truly feels a good joke or work of art to be. The standards by which she judges value are concealed from herself. The values she conceptualizes and describes are not the values by which she in fact operates.

Art and evaluation. The tendency to employ evaluative criteria in the definition of art is a common one. Carroll's narrational approach to the designation of artworks is procedural and theoretically independent of whether those works are good or bad (N. Carroll 1994, 14n22; S. Davies 1991, 42).[23] Nevertheless, Carroll's observation that jokes are not complex, ingenious, or insightful enough to be art implies that artworks are those that fall on the upper end of some scale. Art is not a matter of kind but of degree. Many, perhaps most, philosophers employ evaluative criteria in their characterization of art (e.g., Gaut 2000, 28; Stecker 2000, 51; J. Anderson 2000, 77). Others have opposed the use of such criteria in trying to work out an aesthetic approach (Shusterman 1997, 35). Even those who do not explicitly advocate the use of evaluative criteria, however, often wind up employing evaluative terminology in their considerations. Stephen Davies, for example, while denying the criterion of merit for artworks, still frames the question as whether a piece "qualifies for *elevation* to the status of art" (S. Davies 1991, 41; my emphasis).[24] Other philosophers betray their reliance on notions of value by the examples of artworks that they choose to discuss or avoid.[25] Thus, standards of value explicitly or tacitly determine the application of the *art* label even though the definition or identification of art and the assessment of value could be separate considerations. Like art historians, philosophers sometimes seem lured into framing definitions of art in the promotion or defense of certain canons. Why not entertain the notion that there is much that might be considered art, and much of this muchness is trivial, stale, ephemeral, and worthless? This is certainly the case for jokes. Why not for art as well? In any event, a truly descriptive aesthetic approach, sans evaluation, seems hard to come by.[26]

If evaluative criteria may not be necessary—or even desirable—for a definition of either jokes or art, evaluation is, nevertheless, the inevitable response to both. Jokes and artworks are objects that are regularly evaluated. Jokes are judged good or bad, as are paintings, sonatas, novels, and films. The same is said for particular performances. Evaluation, of course, is not peculiar to aesthetic response. Business plans, forms of government, and people's characters are also evaluated as good or bad, simple or complex, exciting or boring, although such evaluation is not inevitable, nor does such evaluation play a part in the definition of any of these phenomena.

Community. Both jokes and artworks create communities. They can create communities on the basis of the cognitive demands they make. In some respects, a joke is a kind of "understanding test" (Sacks 1974, 350). There are people who have trouble processing jokes. They may not be up to the task of even seeing a joke, let alone appreciating it.[27] These people may be left out of a group that can hear and recognize a joke for what it is. Similarly, communities may be created among those who claim to be able to see the point of an artwork and how the purpose of the artist has been, or has not been, achieved. Because both jokes and artworks are evaluated, they create communities on the basis of the evaluations they provoke. They create communities of taste: social solidarities and disjunctions based on the appreciation, or lack thereof, for particular objects of regard (Bergson 1956, 64; T. Cohen 1983, 125–26).

Unity. There are other similarities in the effects of jokes and art. A joke, like an artwork, is perceived as a unified text, image, or event: as "heterogeneous but interrelated components of a phenomenally objective field" (Beardsley 1958, 527).

A joke may have to be abstracted from a background of disparate actions and utterances in which it is otherwise embedded, as Freud's description of the children's play about the fisherman and his wife was abstracted from a complex social interaction that undoubtedly contained more elements than are represented in his text. Nevertheless, his account of the event can be grasped as a unified whole.[28] As a unified whole, it can be abstracted from the context of its enactment. It can be retold and produce similar effects on a different audience. Such repetition is possible because a joke is first and foremost a coherent structure. Jokes are repeated—if not word for word, at least their basic structure is reprised. Although Carroll did not raise the issue, jokes might not be considered art because they would seem to lack originality and consequently creativity—another criterion regularly employed in the definition and identification of artworks (Beardsley 1958, 562; Alperson 2003, 245–47). But one might think of the structure of a joke as akin to a musical score. A score represents a coherent musical structure. As a musical structure, it can be performed by different musicians, for different audiences, in different settings, and on different instruments. Each score-based performance is to some extent unique. The qualities are not identical. Were one to claim that a joke lacked creativity because it was only a variation of a conventional structure, one should be able to say the same about the performance of a Bach fugue as well.[29]

Disinterestedness. It has often been claimed that art is something made and appreciated "for its own sake" (Beardsley 1958, 562). This notion, which arose in the eighteenth century and finds no place in ancient aesthetic theories, is that the work of art is autonomous and is perceived "disinterestedly," that is, with no thought of possession of the object or of any other consequences arising from the encounter with it. The object has no instrumental value. There is no effect to anticipate beyond the experience of the object itself. In this sense, it is related to the idea that virtue does not derive from the hope of reward or the avoidance of punishment but from the love of good for its own sake (Stolnitz 1961, 131–32; Levinson 2003, 9).

Carroll has argued against the idea that art—or anything—can be valued purely for its own sake (Carroll 2000a, 2002). This would certainly seem true of jokes. Jokes can be used to point to, and even transform, the social interactions in which they are embedded (Emerson 1969; Oring 2003, 85–96). Jokes that seem to have no specific purpose still promote sociability. Joke telling can also be competitive, with tellers attempting to top one another by telling the best jokes and eliciting the most laughter.[30] In other words, jokes can serve the interests of ego gratification. Jokes are forms of rhetoric and they frequently formulate propositions about the world and communicate them with considerable force (Oring 2003, 27–40). They are significant in the entertainment industry and have considerable economic value. Jokes are deeply implicated in the world. They have consequences and these consequences are not unknown to both tellers and audiences.

Nevertheless, when jokes are deployed for some rhetorical, social, or economic end, they generally must prove effective—and not merely recognizable—as *jokes* in order to achieve these ends.[31] The structure must be instantly grasped; the joke must not be mangled in the telling; and the contents cannot be so emotionally charged that the audience cannot recognize the joke or allow itself to be engaged by it. A joke is not merely a token in a social, intellectual, or economic game. To operate in these games, the jokes must work as jokes.

The same might be said for the evaluation of a painting for sale in a gallery. Even though the economic value of the painting may be the primary concern of the gallery owner, the assessment of its value would still require going *through* the painting. How does it look? Is the work original? Is it important? Is it effective? Is it by the artist in question? Is it typical? The painting would be regarded and assessed for its form, textures, subject matter, meanings, originality, authorship, and condition before an economic value could properly be assigned to it.[32] The attention to the painting in these circumstances could not be said to be "disinterested," but to err in the assessment of the painting qua painting might cause the painting to be priced too high or too low. Putting an appropriate economic value on a painting would first depend on an engagement with the painting for what it is as a visual object. It would be assessed perhaps not so much "for its own sake" as "in its own right" (Sparshott 1982, 21).[33]

If disinterestedness is not a necessary or even possible attitude toward the joke, distance is (Morreall 1981, 60). The topics and elements of jokes must be regarded as suitable objects for play. "Q: Why did the dead baby cross the road? A: It was stapled to a chicken." Whatever one feels about babies as real objects, one must be able to deal with them as ideas for playful manipulation. If the topic of a joke or the situation in which it is related is too emotionally charged, it is not likely to be appreciated as a joke. A joke requires "a momentary anesthesia of the heart" (Bergson 1956, 63–64).[34] A joke about the destruction of New York's World Trade Center is not likely to succeed as a joke when told to someone who lost a relative or friend in the attack. An unwillingness to regard certain ideas as matters for playful manipulation will vastly reduce the potential for joke appreciation and perhaps block the possibility of perceiving a joke at all (Dickie 1974, 108).[35]

Contemplation. Although distance may be necessary for discerning and appreciating jokes, the kind of distance that might be associated with contemplation is not. Contemplation has long been identified as a precondition of the experience of art (Beardsley 1958, 529).[36] In fact, if there were preconditions for apprehending and appreciating jokes, a contemplative attitude would be unlikely to even make a list of candidates. Playfulness would seem a much greater possibility. There are, however, too many instances of unexpected jokes disrupting utterly serious interactions to make even playfulness a precondition for joke recognition and appreciation. Nothing obvious seems to condition the experience of a joke other than "getting it"—that is, the sudden apprehension of an appropriate incongruity. It is well known that a significant portion of a joke's effects disappear if getting the joke depends upon explanation and analysis. A joke, on occasion, may be enriched by commentary that results from contemplation, but not in terms of elevating the joke's quotient of humor. New layers of meaning that are discovered retrospectively come too late to alter a joke's humorous effect.[37] Thus it is the immediate and unreflective response that characterizes joke reception, and perhaps such "naïve" responses should play more of a part in the assessment of the experience of art as well (Beardsley 1958, 534; Zangwill 2003, 335). The contemplation of jokes is an activity that is largely restricted to scholars, seasoned joke tellers, and professional comedy writers. What such reflection may bring to the appreciation of jokes, however, is largely prospective (contra Beardsley 1982, 27). It may lead to the creation of new versions in which nuances perceived in the course of contemplation are incorporated into the joke and accentuated in order to enhance the experience of others in a future performance.

Criticism can stand in the way of aesthetic appreciation. I don't think the issue revolves around whether there is such a thing as disinterested attention or a distinct aesthetic attitude (Dickie 1974, 128). It depends upon what is meant by aesthetic appreciation. If appreciation is a synthetic experience (Beardsley 1958, 527–28), then criticism would seem to be opposed to appreciation since criticism is rooted in analysis. The best works of art "grab us" and then provoke a multitude of analytical questions (Eaton 2000, 153). But neither the analytical questions nor their answers constitute appreciation. That is why reading a poem in order to understand the neuroses of the author may prevent an aesthetic appreciation of the poem (contra Dickie 1974, 121).[38] To engage in the analysis of a play or a poem does not ensure that the play or poem will engage the analyst. Yet analysis may lead one to revisit a work and experience it anew. It may lead to greater (or lesser) appreciation. Artworks may be more open to such reencounters than jokes. We may bring our friends to see a painting or hear a symphony and give them the benefit of our insights in an effort to direct them to our enlarged understanding of the work. With jokes we tend not to do this. Instead, we recompose the joke itself and pass it on.

The Avant-garde. As far as I know, there is no avant-garde in the joke world.[39] Although there are metajokes, absurd jokes, and joke parodies, they work as all jokes do (Oring 2003, 13–26; Kelly 2016). Jokes that repel, confound, or puzzle fail as jokes because the structure of a joke must be instantly perceived if it is to be regarded as a joke at all. Of course, there are plenty of jokes that may puzzle and confound individuals, and some people may not recognize them to be jokes even when they are explained.[40] (This is not normally what a joke teller wants to have to do.) Jokes may also shock and disgust. This is a somewhat tricky affair. If the content of the joke is too charged at the onset, a hearer may recoil and withdraw attention and the effort to grasp the joke. Jokes frequently present shocking or disgusting images in their punchlines when there is no longer an opportunity to withdraw attention. A hearer automatically searches for and identifies the appropriate incongruity. Shocking or repulsive images and ideas may be produced as a result of this procedure. The hearer is, in a sense, seduced by this interpretive process into a confrontation with a particular repulsive image or idea. As the joke depends on work performed by a hearer, the hearer is to a great extent an accomplice in the production of the joke.[41] Even if such images are not ultimately enjoyed, the effect of the structure may produce amusement before the import of the image has fully registered. It is not uncommon to hear people begin to laugh and then cut themselves off, saying, "But that's terrible."[42] There is, of course, no consensus on what constitutes a shocking or repulsive image or idea. Nevertheless, some enjoy such images and ideas because they reflect their opinions and ideologies, if only in exaggerated form (Oring 2003, 41–57). Others may enjoy such images and ideas for their transgressive qualities (29–40). That is why there can be jokes about murder, rape, race, disease, dismemberment, and pedophilia that do not depend on some depraved population of joke tellers purveying them.

So the joke may provoke shock and disgust, amusement, and pleasure all at the same time. To achieve this smorgasbord of affects, the conceptual structure must be apprehended and positively experienced at the same time that particular images or ideas contained within this structure shock and repel.[43] We need only recognize that in the successful joke, pleasure can accompany an encounter with otherwise distressing or repulsive images and ideas. If distressing images and ideas can be confined within a frame of pleasure, might this not be the case for other aesthetic objects? Can those avant-garde objects that "perplex, unnerve and disturb" (N. Carroll 2002, 148) also provide pleasure? If apprehension of the structure of a joke can domesticate repulsion, perhaps contemplation is the means by which the disturbing in art is rendered pleasurable. After all, how would one distinguish between a brilliantly repulsive artwork as opposed to one that was merely repulsive?

Novelty. There is a good deal of truth in Carroll's characterization of jokes as "one-shot affairs" (Carroll 2003, 358). Jokes are expected to be novel.[44] Indeed, a common way of keying a joke performance is: "Stop me if you've heard this one" (C. Edwards 1984). But this principle is only occasionally observed. In joke-telling situations, a recognized joke will often be allowed to be completed if it can be ascertained that at least one person in the group has not as yet heard it. Those who quash joke performances by blurting out the punchline tend to be seasoned joke tellers who are hearing a joke from another seasoned teller and who regard their ability to recognize an incipient joke as an index of the size of their repertoires and their joke-recall abilities. The relation between such joke tellers is frequently a competitive one.[45]

If audience members know they have heard a joke before but can't "remember how it goes," they will usually allow a joke to be told. In other words, they have forgotten the punchline, the buildup, or the mechanism by which the appropriate incongruity is achieved. All they know is that they have heard it before. In such cases, not only is the joke permitted to be performed, but the pleasure—cognitive and emotional—may be experienced all over again as though it were being heard for the very first time.

Emotion. If the first experience of the joke is cognitive, the second is affective. The response to a joke is cognitive because a puzzle must be engaged. But the rapid grasping of the "solution" to this puzzle excites a very particular set of responses. When a joke is perceived to be a joke, and when that joke is accorded a measure of positive evaluation, it engenders amusement, an involuntary response. Amusement may be accompanied by an intense and equally involuntary physiological reaction—laughter.[46] When a joke elicits genuine laughter, it might be regarded as literally "breath-taking." Amusement is, or is akin to, an emotion (Sharpe 1975; Roberts 1988; Chafe 2007, 66–68; Palencik 2007; contra Morreall 1987, 212–24). Artworks are also regarded as engendering cognitive and affective responses. With artworks, however, it is difficult to ascertain what responses are peculiar to aesthetic experience. Certainly, feelings of joy, sadness, perplexity, or tranquility are provoked by artworks, but they are not provoked exclusively by artworks (M. Cohen 1977, 486). Amusement is different. It is a type of affective response restricted to a particular type of stimulus. Amusement is not a response apposite to the perception of beauty, sublimity, grace, or even skill.[47] Amusement is the affective concomitant of the perception of an appropriate incongruity. In this sense, the relation of circularity between significant form and aesthetic emotion is broken. Significant form—at least this particular form—produces a particular emotional response and neither the form nor the emotion is defined in terms of the other (Beardsley 1982, 35).

Amusement seems different from other emotions.[48] At one level, it is a more detached response. This is probably attributable to the fact that it is conditioned by a challenging intellectual operation. Also, other emotions depend on a sense of how the world is presumed to work: fear and anger depend upon the belief in real threat; envy upon the belief that certain things are valuable; guilt and shame on the belief that certain actions are wrong; joy on the belief that something valuable has been or will soon be obtained; sorrow on the belief that something valuable has been lost. Amusement does not depend on any class of beliefs about the world (Roberts 1988, 272–73). If anything, amusement seems to depend upon a range of disbeliefs—disbeliefs that the world could operate in the manner represented. It depends upon the sense that certain perceived relations between conceptual domains are incongruous and the appropriate connections between them are to some extent spurious.

If amusement seems to involve a measure of distance, amusement often precedes one of the least-distanced responses imaginable—sustained and uncontrollable laughter. In other words, there are three levels in the reaction to a joke: seeing the joke, being amused by the joke, and laughing at the joke. Although laughter can be feigned or suppressed, laughter is an active and visceral response. Laughter is material; it is of the body (Bakhtin 1984, 20). With laughter, distances collapse, both intellectually and socially. Laughter is participatory. So jokes are doubly oxymoronic formations. In their organization they depend upon relations that are at once appropriate and incongruous. In their reception they demand both emotional distance and corporeal participation (Nuñez-Ramos and Lorenzo 1997, 111).

Although amusement may not prove to be a suitable response to most artworks, it should hold a greater position in aesthetics and art criticism than it does. Philosophers and critics have studiously ignored amusement, when they have not rejected it outright. (One would think that since it contains the word *muse*, it might be of more concern in aesthetics.)[49] They have consistently tried to maintain a distinction between "art" and "entertainment" (Beardsley 1958, 559; Gaut 2000, 28). "Amusement art" has been distinguished from "proper art" (Collingwood 1938, 78–153).[50] It is true that jokes, unlike many artworks, "provide a determinate and preconceived effect" (81). But that may be a virtue. A close study of amusement might pay dividends. It is an emotion that arises from a particular type of understanding. Amusement may be the paradigmatic aesthetic emotion.[51]

CONCLUSIONS

Jokes—and humor more generally—have numerous similarities with artworks. They are aesthetic objects and philosophers should have no trouble regarding them as such. Why not call them art? How might their designation as *art* be important? What difference would it make if jokes were considered art? There is, of course, the practical reason. *Art* is a powerful term. Money, influence, and celebrity may attend those who are capable of persuading institutions and publics that art is their practice, product, or object of study. The social and economic status of jokes, however, is not my major concern. When it comes to jokes, I do not expect to—or care to—see them exhibited in museums anytime soon. I would guess that more people are exposed to jokes on a daily basis through oral communication, the World Wide Web, and the broadcast media than to all the paintings and symphonic music made available by so-called art institutions. The entertainment industry, greeting card industry, and publishing industry depend on the creation and recycling of jokes. They are important and lucrative businesses. It is not the jokes themselves that would benefit from the application of the *art* label.

Rather, I think it is the category of art that might benefit from the inclusion of jokes. A number of philosophers—those supporting narrational or institutional theories—have defined art in such a way that art objects are distinguished from "aesthetic objects." In their view, jokes may be objects that evoke aesthetic responses, but they are not art. Also, art is not necessarily aesthetic.[52] But these approaches seem to create problems. Definitions are constructed around particular social practices—practices that are peculiar to certain social classes in certain types of society. *Art* tends to be the label bestowed by institutions and through discursive practices of a rather narrow bandwidth.[53] This would not be so bad if philosophers were anthropologists. Then one might actually learn something of how such institutions and discourses are constructed and function and the way certain kinds of objects operate within them. The result might be effective pieces of social and linguistic ethnography. But as philosophers are not anthropologists, these institutional and discursive frames are backgrounded. They are used merely to define or identify objects, which then become the center of attention. The frames become peripheral. If what makes some things *art* is their location in particular institutions or incorporation within certain kinds of discourses, then it is the objects that are peripheral and the institutions and discursive practices that are central. To engage art, to study art, or even to think about art would be first and foremost to observe, analyze, and reflect on institutional and discursive practice. The artworks themselves would be of secondary importance.[54]

Aesthetic definitions of art, whatever other problems they may engender, avoid this one. If art is defined in terms of aesthetic response, the focus remains directed at particular kinds of objects and the means by which those objects produce the responses that they do. The objects are not the epiphenomena of institutional or discursive practices. They remain in the foreground because what constitutes an aesthetic experience and how certain objects evoke such experiences are part and parcel of a single consideration.

It might seem that institutional and narrational theories avoid a great deal of the problems that the term *art* creates. But it also seems that these neater definitions and theories of art resemble that attempt to look for a set of lost car keys several blocks from where they were lost because the light is better and the street is cleaner.[55] I am in favor of including jokes in reflections on what constitutes *art*, just as I am for including metaphors (T. Cohen 1978, 7), certain chess games, and certain mathematical proofs. If jokes and a host of other forms were accepted into the category *art*, then philosophers would have to reengage the notion of what art might be. Philosophical inquiry would not proceed from a narrow set of examples chosen by an even narrower set of authorities on the basis of what is—admitted or not—a set of personal or inherited preferences. Philosophy would, I believe, be better served by the proposition that art is everywhere rather than by the supposition that art is rare.

Narrational and institutional definitions of art have tried to bring some order to a messy field. These definitions and theories are nothing if not neat. And neatness does count, unless it leads to sterility. Perhaps it is necessary to do away with the term *art* and refer to everything as an "aesthetic object" (Beardsley 1958, 16) or to do away with the term "aesthetic object" and be prepared to call everything that arrests attention, because of its form and texture, *art*. To employ both terms is to operate with a distinction that presumes what needs to be demonstrated: that there is a categorical distinction between objects of regard that is meaningful and defensible.

CHAPTER TWELVE

Contested Performance and Joke Aesthetics

"I tell it to you," quoth Sancho, "as all stories are told in our country, and I cannot for the blood of me tell it any other way, nor is it fit I should alter the custom."

—MIGUEL DE CERVANTES SAAVEDRA

Of all the aspects of humor that have been addressed by philosophers, scientists, and critics, the aesthetics of humor generally, and of the joke specifically, have perhaps attracted the least attention. The attention of philosophers to jokes has been directed to a narrow range of issues: the structure of humor and the ethics of joking.[1] Some philosophers do not regard jokes as art at all (N. Carroll 1991, 294; 2003, 358). Even Richard M. Dorson, a student of American folk narrative, was equivocal about the aesthetics of the joke: "Jokes seem so ephemeral, topical, and trivial that the literary and the folk critic may well be excused for scorning them" (Dorson 1972, 83).

For folklorists, art is the apprehension of extraordinary arrangements of words, gestures, sounds, colors, forms, textures, or ideas in relation to some ordinary unmarked background.[2] In the context of everyday speech, jokes are extraordinary arrangements of words and ideas. They are art—verbal art—as are folktales, ballads, toasts, proverbs, and jump-rope rhymes (Bascom 1955, 245–52; Ben-Amos 1971, 13). To call something *art* does not necessarily signify its greatness, depth, or importance. It only presumes that for some period of time—brief or enduring—an arrangement calls attention to itself and is apprehended as somehow remarkable.

For the traditional verbal arts, there is no script, score, or artifact to peruse. The aesthetic qualities of these arts are manifested in their oral performance.

Performance is an act of communication that is framed and displayed for an audience. Performers assume responsibility for their communicative skills, and they are assessed on their abilities to communicate effectively and artistically. Every performance is a function of place, time, situation, and personnel. Performances emerge only within the field of dynamic interaction between these variables. Furthermore, performance is a reflexive activity. Performers must be able to see themselves not only as objects of direct contemplation but through the eyes of their audience. Indeed, the notion of performance presumes the notion of feedback—the notion that auditory, visual, and even olfactory messages are constantly being received and shape what is being performed (Bauman 1992, 38–49).[3]

What follows is a small study of folk aesthetics, an attempt to characterize the principles that inform the performances of two accomplished joke tellers based on their evaluations of one another.[4] While these tellers are in many ways socially and culturally similar, they operate with very different ideas of joke performance, ideas that ultimately point to differences between their public personas and individual personalities.

This essay began with a dinner party. Two members of the party were enthusiastic joke tellers. Both—Daniel and Diane—had been at other parties, dinners, and get-togethers that I had previously attended, and both were known by their friends and acquaintances as dedicated joke tellers. All the members of this dinner party knew one another, and knew of Daniel's and Diane's passion for joke telling. While the other guests could and occasionally would tell a joke, no others would have considered themselves—or would have been regarded—as possessing an extensive repertoire of jokes or as being virtuoso performers.

Both Daniel and Diane were in their late fifties or early sixties. Diane was the older and had recently retired. Both had been telling jokes since they were children. Both were Jewish, and while there is no empirical evidence to demonstrate that Jews tell jokes more frequently than non-Jews, or that they are in any way superior joke tellers, both tellers recognized joke telling to be an accepted, and even privileged, discourse in American Jewish culture. Both grew up in kinship and friendship groups where jokes and witty repartee were appreciated and encouraged. Although Daniel and Diane were not religiously observant, neither were they ignorant of Jewish tradition and practice. Both frequently told jokes based upon Jewish characters and themes and rooted in Jewish custom. Both regarded joke telling as part of their personal as well as ethnic personas. They told jokes to friends and to strangers alike, and both had admitted to assessing people in terms of their liking for jokes and on the basis of their responses to particular jokes that they told.

The two joke tellers regularly told jokes to one another. They even shared some jokes by e-mail, but both claimed that the great majority of jokes they received electronically from others were unappealing. Over the years, Diane had compiled lists on small bits of paper to remind her of jokes she knew and wished to tell again. Daniel employed no lists. He claimed that if he were asked to tell the jokes he knew straight out, he would be lucky to remember a dozen. Although his repertoire was much larger than that, he could recall individual jokes only in the context of specific conversations, interactions, or joke-telling exchanges. Most of his jokes needed situational triggers to be recalled to consciousness.

That these two individuals should wind up telling jokes at a dinner party was hardly surprising. Nor was it surprising that their joke telling became somewhat competitive, as this had happened many times before. What was surprising, however, was the criticism that each offered of the other's performance. When Daniel started to tell a joke, Diane interrupted to state that he was telling it wrong, and she went on to describe her objections. When Diane told a joke, Daniel offered his own critique. This exchange of jokes and critical commentary went on for perhaps half an hour. As is often the case with natural performances, there was no opportunity to record the exchange or even to write down what was being said. The best I could do was invite the two tellers to dinner at my house a few weeks later when their jokes—and, more importantly, their critiques—could be elicited and recorded.[5]

Fortunately, at that preplanned dinner, they seemed to go at their joke telling and critique with the same gusto as at the earlier dinner party. The occasion began with about fifteen minutes of general conversation, but both knew they had been invited to exchange jokes. Once we were well into dinner, they both launched into joke telling and evaluation, giving little thought to the tape recorder on the table. A number of the jokes that had been told at the previous dinner party were reperformed and reevaluated. As far as I can recall, both the jokes and their evaluations were essentially the same. Some new jokes were told. Frequently both tellers interrupted one another in the middle of a joke to say what they thought was wrong with it. On two separate occasions in the midst of the joke telling, talk returned to nonhumorous topics, but thirty-five minutes of an hour's recorded tape involved the performance, discussion, and evaluation of jokes.

The joke telling commenced with the following joke:

DANIEL: An old Jewish man is walking down the beach in Tel Aviv, and he stumbles over something. He looks down and picks it up, and it looks like an old artifact, a lamplike thing, with some writing on it. And he starts to rub away the sand. And a genie appears. The genie says: "I'm the genie of the lamp and you can have any one wish that you want."

DIANE: Already I don't like it. Go ahead.

DANIEL: And the man says [*Yiddish accent*], "Well, if I've one wish it's that there's been such strife in the Middle East with the Arabs and the Israelis, the shooting and the killing—it's terrible. Solve the Middle East problem." The genie says, "Well, you know this is a difficult process. It's been a long conflict—100 years we're talking about—that this has been going on. This strife and the animosity is so deep. If you have some other wish that, you know, you'd like me to take care of maybe, you know, that's equally important to you, maybe I'll do that." The guy says [*Yiddish accent*], "Well, all right. Every Friday [*Diane laughs*] night when I come home from work, I should like for my wife to give me a blow job." And the genie says, "What was that first thing again?" [*Diane laughs*] What don't you like about that? . . . Go ahead . . .

DIANE: First of all, it should be a Jewish genie, 'cause I think that's funny in itself. [*Yiddish accent*] "Thank goodness you released me from this lamp. I've been in this lamp for thousands of years, but I'm a Jewish genie and you only get one wish, so make it good, buster!" It raises . . . the . . . "Well, if I only had one wish, I got to make it good. Listen! Let there be peace in the Middle East. Arab and Jew, Palestinian and Muslim and Shiite, and all those guys, they should all get along, they should live and be well." You don't have to call it this "animosity" stuff. [*Diane laughs*]

DANIEL: You didn't understand the word? [*Diane laughs*]

DIANE: There's too many syllables. And he goes, the genie goes, "Whoa, baby! You give me a tough one. I'll tell you what I'm gonna do. I'll give you another choice. This one's too tough." Then he says, not just on Friday nights but "Every night I should come home I want a blow job." The genie sits for a minute, says, "Well, what was that first one again?" [*Diane laughs*]

DANIEL: I would say that when you make the genie a Jewish genie, you don't have any contrast in the speakers. You have two people speaking with a Yiddish accent so it doesn't highlight . . .

DIANE: But we're in Tel Aviv. What's he gonna . . .

DANIEL: He's a genie, a genie . . .

DIANE: The Patrick and Michael joke. Did I tell you that one? Yes, I do. About they're cast adrift in a raft . . .

DANIEL: They wish for the ocean . . .

DIANE: And he finds a lamp and it's an Irish genie. So here he still only gets one wish. So without thinking he says, "I want the . . ." So the Irish genie speaks with [*Irish accent*] a brogue, you know. So he gets one wish and he says quickly, "I want the whole ocean to turn into the finest brew." So the genie disappears . . .

DANIEL: Why does the genie have to be Irish just because the protagonists are Irish, or the genie have to be Jewish because the protagonists are Jewish?

DIANE: Cultural continuity.

DANIEL: [*disdainfully*] Cultural continuity!

DIANE: Cultural continuity, that's my whole explanation.

DANIEL: There's no explanation.

DIANE: It also makes it easier because I don't have to switch brogues . . . and I'm good at the Yiddish one, and I'm good at the Irish one.

DANIEL: Yeah. But you could also do English.

DIANE: It's boring.

DANIEL: It's not boring if one of them is speaking in the accent. I mean, the genie says, "You only have one wish." [*Yiddish accent*] "One wish." There's contrast there.

DIANE: Then I'd make it a godlike one.

DANIEL: Yeah. You could change . . . you could make it a more imperious voice.

DIANE: I like the cultural consistency there. It's a [*Yiddish accent*] Jewish genie.

DANIEL: Well, you've always told it that way. It doesn't necessarily make it a better joke.

DIANE: Oh, yes, it does.

There are several points about which Daniel and Diane are in agreement. Both regard jokes as objects that merit aesthetic evaluation and critical response. There are "good" and "bad" jokes, and for both of these tellers, the joke about the genie in the lamp on the Tel Aviv beach is one of the good ones—one worth telling and repeating. In fact, both said they had told this joke on many occasions.

Not only do they feel that jokes merit aesthetic evaluation, they are able to articulate this evaluation in abstract terms. This is not to say that they possess a systematized aesthetic philosophy or elaborate critical vocabulary. Yet the critical concepts and terminology they employ are more than mere assertions of preference or emotional resonance, and the criteria they invoke can theoretically be extended to very different examples and are, to some extent, empirically verifiable.[6]

Daniel, for example, emphasized notions of contrast. Characters should differ from one another. The genie should not speak with the same accent as the man on the beach.[7] Diane seemed insensitive to or uninterested in such contrast. She regarded the image of an Irish or Jewish genie as funny in itself. In her opinion, this enriched the joke.[8] She also found that making the joke characters of the same ethnicity created an opportunity for extended dialect performance—a type of performance at which Diane felt she excelled. When challenged by Daniel to explain why the genie and the man had to be of the same ethnicity, she came up with the term "cultural continuity." It was meant to sound authoritative, but it was a facetious term invented by Diane on the spur of the moment to justify her preference. Daniel dismissed it immediately, and Diane went on to explain that joke performance was easier when she did not have to switch dialects.

Daniel agreed that the idea of a Jewish genie was in itself funny, but he felt that the joke revolved around the dialogue between the genie and the old Jewish man. Giving a genie a Jewish (or Irish) accent, he thought, reduced the contrast in the exchange and weakened the joke. It called attention away from what the joke had to accomplish. Even if there were a joke in which a Jewish genie appeared, the humor of that image would depend on its contrast with the other characters. "Cultural continuity" was not something that Daniel wanted to establish in the joke.

Daniel also believed that some of Diane's language was protracted and excessive. He didn't see the need for the elaborated dialogue in which the genie expresses his relief at being released from the lamp, his challenge to the man to make his single wish a good one, or the elaboration of the problems that plague the Middle East through the enumeration of various ethnic and religious groups. For Daniel, these elements seemed to lengthen the joke without contributing significantly to its point—to its punchline.

In another joke that was told that evening, the question of contrast arose again. In this case, both tellers formulated their jokes in terms of contrast, but they developed the contrast differently.

> DIANE: This guy gets thrown in jail, and it's on a minor real estate deal, but he gets thrown in a really bad . . . I don't remember this joke. [laughs] I'm faltering. And he gets . . . his cellmate becomes this huge black guy, and his name is Bubba. [laughs] He says [black accent], "While you is in here," he says, "you is either gonna be the man—the husband—or you're gonna be the wife." He says [no accent], "You make your choice right now . . . honky." [laughs] I remember now. "Well, I guess I want to be the husband." See, there's a change there. [black accent] "Well, come over here and suck your wife's dick."
>
> DANIEL: Now, see, the way I told it, there was this Jewish guy who got caught— accountant who got caught—embezzling and sent to the state penitentiary.
>
> DIANE: I wouldn't make him Jewish.
>
> DANIEL: And he was very, very nervous. On the first day he comes in, they give him his uniform, they give him his blanket, and the guard leads him up to his cell, and they close the door.
>
> DIANE: That's good.
>
> DANIEL: And he's standing in there. There's this huge guy, bald, hairy chest, huge prison muscles . . .

DIANE: Is he black?

DANIEL: No. And tattoos. And he sorta nods, the Jewish guy nods to him. And the guy says [*slow, gruff voice*], "One thing we got to get straight in here. You gonna be the husband or you gonna be the wife?" The accountant thinks about it for a few seconds, he says [*higher, quivering voice*], "Well, if it's a matter of choice, I think I'd like to be the husband." He says, "Fine! Get over here and suck your wife's dick."

DIANE: [*laughing*] It's a great joke. No matter. You set the scene better. I haven't told it in a while.

DANIEL: I think the Jewish works better because, you know, you got this frail guy, you know, he's scared. All that comes through.

DIANE: Woody Allen!

DANIEL: Yeah. You get this Woody Allen kind of picture, so the contrast is between this guy in the cell and this accountant guy.

Both tellers recognize the need for contrast in this joke. Diane frames the contrast between the characters as one between a "huge black guy" and a presumably white guy who is sent to jail for some white-collar crime. In the joke, she calls the black guy "Bubba." When Diane told this joke at the first dinner party, Daniel challenged her on the name Bubba, objecting that it wasn't a black name but a redneck one. Another guest at the party—who did not particularly like the joke—agreed with Daniel that "Bubba" seemed inappropriate.[9] Diane owned up to its inappropriateness. However, when she told the joke again at the dinner where she and Daniel were recorded, she continued to use the name. Diane liked the way "Bubba" sounded, even if it was unsuited for the joke character it designated. For her it was a triumph of sound over sense.

Daniel said that he had recast the character in the joke as Jewish. He had not heard it that way. In fact, he thought—although he was not certain—that he first learned the joke from Diane. He felt that the contrast between a timorous Jewish accountant and a hairy, muscle-bound, prison hulk served to polarize the characters better than a mere opposition between white and black figures could. This was a contrast that Daniel felt had to be developed, one that could not be carried by a mere labeling of ethnic or racial differences. To some extent, Diane seems to have agreed with him, as she admitted that Daniel "set the scene better."

DIANE: What's the other one I liked so much? Oh, that's the one. It came from you, but I think I tell it good. It's about the German soldier coming into the French village . . . That's a fine joke . . . This German soldier comes into the French village and finds the French maiden hiding in the barn. And he has his way with her. And as he's zipping up his pants he says [*German accent*], "And if in nine months a beautiful Aryan child should emerge from this union, you might call him Fritz." She says to him [*French accent*], "And if in a couple of weeks some strange spots come up on your private parts, you might call it measles." That's a good one.

DANIEL: First of all, I set it in World War I, not World War II.

DIANE: I didn't set it in World War . . . I didn't say that.

DANIEL: Well, you did. But you did when you said a "beautiful Aryan child." That makes it World War II.[10]

DIANE: Ahhh. That dates it. Oh, silly *moi*.

DANIEL: So I make it in World War I. I have him come across her in the field. He throws her down and has his way with her. And he says [*accent*], "And if in nine months you bear a child you may call him Fritz, if you please." And she says, "And if in three weeks you find a rash all over your body, you may call it measles if you please."

DIANE: Private parts. I like private parts.

DANIEL: It doesn't matter. I think the important thing is the "if you please." In fact, it doesn't end with "You may call it measles"—stop. I think the "if you please" adds something.

DIANE: Oh, I don't. I don't because I think it matches what the German has said. "You might call him Fritz."

DANIEL: So does this. He's also said, "You may call him Fritz, if you please."

DIANE: Oh, he said, "If you please"? Oh, I never, after a rape like that . . .

DANIEL: So there's a balance, a parallelism.

DIANE: That's incongruous. Would you put your panties down?

Daniel thought the reference to an Aryan child relocates the joke from World War I to World War II. He later revealed that he believed this second war was too close and too sensitive for the setting of a joke that involves a rape. Diane seemed to agree with him, although when she was re-recorded almost three months later, she retained the reference to an "Aryan child" in her performance.

In evaluating this joke, both tellers address the issue of parallelism in expression. What the French maiden says to the soldier must be similar to what the soldier said to the maiden. Both Daniel and Diane value such parallelism. This is a joke in which retribution is revealed in the formulation of a verbal expression. Daniel, however, prefers the parallelism of the phrase "if you please," while Diane finds the courteous phrase implausible in the context of the rape.

When asked about it later, Daniel characterized the phrase as consistent with the patronizing demeanor of the soldier. He felt that the seeming courtesy was mere arrogance, and it was fitting that the maiden's retaliation should be couched in the very same terms. Daniel further insisted that it was a matter of meter. The "if you please" extension sounded right. He thought Diane's version ended too abruptly. The three-word extension gave each of the character's expressions a metrical momentum that intensified the parallelism and heightened the sense of revenge.

Matters of contrast and parallelism figure centrally in Daniel's and Diane's evaluation of the following joke.

DIANE: Sir Francis Drake in the *Golden Hind*? I must have told you.

DANIEL: No. I don't think so.

DIANE: Sailing the seven seas, and they look on this man as a noble, wonderful leader. And the modus operandi on the ship is that when the guy in the crow's nest sees an enemy sail, he screams out, "Enemy sail off the port quarter!"

DANIEL: Oh!

DIANE: The first mate goes down . . . You know this?

DANIEL: Go ahead.

DIANE: Goes down to the captain's cabin and says, "Captain, sir [*low-class English accent*], "we spotted an enemy sail." And Sir Francis emerges from the cabin, and he's the picture of nobility and calm. And he comes on the deck and routinely says, "Glass!" And he pops [*claps hands*] the glass in his hand, and he studies the sail, and he pops [*claps hands*] the glass closed, and he hands it back to his first mate. And invariably he'll ask, "Bring me my red cape." And he swirls into this red cape, and he leads them into battle, and they fight like fools for him. Never get a scratch and never lose a battle. One day they were sailing along and the first mate says [*accent*], "Meaning no disrespect, sir," he says, "why is it when we go into battle you always wear that red cape?" And Sir Francis strikes a pose of nobility, and he says [*upper-class English accent*], "Should I shed blood in the course of the battle I wouldn't want our crew to fight with less valor that they need to conquer our foes." So now they think he's godlike, awesome leader. So one day they're sailing along and, a little historic license, but the guy in the crow's nest looks, and they're surrounded by the Spanish Armada. Three hundred and sixty degrees of enemy sail closing in. And he fast loses it. And the crew sees they're in deep trouble. And the first mate as always runs down, but he's so excited he can hardly get it out. "Sir Francis Drake." And he emerges, and just at the mere sight of him on deck the crew starts to settle down because things are in hand. Comes up on the quarter deck and says, "Glass!" Pops the glass in his hand and does a three-sixty of all these enemy sail, really closing in now. Pops the glass closed, and he hands it back to the first mate and says, "Bring me my brown pants."

Daniel then delivered his version of the joke.

DANIEL: In the days of the Barbary pirates, an American man-o'-war was
patrolling in the Mediterranean. One day the first mate comes running up
to the captain, yelling, "Captain, captain! Pirate ship off the starboard bow."
The captain says to the mate, "Fetch me my telescope." The mate fetches the
telescope, and the captain looks though it, and sure enough, there is a pirate
ship off the starboard bow. He commands the mate, "Call the men to their
battle stations, and bring me my sword and my red cape." The mate gives the
order to battle stations, and fetches the sword and cape. The captain dons his
cape, and the ship engages the enemy, and they are victorious. The next day
as they are sailing along, the mate runs up shouting, "Captain, captain! Pirate
ship off the port bow." Captain says, "Bring me my telescope." The mate brings
the telescope. The captain peers through it, and sure enough, there's a pirate
ship off the port bow. The captain says, "Bring me my sword and my red cape."
The mate fetches them, they engage the pirates and are again successful. After
the battle is over and the smoke clears, the mate comes up to the captain and
says, "I understand why you call for your telescope, and I understand why you
call for your sword, but why do you call for your red cape?" The captain says,
"Because if in the course of battle I am wounded, my blood will not show, and
the men will not become demoralized." The mate nods and goes about his
duties. The next day the mate comes running up, "Captain, captain! There's a
pirate fleet off the starboard bow." The captain says, "Bring me my telescope."
The mate brings him the telescope. The captain looks through the telescope
and sees a pirate fleet bearing down on his ship. He looks at his mate and says,
"Bring me my sword and my brown pants." I think the sword works well. You
don't use the sword.

DIANE: I don't. No.

DANIEL: Why not?

DIANE: It's a waste. I mean a battle's a battle.

DANIEL: It's not a waste.

DIANE: Of course they're gonna use weapons, but you don't have to say it. It's
implied.

DANIEL: No, it's not.

DIANE: Gestalt.

DANIEL: Bullshit! Stop making up terms to explain your failure to include the
sword. [*both laugh*] . . . He's going into battle. He wants his sword and his red
cape . . . And you don't set the three-fold pattern in that joke. You only do it
once.

DIANE: Well, I only have limited time when I'm giving my talk, and it's very efficient
to tell it that way. Keeps their attention . . ." "Bring me my sword and brown
pants." It just loses the meter of . . . "bring me my brown pants."

DANIEL: No. It doesn't. No. "Bring me my sword" because it sets up the we're going
to engage in battle, and my brown pants, this time I'm gonna shit. It seems to me
that the sword really helps. Instead of just dumping them with the brown pants.

DIANE: I've told this joke for years.

DANIEL: So have I.

DIANE: Same joke, again and again.

DANIEL: So have I, so have I.

DIANE: And just in terms of stress, and then I work it into my . . . I've never had a
sword in it once.

DANIEL: But this works too. I mean . . .

DIANE: I feel like it's got to be in small, neat packages.

DANIEL: "Bring me my sword" doesn't substantially enlarge the joke.

DIANE: But the focus to me is on the cape.

DANIEL: And the three-fold pattern focuses still upon the cape, because the mate is
willing to put that focus on the cape. He's gonna ask the question, "I understand
why you bring—why you ask—for your sword, but why the red cape?" " 'Cause
if in the course of the battle I'm wounded, you know, blood won't show and my
crew won't become depressed."

The fact that the tellers set the joke in different centuries and different seas is not a
matter of real concern to either of them. The dispute between them focuses upon
issues of contrast and meter. Daniel does not like the fact that Diane's rendition
lacks the threefold structure, with the ship first encountering an enemy vessel on
the right, then on the left, and culminating in a confrontation with an entire fleet.
Daniel feels that the pattern of asking for the sword and cape needs two repeti-
tions to be effectively established (Olrik 1965, 133). Diane is satisfied that a pattern
can be established in a single scene. She claims this is more efficient, although her
rendition of the joke was not shorter than Daniel's.

Daniel also emphasized the importance of the captain asking for his sword *and*
his red cape. Daniel explained that the sword and cape characterize the captain as
a man of action and valor, although the valorous significance of the cape has to be
explicated in the joke text. The sword and cape come to complement one another.
In the punchline, this association is disrupted when the switch from red cape to
brown pants reveals the captain to be a coward. Daniel also felt that the meter was
better with the incremental repetition of "sword and red cape," "sword and red
cape," and "sword and brown pants," while Diane felt the meter was better when
the cape and pants stood alone.

The point is not really to assess which joke version or performance is better. The point is to try to understand why Daniel and Diane—two accomplished joke tellers—develop and prefer the performances that they do, and to grasp something of the aesthetic criteria they employ in the evaluation of jokes. Many of the differences in their approach to the joke texts and performances reported here seem to revolve around a single comprehensive difference: the difference between narrative and theater. Diane's jokes are theatrical. Diane employs changes of voice, dialect, and mimicry to a very high degree. When telling jokes she invariably employs exaggerated facial expressions, gestures, and pronounced bodily movements. For example, in the joke about Sir Francis Drake and the Spanish Armada, Diane did not merely describe the figure of Sir Francis Drake; she acted out the part. When Sir Francis emerges on the deck of the ship cool, calm, and collected, Diane moves her body to portray the character she is describing. She flutters her eyelashes, turns her neck slowly from side to side, and puts up her hands to frame her face and head as though a glow emanated from them in order to convey Sir Francis's calm and self-possession. When Sir Francis pops the telescope open and shut, she claps her hands in accompaniment. She pretends to bring a telescope to her eye to scan for enemy sail. She makes the appropriate motions when Sir Francis swirls into his red cape. She employs high- and low-class British accents to distinguish the speech of Sir Francis from his first mate.

Daniel does little of this. What he conveys he conveys in words. Almost everything is encoded in the joke text. It seems that he stresses the importance of the sword in the joke because the sword represents the captain's courage and martial spirit. This signification is magnified in the explication of the reasons for the red cape. Sword and red cape serve as a formula for courage and intrepidity. The captain's final request for his sword once again would signify these traits, but in the climactic shift to brown pants, the captain's heroic posturing is undone.

Diane does not need a sword because she employed many words and gestures to characterize the nobility and vainglory of Sir Francis. For her, the brown pants alone can serve to shatter her elaborately crafted persona. As Daniel employs no verbal or body language to create the image of a brave or noble hero, the audience's impression of the captain heavily depends on his calling for his weapon, his ordering an attack on the enemy, and his explication of the significance of the red cape. No total persona has been created. There are only the captain's words and his reported actions.

Diane seems to favor jokes that provide latitude for histrionic treatment. Each of the eleven jokes that she told or commented on during the dinner when she was recorded was told with dialect or some other pronounced vocal or bodily mimicry. For Diane, a joke is a vehicle for a theatrical performance. Daniel, while not avoiding dialect and gesture, employs them much more sparingly. He used a low, gruff voice and a higher, tremulous voice to emphasize the difference between the prison cellmate and the Jewish accountant. He also used a Yiddish accent for the man on the beach who releases the genie from the lamp. But dialect, mimicry, and gesture primarily served to accentuate the structure of the joke and to heighten its surprising effect. Daniel prefers jokes that are clever, that is, that depend on an abrupt and unexpected shift in conceptualization. Jokes for Daniel are not primarily theatrical performances but intellectual puzzles that have to be solved. The art of the joke for Daniel would seem to be the delineation of a puzzle with an unexpected, elegant, though immediately accessible solution.[12]

This difference in approach was actually articulated in the course of their dinner conversation. Daniel had finished telling a joke about clergymen and miracles. Diane agreed that it was a wonderful joke. Then Diane brought up a joke about a hunter. Daniel had learned that joke from Diane, and he said he had told it on a number of occasions. He recalled telling it during deer-hunting season to some friends who lived in the country. At that point, Diane started to repeat certain lines from that joke, lines that, even Daniel admitted, demanded vocal and behavioral mimicry if the joke were to succeed. Daniel agreed with Diane that it was a "good joke," but he immediately qualified his praise with "But you know, it's not a clever joke." Referring to the joke he had told about the clergymen and miracles, he continued, "That's conceptually a brilliant joke."

As feedback is a critical force in artistic performance, it seems necessary to ask how much Daniel's and Diane's criticisms ultimately affected the other's performances. After all, Daniel agreed with Diane that the idea of a Jewish genie had good comic possibilities. He was also impressed with her rendition of the captain and his first mate in high- and low-class British accents. Likewise, Diane admitted that there might be some problem in employing the name "Bubba" for the black cellmate and that Daniel had "set the scene better" in that joke. She acknowledged as well that referring to the "Aryan child" in the joke about the German soldier and French maiden might be questionable. How did the criticisms and these admissions affect their subsequent joke-telling behaviors?

As far as I can tell (and I have since had a number of opportunities to observe, since at the time of this writing it is some years since the original dinner party), their joke telling was not affected at all. Daniel never gave the genie a Jewish accent, nor did he try to employ dialect in the joke about the captain and the pirates (which also would have required a switch from an American to a British scenario). Diane did not set the prison joke up with a frightened Jewish accountant, and she continued to characterize the cellmate as black and to name him "Bubba." (She said she liked the sound of the name and the way she vocalized it in the joke.) Nor did she remove the reference to the Aryan child from her joke about the German soldier and the French peasant girl.

This unwillingness to respond to the critique of the other may be rooted, in part, in the competitive nature of their joke telling. For either Daniel or Diane to respond to the other's criticism would be something of an admission of defeat. It would, in effect, establish the other as a superior joke stylist. But it is the fundamental differences in their styles that stand as the greatest impediment to change in performance. These styles are not purely matters of disinterested aesthetic intention. Daniel and Diane are two different personalities, and their joke aesthetics are an extension of their personalities.[13]

Diane performs almost everything. Her performed expressions occur in virtually all situations and venues, from meals to movies to social encounters. At a meal, for example, those around will be sure to learn of her evaluation of the food not merely as a verbal statement but as a performed expression. Prolonged "ahs" and "hmmms" can mark the tasting of each and every dish. At movies, sighs, groans, and laughter leave those around her little doubt as to her opinion of that segment of the film. In meeting new people—waiters, clerks, or even strangers on the street— she will often engage them comically in a loud voice that others in the vicinity can overhear. She creates a situation in which she is in control of a comic scenario.

She seems unable to resist this role. Once, after she underwent a serious surgery, the surgeon told her she needed to rest and not move about. Nevertheless, she insisted on being the center of attention for those who were visiting her, jumping up to engage in some mimicry or other comic antic until one of her guests actually yelled at her to sit down and remain still as the surgeon had instructed. She was able to follow that instruction only for a short while before she was again engaged in some performance with full bodily involvement.

Daniel, no less than Diane, has a comedic persona. Humor is as central to his sense and presentation of self as it is to Diane. But unlike Diane, he does not attempt to hold the center of attention on a full-time basis. He seems to prefer to hang back and let others hold the floor until he can deliver a comic line of appropriateness and force. He is more distant and aloof. Daniel reported that in his youth he was always coming out with one-liners from the back of the classroom. All through school, he liked sitting in the back of the classroom because he could see everything yet not be seen. He envisioned his comic interjections at school as emanating from a "disembodied voice," although he was well aware that everyone in the class knew who made them. Daniel's humor puts an emphasis on the verbal and serves more as a commentary on what is going on than as the driving force of the social action. Even Daniel's tellings of canned jokes tend to be triggered by an association to or commentary on the ongoing social interaction.

Daniel is more of a jester, while Diane is more of a clown. Like a jester, Daniel listens to what others are saying and then offers a humorous remark or retort. Diane, however, is more likely to be the entire act. Like a clown, she employs an array of verbal, vocal, and kinetic techniques to create a scenario that can stand on its own. She is both the performer and the performance. So when it comes to joke telling, the joke narrative itself is only a facet of a more comprehensive comedic expression.

This, I suspect, is largely why their criticisms provoked no changes in the other's performances. Their joke-telling performances are expressions of their comedic personas and ultimately their personalities. They are no more likely to change their styles of performance then they are to change from being right-handed to left-handed. One changes handedness in the event of some trauma that renders the preferred hand unusable. What might make Daniel and Diane change their joke-telling styles would be the trauma of repeated joke-performance failure. But because Daniel and Diane tell jokes frequently and regularly receive positive feedback from their audiences, neither is likely to change a performance strategy that has proven successful *and* seems so much a product of who they are.[14]

Philosopher Noël Carroll believes jokes to be less than art because there is so little room for interpretive play in them: "The organization of the joke is . . . so parsimonious that any attempt to reflect upon the text and its interpretation for any period of time is likely to be very unrewarding. Jokes are not designed for contemplation—one cannot standardly review them in search of subtle nuances that inflect, enrich, or expand our interpretations" (Carroll 1991, 294).[15] In fact, the minutiae of joke construction and expression are precisely what Daniel and Diane argue about. For these performers, "subtle nuances" are at the core of joke aesthetics. Both feel that a word, an intonation, a repetition, a parallelism, or a heightened contrast makes a joke succeed or fail. The change of a word or inflection can, in fact, radically alter the interpretation of a joke and the ability to articulate what its message might be (Oring 2003, 27–40).[16] Of course, Carroll has considered the joke as a type, not as an individual expression. The interpretative possibilities of a novel, poem, or painting might look equally limited were the genres themselves the objects of contemplation rather than particular novels, poems, or paintings. The formulation "initial situation, complication, resolution" might appear as thin a basis for an aesthetic evaluation of the dramatic novel as "appropriate incongruity" or "incongruity resolution" might for an aesthetic evaluation of the joke. When philosophers seek to write about jokes as art, perhaps it would be a good idea to base their reflections on joke performances—that is, the observation of real joke tellers telling real jokes in real joke-telling situations—rather than contemplate formulations of what jokes are supposed to be.

Afterword

> The question is always whether in the end the spirit of contradiction is not on the whole more useful than unity in agreement.
> —GEORG CHRISTOPH LICHTENBERG

Although the essays in this book constitute a series of reflections on and studies of fairly specific questions, there are several broad issues in the study of jokes and humor that are brought to the fore. The first is that the problem of what humor is—what provokes amusement—remains unresolved. Four recent theories of humor, the General Theory of Verbal Humor, Conceptual Integration or Blending Theory, Benign Violation Theory, and False-Belief Theory, all betray serious weaknesses. The General Theory of Verbal Humor, which is basically a form of appropriate incongruity theory—fails because of its formalizing aspirations. The presumption that all jokes could be reduced to a set of well-delineated components and conceptualized in terms of simple binary oppositions blinded theorists to how jokes actually work in favor of views of how they should work. Even joke examples employed to advance the theoretical structure were misperceived and incorrectly analyzed. It is a classic case of a theory advancing despite its misalignment with the facts.

Conceptual Integration or Blending Theory falls short because there are all sorts of blends that are not humorous. A great deal of serious poetry is expressed in blended language and images: "Upon my belly sat the sow of fear" (Shapiro 1978, 37), "Our eunuch dreams, all seedless in the light" (Thomas 2003, 104).[1] Akira Kurosawa's film *Throne of Blood* [*Kumonosu-jō* = "Spider Web Castle"], a version of Shakespeare's *Macbeth* set in feudal Japan and employing stylistic elements of Noh drama, is an obvious but decidedly nonhumorous example of a blend. Blending does go on in jokes, but often in what Sigmund Freud labeled "condensation" jokes, which depend on a "composite structure made up of two components" (Freud 1960, 8:19–33). Blending does not seem to describe "displacement" jokes, which depend upon "the diversion of the train of thought" from one topic to another (8:51). Conceptual Integration Theory sets out to show that *all* human thought proceeds in terms of blending. It is, therefore, not surprising that the theory has difficulties in distinguishing humor from other types of expression.

Benign Violation Theory fails because it claims to infer the emotional dispositions underlying various texts and behaviors. The evidence for an emotional basis for all humor remains weak. The theory would have to account for jokes that focus on very different topics and presumably depend upon moral violations of very different degrees that nevertheless prove to be equally funny. Second, the experimental data amassed to evidence the theory can be explained in other ways. Humor theorists of every stripe would acknowledge that emotion may influence humor perception and appreciation. This, however, is a far cry from claiming that humor is fundamentally an emotional affair. False-Belief Theory proposes that humor resides in the discovery of errors in our tacit assumptions in the course of making sense of everyday speech and behavior. The errors are there, but there would seem to be a lot more besides.

All told, humor scholars are pretty far from conclusively answering the question "What is humor?" with some concise and felicitous formula. Even *appropriate incongruity*, I claim, is only a *better* formulation of what is going on. It still leaves some questions—big and small—unresolved. The big questions might be: What, other than identity, is not incongruous? And what, other than identity, is appropriate? Is any connection whatsoever capable of transforming an incongruity into humor? If not, what kinds of appropriateness fail and which succeed? Small questions would be directed at the explanation of particular problematic humor examples. It is important to keep in mind that despite all the efforts to theorize humor and all the attempts to apply theories from a variety of disciplines, the questions first raised by the ancients are far from being definitively answered. The conversation continues, and I am happy to be a part of it.

A second point to be derived from these essays is that the analysis of jokes requires studious attention. "Why did the chicken cross the road?" or "How many Polacks does it take to change a light bulb?" are not as simple as they might first appear. Even scholars of humor have gotten them wrong. Some jokes are simple, but many are not. A number of philosophers have dismissed jokes as not worthy of contemplation. One wonders, however, how many of them have sat down with a decent corpus of jokes and tried to sort out how each specimen actually works.

A presumption exists that the study of humor cannot really be a serious affair. It seems to suffer from the same debility as pediatrics. This medical subspecialty does not rank high in the estimation of many physicians because, after all, it deals with caring for small children, which is devalued as "women's work" ("What Influences" 2009).² This, however, is magical, not rational, thinking. The science is stigmatized because its object of study is devalued in some greater scheme of things. I will not defend the importance of humor here. I will merely suggest that with all that has been written about Shakespeare's *Hamlet*, Cervantes' *Don Quixote*, and a thousand other literary works, one might realize that it is possible to say silly things about interesting and important texts and to say interesting and important things about ostensibly silly ones.

A third point is that humanists who work in humor research can and should formulate and test hypotheses. Hypothesis building and testing need not and should not be left solely to experimental psychologists and sociologists. There is no need to work pigeons to death or run rats through mazes to be allowed to employ the word *hypothesis*. In this book, I propose a number of hypotheses that can be tested using literary, historical, and fieldwork materials. I have also tried to examine a number of long-standing hypotheses in humor theory, have submitted seemingly contrary evidence for discussion, and offered possible alternatives (e.g., Oring 2003, 41–57, 58–70, 71–84). Others, I am sure, could do the same.

A fourth point that emerges from these essays is that, to a great extent, the whole area of history is missing from the study of jokes. Of course, there are histories—chronicles, actually—of the theories of humor and laughter (e.g., Piddington 1933, 132–221; Morreall 1987, 9–172; B. Sanders 1995; Carrell 2008). There are historical surveys of literary parody and satire (e.g., M. Rose 1993; Griffin 1994), fools and jesters (Otto 2001), political cartoons (Hess and Northrop 1996), and comics (Robinson 1974). There are studies of humor in particular historical periods (Beard 2014). There is, however, very little material on the history of jokes or their relation to oral and literary tales. Occasionally, folklore and literary scholars have traced the peregrinations of individual texts through time and place (Baum 1917; Brown 1922; W. Anderson 1923; R. Raskin 1992, 186–240), but we still do not have any firm grasp of the history of the genre.³ Jokes are usually treated as psychological and sociological phenomena and studied largely from a synchronic perspective. This is probably due to the fact that jokes appear to be expressions of the moment. They are oral, anonymous, seemingly ephemeral, and inconsequential. Only occasionally in earlier periods were they written down, and only some of those records have survived. Joke remains lay scattered over wide expanses of space and time. Such intermittent documentation does not beget a historical consciousness or promote historical reflection.

Jokes should not be analyzed only as commentaries on the contemporary. They need a history of their own.

The fifth point is that the joke is a literary form that merits literary analysis. Just as the joke has been ignored as a historical fact, it has been ignored as an artistic one. The joke is art to the extent that it is a form that arrests attention. There are probably no grounds for negotiation with those who would hold art to be something else—something that subsumes only those objects that move them (although, other than dance, I cannot think of another form that is as literally *moving* as a joke). I reject axiological approaches to the term *art*. Bad art, mediocre art, and great art are no less art than bad business, mediocre business, and good business are all business. (The Internal Revenue Service allows business deductions even when your business is poorly run.) My point is not to put forth jokes as great art, although I would not exclude the possibility that some jokes are great. When it comes to the question of what makes a particular art form good, one undertakes research in ethno- or folk-aesthetics. As a folklorist, it is not my task to prescribe a set of universal criteria for the production of good jokes. Nor should I be purveying my own preferences. It is my job, however, to try to describe the criteria that people employ in crafting a successful joke in their particular social environments. It is my job to try and understand why someone might be considered a good or bad joke teller. Folklorists want to identify those forms that arrest attention and those that do not. They want to know the reasons people make the choices they do and how changes in aesthetic preference come about. Why does Diane emphasize dialect in her joke telling, and why is Daniel so insistent on threefold repetition? Why did the medieval Scandinavians and Anglo-Saxons reject rhyme for their poetry?

Joking Asides is my third collection of essays and fifth book on the subject of humor. Nonetheless, I have not exhausted the questions I want to raise, the observations I would hope to emphasize, and the comments I wish to make. In some sense, humor has proven an intractable subject. Were this not so, we would not still be talking about it after 2,500 years. Psychologists would not be running hundreds of experiments on hapless college freshmen; critics would have ceased identifying humor in major and minor literary texts; computational linguists would have successfully programed computers to recognize and produce jokes; and anthropologists, sociologists, and folklorists would have forged the master keys to unequivocally unlock the social and cultural meanings of jokes. But the conversation continues. Whatever understandings we claim to possess remain tentative. Each proposition about the workings of humor invariably runs up against recalcitrant facts and antinomies. This is all well and good, however. An agreeable conversation may be agreeable, but it very soon ceases to be conversation.

This volume is meant to offer challenges to our conventional understandings of humor: understandings of what humor is; how jokes function; who the targets of comedy are; what the basis might be for the identification of a humorous repertoire with a particular social group; how the subgenres of jokes might be defined; and how jokes might relate to those forms of expression considered to be art. Hopefully, there will be those who will respond to my challenges and challenge my own propositions.

It would be fair to ask, consequently, whether there have been any advances in thinking over the millennia. Has it just been a matter of point and counterpoint? I would think the separation of laughter from humor would be one advance. *Humor*, as the term is currently employed, only emerges in the eighteenth century. The ancient philosophers theorized about laughter. Nevertheless, it seems clear from looking at ancient comedies and old joke books that people of the past were responsive to many of the same stimuli that provoke amusement today (Beard 2014, 211–12). It is true that the ancients tended to regard laughter as a response to the ugly and held it, for the most part, in rather low esteem. The point is not that humor and laughter have finally achieved their esteemed status—although in the West for the most part they have—but that there is a separation of the behavioral response from the internal sensibility that provokes it. The question today is now a bifurcate one: what is it that engenders the sense of amusement, and why is laughter often involuntarily provoked by that sensibility?

A second advance occurred when the questions of what humor is and how it operates were separated from issues of morality. From ancient times, the analytic questions have been interwoven with the question of whether laughter and amusement could be considered right conduct. Prejudgments about the ethics of laughter and humor influenced attempts to understand the phenomena themselves. Even today, it is difficult to find a paper written on jokes by a philosopher that does not have a substantial section devoted to ethical considerations (e.g., N. Carroll 1991, 295–98; 2003, 358–64; Gaut 1998). Nevertheless, the two questions became detached, allowing for the formulation of theories rooted solely in a consideration of causes and independent of their presumed moral consequences.

Finally, the escape of humor from the exclusive confines of speculative philosophy to the disciplines of psychology, sociology, anthropology, folkloristics, and linguistics also seems a progressive step. Theorizing based on a narrow range of handpicked—often ersatz—examples no longer serves to ground inquiry. The cultural and social sciences have described—often in great detail—humor from real life and from a wide range of social and cultural groups along with the circumstances of its expression. Comparative and experimental frameworks have been put to work in an effort to test propositions about the nature of humor and the effects of its deployment. The development of the neurosciences and imaging technology will likely have a part to play in unraveling the secrets of humor as well. If all this attention from an array of disciplines has yet to dispose of fundamental problems surrounding humor, it is well to remember that fundamental problems in the physical sciences, social sciences, and mathematics still await resolution. Meanwhile, the conversation is ongoing and those who would acquaint themselves with the issues, the materials, and previous research are more than welcome to put their two cents in.

Notes

PREFACE

1. Aristotle wrote that "the ludicrous . . . is a failing or a piece of ugliness which causes no pain or destruction; thus, to go no farther, the comic mask is something distorted but painless" (1970, 23–24). Laurent Joubert wrote in *Traité de ris* (Treatise on Laughter) in 1579 that "laughter is made up of the contrariety or battle of two feelings, holding the middle ground between joy and sadness . . . Laughter can therefore be called false joy with false displeasure (1980, 44). Also see Eastman (1921, 211–23) for other theories based on a mixture of emotions, but Benign Violation Theory does not seem aware of these predecessors and, consequently, does not seem to have developed from them.

CHAPTER 1

1. Over the years, Freud substantially revised and updated *The Interpretation of Dreams* (first published in 1900), *The Psychopathology of Everyday Life* (1903), *and Three Essays on the Theory of Sexuality* (1905). *Jokes and Their Relation to the Unconscious* did not attract similar attention. After very minor additions in the 1912 edition, the book was thenceforth published unchanged (Freud 1960, 8:3).

2. Eastman was in many respects critical of Freud's approach to jokes (1936, 248–53).

3. Patricia Keith-Spiegel does not actually include Freud's theory under the section "Release and Relief Theories" in her survey of theories of humor, but she includes Freud among those who see laughter as the sudden liberation of "repressed energy" or "pent-up emotion." She probably did not include Freud under release and relief theories because she allocates a separate section to "Psychoanalytic Theory" (Keith-Spiegel 1972, 10–11, 12–13, 20–21).

4. In *On Dreams*, the shorter exposition of his dream theory, Freud refers to "conditions of intelligibility" rather than to "secondary revision," which is what he discusses in *The Interpretation of Dreams*, but they both refer to the transformation in dream content to make the dream somewhat orderly and reportable (Freud 1953, 5:488–508).

5. In Freud's view, the third person does not ever seem to be the object of aggression even though he may be the sole obstacle to a successful seduction. The hostility is turned toward the woman despite her potential willingness.

6. The joke is ancient and was told about the emperor Augustus (Beard 2014, 131).

7. The joke is made, it is deciphered, and the inhibited thought emerges, at which point the inhibition in place to suppress the thought becomes superfluous. The joke tricks the hearer. Freud does not state the matter in exactly this way (Freud 1960, 8:152). I don't hold with Neal Schaeffer's view that because of the joke-work, a matter that is "repressed" in the unconscious no longer has to be "taken seriously," allowing that energy to be spent in the pleasure of laughter (Schaeffer 1981, 12). Schaeffer, however, is right in questioning why the surplus energy should be channeled into laughter.

8. Freud goes on to describe play in which various words are strung together by a child without any concern as to their meaning or coherence. The child revels in the wild romp with the rediscovery of what is familiar. A jest involves the putting together of thoughts that have some measure of sense. In a joke, that thought must contain something valuable or new. Both the jest and the joke, because of the thoughts they contain, manage to circumvent the censorship and thus release energy that had been dedicated to the suppression of undisciplined and unreasoned expression (Freud 1960, 8:128–29).

9. Paul Kline is one of the few writing about *The Interpretation of Dreams* who registered the important differences between dreams and jokes rather than glossing over them (Kline 1977, 8–9).

10. J.Y.T. Grieg, in responding to someone who characterized Freud's theory of jokes and humor as "letting the cat out of the bag," properly asked: "But what cat, what bag, and what are the means?" (Grieg 1923, 200).

11. Likewise, it may be true that constant energy from the sun and the earth's rotation underlie the earth's system of weather, but no particular weather phenomena are likely to be directly reducible to these two principles alone.

12. *Jokes and Their Relation to the Unconscious* relies upon and responds to Theodor Lipps's (1922) *Komik und Humor* (originally published in 1898), which also invokes notions of psychical energy, as did other theories of the day. Freud proposed that psychology and psychopathology could be reduced to neurophysiology and matters of energy excitation, conversion, and discharge. He elaborated this view at length in the manuscript "Project for a Scientific Psychology" in 1895 (Freud 1966, 1:283–397). He never finished the manuscript, but his thinking makes its way into the last chapter of *The Interpretation of Dreams*.

13. One might be surprised to discover that when jokes are formed to fulfill unconscious purposes, Freud identifies "cynical jokes" as the prime examples rather than sexual or aggressive jokes (Freud 1960, 8:176). See Freud's discussion of the Schnorrer and Schadchen jokes to understand why (105–9, 112–13). Also see Freud's analysis of the *familionär* joke made by Heinrich Heine's character Hirsch-Hyacinth (12–13, 140–42).

CHAPTER 2

1. The manner in which the KRs are derived suggests they are *components* of the joke. In fact, they are sometimes called "aspects" of the joke (Attardo and Raskin 1991, 295).

2. I do agree with Morreall that GTVH is not explanatory. If it could serve as the basis of computational models of jokes, that would be another matter. Linguistic models of jokes will prove

themselves when a computer can generate jokes, another computer can identify those products as jokes, and both production and identification reasonably duplicate what humans do. With a large enough encyclopedia and a few rules about opposition and overlap, a computer, I would imagine, could find script overlap in almost any text. The question is whether it could identify the jokes that humans identify and ignore the ones that humans ignore.

3. *Stereotype* may not be the best word to use because it suggests that the image of the person or group is believed and consequently conditions social interaction (Oring 1992, 8–9). In Polish jokes, the association established between Poles and stupidity was created by the jokes themselves and became part of general social knowledge. In the 1960s, these jokes were not a representation of a prior presumption about the intelligence of Poles (see C. Davies 1990, 40–83). Attardo and Raskin (1991, 304) are aware of the problem.

4. There are such jokes:

> There was a blonde who found herself sitting next to a lawyer on an airplane. The lawyer just kept bugging the blonde wanting her to play a game of intelligence. Finally, the lawyer offered her 10 to 1 odds, and said every time the blonde could not answer one of his questions, she owed him $5.00, but every time he could not answer hers, he'd give her $50.00. The lawyer figured he could not lose, and the blonde reluctantly accepted. The lawyer first asked, "What is the distance between the Earth and the nearest star?" Without saying a word the blonde handed him $5.00.
>
> Then the blonde asked, "What goes up a hill with 3 legs and comes back down the hill with 4 legs?" Well, the lawyer looked puzzled. He took several hours, looking up everything he could on his laptop and even placing numerous air-to-ground phone calls trying to find the answer. Finally, angry and frustrated, he gave up and paid the blonde $50.00. The blonde put the $50.00 into her purse without comment, but the lawyer insisted, "What is the answer to your question?"
>
> Without saying a word, the blonde handed him $5.00 ("Game of Intelligence" n.d.).

5. Attardo and Raskin dismiss this possibility by stating that such a joke would not be funny (Attardo and Raskin 1991, 342–43). I do not recall that SSTH or GTVH demands that a joke be found funny—only that it be recognized as "joke-carrying text" (V. Raskin 1985b, 99). Nevertheless, I think the joke would still be funny—although perhaps not as funny.

6. For example, see G. C. von Lichtenberg's joke: "Not only did he disbelieve in ghosts; he was not even frightened of them" (Freud 1960, 8:92). It would be difficult to delineate a precise "mechanism" for this joke.

7. If the mechanisms are too general or abstract—for example, indirect representation, allusion (Freud 1960, 74, 89)—they may not be of much use. It is possible that the basic processes of the joke are not easily dissected or categorized.

8. It is not enough: for example, "'How are you?' 'Is that a trick question?'"

9. Attardo and Raskin (1991, 321) are fully aware that the variants differ in LA.

10. Ruch, Attardo, and Raskin (1993, 134) are also aware that the degree to which a variant differs from its anchor itself varies. Thus, in creating joke 2, which differs from the anchor joke in NS, the experimenters made only a very small change to the grammatical structure of the anchor. They turned a question into an assertion. The two jokes are otherwise identical. But the changes in creating variants that were supposed to differ from the anchor in terms of LM and SO were not minor at all. Completely new elements were introduced in the joke texts (135). So one wonders why in creating a NS variant they did not recast the anchor joke, for example, as a genuine narrative to ensure that the scale of transformation in the NS variant might parallel the scale of transformation of the LM and SO variants.

11. "The script of DUMBNESS opposes the ethnic group or groups to which the speaker and hearer(s) belong as the non-dumb, reasonable, natural, regular people to the targeted group which

is depicted as dumb, unreasonable, irrational, irregular, etc. It is a typical good/bad kind of oppositeness" (V. Raskin 1985b, 186).

12. This would not be the most salient script for a joke involving eunuchs. One would more likely expect an answer like, "None. They can't screw anything at all."

13. The "Self-Operating Napkin" is activated when the soup spoon (A) is raised to mouth, pulling string (B) and thereby jerking ladle (C) which throws cracker (D) past parrot (E). Parrot jumps after cracker and perch (F) tilts, upsetting seeds (G) into pail (H). Extra weight in pail pulls cord (I), which opens and lights automatic cigar lighter (J), setting off skyrocket (K) which causes sickle (L) to cut string (M) and allow pendulum with attached napkin to swing back and forth, thereby wiping chin" ("Rube Goldberg Machine" n.d.).

14. I am not fond of the term *resolution* because nothing in a joke is truly resolved (Oring 2003, 2).

15. On occasion, the light-bulb joke works on the principle of sufficiency versus insufficiency: "How many Jewish mothers does it take to screw in a light bulb? None. 'The dark is all right.'"

16. For examples of actual light-bulb jokes, see Dundes 1987, 143–49.

17. In fact, this was not originally a Polish joke or any other kind of ethnic joke. The characters were made Polish for the purposes of this example.

18. Even so, there is likely to be another aspect to the appropriateness besides stupidity. Conceptually, one might screw in the bulb by men turning the table. In other words, the stupid activity must still relate to the problem described because it needs to create the notion of excessive activity *for the task at hand*. The following would probably not work well as a joke: "How many Poles does it take to screw in a light bulb? Five. One to screw in the bulb and four to learn how to read." While learning how to read might invoke the stupidity script, it would not contribute to making the incongruity appropriate since learning how to read is unrelated to the task of screwing in the bulb. However, if the answer were "Five. One to screw in the bulb and four to learn to read the directions on the package," the joke would probably work well.

19. The joke relies on the perception that senators are politicians and therefore arrogant, deceitful, unscrupulous, and concerned with power, money, and reelection rather than the welfare of those they represent.

20. An incongruity can always be formulated as an opposition in terms of some semantic component. For example, *tomato* versus *carburetor* can be generalized as organism versus machine—living versus not living—but it is not clear that this will necessarily prove relevant to the production or understanding of a joke that refers to these objects.

21. Attardo (1997) addresses the serial nature of the joke in his attempt to reconcile GTVH and "incongruity resolution" theories of humor.

CHAPTER 3

1. The term linguists employ is *online*. It is meant to designate real-time, face-to-face communication but maps Internet-situated communication onto everyday speech.

2. Thus, in the sentence "Liz thinks Richard was wonderful," there is a mental space for Liz's beliefs—which is pretty unstructured—except that it contains a mental space for Richard's wonderfulness. In the sentence "Liz thinks that last year Richard was wonderful," there is a mental space for Liz's belief in which is embedded a space for "last year" as well as a space for Richard's wonderfulness (Fauconnier 1997, 11).

3. It seems surgeons *are* prone to see patients as meat (Kramer 1983).

4. Arvo Krikmann 2007 also offers a critique of the "digging your own grave blend" analyzed by Fauconnier and Turner (1998, 149–51) and Coulson (2001, 168–72).

5. Except for Brandt and Brandt 2005.

6. It seems to me that a similar problem arises in the analysis of some humorous insults. Geert Brône and Kurt Feyaerts offer an analysis of German insults in terms of "metonymic chaining." I believe, however, that some of these insults depend on a conventional meaning that might well be missed were they presented as novel expressions. For example, "Ihm haben sie wohl eine Ecke abgefahren" would probably be puzzling to an English speaker if presented in translation: "Someone must have cut off one of his edges" (Brône and Feyaerts 2003, 28). The analysis proceeds easily, however, because the imputation of stupidity is conventional and well known. In "He is a few fries short of a Happy Meal," the imputation of stupidity might not be immediately grasped, although it would become more likely were one aware of "He is a few beers short of a six-pack" or other similar constructions.

7. Coulson imagines that the pig summons the server because the pig finds the food distasteful (Coulson 2005b, 110). That is one possible interpretation. The joke does not depend on it, however. For all one knows, the pig might wish to ask for the wine list.

8. Even if the joke were located on one of these streets, it would remain substantially the same. The name of the street would merely be a diversion.

9. This joke goes back at least a thousand years. See Baldwin (1983, 29).

10. In actual speech, some of these might be regarded as efforts to conceal information, but they are also jokes.

11. One could argue that there is a blend between the pragmatic and definitional senses of the *wh* questions, but this simply seems a way to suggest that the questions have semantic ambiguities exploited in the production of incongruities.

12. Giora knows that these types of jokes exist, and she even provides an example: "Outside the Jewish Quarter in the Old City of Jerusalem a tourist asks a local boy: 'Where is the Wailing Wall?' The boy answers, 'In Israel'" (Giora 1991, 470n4). But she does not discuss them because most jokes seem to move to marked informativeness. Also, Giora has limited her consideration only to jokes that depend upon semantic ambiguity (466). When other kinds of jokes are considered, an informativeness principle will not necessarily apply.

13. In fact, the linguist's construal of the chicken-crossing-the-road joke was based on an analysis by a humor scholar, although "street" and not "road" was used in the original example (Lewis 1989, 9).

14. Yet the analyses of jokes like these take place without the reduction to input and blending spaces (e.g., Coulson 2001, 49–70). As such, they resemble analyses performed by scholars in a variety of disciplines.

15. One could rewrite the text as "There is *one* rule for succeeding in business. Never tell them everything you know." This may or may not be a joke, depending on the perception of the listener. It might pass entirely as a serious principle of business philosophy. There is no incongruity because the speaker promises only one rule and offers only one rule. This formulation might be perceived by others as a joke, however, since the speaker betrays his own principles by revealing all he knows about the rules of business.

16. Some cognitive linguists (Brône and Feyaerts 2003) do make use of incongruity, however.

17. Note that the usage of the elements of the attack in retaliation is what makes the joke. Retaliation in and of itself is not funny: "You are vain." "You are ugly."

18. This technique does not actually have a name, but it is not really an "exchange of roles" (Paolillo 1998, 271).

19. A shift in perspective does not in itself produce humor. The shift must produce an incongruity that is rooted in a failure to recognize the extent to which objectivity is subjective and yet prove in some measure spurious.

20. Christie Davies holds a different position (C. Davies 2004, 367). See my response to this position (Oring 2011).

21. One example of this is Tony Veale's (2007) suggestion that figure-ground reversal is a pervasive mechanism in humor. What he calls "figure-ground" reversal, however, might just as well be called "displacement" (see Freud 1960, 8:51).

22. An appropriate incongruity perspective does provide a method of analysis. The method is simple. Go through the joke and note incongruities that may arise. Discover whether these incongruities are made appropriate by the joke's end. This is, of course, more related to comprehension than production, but blending does not offer any real insight into production either.

23. Giora's "marked informativeness" hypothesis (Giora 1991) would also seem to be connected to semantic distance, as the punchline of the joke is supposed to be its least predictable element and therefore the most distant from those domains established in the joke setup.

24. Tim Hillson and Rod Martin show that semantic distance—measured in terms of loadings for three factors—is correlated with the funniness of jokes. However, the same semantic distance is correlated with the aptness of metaphors (Hillson and Martin 1994).

25. It is difficult but not impossible.

26. Another inverted metaphorical pair is also meaningful, although again on different grounds. "Italian is the daughter of Latin" may be interpreted in a historical sense. "Latin is the daughter of Italian" may be understood to mean the study of Italian leads to the study of Latin (Fauconnier and Turner 1998, 157). Another pair is "Necessity is the mother of invention" and my own creation "Invention is the mother of necessity," the latter implying that when something is invented, it often becomes something people cannot do without.

27. One could of course imagine statements in which the assignment of an occupation to a shark might not be humorous at all. A marine biologist who states, "My shark is a teacher" might be perfectly understood. "My teacher is a shark" would be perfectly understood as well, although in two different senses. The first is simply a restatement "My shark is a teacher"—that is, my shark teaches me about mysteries of biology or behavior. The other would be somewhat equivalent to saying that a lawyer is a shark—that is, the teacher is vicious and bloodthirsty. In the second formulation, "My shark is a teacher" and "My teacher is a shark" are two different metaphors, as the attributes invoked in the interpretation of each would be very different.

28. It has been suggested that metaphors dissolve domain boundaries while humor highlights them (Mio and Graesser 1991, 94; Pollio 1996, 248; Kyratzis 2003). It is an interesting statement of the difference. There is no indication of how this is achieved, however.

29. In this sense it is like an Aristotelian syllogism, which stands or falls on its internal structure and not on the relations of its propositions to the real world.

30. Knowledge about the world, however, can serve to make an incongruity spuriously appropriate. G. C. von Lichtenberg's remark "Not only did he disbelieve in ghosts; he was not even frightened of them" (Freud 1960, 8:92) is incongruous because not believing in ghosts should preclude a fear of them so that the phrase "he was not *even*" should prove unnecessary. But what one claims intellectually and what one feels emotionally may be different. To claim a lack of belief does not assure that one cannot be afraid. But this justification, this appropriateness, is spurious, since if one can be afraid of ghosts, one cannot claim to be altogether free of some degree of belief in them.

31. This graphic representation of the blend is not exactly what is presented by Coulson in her discussions (Coulson 2001, 179–85, 2005b, 3–4). She frames her analysis in terms of target and source domains rather than input spaces. In that respect, it does not quite mirror her analysis of "The surgeon is a butcher" metaphor or the chicken-crossing-the-road joke. Nevertheless, this representation captures the essential ideas necessary for the discussion of emergent structure.

32. Liisi Laineste (2002, 21) regards certain, but not all, jokes as blending humor.

CHAPTER 4

1. McGraw and Warner's book is not a serious effort to demonstrate Benign Violation Theory or a thoughtful piece of humor research. Rather, the authors travel all over the world rehashing findings registered by other humor researchers while appending anecdotes of their own in an effort to entertain readers. It was conceived, written, and marketed as a popular book. They also frame their efforts between chapters describing McGraw's attempts at stand-up comedy, although Benign Violation Theory is such a general formulation that it is unlikely to be able to serve as a protocol for the production of quality humor.

2. I actually feel that a small measure of humor in this sentence can be perceived. The semantic nonsense is made somewhat appropriate by the syntactic sense. All the parts of speech are appropriately combined. It is very different from the sentence "Ideas colorless furiously green sleep."

3. I continue to refer to appropriate incongruity as a perspective rather than a theory (Oring 1992, 1–2). The term is meant to label a line of thought that goes back to the eighteenth century (Beattie 1778, 347). It is more a characterization or description than a proper theory. It does not so much explain as describe what has to be explained in a theory of humor. The term stands for all those perspectives that argue for the existence of a relation between incongruous or incompatible domains: *bisociation* (Koestler 1964, 35), *appropriateness in the inappropriate* (Monro 1951, 255), *script overlap* (V. Raskin 1985b, 100), *incongruity resolution* (Suls 1972).

4. Other jokes exist that depend upon thwarting the expectation of an absurd joke by retreating from absurdist conventions to more direct and literal ones (Oring 1992, 25–26).

5. A suppressed thought is one that is inappropriate for public expression and deliberately avoided by speakers. A repressed thought is one that individuals conceal even from themselves.

6. Actually, Abrahams and Dundes's essay would have allowed Veatch to come up with more possible violations to consider in trying to frame an emotional hypothesis for the elephant joke. My essay on elephant jokes was a reaction to the one by Abrahams and Dundes.

7. The joke was likely some variant of "What squeals and goes around at 100mph? A baby in an electric fan" ("Collection" n.d.).

8. Jews, of course, tell and greatly enjoy jokes about Jews, and lawyers are the greatest purveyors of lawyer jokes (Galanter 2005, 22).

9. "Sexist humor" is in scare quotes because it is not clear that blonde jokes count as sexist humor (Oring 2003, 58–70).

10. Strangely, men who rated higher in feminist sympathies did not rate their appreciation of the humor higher than those with lower sympathy levels (Gallivan 1992, 372).

11. The results of experiments on the funniness of jokes in relation to joke tellers and joke targets are equivocal. Other experiments suggest a strong relationship between the funniness of jokes and the social distance of the joke target. See Thomas and Esses 2004.

12. Also see Wyer and Collins 1992—cited by Veatch—on comprehension difficulty.

13. The notion that jokes are a species of puzzle was explored by Schiller 1938.

14. It seems that Oak Ridge stopped processing plutonium after World War II.

15. Although the appreciation of a *New Yorker* cartoon may benefit from knowledge of the magazine's self-presentation and cartoon style.

16. Veatch ignores or is unaware of the argument that puns often elicit groans because their mechanism is too transparent, and they require too little in the way of intellectual effort. People groan to register their intellectual superiority to the proffered humor (Sherzer 1985, 219).

17. Freud, who seems to have thought about everything, discussed a version of peekaboo played by an eighteen-month-old child in *Beyond the Pleasure Principle* (1955, 18:14–15).

18. In fact, there is evidence that jokes that would seem almost devoid of "wrongness" are funnier than those charged scenarios employed by McGraw et al. See Earleywine and Mankoff 2013.

19. The joke could actually end with the wife's exclamation since the pun is already present. I would suggest, however, that the husband's response adds significantly to the joke's humor—and BVT is unlikely to be able to explain why.

20. These theorists do not seem to recognize that this is not only a statement about human psychology, it is also a joke. An obviously exaggerated characterization of comedy and tragedy (incongruity) uses a truth about the effects of psychological distance (appropriateness) to produce humor. As a literal characterization of comedy and tragedy, it is not taken seriously.

21. The fourth and fifth experiments in the series seem problematical from the point of view of the experimental materials. These are two doctored photographs—one shows a man with a frozen beard from which long icicles are hanging (mild violation); the other is of a man inserting his finger deeply into his nose so that it emerges from his eye socket (severe violation). The fourth experiment is concerned with framing these photographs for the subjects as "fake" or "real," but it is not clear that this framing would have been accepted by all subjects. This may have something to do with the reason the correlations were not significant (McGraw et al. 2012, 7). The fifth experiment used the same photographs but they were manipulated in terms of size and position. The size in the distant position was only 1.5 × 1.7 inches. I wonder whether all subjects would have been able to see the photo in the distant position clearly enough to fully comprehend the image.

22. Professors who regularly give tests to college students should know that answers received often bear little relation to questions posed.

23. It is well to remember the journalist's sense about what constitutes news: immediacy, proximity, prominence, oddity, conflict, suspense, emotion, consequence (Warren 1959, 15–27). Clearly, emotion is an important factor, but there are other factors that generate interest. News cannot be defined as *any* recent emotion-provoking account. The human-interest story is often intended to arouse emotion, but it is distinguished from hard news.

24. Upsetting and offensive were collapsed into an index called "threat perception" (McGraw, Williams, and Warren 2013, 3). Why this is labeled "threat" is a mystery. Why not simply label it "offensiveness"? The researchers also looked at the geographical location of the respondents to see whether distance from the disaster proved to be a factor in their assessments of the tweets, but it did not. This should raise questions about the principle that psychological distance normalizes a violation, but the matter is not addressed.

25. McGraw, Williams, and Warren speak of "pure violation," "purely benign," and "completely benign" (McGraw, Williams, and Warren 2013, 4–5), but these terms are never quantified or defined.

26. There is a continued interest in all things related to the sinking of the *RMS Titanic* more than a century after the event. There is a voluminous literature on the tragedy and more than a score of films have been produced ("List of Films about the RMS *Titanic*" n.d.). There are *Titanic* societies, *Titanic* journals, *Titanic* artifacts (which are sold for fantastic sums) as well as *Titanic* T-shirts, sweatshirts, and coffee mugs. *And* there are *Titanic* jokes on websites ("Best Ever Titanic Jokes" 2009) and published in books (Anderson and Furlow 2006). The jokes are recent creations, not materials that were circulated immediately after the event or throughout the intervening decades. Except perhaps for diehard enthusiasts, the disaster generates little emotion today. The disaster should have become, to use BVT's terminology, "totally benign." Nevertheless, the event is still a recognized *idea*, and humor is fundamentally about the structuring of ideas—the structuring of appropriate incongruities.

CHAPTER 5

1. Freud's is a book that the authors seem not to have read, however, and from which they might have benefited.

2. Nevertheless, the belief that a restaurant will be open is not considered an epistemically committed one, even though one drives across town on its basis. Epistemic commitment characterizes beliefs "you would bet your life on" (Hurley, Dennett, and Adams 2011, 109), but it remains to be seen that the beliefs in jokes begin to approach this level of commitment.

3. I am not all that fond of the word *mirth*. Both in the past and the present day, the term refers to feelings of joy, gratification, happiness, celebration, and gaiety. Mirth may erupt in the course of a convivial meal or during play activities, and while such responses may be related to reactions to a joke or humorous story, they also seem to differ. I prefer the term *amusement*.

4. The authors regard cognition as a behavior that differs from other kinds of behaviors in that the output is inhibited from producing actual movement (Hurley, Dennett, and Adams 2011, 77).

5. This second, socially embedded joke scenario depends upon an intentional stance or a theory of mind, while the textual joke does not. Yet the text and the social experience would appear in every other respect to be the same joke. The second would be regarded by Hurley, Dennett, and Adams as "higher-order" humor, while the first is "basic or primitive" humor since it is based in the discovery of a false belief in one's own mental space. However, the development of jokes, and the text assuredly is one, is supposed to be of a higher order as it allows for the exploration of mental spaces other than one's own (Hurley, Dennett, and Adams 2011, 117, 127, 145).

6. This characteristic of jokes has been noted by previous theorists. Freud points out that when a connection is legitimate, it produces an inferior joke (Freud 1960, 8:46).

7. The connection is not entirely phonological, as the term for the armored vehicle is based on its resemblance to a cistern or tank (*Oxford English Dictionary*, s.v. "tank"). That historical connection, however, is generally absent in both working and long-term memory. Someone who grasped the semantic connection might not see the joke (Oring 2003, 8). I first encountered a version of this joke in an article by Graeme Ritchie (2006, 254): "There are the two goldfish in a tank. One says to the other, 'How do you drive this thing?'" I did not take "tank" to refer to an armored vehicle but to a fish tank and the joke depended on the fish thinking about their tank as humans would think about their cars: as an enclosed container that has glass on all four sides with a view in all directions. So the question about driving this object is incongruous (it is not a motorized vehicle) but spuriously appropriate (in that it bears some structural resemblance to a motorcar).

8. The mathematical truth is perhaps cognitively more challenging than the joke: the difference between a 0 and an 8 is 8.

9. This is, in essence, the principle of *nonreplacement* (Wyer and Collins 1992, 666, following a lead from Michael Apter [1982, 193]), of which Hurley, Dennet, and Adams are aware (Hurley, Dennett, and Adams 2011, 50, 203). As for the principle of *diminishment*, on which Wyer and Collins also follow Apter (Wyer and Collins 1992, 667; Apter 1982, 180), I am less certain. Apter's principle seems similar to Herbert Spencer's notion of "descending incongruity" proposed in his essay "The Physiology of Laughter" (Spencer 1860, 400), but I think the definition of diminishment is somewhat vague, and it is not really relevant to this discussion.

10. There was a time when a question about the speed of light would probably have evoked dumb stares.

11. If these questions seem fundamentally wrong because they ask about the speed of general categories rather than specific members of those categories, why doesn't the sense that they are wrong make them funny?

12. Although that "thing" called "peace" would seem to be an absence of "war," it would not be amiss to speak of the "spread of peace" as well as the "spread of war." Perhaps demonstrations of the existence of dark matter may, in time, eliminate the humor of the "speed of dark" question.

13. Hurley, Dennett, and Adams also propose to distinguish wit from humor, suggesting that wit is often more thought provoking than laugh inducing. There is nothing, however, that should keep a joke from being thought provoking, nor are the examples of wit they put forward deficient in humor. They also reject regarding visual puns as humorous since no false beliefs are discon-

firmed (Hurley, Dennett, and Adams 2011, 247). Actually, visual puns are often used as riddles in which the visual and textual elements must be combined (like a rebus) to discover the word or idiomatic expression it represents. It is also not clear to me why these are only "clever" but not funny.

14. Of course I am claiming to know how and what people think, but Hurley, Dennett, and Adams do this, necessarily, throughout their book as well.

15. This is not the three-rope trick I am somewhat familiar with (see YouTube for "Three Rope Trick"), but we can presume it exists.

16. Special pleading, as far as I can tell, is something in which all humor theorists engage at some point. I would suggest that humor might have resulted if the audience showed up to a Dennett presentation only to discover that he was speaking on "unconsciousness." Nevertheless, since the audience member based his action of going to the session on the belief that Dennett would be speaking on consciousness, it would seem to resemble a committed belief in their sense of the word.

17. Again, all humor theorists seem to decide what is funny and provokes laughter and what is not funny and fails to provoke laughter in the absence of any ethnographic evidence whatsoever.

18. This would seem empirically testable. Are the moments of failed capture the ones that specifically elicit the "laughter" response or is the response distributed throughout the play activity?

19. Chemically or electronically induced laughters clearly would not count in this consideration.

20. Given their propensity to see analogies between humor and scientific investigation—that is, scientists and comedians try to diagnose and fix errors in world knowledge—Hurley, Dennett, and Adams wonder whether bankers would propose theories of humor in terms of risk management and plumbers in terms of pressure and leaks (Hurley, Dennett, and Adams 2011, 112, 113n10). Actually, they do not seem to be scientists so much as computer programmers.

21. Hurley, Dennett, and Adams might argue that what constitutes humor today is an outgrowth of the original error-checking mechanism and not identical with it. Humor is, after all, a *supernormal stimulus* that is no longer identical with its primeval forebear and no longer fulfills its original function. But if humor has become something different, what sort of explanation of humor are Hurley, Dennett, and Adams really offering?

22. It should be pointed out that FBT would have to struggle with metaphors, as do other cognitive theories (see chapter 4).

23. I believe that the reviews of *Inside Jokes* that have appeared in the humor journals to date are simply dismissive and do not do justice to the theory (see Sohval and Attardo 2013; V. Raskin n.d.).

CHAPTER 6

1. It was previewed at the 2006 Comic-Con International in San Diego on July 21, 2006. Its official debut was on September 7, 2006, in Toronto, where Borat appeared in a cart pulled by women dressed as peasants. It was first publicly released in Belgium on November 1, 2006, and had limited public release in the United States and Canada and various European countries on November 3, 2006 ("*Borat*" n.d.).

2. According to the Internet Movie Database, the film grossed more than $128 million, putting it in the top 260 films in terms of gross receipts (Internet Movie Database 2009). Wikipedia puts the figure at $261,752.44 ("*Borat*" n.d.).

3. A "*not* joke" is a joke in which someone says something, perhaps outrageous, and then adds, after a slight pause, "*not*," thus negating the statement. It might be considered a form of explicit irony.

4. An interesting comparison may be made with the Ukrainian character Alex in the film *Everything Is Illuminated* (2006) who refers to African Americans as "Negroes" and is cautioned by the American character Jonathan that that word is not acceptable. Alex responds, "Why? The Negroes are a premium people."

5. "Little Moron" jokes of the 1950s did not target a particular social group, but these were children's jokes. The Polish jokes were not originally children's jokes.

6. It probably derives from her book *And Keep Your Powder Dry*, where she states: "Significantly, we began to question our own image of ourselves as a people who were rich, overgenerous, and careless, a people who were being played for a sucker by the rest of the world" (Mead 2000, 172).

7. In one outtake of the film on YouTube, an animal shelter employee does confront Borat's anti-Semitism, saying that the "Jews are Jesus's children. She [the dog at the animal shelter] probably loves Jews" ("Borat Visiting" 2009).

8. The latest of these is a suit by a New Yorker who appears in the film running away from Borat as he tries to hug and kiss him in greeting ("NY Businessman" 2007). I have seen the film several times, and I would not be able to identify the person who was fleeing.

9. In the film, the people thanked were from Glod, Romania. In the DVD, the name of the village was Moroeni, Romania. Glod seems to be a little over a mile up highway 71 from Moroeni. "Glod" in Romanian means "mud."

10. Not overlooking the fact that Shakespeare's play did not accurately reflect the historical record in the first place. King Duncan was killed in battle and was not assassinated.

11. Davidian speaks a broken Armenian combining elements of Russian and western Armenian. Some of his speech is translated correctly in the subtitles, but much is not. His cursing is not translated (Hrag Varjabedian, personal communication, April 1, 2007).

12. One might argue that satire always breaks its humorous frame as it is evaluated in terms of the aptness of its characterization of something in the real world. But a format does not need to be satiric to require the breaking of the frame. Allan Funt's television show *Candid Camera* also demanded an evaluation outside the humorous frame, although the show could not really be described as satiric.

13. In fact, the film has been criticized for being too easy on blacks and gays (Saunders 2006).

CHAPTER 7

1. Captain Ernie Blanchard told such jokes at a banquet, and the backlash was so fierce that he eventually killed himself (M. Thompson 1996). Actor Ted Danson appeared in blackface at a Friar's Club banquet in 1993 and was roundly condemned for it ("Ted Danson" 1993).

2. Sigmund Freud also cites a version of this joke (Freud 1960, 8:74). A death sentence for telling jokes in Nazi Germany was rare, although it did occur. When it happened, there were other reasons the regime wanted to target the accused joke teller. Usually joke tellers received warnings or prison sentences (Herzog 2010, 164–71).

3. Two U.S. secretaries of agriculture lost jobs and ended their political careers because of their joking remarks. Earl L. Butz resigned his position in 1976 when a racial joke he told in private conversation was reported by the press. When asked why the Republican Party was not able to attract more blacks, he said, "The only thing coloreds are looking for are tight pussy, loose shoes, and a warm place to shit" ("Nation" 1976, 23). James Watt resigned in 1983 after he jokingly referred to the diversity of his coal-leasing review commission, which he said consisted of "a black, two Jews, a woman, and a cripple" ("Essay" 1983, 100).

4. Control of humor in the press was a big concern of the Prussian government in the nineteenth century, but it does not seem that the authorities were equally concerned with the control of humor in everyday life (Townsend 1992).

5. Marianne Elise K. was tried and executed for telling this joke (Herzog 2010, 167–68).

6. This joke would have undermined the "Lenin with children" (*Lenin i deti*) representations that were officially promoted in sculpture and portraiture in the late 1960s (Yurchak 2006, 55). Lenin was a figure of overarching importance, and it has been argued that jokes about him appeared when the system was already unraveling in the 1980s (73, 97–98). It would be interesting to know when this joke about Lenin first circulated. Davies first heard it in the 1980s (C. Davies 1998, 178). Collections of jokes rarely fix dates. Jokes about Lenin were created or infused with new life at the time of the anniversaries of his birth and death in the 1970s (see below).

7. The phrase "repressive regime" is not a product of the twentieth century. It was already used in the mid-nineteenth century to refer, for example, to the French government's intervention in religious affairs and its efforts to control the press (de Félice 1851, 601; "Paris en Amérique" 1864, 910).

8. *Anekdot* (pl. *anekdoty*) is the Russian word for a story about an actual personal experience. It became the designation of a folkloric genre that we would call a canned joke (Draitser 1982, 233; Tiupa 2009). Graham (2009, 20–43) gives the most complete account of the history of the anekdot.

9. For some examples of the lengths to which the KGB would go to trap people, see Deriabin and Gibney (1959, 300–306).

10. To grasp the role such jokes might play in a state security investigation, see the sample report in Deriabin and Gibney (1959, 296–97).

11. Such surreptitious communication was regarded by James C. Scott as part of the "hidden transcript" in systems of domination (Scott 1990, 37).

12. Since the 1800s, Odessa has had a significant Jewish population. By 1900, Jews comprised more than 35 percent of the city's population and gave a distinctive character to the culture of the city. In 1941, the city was occupied by German and Romanian armies and thousands of Jews fled. Thousands of others were massacred or transported, making the city *Judenrein*. But after the war, Jews returned, making the city one of the Jewish centers in the Soviet Union, although there were no public expressions of Jewish communal or cultural life. By 1959, Jews comprised some 16 percent of the population (C. Roth 1972, 12:1319–28) There is even a joke about the Jewish character of Odessa:

> How many people live in Odessa?
> One and a half million.
> And how many Jews?
> What are you, deaf?

13. In fact, the hundredth anniversary of Lenin's birth would have been 1970. The fiftieth anniversary of his death would have been 1974. Klava was sure that the year in which the incident took place was 1974, and when questioned admitted that the occasion could have been the anniversary of his death. In any event, there were many jokes going around about Lenin at that time. See the description of Lenin jokes around the time of the 1970 centenary in Adams 2005, 123–31.

14. This joke is well known and versions have been printed in a number of collections (Lukes and Galnoor 1985, 10; Banc and Dundes 1989, 9; Lipman 1993, 35, 49; Adams 2005, 126).

15. This is not entirely true. KGB officer Peter Deriabin almost got in serious trouble for telling a joke about Stalin's son (Deriabin and Gibney 1959, 173).

16. Two informants also communicated to me that when they applied to leave the Soviet Union, they had no way of determining whether they would be successful. Permissions were granted in a seemingly random manner. People with security clearances might be allowed to leave while ordinary

people of no particular value to the state might be denied. Leon believed that the arbitrariness was deliberate and designed to intimidate (June 18, 2003).

17. Saul Bellow's novel *The Dean's December* captures something of the anomaly of this situation in the character of Ioanna, the building concierge (Bellow 1982, 72, 212–13).

18. Graham speaks of the fetishizing of the anekdot (Graham 2009, 140).

19. George Mikes refers to the humorist's cowardice (Mikes 1971, 37).

20. As happened to Leonid Z., who in 1936 began to be investigated because of an anecdote he told at a drunken party (Solzhenitsyn 1973, 200).

21. KGB officer Peter Deriabin estimated that 80 percent of the Soviet population at one time or another acted as agents or informers (Deriabin and Gibney 1959, 75).

22. Unsurprisingly, there is a joke about this: "'What are you in for?' 'For being talkative: I told some jokes. And you?' 'For laziness. I heard a joke and thought: I'll tell them tomorrow, but a comrade didn't waste time'" (Fitzpatrick 1999, 185; Adams 2005, 49).

23. See, for example, his discussion of a joke about Serenissimus (Freud 1960, 8:68–69, 104).

24. It is worth noting that the energy released in laughter is not the energy of the impulse but the energy devoted to the inhibition of that impulse. In other words, Freud's theory is not a straightforward release or relief theory of joking, as is usually maintained (see chapter 1).

25. See Scott for a critique of safety-valve theory (Scott 1990, 177–79, 186).

26. Fitzpatrick refers to this type of speech as "kitchen table" (Fitzpatrick 1999, 166). The association of such conversations with the kitchen probably dates the expression to the period in which people had individual apartments with private kitchens. Such conversations could not have taken place in the period when many lived in communal apartments with a single, multipurpose room and shared bathrooms and kitchens. Adams sets these kitchen conversations, in which anecdotes were "reeled out," in the Brezhnev period (Adams 2005, 60).

27. Literally "self-publishing house," *samizdat* referred to those works that circulated from person to person in typescript. For information on the circulation of Solzhenitsyn's works in samizdat, see Schammel 1984, 507–9.

28. "Tiny revolutions" is used in the title of Bruce Adams's book on Soviet jokes (Adams 2005).

29. Witness the tenacity of President Bill Clinton in the face of the torrent of jokes about his affair with Monica Lewinsky and his misrepresentations under oath during his deposition in the sexual harassment suit of Paula Jones. He did not resign his presidency (Oring 2003, 129–40).

30. Speier thought that this forbearance came largely through their venting of their aggression. This hypothesis was examined above.

31. There are interesting dialogues in Gerald Seymour's novel *Archangel* concerning the merits of real resistance versus humor and other forms of symbolic resistance (Seymour 1982, 137–38, 305).

32. Not all anthropologists would agree. See R. Rappaport 1967.

33. Such expressions would have been part of what Scott has called the "public transcript" and would have constituted powerful acts of political resistance (Scott 1990, 45–69, 202–27).

34. Curiously, a joke that Stokker cites as reflecting a high degree of anti-Nazi sentiment in Norway (Stokker 1995, 132) is also cited by Egon Larsen in describing the early years of Nazi rule in Germany. Larsen claimed, however, that jokes of this type gave people an unwarranted feeling of confidence that Hitler's regime could not last very long as there were so many anti-fascists in governmental and administrative institutions. In other words, it communicated that active resistance was not really necessary at all (Larsen 1980, 44–45).

35. Yurchak does not use this term.

36. "Repression" seems too strong a term. "Suppression" would be a more accurate term from the Freudian lexicon as it suggests something that is accessible to consciousness.

37. There were other indications that joke tellers were fully aware of the impositions of the system and that pretense was not involved: bureaucratic language was referred to as "oaken"

(*dubovyi iazyk*); participation in official events was recognized as pro forma; the distinction between bureaucratic work and "work with meaning" was kept clearly in mind (Yurchak 2006, 61, 96, 287).

38. Indeed, Leszek Kolakowsi characterized the split between the spheres of Soviet life and the misrecognition as characteristic of the Stalin era: "Half-starved people, lacking the bare necessities of life, attended meetings at which they repeated the government's lies about how well off they were, and in a bizarre way they half-believed what they were saying . . . Truth, they knew, was a Party matter, and therefore lies became true even if they contradicted the plain facts of experience. The condition of their living in two separate worlds at once was the remarkable achievement of the Soviet system" (quoted in Amis 2002, 152–53).

39. Yurchak gives a number of indications that the atmosphere in late socialism was more open: the risk attached to copying and distributing the poems of older Russian poets faded (Yurchak 2006, 145); musicians ignored state restrictions on rock music (146); and joke-telling sessions became frequent, protracted, and open (274).

40. Martin Amis would seem to agree: "*Glasnost*, which was a euphemism for not lying, laughed the Bolsheviks off the stage. The poets had talked about the inhuman power of the lie—but there is an antithesis to that: the human power of truth. Lying could no longer be enforced, and the regime fell. And the leaders had become too evolved, and were incapable of the necessary cruelty—the cruelty of Lenin and Stalin" (Amis 2002, 48). Adams also characterizes the Brezhnev era as led by people "who no longer believed in the goals and values of the 1917 Revolution" (Adams 2005, 107). Also see Graham 2009, 61.

41. Note Graham's (2009, 13) quotation from a notebook of Sergei Dovlatov: "I call [Anatoli] Naiman and say, 'Tolia, let's go visit Leva Druskin.' 'No way,' he says, 'that guy is so Soviet.' 'What do you mean, Soviet? You're making a mistake.' 'Anti-Soviet, then. What's the difference?'"

42. The jokes were also about the way Lenin anniversaries were packaged and presented by the state (Graham 2003, 44).

43. It is odd, no doubt, that buried within *Jokes and Their Relation to the Unconscious* is a rationale for humorous expression that rests upon a notion of self. Freud paid little attention to the concept of self in his work (Jackson 1984, 108–10).

44. Obrdlik was not merely equating the lifting of mood with the laughter that normally follows a joke. He reported a general increase in good spirits.

45. Contrary to Scott 1990, 19–20. The domination was not so complete, however, as to keep such jokes from being generated in the first place.

46. For example, see Wertheim 1965, 31; Speier 1969, 180; Lukes and Galnoor 1985, xii. When there have been specific references to support the allegation, they usually concern the use of official humor magazines or the establishment of cabarets to damp down dissent (A. Rose 2001–2002, 67). Fitzpatrick (1999, 183) also notes that under Stalin some people believed that the NKVD started rumors because "people liked to hear them." Also see Deriabin and Gibney 1959, 61, 74, 80, 141, 173, 175, 227–28. Graham (2009, 63) mentions a rumor that the KGB conducted experiments in 1970 to see how quickly an anekdot could spread (supposedly throughout a city the size of Moscow within six to eight hours). It is interesting that the *World Upside Down* graphic prints that began to be circulated in the sixteenth century were also regarded as a conspiracy of the dominant class (Scott 1990, 167–68).

47. It would require some independent protocol to assess if those who told jokes were psychologically, and perhaps also socially, different from those who did not.

48. All of the explanations of underground political jokes that have been offered by scholars are formulated as functional explanations. Functions are the effects of social behaviors, and while functions are real and important, their use as explanations is problematic. See Jarvie 1965, 18–34; Cancian 1968, 29–43; and Oring 1976, 67–80. However, as these explanations of political jokes have been framed as individual psychological functions, they can escape the charges of illegitimate

teleology or tautology (Turner and Maryanski 1979, 118–26). The tellers of the jokes, consciously or unconsciously, *mean* to speak surreptitiously or discharge aggressive energies or destabilize the regime from below or elevate their spirits. These are first and foremost intentions, and they are functions only to the extent that these intentions are realized.

49. Perhaps the telling of anecdotes is like Tanya Luhrmann's characterization of prayer (slightly but deliberately misquoted here): "It makes you feel like you are doing something, even if it doesn't help" (Newcott 2015, 46).

CHAPTER 8

1. Alan Dundes (1965, 3) would seem to have done so in *The Study of Folklore*, but as this was an introductory text, he was merely illustrating the kinds of material that constituted folklore. He never did offer a definition of the subject matter, however.

2. In fact, folklore can appear in all of these sites, but it is apart from or grafted onto the official business of the organization.

3. It might be argued that there could be processes that are unique to the Web that generate folklore. However, while there may indeed be unique processes, it is hard to imagine why they would generate anything that should be called *folklore*. If that word is used, it can only be because some analogy with older meanings of the term is recognized. If there are unique processes that generate unique products on the Web, these would necessarily be identified with a unique name.

4. This is not to say that their identity could not be found out (see Oring 2003, 129–40).

5. Humor may be expected from the very beginning, but *how* the humor is achieved is surprising.

6. Eye movements can be tracked to determine the order in which visual jokes are processed so that it can be determined how the humor is apprehended.

7. The viewable list of recipients can change in the course of the forwarding.

8. There are people who forward joke e-mails without having read them. Theoretically it would be possible for a joke to be distributed to hundreds, even thousands, of people without the joke being read.

9. Jokes are undoubtedly told on the telephone and via Web-based platforms that enable voice and visual transmission. The characteristics of joke telling in these situations would more likely resemble oral telling in face-to-face environments, but the research remains to be done.

10. I presume it was, in some early version, "next to the water pitcher."

11. It seems significant that when the errors are extended beyond three examples, they are contained in a *written* list posted on the office door. The older priest does not enumerate the younger priest's errors orally in a face-to-face situation.

12. These are the names of Renaissance artists, but the allusion is to the Teenage Mutant Ninja Turtles popular in comic books, television, and movies in the 1980s and 1990s. This line does not seem to appear on any other website today.

13. It might be thought that these two choices predominate because they are sexual in nature, but that would not explain the fact that "Eat me," which is also sexual, served to end only 2 percent of the examples.

14. Narrative jokes sometimes seem to undergo radical structural change, but this process is neither well documented nor understood.

15. Certain legends circulate in list form (Fine and O'Neill 2010), but humorous lists would seem to far surpass them both in number and popularity.

16. Goody thinks that because lists have a precise beginning and end, they are bounded (Goody 1977, 81), but while lists have a precise beginning, they do not have a precise end. They can always be extended (Belknap 2004, 31; Eco 2009, 15).

17. It is not always completely invisible. In the "Number of the Beast" list in the 2006 e-mail, the forwarder suggested his own contribution to the list: "OSDCLXVI = the new Mac Operating system of the Beast." It was not placed at the end of the list but at the beginning of the forwarded message. It does not seem to have gained any currency, as it does not show up in any Web searches. Both "DCLXVI = the Roman numeral of the Beast" and "Win666 = the operating system of the Beast" do, however.

18. There are many old tales about parsons' sermons (Uther 2011, ATU 1824–1839), and there is a possible precursor in tale 55 in *One Hundred Merry Tales*, published in 1525 (Klaf and Hurwood 1964, 84–86).

19. In Tristan Cafe Pinoy Forums, where it appears on three different pages ("Tristan Cafe" n.d.). It seems to be associated only with this Filipino website. One version is interspersed with little animated emoticons.

20. The grace is, in part, a parody of the nursery rhyme that begins "Rub-a-dub-dub, three men in a tub." A similar and well-known type of grace "Good bread, good meat, good God, let's eat!" ("Grace before Meals" n.d.).

21. It is not just the market that captures folklore for commercial purposes; folklore captures elements of the market for use in jokes and other genres. One example is the enormous number of video clips on YouTube that attach humorous subtitles to Adolf Hitler's rants in the German film *Downfall* (*Der Untergang*). There is even a clip where Hitler rants about the enormous number of parodies that have been posted on YouTube ("Downfall" 2009).

22. I presume the cartoonist hoped that his readers had never seen it before.

23. While all kinds of verbal humor abound in synchronous chat, it would seem that canned jokes are rarely exchanged (Baym 1995; Nilsen and Nilsen 2000, 167).

24. There is no etymological connection between *surf* and *surface*, the latter deriving from the French *sur* + *face*—that is, "on the face of."

25. "Mother" is used not in the sense of ancestor but in the sense that Saddam Hussein used the term to refer to the forthcoming 1991 Gulf War as "the mother of all battles"—that is, the greatest battle of all.

26. Should the exchanges on book discussion websites, for example, be considered folklore because they are "unofficial" or "vernacular"—not taking place in such institutional settings as university classrooms or the corporate offices of a publishing house? Why would a folklorist be interested in these exchanges? The term *vernacular*—dialectically defined—is likely to include almost everything under the sun (Howard 2005, 328–31).

CHAPTER 9

1. Some folklorists seem to regard *any* joke as a narrative, including knock-knock jokes, blonde jokes, and light-bulb jokes, even though they are framed as questions and answers and lack even a situational setup (Thursby 2006, 50–51).

2. E. M. Forster considers a recounting of events in a chronological series a *story*, but a series of consequential events a *plot* (Forster 2005, 87).

3. Consequently, Esar's distinction between the gag and the joke is anything but clear. Should the exchange "'Why do you drink liquor?' 'What do you suggest I do with it?'" be considered a gag and "A guy walks up to a man in a bar and asks, 'Why do you drink liquor?' 'What do you suggest I do with it'" be considered a joke because there is the initial incident of the man walking up and asking that question?

4. Leitch introduces jokes only to illustrate something about the worlds they create (Leitch 1986, 113–14). Nevertheless, he considers them narratives.

5. Leitch at times is ready to call almost anything a story. "'The king died' is a narrative—a news 'story' which, fleshed out merely with a time and proper name would probably hold the interest of the king's subjects for days on end" (Leitch 1986, 24). The fact that newspapers call their products "stories" doesn't necessarily make them narratives. All sorts of things may hold the interest of readers that are not even remotely narratives. People living in California might be interested in earthquake preparedness. A list of recommended preparations published in a newspaper, however, would still be a list, not a narrative. The ersatz joke about the queen stating she would drink dark wine is based on joke #227 in *The Philogelos* (Baldwin 1983, 43).

6. Nevertheless, see "The Story of Asdiwal," although the hero does many things before becoming stuck halfway up a mountain (Lévi-Strauss 1976, 149–52). The conclusion of a modern novel or short story can be very different from that of a folktale. A character might very well be found stuck in some position, having achieved nothing.

7. The appropriateness is spurious, however, because "Yeah, yeah" is not a true grammatical construction but an ironic comment.

8. The text actually begins "A floozy and her floo-zer," but I have changed it to make the text more consistent with the nature of the characters. The jokes in this book were "sanitized" in order to avoid giving offense (R. Edwards 1993, i).

9. Edwards's book has no pages numbers. I have numbered the pages myself.

10. Daniel Barnes (1986) has discussed concealed functions in urban legends and he has related these types of legends to certain kinds of jokes.

11. In operas, the disguise is usually not a gorilla suit. Generally it involves an exchange of clothes—between a master and a servant or a mistress and a maid, as in Mozart's *The Marriage of Figaro*.

12. According to Taylor, a true riddle compares an object to another entirely different object using contradictory elements, one of which must be taken literally and one figuratively for the contradiction to be resolved. The true riddle is to be distinguished from the neck riddle, the conundrum, arithmetical puzzle, and clever question.

13. Note that the exchange between George and his father is a narrative and not merely a conversation. George has *chopped down* a cherry tree. George is *interrogated* by his father about the chopping of the tree. George *confesses* to the act. George *escapes punishment* because of his honesty. There is a chain of events that results in a new situation that marks the conclusion (Bordwell and Thompson 2004, 69).

14. One exception is a version first published by Giraldi Cintio as the third tale of the first decade in his *Ecatommiti* in 1565. The soldier reveals that he ate the cake only in recounting his dream. The two travelers then agree they should divide it equally but find that the cake is missing. They confront the soldier, who justifies his action on the basis of the spiritual worlds that the two travelers visited in their dreams where food and drink were unnecessary. His dream was about his exertions on earth, for which physical sustenance is necessary. The narrative goes on to say that the travelers were angry with the soldier but could not vent their anger because they were weak from not having eaten anything (Baum 1917, 393–95). This text, however, is a comic tale and not a joke ending with a punchline, which is why the narrative continues beyond the soldier's revelation of having eaten the cake.

15. While Baum is sensitive to a variety of differences in the versions of "Dream Bread," he is totally oblivious to the differences in story structure—that is, when the tale audience learns that the bread has been eaten.

16. Baum also summarizes a joke version told by a Romanian Jew, who had recently come to the United Sates, which was used as a parable by Jewish Zionists in Romania. He also cites, but does not reproduce or summarize, a version in a Jewish joke book published in New York in 1906 (Baum 1917, 403–4, 408n1). For Internet texts, see "Red Rider" 2007; "Two Pendejos" 2010; and a narrative song, "Bologna" n.d., based on the tale.

17. There is another joke based on "The Silence Wager." It is a narrative joke, but no element of action is hidden so it is not a *true* narrative joke (Legman 1975, 168).

18. There are 265 numbered texts in *The Philogelos*, but numbers 151, 158, and 175 give different *a* and *b* texts, which gives a total number of 268 texts. Text 42 is incomplete but is completed in text 132 so it is not counted. Texts numbered 128–31, 143, 152, 155–58b, 175b, 252, 257, and 260 duplicate other texts, so sixteen texts are subtracted from the total of 268, to give 252 different texts. Hasan Javadi's English translation of *Resaleh-ye Delgosha* (Zakani 2008, 89–150) contains two sections, "Stories from the Arabic" and "Persian Anecdotes." Together these sections contain 142 texts (Javadi's numbering is slightly off; he numbers only 140 but he uses some numbers twice). More texts have been attributed to Zakani, but they do not exist in an English translation. *A Hundred Merry Tales*, edited by Franklin S. Klaf and Bernhardt J. Hurwood, presents only eighty-five texts; fifteen fewer than published by Paul Zall (1963, 64–150). There are eighteen texts in Zall that are not found in Klaf and Hurwood, and three texts in Klaf and Hurwood that are not found in Zall. Sixteen of the eighteen texts in Zall end in direct discourse, and eleven are narratives, but none of these narratives contain a hidden narrative function. *The American Joe Miller* contains 671 texts and is meant to be an example of jokes from the mid-nineteenth century. While there are many texts that would qualify as jokes—usually dialogic—there are also examples of humorous poetry; extracts from American comic writers such as Sam Slick and Artemus Ward; news items, advertisements, misprints, and announcements from newspapers; and anecdotes about Abraham Lincoln or officers and soldiers in the Union military. There are even a few items that are not humorous and were not meant to be. I was unfamiliar with the book before using it for this project. I also chose *The Bathroom Joke Book* (R. Edwards 1993), published in the United States, because it provided several hundred joke examples, and I had not previously read it. Despite its title, it is a book of "clean" jokes and in many cases the editor has modified texts in order not to give offense (for example, ethnic and blonde jokes are attributed to "Joke Book Publishers"). The jokes and even the pages in this book are unnumbered. I numbered them all; however, on a very few occasions I numbered texts that were not meant to be jokes. In a few instances I skipped some "boxed" texts that were meant to be humorous. The texts that I numbered came to 306. But I eliminated 122 jokes from the analysis as they were chains of one-liners, riddles, joke lists, puzzles, and whatnot. Not all jokes of these types were removed from the final set, only those that the editor seems to have included as a group.

19. Eric Eliason claims that J. Golden Kimball anecdotes show J. Golden to be a "man of words" and thus a "performer-hero" rather than a doer of deeds characteristic of the hero of tradition. In fact, the characters in most jokes and anecdotes are men of words or "performer-heroes" (Eliason 2007, 31–34).

20. It is not clear to me why Baum (1917) did not include it in his survey of the tale. Perhaps he did not have access to a translation that included it.

21. This analysis is only a first approximation. I have conveniently skipped over a number of crucial problems that are essential to such discussion but could not be entered into here. The first concerns the translation of the texts in the collections I have examined. I do not read Greek, Persian, or Chinese. Consequently, I am not certain whether the translators of the texts may have made accommodations for what they perceived as the sensibilities of modern English readers.

The second problem concerns what constitutes the chain of events necessary to classify a joke as a narrative. For example, consider the following joke. "How long have you been working here? Ever since they threatened to fire me" (R. Edwards 1993, 19). This might be considered a verbal exchange and not a narrative joke. But the setup is clearly open to elaboration. "A new worker at a corporation meets another worker at the water cooler. He asks questions about the company, the character of their supervisor, the schedule of pay raises, vacation, and medical benefits, to which he receives short but informative answers. The other worker seems eager to go back to his workstation. As he is leaving, the new worker says, 'One last question. How long have you been working here?' The guy looks back over his shoulder and says, 'Ever since they threatened to fire me.'" Is this more of a narrative than the previous example? Finally, "Walter has been on the job only two weeks at Steele Corporation. He has spent much of his time in his office surfing the Web and playing computer games. Finally, his supervisor calls him in and chews him out for failing to follow up those accounts that were more than thirty days overdue as he was instructed. He goes back to his office and, feeling particularly miserable, goes to the water cooler and pops a Valium to help him relax. Just then another worker comes up to get a cup of water. Walter introduces himself and finds out the other guy is named Paul. He asks Paul how long he has been working at Steele. Paul says, "'Ever since they threatened to fire me.'" Clearly, there is a greater chain of consequential events in this third example than in the first, but ultimately the point of the joke and the humor in it are the same. Indeed, some of the texts that I classified as narratives have fairly weak narrative lines.

The third problem that should be considered is what constitutes the final line in a humorous text. In some early texts, the humorous story is followed by an apothegm, a discussion of a moral principle tacked on and supposedly relevant to the narrative. But the humor in the text may be some distance away from the close of the apothegm. Should the final line of the apothegm be considered the final line, or should only the last line that provokes humor be considered the final line? After a humorous comic statement by a joke character, a text might conclude, "And so-and-so was convulsed with laughter" (e.g., Kowallis 1986, 30). Clearly, this last line does not produce humor but explicitly acknowledges the humor engendered by the preceding line. Which should be considered the final line in the humorous text? Should the final line be categorized as direct discourse because it is the final comic line, or as a descriptive statement because it is, in fact, the very last line of the text?

CHAPTER 10

1. In 1893, for example, Rabbi Hermann Adler commented on the aggressive nature of some Jewish humor and noted its contribution to the survival of an oppressed people (Adler 1893, 458, 464). His essay, however, was in large measure meant to counter Ernest Renan's and Thomas Carlyle's observations that the Jews lacked humor, and intended to show that the Jews had, in fact, evidenced a humorous spirit for millennia.

2. Irving Howe, in his discussion of Jewish humor, notes that Yiddish was brought to Poland by refugees from the Crusades in Germany. He does not suggest, however, that they brought their humor with them (Howe 1987, 18).

3. And indeed, there has been something of a cottage industry in identifying and analyzing instances of humor in the Bible, Talmud, and Midrash (e.g., Isbell 2011; Brodsky 2011; Diamond 2011; Friedman and Friedman 2014).

4. "'Why do you Jews answer a question with another question?' a Gentile asks. 'Why should we not answer with a question?' the Jew replies" (Reik 1962, 117). Chaim Bermant sees this joke as already prefigured in Cain's response to God's question concerning the whereabouts of his brother Abel (Bermant 1986, 6). Interestingly, this characteristic—indeed, this particular joke—is attributed to a Yankee in an American joke book published in 1865 (Kempt 1865, 32). I would be interested to know whether there is an earlier Jewish example in print. There are a couple of other jokes in this collection that parallel and perhaps antedate well-known Jewish jokes (see 71–72, 144).

5. Also overlooked is that Jewish jokes are unevenly distributed in Freud's work (Oring 2003, 122–24). They were employed only in his discussion of the joke (der Witz). Jewish examples are singularly absent in his later discussions of the comic (das Komische) and of humor (Humor).

6. Classical Latin was also written without punctuation and even without spaces between words. Did this have an effect on Roman humor or later Italian humor? Arab and Persian humor

also had to deal with the problem of vocalization of written texts and employed some of the same hermeneutic principles that were characteristic of rabbinical interpretation. Where does their humor stand in the scheme of things?

7. During a gigantic celebration in Red Square, after Trotsky had been exiled, Stalin, on Lenin's great tomb, excitedly raised his hand to still the acclamations: "Comrades! A most historic event! A cablegram—of congratulations—from Trotsky!" The hordes cheered, and Stalin read the historic cable aloud:

STALIN,
　YOU WERE RIGHT AND I WAS WRONG. YOU ARE THE TRUE HEIR OF
LENIN. I SHOULD APOLOGIZE.
　TROTSKY

A roar of triumph erupted. But in the front row, a little tailor called, "Pst, Comrade Stalin. A message for the ages! But you didn't read it with the right feeling!"

Whereupon, Stalin stilled the throng once more. "Comrades! Here is a simple worker, a loyal communist, who says I haven't read the message with enough feeling. Come, Comrade, read the historic communication!"

The little tailor went up to the podium, took the telegram, and read:

"Stalin, *you* were right, and *I* was wrong? *You* are the true heir of Lenin?! *I* should apologize?! Trotsky!" (Brodsky 2011, 16–17)

8. I have casually made a similar observation (Oring 2005–2006, 107).

9. Freud certainly used jokes this way. See, for example, the appendix in Oring (2003, 147–62).

10. It is worth noting that Saphir does not seem to distinguish between *Witz* and *Humor*, as others do; he uses the terms interchangeably (e.g., Chase 2000, 238).

11. Ludwig Börne, writing in 1807 about his visit to the ghetto in Frankfurt am Main—from which he had escaped—characterizes the conversations of the Jews as "overflowing with sophisticated witticisms and witty sophistications" (quoted in Chase 2000, 244).

12. Chase does not state when the term and the notion of *Judenwitz* first became current, but the distinction of *Humor* as something apart in German *Kultur* was registered in Jean Paul Richter's *Die Vorschule der Aesthetik* (The School for Aesthetics), first published in 1804 and substantially expanded in 1813. For Richter, the ordinary mocker is distanced from the traits that he derides. "He is narrowly and selfishly aware of his own superiority." True humor, however, "recognizes no individual foolishness, no fools, but only folly and a mad world" (Richter 1973, 88). Humor is tolerant of individual follies because of the humorist's sense of kinship with humanity (91). Richter's distinction, it must be noted, invokes no racial discourse. Jews are not mentioned in his work at all.

In 1758, Moses Mendelssohn contrasted "ordinary, caviling wit" that "is more blinding than illuminating" with "higher forms of wit" that are "beautiful, noble, and important" (Mendelssohn 1997, 219). This does not seem to be a distinction made by Mendelssohn's idol, the third Earl of Shaftesbury, some half century before (112). Shaftesbury seemed more open to "raillery" of all types, which increases the pleasantness of conversation and promotes sociability on the one hand, and serves as a touchstone of truth on the other (Shaftesbury 1963, 1:49, 54). Shaftesbury admits that there can be a "gross sort of raillery that is offensive in good company," but he is confident that such forms will be recognized for what they are (1:45). Moreover, Shaftesbury does not seem to distinguish between "wit," "ridicule," "raillery," and "humor." He employs all the terms fairly equally. That humor is something special and superior is a distinction made in German letters.

Wit and *humor* are often interchangeable terms in England in the late seventeenth and early eighteenth centuries. The distinction becomes more important in the late eighteenth century. Wit is associated with the aristocracy and emphasizes verbal expertise. Wit was artificial, intellectual, and less grounded in reality. Humor was more bourgeois and emphasized benevolence and universality. It promotes a tolerant view. Wit is antipathetic, while humor is sympathetic (Wickberg 1998, 57–64). In the United States in the late nineteenth and early twentieth century, women, like the Jews in Germany, were held to lack a sense of humor. Humor was often considered a strictly masculine trait (91–98).

13. It was printed in Elberfeld, since 1929 merged into Wuppertal.

14. Why is this not a matter of common knowledge in Jewish studies?

15. In his autobiography, published in 1793, Solomon Maimon reports that after becoming adept in the Zohar, he attempted to master, with the aid of a teacher, the *kabbalah ma'asit* (practical kabbalah). He eagerly learned to make himself invisible so that he "might practice some wanton on . . . [his] comrades." In preparation, Maimon fasted for three days and uttered prayers, but when he finally went to the *beis hamedresh* (house of study) and gave his friend a box on the ears, he was astounded when he was immediately given one in return (Maimon 1888, 100–102). Maimon does not relate this as an amusing anecdote; he recounts it to explain his loss of confidence in kabbalah and ultimately in Jewish learning in general.

16. Hirsz Abramowicz does mention the use of such humor, but his memoir, although it is set in the period before World War I, was composed in the New World around 1925. Interestingly, most of his examples focus on the ignorance of rural Jews in the jokes of the townsfolk (Abramowicz 1999, 59, 64–65, 68–69, 83).

17. The collection of Anglo-American balladry was less connected with expressions of national identity than with matters of antiquity.

18. Druyanow discovered the importance of jokes when he was sick near Dresden and picked up the book *Der Yidishe Humorist: Yidishe Vitsen un Anekdoten,* published by M. Krinski in Warsaw in 1908 (Bar-Itzhak 2010, 116). B. Rohatyn, who ignored Jewish jokes in his collection of folklore, was also brought to their consideration when he saw how they might alleviate Jewish suffering (Rohatyn 1911, 122).

19. Richard Raskin contends that the very best Jewish jokes can be understood in multiple ways (Raskin 1992, 183). I think Raskin is wrong on this count, but more to the point, the aesthetic preferences of an analyst are a very uncertain standard for measuring the qualities of jokes.

20. It need not necessarily be compared only with other ethnic or national groups. Perhaps some geographical, occupational, religious, or other group will prove to have a high number of self-critical jokes or employ logics similar to those that are said to exist in Jewish joke repertoires.

21. Even when comparative statistical studies are attempted, the definitions of the terms under discussion are not always clear. Juni, Katz, and Hamburger (1996) attempt such a study, but they leave the question of whether a joke is self-critical or outwardly aggressive to the raters of the sample jokes. They identify other problems in categorizing jokes as well.

22. There may be numerous jokes that appear in joke books that never circulate orally.

23. Whether Büschenthal was correct in his assessment is an entirely different matter.

24. Moses Mendelssohn, writing in Berlin, is often considered to be the "father" of the Haskalah movement, although there were individuals before him who promoted secular studies and argued for the integration of Jews into civil society (C. Roth 1972, 7:1433–34).

25. Heda Jason pointed out long ago that the societal conditions of Jews in eastern Europe, western Europe, and the United States were very different, and that studies of the Jewish joke never explore these differences (Jason 1967, 53–54).

26. There have been studies of the effects of humor on stress. These, of course, have been of laboratory-induced mild stresses, and the positive effects of humor—when they are shown to exist at all—are short-lived. In other words, the experimental data is highly equivocal (R. Martin 2006, 269–307). See chapter 7 of this book on the evaluation of functional hypotheses to explain political joking.

27. And what is that relationship? Jewish jokes register deformities in Jewish character as a result of oppression; they serve as a means of defense and retaliation; and they offer consolation. In other words, the jokes are seen as pathological, defensive, or transcendent (Oring 1992, 118–19).

28. Bascom (1954, 336) actually was more interested in cultural context than social context. Dundes, who advocated attention to social context and made his students describe that context in their fieldwork, never made use of it in his own interpretations.

29. Yigal Zan's article on this subject was a contribution to the debate on text and context that appeared in the pages of *Western Folklore* in 1979 and 1980 (S. Jones 1979a, 1979b; Ben-Amos 1979; Georges 1980). Zan's article seems the most astute and carefully argued, but it is rarely cited and never engaged. Also see Kenneth Ketner (1973) on hypotheses in folklore.

30. The compilations of jokes about Jews by Gentiles are not irrelevant to this hypothesis. The self-image of the Jews was crafted in part from how Jews believed others saw them. It may be that Jewish jokes reacted against Gentile images of Jews in jokelore, accepted Gentile images of Jews in jokelore, or domesticated Gentile images of Jews in jokelore. The matter needs to be sorted out, but to date it does not seem that there has been a rigorous and comprehensive study of the tales and jokes that circulated in Gentile society about the Jews.

31. Some may recognize in this formulation a relation to Clifford Geertz's (1973, 90) definition of religion.

32. The Pew survey of American Jews asked what it means to be Jewish: 74 percent said remembering the Holocaust; 56 percent said working for justice and equality; 43 percent said caring about Israel; *42 percent said having a good sense of humor*; and 19 percent said observing Jewish law (Heilman 2013; my emphasis).

CHAPTER 11

1. *Humor* is a late term for that which provokes laughter. See Wickberg 1998, 13–45 for a discussion of how the term developed. For a review of the philosophical commentary on humor, see Morreall 1987, 10–126.

2. Nevertheless, entries for "humor" are absent in encyclopedias of ethics (Chadwick 1998; Becker and Becker 2001; J. Roth 2005).

3. Carroll (1991, 294) made these claims long before he wrote his chapter, and Berys Gaut (1998, 64) quotes them favorably. Although I don't agree with him, Richard Raskin felt that it was precisely jokes open to multiple interpretations that were the "classics" (Raskin 1992, 26–32). See chapter 2 in this volume on complexity in the analysis of jokes.

4. Carroll claims to remain an agnostic on this issue (Carroll 1994, 9, 14).

5. This, of course, begs the question of how those antecedents—or their antecedents—came to have the status of art.

6. The question of whether the account is truthful seems beside the point (Bailey 2000, 169). The historical account need only appear truthful. I think it would be better to speak of Carroll's theory as a rhetorical theory of art. It is about arguments, not history. Historical references are simply the tropes of this rhetoric.

7. I would also suggest that it is wrong.

8. Unless one allows that there is one theory of art for the avant-garde and another for everything else.

9. Nevertheless, if some jokes are art, why cannot the remainder become art by constructing narratives about their formal and stylistic similarities?

10. My definition of art, as I give it in chapter 12 below, is "the apprehension of extraordinary arrangements of words, gestures, sounds, colors, forms, textures, or ideas in relation to some ordinary, unmarked background." Ultimately, what is apprehended depends upon what individuals

find remarkable—even if only briefly. Consequently, my definition depends not on the object, the intention of a creator, or institutional framing. The definition is a subjective one. Art *is* in the eye of the beholder.

11. In fact, this approach has been taken by both Ted Cohen (1983) and John Morreall (1981). Cohen, however, focuses on other issues: the resemblance of jokes to logical arguments—an interesting but tangential matter in aesthetic discussion—and the ethics of joking. Morreall is focused on the play and imagination necessary for the creation and appreciation of humor and their role in child education.

12. There are scholarly narratives (e.g., Baum 1917; Brown 1922) that link contemporary jokes to the tales found in literary collections of the past: those of Petrus Alphonsi, Geoffrey Chaucer, Poggio Bracciolini, Gianfrancesco Straparola, Giambattista Basile, Giovanni Boccaccio, and medieval Arab and Persian authors.

13. I have not found a photo of this sign on the Internet, and it has been attributed to locations other than Nairobi. These signs become joke traditions, and it is difficult to know whether they are based on real signs. Of course, unintended humorous signs exist nevertheless.

14. Freud intended his account of the event to be humorous. In fact, the account has the form of a joke. But such a story might be told without any humorous intention whatsoever. For example, someone might offer the account of the children's theatrical without recognizing its humorous dimension. The event would be intentionally artifactualized as a narrative but not as a joke.

15. This has also been characterized as "bisociation" (Koestler 1964, 35), "incongruity resolution" (Suls 1972, 84), and "script overlap" (V. Raskin 1985b, 100), although there are differences between these formulations.

16. This is why Victor Raskin (1985b) can write a book titled *Semantic Mechanisms of Humor*.

17. The cognitive aspect of the joke that I am speaking of is its puzzle-solving aspect. A joke may also make observations and register truths about the world that are a consequence of solving the puzzle. For some discussion of the propositions conveyed by jokes, see Oring 2003, 27–40.

18. Joke tellers are aware of aspects of their performances and can analyze and criticize them in theoretical terms. See chapter 12.

19. These different properties are often collapsed—inappropriately, I believe—into the term *comic timing*.

20. Whether incongruity is first perceived and then appropriateness is recognized, or an appropriate idea or behavior is suddenly recognized to be incongruous depends on the individual joke (Oring 2003, 2–3).

21. There is an interesting example of a cartoon that some viewers regard as a joke and others as a puzzle (Morreall 1987, 198). It seems to depend on whether one assumes the point of view of a character in the cartoon or whether one switches between that character's perspective and one's own.

22. In the Netherlands, the joke genre is generally held in low esteem in educated classes (Kuipers 2006, 47–50).

23. Nevertheless, when one thinks about the narratives that would be proposed to confer art status on some object, it is difficult to imagine that criteria of value would be absent. Value would likely be at the basis of any historical argument. Art would be determined by value de facto if not de jure.

24. The *baptism, christening,* and *consecration* of objects as art show up in philosophical discussion as well.

25. References to paintings by Renoir or symphonies by Mozart abound. Cigarette advertisements (Eaton 2000, 150), detective stories (Collingwood 1938, 86; Beardsley 1982, 26), or photojournalism (Tolhurst 1984, 266) are deeply suspect. Carroll (1994, 36) considers the tap dancing of Honey Coles to be art, but on what basis can he make this suggestion other than his own response

to the qualities of the dancing? True, Carroll admits, it would require some art-historical background to create the necessary narratives to classify it as art, but what impels the creation of such narratives? It would seem to result from a positive evaluation of the experience.

26. Weitz maintains that aesthetic theories are about value (Weitz 1956, 35), as does J. Anderson (2000, 81).

27. Sometimes this is purely situational. No one is likely to grasp every joke every time (see Larson 1989, 155–57). Yet some people seem to lack an aptitude for jokes. A very intelligent and talented colleague of mine admits weakness when it comes to both telling jokes and understanding them.

28. This is not to say that the understanding and appreciation of a joke never depend on the contexts in which the joke occurs. It means only that the joke can be abstracted from its context and never constitutes the whole of one's experience in a particular time and place.

29. Dickie (1974, 47) believes originality is necessary for something to be art. I do not see why. Only in certain cases would it even be possible to determine whether something were original.

30. I presume that there is also a competitive aspect to artistic exhibition, although I don't know if competitive aspects are much of a focus in critical or philosophical discussion.

31. A possible exception is when someone deliberately tells a joke poorly in order to demonstrate that he is not a good joke teller in order to escape the social obligation to perform in the future. The teller thereby steps out of the social spotlight to permit someone else to be the center of attention.

32. Even a painting that was used to cover a hole in a wall would have to be judged preferable to the appearance of the hole.

33. It would demand "sympathetic attention" (N. Carroll 2000a, 195).

34. This distance is not a special aesthetic attitude. It is the distance necessary for attending to the joke (Dickie 1974, 108–9).

35. It may even cause audience members to disengage socially and remove themselves physically from the scene without staying long enough to hear the joke.

36. This has been challenged by Marshall Cohen (1977, 489–90) and others.

37. For example, see Freud's (1960, 8:113) and Cohen's (1983, 125–26) discussions of particular Jewish jokes. In each case a new layer is added to the joke. Those layers, however, resonate only for those who are aware of them when the joke is first told. The layer is optional in understanding a joke, and it would not seem to heighten the joke's humorous effect post-factum.

38. Having analyzed jokes with this particular aim in mind, I can say that my appreciation of the jokes was irrelevant to the task. I attended to details of content, structure, mechanism, and message without caring, or sometimes even noticing, whether the joke was a good one. One joke was as good as another (Oring 1984).

39. It is not entirely clear that there is an avant-garde in art either (Horowitz 2003, 748).

40. I remember telling the joke "Q: Why is there only one Eiffel Tower? A: Because it eats its young" to a person who did not get it and who was sure that it was some kind of trick to get the hearer to laugh at utter nonsense. For a discussion of this joke, see Oring 2003, 20. Freud also believed that absurd jokes were "idiocy masquerading as a joke" (Freud 1960, 8:138–39), but I think he was wrong (Oring 2003, 17–18, 168n26).

41. That is why Freud thought that any inhibitions associated with such images or ideas are made superfluous by the joke, and the energy employed in maintaining those inhibitions is discharged as laughter (Freud 1960, 8:103, 148).

42. This is different from the response "That's not funny!" which recognizes the existence of a joke without acknowledging any feeling of amusement.

43. It was in this sense that Freud distinguished between the thought of a joke and the envelope within which the thought was expressed. For Freud, the envelope allowed the expression of thoughts that would otherwise have remained inaccessible (Freud 1960:103), but it is not necessary to agree with Freud on this point.

44. There are exceptions to this notion (Oring 1992, 56).

45. In competitive situations, a performer may have to address repeated challenges about the joke's novelty (Sacks 1974, 337–44).

46. Amusement and laughter can be suppressed. They can be feigned for the benefit of others. But it does not seem as though one can generate amusement and amusement-based laughter without an awareness of something that is actually perceived to be humorous.

47. The experiences of beauty or sublimity are named not for the experiences but for qualities of the objects that supposedly arouse these experiences. Amusement, however, is not a property of the object.

48. The term *amusement* has a number of meanings. I am not referring to the kind of amusement suggested by "amusement park," which suggests diversion and enjoyment. This latter type of amusement correlates with "fun." The amusement I am speaking of correlates with "funny." "Funny" is a kind of fun, but "fun" is not a kind of funny.

49. Even though there would seem to be no etymological connection between the words.

50. Collingwood is at least willing to call both species of "art," although he considers amusement art to be false art (Collingwood 1938, 105).

51. Amusement is a "cognitive emotion." Israel Scheffler regards the "joy of verification" and "surprise" as more basic cognitive emotions than amusement, however. In fact, he sees surprise as contributing to amusement (Scheffler 1991, 11). Although jokes depend upon surprise, a good deal of humor does not. Nevertheless, the joy of verification and surprise both play a part in jokes: surprise in the initial incongruity and joy in finding appropriate connections. Joy, however, may result from any number of causes, and surprise is not always, or even usually, amusing (or even pleasurable). Also, when a joke is successful, amusement affects us like a "stroke of an apoplexy," contrary to what Pouivet suggests is characteristic of cognitive emotions (Pouivet 2000, 52).

52. I am not sure I accept this last proposition. I would think that anything designated *art* would at the very least demand that we make an effort to engage it aesthetically. One would be predisposed to attend to its form, textures, and meanings. In doing so, it would become an aesthetic object.

53. Actually, Dickie is willing to acknowledge the existences of *artworlds*, such that the artworld "is the totality of all artworld systems" (Dickie 2000, 96). So, theoretically, it would be possible to have a five-string-banjo-music artworld, a joke artworld, and an avant-garde artworld. But these artworlds would remain isolated and not merged into any total system. Who would be in a position to unite these worlds? That is why jokes remain in their own jokeworld and are not considered art.

54. Davies criticizes Dickie for not attending more to the structure of the institution that bestows art status, "though his aim is neither that of a social anthropologist or historian" (S. Davies 1991, 94–95).

55. Paradoxically, identifying art in terms of historical narratives would seem to cut art off from history. *Beauty, sublimity,* and *truth* are terms with which the philosophy of art developed. These are aesthetic terms. How does one argue for a theory of art that cuts itself off from connections to that past in the name of historical narration?

CHAPTER 12

1. See, for example, Morreall 1981; M. Martin 1987; T. Cohen 1983, 1998; Gaut 1998; and N. Carroll 2003. While these concerns have also been of interest to scholars in other disciplines, they have not been generally conceptualized as aesthetic issues.

2. This view would be close to the notion of art as "significant form" (Bell 1958, 19), but it does not presume that the aesthetic experience is purely a formal one. Form is what characterizes some-

thing as art. It is what provokes aesthetic attention. The aesthetic experience, however, depends upon the interrelation of form and content and their resonances for the individual—including purely subjective factors. The parts, the ideas and values connoted by the parts, their emotional valences, and their organization mutually influence one another and bear upon this experience. The experience is a synthetic one (Beardsley 1958, 527–28).

3. I have no problem with the notion that performers' audiences may on occasion consist only of themselves, as when magicians, mimes, or dancers practice routines alone in front of a mirror.

4. Folk aesthetics deals with the principles that govern aesthetic expression and reception in particular social or cultural groups. I use the term here to refer to any native aesthetic, even if ascribed only to a single individual. See M. Jones 1971.

5. This was the creation of an "induced natural context" (Goldstein 1967).

6. This is different from the kinds of evaluations that, for example, Michael Owen Jones (1971, 96–99) heard from the chair makers he studied in Kentucky or that Kenneth S. Goldstein (1991) was able to elicit from his Anglo-American informants over a period of some forty years.

7. This conforms, it would seem, with Axel Olrik's (1965, 135) "Law of Contrast" for characters in a folk narrative.

8. We might refer to this as *comic embedding*, the embedding of humorous images and phrases in a joke that are not essential to the success of the punchline.

9. "Bubba" is a southern nickname derived from the word "brother" that is generally applied to elder brothers. It is often attached to large men of intimidating mien (see "Bubba" n.d.). Often a white—indeed "redneck"—sobriquet (Jenkins 1993), it is also applied to and used by blacks: William "Bubba" Paris, Charles Richard "Bubba" Wells, Daniel Lamont "Bubba" Franks, and Richard Stephen "Bubba" Crosby. It is also the name of Forrest Gump's black friend—Benjamin Buford "Bubba" Blue—in the 1994 film *Forrest Gump*.

10. Actually, "Aryan" was a recognized term for a racial category in the nineteenth century. The term was originally a linguistic term. Later it became conflated with biology. Max Müller may have been the first to speak of an Aryan "race," but he meant a group of people rather than a biologically distinct line. It was employed as part of racial superiority theories before World War I, notably in the works of Houston Stewart Chamberlain. It was most frequently contrasted with "Semite." The politicization of these racial distinctions during the Nazi period gave the term a greater association with World War II ("Aryan Race" n.d.).

11. Diane had said that she used this joke to open her workshops on stress management. She characterized it as a "stress joke," and she would tell her audiences that she hoped their levels of stress did not require a change of costume. Daniel claimed never to have heard Diane tell this joke before. He was surprised that she knew it. He had learned his version many years before and was surprised that he had never told it to Diane.

12. Although I have no reason to believe that the differences between Daniel and Diane are attributable to their genders, it has been remarked that the styles of male and female comedians in Tubetube in Milne Bay Province, Papua New Guinea, seem to turn on just such differences (Macintyre 1992, 142).

13. I have not subjected either Daniel or Diane to any standardized personality assessment protocols. The differences I note are based on my own long-term personal observations. For an example of such protocols in the analysis of jokes, see Burns with Burns 1976.

14. For another comparative assessment of joke performance that seems to depend on a difference in the personalities of the joke tellers, see Bronner 1984.

15. I do not understand why art demands "contemplation"—a position that even Henry Glassie (1989, 86) would seem to endorse. The contemplative response seems to limit art to the domain of Western fine arts and the museum and gallery experience. That is why Robert Plant Armstrong (1971) tried to replace the term *art* with *affecting presences*.

16. Richard Raskin holds that some jokes are open to multiple interpretations. He also believes such jokes to be aesthetically superior to "closed" jokes, but there is no reason to accept his view on this point (Raskin 1992, 25, 30–32). Carroll also recognizes the possibility of multiple interpretations of jokes (Carroll 2003, 359).

AFTERWORD

1. Here we are not all that far from Chomsky's "Colorless green ideas sleep furiously."

2. Pediatrics ranks among the worst-compensated medical subspecialities ("Medscape Physician Compensation Report" 2015, 3).

3. Googling "History of the Joke" produces no work by this name or on this topic other than a DVD of a television show produced for the History Channel hosted by Lewis Black in which the comedian interviews other comedians about their favorite jokes and how they got into comedy (Black 2008). History scarcely enters into it. Despite its title, Albert Rapp's (1951) *The Origins of Wit and Humor* is not a history but a survey of forms and techniques with entertaining joke examples. Jim Holt's (2008) *Stop Me If You've Heard This: A History and Philosophy of Jokes* recognizes the problem of an absence of history, but he does not contribute much to its solution. His history is far too casual, familiar, and sketchy to be of substantive value.

Works Cited

"666A The Tenant of the Beast." n.d. Accessed 3 February 2011. http://tenantofthebeast.tumblr.com /post/671443190/han-solo-p-i.

"668 Neighbor of the Beast [album]." n.d. Accessed 3 February 2011. http://www.swapacd.com /Travis-Shredd-The-Good-Ol-668-Neighbor-Beast/cd/13178694/.

"668 Neighbor of the Beast [beer]." n.d. Accessed 3 February 2011. http://www.craftcans.com/668 -neighbor-of-the-beast-new-england-brewing-company.

"668 Neighbor of the Beast [lyric]." n.d. Accessed 3 February 2011. http://www.travisshredd.com/cz /Band/668.htm.

Abrahams, Roger D., and Alan Dundes. 1969. "On Elephantasy and Elephanticide." *Psychoanalytic Review* 56 (2): 225–41.

Abramowicz, Hirsz. 1999. *Profiles of a Lost World: Memoirs of East European Jewish Life before World War II*, ed. Dina Abramowicz and Jeffrey Shandler. Trans. Eva Zeitlin Dobkin. Detroit: Wayne State University Press.

Abrams, Jessica R., and Amy M. Bippus. 2011. "An Intergroup Investigation of Disparaging Humor." *Journal of Language and Social Psychology* 30 (2): 193–201.

Abrams, Jessica R., and Amy M. Bippus. 2014. "Gendering Jokes: Intergroup Bias in Reactions to Same- Versus Opposite-Gender Humor." *Journal of Language and Social Psychology* 33 (6): 692–702. http://dx.doi.org/10.1177/0261927X14544963.

Adams, Bruce. 2005. *Tiny Revolutions in Russia: Twentieth-Century Soviet and Russian History in Anecdotes*. New York: RoutledgeCurzon.

ADL. 2006. "Statement on the Comedy of Sacha Baron Cohen a.k.a. 'Borat.'" Accessed 2 July 2014. http://archive.adl.org/presrele/mise_00/4898_00.html#.VXjfB0aWM-Y.

Adler, Hermann. 1893. "Jewish Wit and Humour." *Nineteenth Century* 33:457–69.

Allport, Gordon M. 1958. *The Nature of Prejudice*. Abr. ed. Garden City, NY: Doubleday Anchor.

Alperson, Philip. 2003. "Creativity in the Arts." In *The Oxford Handbook of Aesthetics*, ed. Jerrold Levinson, 245–57. Oxford: Oxford University Press.

Alter, Robert. 1987. "Jewish Humor and the Domestication of Myth." In *Jewish Wry: Essays on Jewish Humor*, ed. Sarah Blacher Cohen, 25–36. Detroit: Wayne State University Press.

Altman, Sig. 1971. *The Comic Image of the Jew: Explorations of a Pop Culture Phenomenon*. Rutherford, NJ: Farleigh Dickinson Press.

Amis, Martin. 2002. *Koba the Dread: Laughter and the Twenty Million*. New York: Vintage.

Anderson, Brian, and Bill Furlow. 2006. *The Titanic Joke Book*. Seabrook, TX: Towers.

Anderson, James C. 2000. "Aesthetic Concepts of Art." In *Theories of Art Today*, ed. Noël Carroll, 65–92. Madison: University of Wisconsin Press.

Anderson, Walter. 1923. *Kaiser und Abt: Die Geschichte des Eines Schwank. Folklore Fellows Communication No. 42*. Helsinki: Suomalainen Tiediekatemia.

Applebaum, Annie. 2003. *Gulag: A History*. New York: Doubleday.

Apter, Michael J. 1982. *The Experience of Motivation: The Theory of Psychological Reversals*. London: Academic Press.

Aristotle. 1970. *Poetics*. Trans. Gerald F. Else. Ann Arbor: University of Michigan Press.

Armstrong, Robert Plant. 1971. *The Affecting Presence: An Essay in Humanistic Anthropology*. Urbana: University of Illinois Press.

"Aryan Race." n.d. *Wikipedia*. Accessed 22 June 2015. https://en.wikipedia.org/wiki/Aryan_race.

Athenaeus. 1959. *The Deipnosophists*. Vol. 6. Trans. Charles Burton Gulick. Cambridge, MA: Harvard University Press.

Attardo, Salvatore. 1997. "The Semantic Foundations of Cognitive Theories of Humor." *Humor: International Journal of Humor Research* 10 (4): 395–420. http://dx.doi.org/10.1515/humr .1997.10.4.395.

Attardo, Salvatore. 2001. *Humorous Texts: A Semantic and Pragmatic Analysis*. Berlin: Mouton de Gruyter. http://dx.doi.org/10.1515/9783110887969.

Attardo, Salvatore. 2006. "Cognitive Linguistics and Humor." *Humor: International Journal of Humor Research* 19 (3): 341–62. http://dx.doi.org/10.1515/HUMOR.2006.017.

Attardo, Salvatore. 2007. "Humorous Metaphors." Paper presented at the Tenth Conference of International Linguistics, 19 July, Kraków, Poland.

Attardo, Salvatore, Christian F. Hempelmann, and Sara Di Maio. 2002. "Script Oppositions and Logical Mechanisms: Modeling Incongruities and Their Resolutions." *Humor: International Journal of Humor Research* 15 (1): 3–46. http://dx.doi.org/10.1515/humr.2002.004.

Attardo, Salvatore, and Victor Raskin. 1991. "Script Theory Revis(it)ed: Joke Similarity and Joke Representation Model." *Humor: International Journal of Humor Research* 4 (3/4): 293–347.

Ausubel, Nathan, ed. 1948. *A Treasury of Jewish Folklore*. New York: Crown.

Bailey, George W. S. 2000. "Art: Life after Death?" In *Theories of Art Today*, ed. Noël Carroll, 160–74. Madison: University of Wisconsin Press.

Baker, Ronald L. 1986. *Jokelore: Humorous Tales from Indiana*. Bloomington: Indiana University Press.

Bakhtin, Mikhail. 1984. *Rabelais and His World*. Bloomington: Indiana University Press.

Bal, Mieke. 1985. *Narratology: Introduction to the Theory of Narrative*. Trans. Christine van Boheemen. Toronto: University of Toronto Press.

Baldwin, Barry. 1983. *The Philogelos or Laughter-Lover*. Amsterdam: J. C. Gieben.

Banc, C. [pseud.], and A. Dundes. 1989. *First Prize: Fifteen Years! An Annotated Collection of Romanian Political Jokes*. Rutherford, NJ: Fairleigh Dickinson University Press.

Bar-Itzhak, Haya. 2010. *Pioneers of Jewish Ethnography and Folkloristics in Eastern Europe*. Ljubljana: Scientific Research Center of the Slovenian Academy of Sciences and Arts.

Barnes, Daniel. 1986. "Interpreting Urban Legends." *Arv: Scandinavian Yearbook of Folklore* 40:67–78.

Barrick, Mac E. 1974. "The Newspaper Riddle Joke." *Journal of American Folklore* 87 (345): 253–57. http://dx.doi.org/10.2307/538740.

Bascom, William R. 1954. "Four Functions of Folklore." *Journal of American Folklore* 67 (266): 333–49. http://dx.doi.org/10.2307/536411.

Bascom, William R. 1955. "Verbal Art." *Journal of American Folklore* 68 (269): 245–52. http://dx.doi.org/10.2307/536902.

Bateson, Gregory. 1972. *Steps to an Ecology of Mind*. New York: Ballantine.

Baum, Paull Franklin. 1917. "The Three Dreams or 'Dream Bread' Story." *Journal of American Folklore* 30 (117): 378–410. http://dx.doi.org/10.2307/534381.

Bauman, Richard. 1992. "Performance." In *Folklore, Cultural Performances, and Popular Entertainments*, ed. Richard Bauman, 41–49. New York: Oxford University Press.

Baym, Nancy K. 1995. "The Performance of Humor in Computer-Mediated Communication." *Journal of Computer-Mediated Communication* 1 (2). Accessed 16 February 2011. http://onlinelibrary.wiley.com/doi/10.1111/j.1083-6101.1995.tb00327.x/full.

Beard, Mary. 2014. *Laughter in Ancient Rome: On Laughing, Tickling, and Cracking Up*. Berkeley: University of California Press.

Beardsley, Monroe C. 1958. *Aesthetics: Problems in the Philosophy of Criticism*. New York: Harcourt, Brace.

Beardsley, Monroe C. 1982. *The Aesthetic Point of View: Selected Essays*, ed. Michael J. Wreen and Donald M. Callen. Ithaca, NY: Cornell University Press.

Beattie, James. 1778. *Essays: On Poetry and Music, as They Effect the Mind; On Laughter and Ludicrous Composition; On the Utility of Classical Learning*. Edinburgh: for W. Creech and E. Dilly in London.

Becker, Lawrence C., and Charlotte B. Becker, eds. 2001. *Encyclopedia of Ethics*. 3 vols. New York: Routledge.

Belknap, Robert E. 2004. *The List: The Uses and Pleasures of Cataloguing*. New Haven, CT: Yale University Press. http://dx.doi.org/10.12987/yale/9780300103830.001.0001.

Bell, Clive. (Original work published 1913) 1958. *Art*. New York: Capricorn.

Bellow, Saul. 1982. *The Dean's December*. New York: Harper & Row.

Ben-Amos, Dan. 1971. "Toward a Definition of Folklore in Context." *Journal of American Folklore* 84 (331): 3–15. http://dx.doi.org/10.2307/539729.

Ben-Amos, Dan. 1973. "The Myth of Jewish Humor." *Western Folklore* 32 (2): 112–31. http://dx.doi.org/10.2307/1498323.

Ben-Amos, Dan. 1979. "The Ceremony of Innocence." *Western Folklore* 38 (1): 47–52. http://dx.doi.org/10.2307/1498984.

Ben-Amos, Dan. 1991. "Jewish Folklore Studies." *Modern Judaism* 11 (1): 17–66. http://dx.doi.org
/10.1093/mj/11.1.17.

Bergen, Benjamin, and Kim Binsted. 2003. "The Cognitive Linguistics of Scalar Humor." In
Language, Culture, and Mind, ed. Michel Achard and Suzanne Kemmer, 79–92. Stanford:
CSLI.

Bergen, Benjamin, and Kim Binsted. 2015. "Embodied Grammar and Humor." In *Cognitive
Linguistics and Humor Research*, ed. Geert Brône, Tony Veale, and Kurt Feyaerts, 49–68. Berlin:
Mouton de Gruyter. http://dx.doi.org/10.1515/9783110346343-003.

Berger, Arthur Asa. 1997. *The Art of Comedy Writing*. New Brunswick, NJ: Transaction.

Bergler, Edmund. 1956. *Laughter and the Sense of Humor*. New York: Grune & Stratton.

Bergson, Henri. (Original work published 1900) 1956. "Laughter: An Essay on the Significance of
the Comic." In *Comedy*, ed. Wylie Sypher, 61–190. Garden City, NY: Doubleday Anchor.

Bermant, Chaim. 1986. *What's the Joke? A Study of Jewish Humor through the Ages*. London:
Weidenfeld & Nicolson.

"Best Ever Titanic Jokes." 2009. Accessed 27 September 2014. http://ezinearticles.com/?Best-Ever
-Titanic-Jokes---Essential-Reading-For-Your-Cruise-Vacation&id=3340989.

Billig, Michael. 2005. *Laughter and Ridicule: Towards a Social Critique of Humour*. Los Angeles:
Sage.

Bisberg-Youkelson, Feigl, and Rubin Youkelson. 2000. *The Life and Death of a Polish Shtetl*. Trans.
Gene Bluestein. Lincoln: University of Nebraska Press.

"Bizarro." 2011. *Los Angeles Times*, 4 February, D23.

Black, Lewis. 2008. *History of the Joke*. Produced by Marc Etkind. 100 min. DVD. AAEE117200.
History Channel.

"Blonde Jokes." n.d. Accessed 16 February 2011. http://www.jokeforum.com/jokes_Blonde-jokes
.html.

"Bologna." n.d. Accessed 25 January 2012. http://sniff.numachi.com/pages/tiBOLOGNA
;ttWEASLPOP.html.

"*Borat*." n.d. *Wikipedia*. Accessed 2 July 2014. http://en.wikipedia.org/wiki/Borat.

Borat: Cultural Learnings of America for Make Benefit Glorious Nation of Kazakhstan. 2007. Dir.
Larry Charles. DVD. 84 min. Twentieth-Century Fox.

"*Borat* Spoof Film Banned in Russia." 2006. *BBC News*, 9 November. Accessed 2 July 2014. http://
news.bbc.co.uk/2/hi/europe/6130918.stm.

"Borat Visiting Animal Control Centre." 2009. YouTube. Accessed 2 July 2014. http://www.youtube
.com/watch?v=q0r7yQ-3Kdg.

Bordwell, David, and Kristin Thompson. 2004. *Film Art: An Introduction*. Boston: McGraw-Hill.

Brandes, Stanley. 1977. "Peaceful Protest: Spanish Political Humor in a Time of Crisis." *Western
Folklore* 36 (4): 331–46. http://dx.doi.org/10.2307/1499197.

Brandt, Line, and Per Aage Brandt. 2005. "Making Sense of a Blend: A Cognitive-Semiotic
Approach to Metaphor." *Annual Review of Cognitive Linguistics* 3 (1): 216–49. http://dx.doi.org
/10.1075/arcl.3.12bra.

Bremmer, Jan. 1997. "Jokes, Jokers, and Jokebooks in Ancient Greek Culture." In *A Cultural History
of Humour*, ed. Jan Bremmer and Herman Roodenburg, 11–28. Cambridge: Polity.

Bressler, Eric R., and Sigal Balshine. 2006. "The Influence of Humor on Desirability." *Evolution and
Human Behavior* 27 (1): 29–39. http://dx.doi.org/10.1016/j.evolhumbehav.2005.06.002.

Brewer, Derek. 1997. "Prose Jest-Books Mainly in the Sixteenth to Eighteenth Centuries in England." In *A Cultural History of Humour*, ed. Jan Bremmer and Herman Roodenburg, 90–111. Cambridge: Polity.

Brodsky, David. 2011. "Why Did the Widow Have a Goat in Her Bed? Jewish Humor and Its Roots in the Talmud and Midrash." In *Jews and Humor*, ed. Leonard J. Greenspoon, 13–32. Studies in Jewish Civilization 22. West Lafayette, IN: Purdue University Press.

Brône, Geert, and Kurt Feyaerts. 2003. "The Cognitive Linguistics of Incongruity Resolution: Marked Reference-Point Structures in Humor." University of Leuven, Department of Linguistics preprint no. 205. Accessed 18 June 2015. http://www.researchgate.net/publication /242679703_The_cognitive_linguistics_of_incongruity_resolution_Marked_reference-point_ structures_in_humor.

Brône, Geert, Kurt Feyaerts, and Tony Veale. 2006. "Introduction: Cognitive Linguistic Approaches to Humor." *Humor: International Journal of Humor Research* 19 (3): 203–28. http:// dx.doi.org/10.1515/HUMOR.2006.012.

Bronner, Simon J. 1984. "'Let Me Tell It My Way': Joke Telling by a Father and Son." *Western Folklore* 43 (1): 18–36. http://dx.doi.org/10.2307/1499427.

Bronner, Simon J. 1985. "What's Grosser than Gross?" *Midwestern Journal of Language and Lore* 11 (1): 39–49.

Bronner, Simon J. 1988. *American Children's Folklore*. Little Rock, AR: August House.

Bronner, Simon J. 2009. "Digitizing and Virtualizing Folklore." In *Folklore and the Internet*, ed. Trevor J. Blank, 21–66. Logan: Utah State University Press.

Bronner, Simon J. 2012. "The Jewish Joke Online: Framing and Symbolizing Humor in Analog and Digital Culture." In *Folk Culture in the Digital Age: The Emergent Dynamics of Human Interaction*, ed. Trevor J. Blank, 119–49. Logan: Utah State University Press.

Brown, W. Norman. 1922. "The Silence Wager Stories: Their Origin and Their Diffusion." *American Journal of Philology* 43 (4): 289–317. http://dx.doi.org/10.2307/288930.

Brunvand, Jan Harold. 1998. *The Study of American Folklore*. 4th ed. New York: W. W. Norton.

"Bubba." n.d. *Wikipedia*. Accessed 22 June 2015. https://en.wikipedia.org/wiki/Bubba.

Burns, Thomas A., with Inger H. Burns. 1976. *Doing the Wash: An Expressive Culture and Personality Study of a Joke and Its Tellers*. Norwood, PA: Norwood.

Büschenthal, Lippmann Moses. 1812. *Sammlung witziger Einfälle von Juden, als Beyträge zur charakteristik der jüdischen Nation* [Collection of Comic Thoughts about Jews as a Contribution to the Characterization of the Jewish Nation]. Elberfeld, Germany: H. Büschler in Kommission.

Butler, Christopher. 2004. *Pleasure and the Arts: Enjoying Literature, Painting, and Music*. Oxford: Oxford University Press.

Cancian, Francesca. 1968. "Functional Analysis II: Varieties of Functional Analysis." In *International Encyclopedia of the Social Sciences*, ed. David Sills, 6:29–41. New York: Macmillan and the Free Press.

Cann, Arnie, Lawrence G. Calhoun, and Janet S. Banks. 1997. "On the Role of Humor Appreciation in Interpersonal Attraction." *Humor: International Journal of Humor Research* 10 (1): 77–89. http://dx.doi.org/10.1515/humr.1997.10.1.77.

Carrell, Amy. 2008. "Historical Views of Humor." In *The Primer of Humor Research*, ed. Victor Raskin, 303–32. Berlin: Mouton de Gruyter. http://dx.doi.org/10.1515/9783110198492.303.

Carroll, Larry. 2006. "Was Pamela Anderson in on the Joke? A *Borat* Investigation." *MTV Movie News*, 6 November. Accessed 19 June 2015. http://www.mtv.com/news/1544909/was -pamela-anderson-in-on-the-joke-a-borat-investigation/.

Carroll, Noël. 1991. "On Jokes." *Midwest Studies in Philosophy* 16 (1): 280–301. http://dx.doi.org/10 .1111/j.1475-4975.1991.tb00244.x.

Carroll, Noël. 1994. "Identifying Art." In *Institutions of Art: Reconsiderations of George Dickie's Philosophy*, ed. Robert J. Yanal, 3–38. University Park: Pennsylvania State University Press.

Carroll, Noël. 2000a. "Art and the Domain of the Aesthetic." *British Journal of Aesthetics* 40 (2): 191–208. http://dx.doi.org/10.1093/bjaesthetics/40.2.191.

Carroll, Noël. 2000b. Introduction to *Theories of Art Today*, ed. Noël Carroll, 3–24. Madison: University of Wisconsin Press.

Carroll, Noël. 2002. "Aesthetic Experience Revisited." *British Journal of Aesthetics* 42 (2): 145–68. http://dx.doi.org/10.1093/bjaesthetics/42.2.145.

Carroll, Noël. 2003. "Humor." In *The Oxford Handbook of Aesthetics*, ed. Jerrold Levinson, 344–65. Oxford: Oxford University Press.

Chadwick, Ruth, ed. 1998. *Encyclopedia of Applied Ethics*. 4 vols. San Diego: Academic Press.

Chafe, Wallace. 2007. *The Importance of Not Being Earnest: The Feeling behind Laughter and Humor*. Amsterdam: John Benjamins. http://dx.doi.org/10.1075/ceb.3.

Charney, Maurice. 1983. "Comic Creativity in Plays, Films, and Jokes." In *Handbook of Humor Research*, ed. Paul E McGhee and Jeffrey Goldstein, 2:33–40. New York: Springer-Verlag. http:// dx.doi.org/10.1007/978-1-4613-8236-2_3.

Chase, Jefferson S. 2000. *Inciting Laughter: The Development of "Jewish Humor" in 19th Century German Culture*. Berlin: Walter de Gruyter. http://dx.doi.org/10.1515/9783110813838.

Child, Francis James. (Original work published 1884–1898) 1965. *The English and Scottish Popular Ballads*. 5 vols. New York: Dover.

"Children's Answers to Sunday School Questions." n.d. Accessed 1 February 2011. http://www .virtualchristiancenter.com/humor/childrensanswers.htm.

Chotzner, J. 1905. *Hebrew Humour and Other Essays*. London: Luzac.

Clement, Paul A., and Herbert B. Hoffleit. 1969. *Plutarch's Moralia*. Vol. 8. Cambridge, MA: Harvard University Press.

Clements, William M. 1969. "The Types of the Polack Joke." *Folklore Forum*. Bibliographic and Special Series no. 3.

Clements, William M. 1973. "Unintentional Substitution in Folklore Transmission: A Devolutionary Instance." *New York Folklore Quarterly* 29 (4): 243–73.

Cochran, Robert. 1989. "'What Courage!'; Romanian 'Our Leader' Jokes." *Journal of American Folklore* 102 (405): 259–74. http://dx.doi.org/10.2307/540637.

Cochran, Robert. 1991. "Laughter's Low: Political Jokes and the Heart of Romanian Life." Hartman Hotz Lectures in Law and Liberal Arts, 27 March, University of Arkansas, Fayetteville, AR.

Cohen, Marshall. 1977. "Aesthetic Essence." In *Aesthetics: A Critical Anthology*, ed. George Dickie and R. J. Sclafani, 484–99. New York: St. Martin's.

Cohen, Sarah Blacher. 1987. "Introduction: The Varieties of Jewish Humor." In *Jewish Wry: Essays on Jewish Humor*, ed. Sarah Blacher Cohen, 1–15. Detroit: Wayne State University Press.

Cohen, Ted. 1978. "Metaphor and the Cultivation of Intimacy." *Critical Inquiry* 5 (1): 3–12. http:// dx.doi.org/10.1086/447969.

Cohen, Ted. 1983. "Jokes." In *Pleasure, Preference, and Value: Studies in Philosophical Aesthetics*, ed. Eva Schaper, 120–36. Cambridge: Cambridge University Press.

Cohen, Ted. 1998. "Jokes." In *Encyclopedia of Aesthetics*, ed. Michael Kelly, 3:1–12. New York: Oxford University Press.

Cohen, Ted. 1999. *Jokes: Philosophical Thoughts on Joking Matters*. Chicago: University of Chicago Press. http://dx.doi.org/10.7208/chicago/9780226112329.001.0001.

"Collection of Dead Baby Jokes." n.d. Accessed 3 September 2014. http://www.ebaumsworld.com /jokes/read/80728222/.

Collingwood, R. C. 1938. *The Principles of Art*. Oxford: Oxford University Press.

Corbeill, Anthony. 1996. *Controlling Laughter: Political Humor in the Late Roman Republic*. Princeton, NJ: Princeton University Press.

Coulson, Seana. 2001. *Semantic Leaps: Frame-Shifting and Conceptual Blending in Meaning Construction*. Cambridge: Cambridge University Press. http://dx.doi.org/10.1017/ CBO9780511551352.

Coulson, Seana. 2005a. "Extemporaneous Blending: Conceptual Integration in Humorous Discourse from Talk Radio." *Style* 39 (2): 107–22.

Coulson, Seana. 2005b. "What's So Funny? Conceptual Integration in Humorous Examples." Accessed 19 June 2015. http://www.cogsci.ucsd.edu/~coulson/funstuff/funny.html.

Cray, Ed. 1964. "The Rabbi Trickster." *Journal of American Folklore* 77 (306): 331–45. http://dx.doi .org/10.2307/537381.

Cray, Ed, and Marilyn Eisenberg Herzog. 1967. "The Absurd Elephant: A Recent Riddle Fad." *Western Folklore* 26 (1): 27–36. http://dx.doi.org/10.2307/1498485.

Danto, Arthur. 1964. "The Artworld." *Journal of Philosophy* 61 (19): 571–84. http://dx.doi.org /10.2307/2022937.

Davies, Christie. 1986. "Jewish Jokes, Anti-Semitic Jokes and Hebredonian Jokes." In *Jewish Humor*, ed. Avner Ziv, 75–96. Tel Aviv: Papyrus.

Davies, Christie. 1990. *Ethnic Humor around the World: A Comparative Analysis*. Bloomington: Indiana University Press.

Davies, Christie. 1998. *Jokes and Their Relation to Society*. Berlin: Mouton de Gruyter. http://dx.doi. org/10.1515/9783110806144.

Davies, Christie. 2002. *The Mirth of Nations*. New Brunswick, NJ: Transaction.

Davies, Christie. 2004. "Victor Raskin on Jokes." *Humor: International Journal of Humor Research* 17 (4): 373–80. http://dx.doi.org/10.1515/humr.2004.17.4.373.

Davies, Stephen. 1991. *Definitions of Art*. Ithaca, NY: Cornell University Press.

Davis, Murray S. 1993. *What's So Funny? The Comic Conception of Culture and Society*. Chicago: University of Chicago Press.

Deckers, Lambert, and Robert Thayer Buttram. 1990. "Humor as a Response to Incongruities within or between Schemata." *Humor: International Journal of Humor Research* 3 (1): 53–64. http://dx.doi.org/10.1515/humr.1990.3.1.53.

de Félice, G. 1851. *History of the Protestants of France from the Reformation to the Present Time*. Trans. Henry Lobdell. New York: Edward Walker.

Deriabin, Peter, and Frank Gibney. 1959. *The Secret World*. Garden City, NY: Doubleday.

Deutsch, Nathaniel. 2011. *The Jewish Dark Continent: Life and Death in the Russian Pale of Settlement*. Cambridge, MA: Harvard University Press. http://dx.doi.org/10.4159/harvard .9780674062641.

Diamond, Eliezer. 2011. "But Is It Funny? Identifying Humor, Satire, and Parody in the Rabbinic Literature." In *Jews and Humor*, ed. Leonard J. Greenspoon. Studies in Jewish Civilization 22. West Lafayette, IN: Purdue University Press.

Dickie, George. 1974. *Art and the Aesthetic.* Ithaca, NY: Cornell University Press.

Dickie, George. 2000. "The Institutional Theory of Art." In *Theories of Art Today,* ed. Noël Carroll, 93–108. Madison: University of Wisconsin Press.

Dore, Margherita. 2007. "Metaphor, Humour, and the Characterisation of the TV Comedy Programme *Friends.*" Paper presented at the Tenth International Cognitive Linguistic Conference, 19 July, Kraków, Poland.

Dorson, Richard M. 1968. "What Is Folklore?" *Folklore Forum* 1(4): 37.

Dorson, Richard M. 1972. *Folklore: Selected Essays.* Bloomington: Indiana University Press.

Dorst, John. 1990. "Folklore in the Telectronic Age." *Journal of Folklore Research* 27 (3): 179–90.

Douglas, Mary. 1968. "The Social Control of Cognition: Some Factors in Joke Perception." *Man* 3 (3): 361–76. http://dx.doi.org/10.2307/2798875.

"Downfall." 2009. YouTube. Accessed 15 February 2011. http://www.youtube.com/watch?v =vT2-AuEb7Bc.

Draitser, Emil, ed. 1978. *Forbidden Laughter: Soviet Underground Jokes.* Trans. Jon Pariser. Los Angeles: Almanac.

Draitser, Emil. 1982. "The Art of Storytelling in Contemporary Russian Satirical Folklore." *Slavic and East European Journal* 26 (2): 233–38. http://dx.doi.org/10.2307/308092.

Dresner, Eli, and Susan C. Herring. 2010. "Functions of the Nonverbal in CMC: Emoticons and Illocutionary Force." *Communication Theory* 20 (3): 249–68. http://dx.doi. org/10.1111/j.1468-2885.2010.01362.x.

Druyanow, Alter. 1963. *Sefer ha-Bediḥah ve-ha-Ḥidud* [The Book of the Joke and the Witticism]. 3 vols. Tel Aviv: Dvir.

Druyanow, Alter. (Original work published 1922) 2010. "Jewish Folk Humor." In *Pioneers of Jewish Ethnography and Folkloristics in Eastern Europe,* ed. Haya Bar-Itzhak, 119–56. Ljubljana: Scientific Research Center of the Slovenian Academy of Arts and Sciences.

Dundes, Alan. 1964. "Texture, Text, Context." *Southern Folklore Quarterly* 28:251–65.

Dundes, Alan. 1965. *The Study of Folklore.* Englewood Cliffs, NJ: Prentice-Hall.

Dundes, Alan. 1971a. "Laughter behind the Iron Curtain: A Sample of Rumanian Political Jokes." *Ukrainian Quarterly* 27:50–9.

Dundes, Alan. 1971b. "A Study of Ethnic Slurs: The Jew and Polack in the United States." *Journal of American Folklore* 84 (332): 186–203. http://dx.doi.org/10.2307/538989.

Dundes, Alan. 1979. "The Dead Baby Joke Cycle." *Western Folklore* 38 (3): 145–57. http://dx.doi .org/10.2307/1499238.

Dundes, Alan. 1981. "Many Hands Make Light Work; or, Caught in the Act of Screwing in Light Bulbs." *Western Folklore* 40 (3): 261–66. http://dx.doi.org/10.2307/1499697.

Dundes, Alan. 1987. *Cracking Jokes: Studies of Sick Humor Cycles and Stereotypes.* Berkeley, CA: Ten Speed.

Dundes, Alan, and Meegan Brown. 2002. "Viola Jokes: A Study of Second String Humor." *Midwestern Folklore* 28 (2): 5–17.

Dundes, Alan, and Carl R. Pagter. 1975. *Work Hard and You Shall Be Rewarded: Urban Folklore from the Paperwork Empire.* Bloomington: Indiana University Press.

Dundes, Alan, and Carl R. Pagter. 1987. *When You're Up to Your Ass in Alligators . . .: More Urban Folklore from the Paperwork Empire*. Detroit: Wayne State University Press.

Dundes, Alan, and Carl R. Pagter. 1991. *Never Try to Teach a Pig to Sing: Still More Urban Folklore from the Paperwork Empire*. Detroit: Wayne State University Press.

Dundes, Alan, and Carl R. Pagter. 1996. *Sometimes the Dragon Wins: Yet More Folklore from the Paperwork Empire*. Syracuse: Syracuse University Press.

Dundes, Alan, and Carl R. Pagter. 2000. *Why Don't Sheep Shrink When It Rains? A Further Collection of Photocopier Lore*. Syracuse: Syracuse University Press.

Earleywine, Mitch, and Robert Mankoff. 2013. "Are Benign Violations Necessary for Humor?" Accessed 25 February 2015. http://www.albany.edu/~me888931/earleywinemankoffbenignviolationsextension.pdf.

Eastman, Max. 1921. *The Sense of Humor*. New York: Charles Scribner's Sons.

Eastman, Max. 1936. *Enjoyment of Laughter*. New York: Halcyon.

Eaton, Marcia Muelder. 2000. "A Sustainable Definition of 'Art.'" In *Theories of Art Today*, ed. Noël Carroll, 141–59. Madison: University of Wisconsin Press.

"eBaum's World Forum." n.d. Accessed 5 February 2011. http://forum.ebaumsworld.com/archive/index.php.

Eco, Umberto. 2009. *The Infinity of Lists*. Trans. Alastair McEwen. New York: Rizzoli.

Edwards, Carol L. 1984. "'Stop Me if You've Heard This One': Narrative Disclaimers as Breakthroughs into Performance." *Fabula* 25 (3/4): 214–28. http://dx.doi.org/10.1515/fabl.1984.25.3-4.214.

Edwards, Russ "The Flush." 1993. *The Bathroom Joke Book*. Saddle River, NJ: Red Letter.

Eilbirt, Henry. 1993. *What Is a Jewish Joke? An Excursion into Jewish Humor*. Northvale, NJ: Jason Aronson.

Eliach, Yaffa. 1998. *There Once Was a World: A Nine-Hundred Year Chronicle of the Shtetl of Eishyshok*. Boston: Little, Brown.

Eliason, Eric A. 2007. *The J. Golden Kimball Stories*. Urbana: University of Illinois Press.

Emerson, Joan. 1969. "Negotiating the Serious Import of Humor." *Sociometry* 32 (2): 169–81. http://dx.doi.org/10.2307/2786261.

"Emoticons." n.d. *Wikipedia*. Accessed 5 February 2011. http://en.wikipedia.org/wiki/Emoticons.

Esar, Evan. 1952. *The Humor of Humor*. New York: Bramhall House.

"Essay." 1983. *Time*, 17 October, 100.

Everything Is Illuminated. 2006. Dir. Liev Schreiber. DVD. 105 min. Warner Bros. Entertainment.

Fauconnier, Gilles. 1997. *Mapping in Thought and Language*. Cambridge: Cambridge University Press. http://dx.doi.org/10.1017/CBO9781139174220.

Fauconnier, Gilles. 2001. "Conceptual Integration." Workshop. Emergence and Development of Embodied Cognition (EDEC2001). Accessed 17 February 2016. http://citeseerx.ist.psu.edu/viewdoc/download?doi=10.1.1.90.8028&rep=rep1&type=pdf.

Fauconnier, Gilles. 2003. "Cognitive Linguistics." In *Encyclopedia of Cognitive Science*, ed. Lynn Nadel, 1:539–43. London: NPG.

Fauconnier, Gilles, and Mark Turner. 1998. "Conceptual Integration Networks." *Cognitive Science* 22 (2): 133–87. http://dx.doi.org/10.1207/s15516709cog2202_1.

Fauconnier, Gilles, and Mark Turner. 2002. *The Way We Think: Conceptual Blending and the Mind's Hidden Complexities*. New York: Basic Books.

Fesmire, Steven A. 1994. "What Is 'Cognitive' about Cognitive Linguistics?" *Metaphor and Symbolic Activity* 9 (2): 149–54. http://dx.doi.org/10.1207/s15327868ms0902_4.

"Fifty Dollars Is Fifty Dollars." 2014. Accessed 15 June 2014. http://www.aish.com/j/j/51475727.html.

Fine, Gary Alan, and Barry O'Neill. 2010. "Policy Legends and Folk Lists: Traditional Beliefs in the Public Sphere." *Journal of American Folklore* 123 (488): 150–78. http://dx.doi.org/10.1353/jaf.0.0133.

Finkin, Jordan. 2011. "Jewish Jokes, Yiddish Storytelling, and Sholem Aleichem: A Discursive Approach." In *Jews and Humor*, ed. Leonard J. Greenspoon, 83–106. Studies in Jewish Civilization 22. West Lafayette, IN: Purdue University Press.

Fischman, Fernando. 2011. "Using Yiddish: Language Ideologies, Verbal Art, and Identity among Argentinian Jews." *Journal of Folklore Research* 48 (1): 37–61. http://dx.doi.org/10.2979/jfolkrese.48.1.37.

Fitzpatrick, Sheila. 1999. *Everyday Stalinism: Ordinary Life in Extraordinary Times; Soviet Russia in the 1930s*. Oxford: Oxford University Press.

"Flowgo." n.d. Accessed 15 February 2011. http://www.flowgo.com/funny/12673_blondes-year-in-review.html (site discontinued).

Forster, E. M. (Original work published 1927) 2005. *Aspects of the Novel*. London: Penguin.

"Fortune City." n.d. Accessed 31 January 2011. http://www.fortunecity.com/bennyhills/proops/125/Jokes/Religion_Jokes/First_Mass.htm (site discontinued).

Frank, Russell. 2009. "The *Forward* as Folklore: Studying E-mailed Humor." In *Folklore and the Internet*, ed. Trevor J. Blank, 98–122. Logan: Utah State University Press.

Freud, Sigmund. 1953–1974. *The Standard Edition of the Complete Psychological Works of Sigmund Freud*. 24 vols. Ed. and trans. James Strachey. London: Hogarth Press and the Institute of Psycho-Analysis.

Freud, Sigmund. 1954. *The Origins of Psycho-analysis: Letters to Wilhelm Fliess, Draft and Notes, 1887–1902*, ed. Marie Bonaparte, Anna Freud, and Ernst Kris. New York: Basic Books. http://dx.doi.org/10.1037/11538-000.

Friedman, Hershey H., and Linda Weiser Friedman. 2014. *God Laughed: Sources of Jewish Humor*. New Brunswick, NJ: Transaction.

Galanter, Marc. 2005. *Lowering the Bar: Lawyer Jokes and Legal Culture*. Madison: University of Wisconsin Press.

Gallivan, Joanne. 1992. "Group Differences in the Appreciation of Feminist Humor." *Humor: International Journal of Humor Research* 5 (4): 369–74. http://dx.doi.org/10.1515/humr.1992.5.4.369.

"Game of Intelligence." n.d. Accessed 26 August 2011. http://www.coolblondejokes.com/DumbJokes/GameOfIntelligence.shtml.

Gaut, Berys. 1998. "Just Joking: The Ethics and Aesthetics of Humor." *Philosophy and Literature* 22 (1): 51–68. http://dx.doi.org/10.1353/phl.1998.0014.

Gaut, Berys. 2000. "'Art' as a Cluster Concept." In *Theories of Art Today*, ed. Noël Carroll, 25–44. Madison: University of Wisconsin Press.

Geertz, Clifford. 1973. *The Interpretation of Cultures*. New York: Basic Books.

Georges, Robert A. 1980. "Toward a Resolution of the Text/Context Controversy." *Western Folklore* 39 (1): 34–40. http://dx.doi.org/10.2307/1499762.

Gibbs, Raymond W., Jr. 2000. "Making Good Psychology out of Blending Theory." *Cognitive Linguistics* 11 (3/4): 347–58.

Gilman, Sander L. 1984. "Jewish Jokes: Sigmund Freud and the Hidden Language of the Jews." *Psychoanalysis and Contemporary Thought* 7 (4): 591–614.

Giora, Rachel. 1991. "On the Cognitive Aspects of the Joke." *Journal of Pragmatics* 16 (5): 465–85. http://dx.doi.org/10.1016/0378-2166(91)90137-M.

Glassie, Henry. 1989. *The Spirit of Folk Art: The Girard Collection at the Museum of International Folk Art*. New York: Harry N. Abrams.

Glucksberg, Sam. 1998. "Understanding Metaphors." *Current Directions in Psychological Science* 7 (2): 39–43. http://dx.doi.org/10.1111/1467-8721.ep13175582.

Golden, Harry. 1972. *The Golden Book of Jewish Humor*. New York: G. P. Putnam's Sons.

Goldsmith, Emmanuel S. 1993. "Sholom Aleichem's Humor of Affirmation and Survival." In *Semites and Stereotypes*, ed. Avner Ziv and Anat Zajdman, 13–27. Westport, CT: Greenwood.

Goldstein, Jeffrey H., Jerry M. Suls, and Susan Anthony. 1972. "Enjoyment of Specific Types of Humor Content: Motivation or Salience?" In *The Psychology of Humor: Theoretical Perspectives and Empirical Issues*, ed. Jeffrey H. Goldstein and Paul E. McGhee, 159–71. New York: Academic Press. http://dx.doi.org/10.1016/B978-0-12-288950-9.50014-6.

Goldstein, Kenneth S. 1967. "The Induced Natural Context: An Ethnographic Folklore Field Technique." In *Essays on the Verbal and Visual Arts: Proceedings of the 1966 Annual Spring Meeting of the American Ethnological Society*, ed. June Helm, 1–6. Seattle: University of Washington Press.

Goldstein, Kenneth S. 1991. "Notes towards a European-American Folk Aesthetic: Lessons Learned from Singers and Storytellers I Have Known." *Journal of American Folklore* 104 (412): 164–78. http://dx.doi.org/10.2307/541226.

Goody, Jack. 1977. *The Domestication of the Savage Mind*. Cambridge: Cambridge University Press.

Gordon, Mel. 2012. "Nazi 'Proof' That the Jews Possessed the Worst Humor in the World." *Israeli Journal of Humor Research* 1 (2): 97–100.

Gottesman, Itzik Nakhmen. 2003. *Defining the Yiddish Nation: The Jewish Folklorists of Poland*. Detroit: Wayne State University Press.

"Grace before Meals." n.d. Children's Graces. Accessed 2 February 2011. http://home.pcisys.net /~tbc/mealpryr.htm#prayer11_26.

Grady, Joseph E., Todd Oakley, and Seana Coulson. 1999. "Blending and Metaphor." In *Metaphors in Cognitive Linguistics*, ed. G. Steen and R. Gibbs, 101–24. Amsterdam: John Benjamins. http://dx.doi.org/10.1075/cilt.175.07gra.

Graham, Seth. 2003. "The Wages of Syncretism: Folkloric New Russians and Post-Soviet Popular Culture." *Russian Review* 62 (1): 37–53. http://dx.doi.org/10.1111/1467-9434.00262.

Graham, Seth. 2009. *Resonant Dissonance: The Russian Joke in Cultural Context*. Evanston, IL: Northwestern University Press.

Greengross, Gil, and Robert Mankoff. 2012. "The Hidden Side of the Joke: Review of *Inside Jokes* by Matthew M. Hurley, Daniel C. Bennett, and Reginald B. Adams, Jr." *Evolutionary Psychology* 10 (3): 443–56.

Greengross, Gil, and Geoffrey Miller. 2011. "Humor Ability Reveals Intelligence, Predicts Mating Success, and Is Higher in Males." *Intelligence* 39 (4): 188–92. http://dx.doi.org/10.1016/j.intell .2011.03.006.

Greenwood, Dara, and Linda M. Isbell. 2002. "Ambivalent Sexism and the Dumb Blonde: Men's and Women's Reactions to Sexist Jokes." *Psychology of Women Quarterly* 26 (4): 341–50. http:// dx.doi.org/10.1111/1471-6402.t01-2-00073.

Grieg, J. Y. T. 1923. *The Psychology of Laughter*. New York: Cooper Square.

Griffin, Dustin. 1994. *Satire: A Critical Reintroduction*. Lexington: University Press of Kentucky.

Gross, Naftoli. 1955. *Ma'aselach un Mesholim* [Tales and Parables]. New York: Aber.

Grotjahn, Martin. 1966. *Beyond Laughter: Humor and the Subconscious*. New York: McGraw-Hill.

Grotjahn, Martin. 1970. "Laughter and Sex." In *A Celebration of Laughter*, ed. Werner M. Mendel, 161–72. Los Angeles: Mara.

Gruner, Charles R. 1978. *Understanding Laughter: The Workings of Wit and Humor*. Chicago: Nelson-Hall.

Haig, Robin Andrew. 1988. *The Anatomy of Humor: Biopsychological and Therapeutic Perspectives*. Springfield, IL: Charles C. Thomas.

Halkin, Hillel. 2006. "Why Jews Laugh at Themselves." *Commentary* 121 (April): 47–54.

Handelman, Don. 1974. "A Note on Play." *American Anthropologist* 76 (1): 66–8. http://dx.doi.org /10.1525/aa.1974.76.1.02a00140.

Harris, David A., and Izrail Rabinovich. 1995. *The Jokes of Oppression: The Humor of Soviet Jews*. Northvale, NJ: Jason Aronson.

Heilman, Uriel. 2013. "Pew Survey of U.S. Jews: Soaring Marriage, Assimilation Rates." Accessed 18 March 2013. http://www.jta.org/2013/10/01/news-opinion/united-states/pew-survey-u-s-jewish -intermarriage-rate-rises-to-58-percent.

Herzog, Rudolph. 2010. *Dead Funny: Humor in Hitler's Germany*. Trans. Jefferson Chase. Brooklyn: Melville House.

Hess, Stephen, and Sandy Northrop. 1996. *Drawn and Quartered: The History of American Political Cartoons*. Montgomery, AL: Elliott & Clark.

Hillson, Tim R., and Rod A. Martin. 1994. "What's So Funny about That? The Domains-Interaction Approach as a Model of Incongruity and Resolution in Humor." *Motivation and Emotion* 18 (1): 1–29. http://dx.doi.org/10.1007/BF02252473.

"Hitler Emoticons." 2008. Accessed 5 February 2011. http://www.buzzfeed.com/expresident /hitler-emoticons.

"HK Expats." n.d. Accessed 5 February 2011. http://hkexpats.com/showthread.php?p=76099 (site discontinued).

Hoffman, Eva. 1997. *Shtetl: The Life and Death of a Small Town and the World of Polish Jews*. Boston: Houghton Mifflin.

Holland, Norman N. 1982. *Laughing: A Psychology of Humor*. Ithaca, NY: Cornell University Press.

Holt, Jim. 2008. *Stop Me If You've Heard This: A History and Philosophy of Jokes*. New York: W. W. Norton.

Horowitz, Gregg. 2003. "The Aesthetics of the Avant-Garde." In *The Oxford Handbook of Aesthetics*, ed. Jerrold Levinson, 748–60. Oxford: Oxford University Press.

Howard, Robert Glenn. 2005. "Toward a Theory of the World Wide Web Vernacular: The Case for Pet Cloning." *Journal of the Folklore Institute* 42 (3): 323–60. http://dx.doi.org/10.2979/JFR .2005.42.3.323.

Howe, Irving. 1987. "The Nature of Jewish Laughter." In *Jewish Wry: Essays on Jewish Humor*, ed. Sarah Blacher Cohen, 16–24. Bloomington: Indiana University Press.

Howe, Irving, and Ruth R. Wisse, eds. 1979. *The Best of Sholem Aleichem*. Washington, DC: New Republic.

Hugill, Stan. 1969. *Shanties and Sailor's Songs*. New York: Praeger.

Hunt, Margaret. 1884. *Grimm's Household Tales*. 2 vols. London: George Bell & Sons.

Hurley, Matthew M., Daniel C. Dennett, and Reginald B. Adams Jr. 2011. *Inside Jokes: Using Humor to Reverse-Engineer the Mind.* Cambridge, MA: MIT Press.

Internet Movie Database. 2009. "All-Time USA Box Office." Accessed 2 July 2014. http://www .imdb.com/boxoffice/alltimegross.

Isaacs, Abram S. (Original work published 1893) 1911. *Stories from the Rabbis.* New York: Bloch.

Isbell, Charles David. 2011. "Humor in the Bible." In *Jews and Humor,* ed. Leonard J. Greenspoon, 1–11. Studies in Jewish Civilization 22. West Lafayette, IN: Purdue University Press.

Ismenger, Gary. 2003. "Aesthetic Experience." In *The Oxford Handbook of Aesthetics,* ed. Jerrold Levinson, 99–116. Oxford: Oxford University Press.

Jackson, Michael R. 1984. *Self-Esteem and Meaning: A Life Historical Investigation.* Albany: State University of New York Press.

Jarvie, I. C. 1965. "Limits to Functionalism and Alternatives to It in Anthropology." In *Functionalism in the Social Sciences: Strengths and Limits of Functionalism in Anthropology, Economics, Political Science, and Sociology,* monograph 5, ed. Don Martindale, 18–34. Philadelphia: American Academy of Social and Political Sciences.

Jason, Heda. 1967. "The Jewish Joke: The Problem of Definition." *Southern Folklore Quarterly* 67 (1): 48–54.

Jenkins, Dan. 1993. *Bubba Talks of His Life, Love, Sex, Whiskey, Food, Foreigners, Teenagers, Football and Other Matters That Occasionally Concern Human Beings.* New York: Doubleday.

Jenkins, Elijah. (Original work published 1739) 1963. *Joe Miller's Jests; or, The Wit's Vade-Mecum.* New York: Dover.

Jones, Michael Owen. 1971. "The Concept of 'Aesthetic' in the Traditional Arts." *Western Folklore* 30 (2): 77–104. http://dx.doi.org/10.2307/1499067.

Jones, Steven. 1979a. "Dogmatism in the Contextual Revolution." *Western Folklore* 38 (1): 52–55. http://dx.doi.org/10.2307/1498985.

Jones, Steven. 1979b. "Slouching Towards Ethnography: The Text/Context Controversy Reconsidered." *Western Folklore* 38 (1): 42–47. http://dx.doi.org/10.2307/1498983.

Joubert, Laurent. (Original work published 1579) 1980. *Treatise on Laughter.* Trans. Gregory David de Rocher. Tuscaloosa: University of Alabama Press.

Juni, Samuel, Bernard Katz, and Martin Hamburger. 1996. "Identification with Aggression vs. Turning against the Self: An Empirical Study of Turn-of-the-Century European Jewish Humor." *Current Psychology (New Brunswick, NJ)* 14 (4): 313–28. http://dx.doi.org/10.1007/BF02686920.

Kaplan, Abraham. 1964. *The Conduct of Inquiry.* San Francisco: Chandler.

"Kazakhstan in the 21st Century." 2006. *New York Times,* 27 September, A11–A14.

"Kazakhstan Thanks Borat for 'Boosting Tourism.'" 2012. *BBC,* 24 April. Accessed 2 July 2014. http:// www.bbc.co.uk/newsbeat/article/17826000/kazakhstan-thanks-borat-for-boosting-tourism.

Keillor, Garrison. 2005. *The Pretty Good Joke Book.* 4th ed. Minneapolis: Highbridge.

Keith-Spiegel, Patricia. 1972. "Early Conceptions of Humor: Varieties and Issues." In *The Psychology of Humor: Theoretical Perspectives and Empirical Issues,* ed. Jeffrey H. Goldstein and Paul E. McGhee, 3–39. New York: Academic Press. http://dx.doi.org/10.1016/B978-0-12-288950 -9.50007-9.

Kelly, Greg. 2016. "'The Joke's on Us': An Analysis of Metahumor." In *Folkloresque: Reframing Folklore in a Popular Culture World,* ed. Michael Dylan Foster and Jeffrey A. Tolbert, 205–20. Logan: Utah State University Press.

Kempt, Robert, ed. 1865. *The American Joe Miller: A Collection of Yankee Wit and Humour.* London: Adams & Francis.

Kennick, William E. 1958. "Does Traditional Aesthetics Rest on a Mistake?" *Mind* 67 (267): 317–34. http://dx.doi.org/10.1093/mind/LXVII.267.317.

Ketner, Kenneth Laine. 1973. "The Role of Hypotheses in Folkloristics." *Journal of American Folklore* 86 (340): 114–30. http://dx.doi.org/10.2307/539745.

Kirsch, Jonathan. 2001. *The Woman Who Laughed at God: The Untold History of the Jewish People.* New York: Penguin Compass.

Kirshenblatt-Gimblett, Barbara. 1974. "The Concept and Varieties of Narrative Performance in East European Jewish Culture." In *Explorations in the Ethnography of Speaking,* ed. Richard Bauman and Joel Sherzer, 283–308. Cambridge: Cambridge University Press.

Kirshenblatt-Gimblett, Barbara. 1995. "From the Paperwork Empire to the Paperless Office." In *Folklore Interpreted: Essays in Honor of Alan Dundes,* ed. Regina Bendix and Rosemary Levy Zumwalt, 69–92. New York: Garland.

Kishtainy, Khalid. 1985. *Arab Political Humour.* London: Quartet.

Klaf, Franklin S., and Bernhardt J. Hurwood, eds. 1964. *A Hundred Merry Tales.* New York: Citadel.

Kline, Paul. 1977. "The Psychoanalytic Theory of Humor and Laughter." In *It's a Funny Thing, Humour,* ed. Anthony J. Chapman and Hugh C. Foot, 7–12. Oxford: Pergamon. http://dx.doi .org/10.1016/B978-0-08-021376-7.50006-1.

Knox, Israel. 1969. "The Traditional Roots of Jewish Humor." In *Holy Laughter,* ed. M. Conrad Hyers, 150–65. New York: Seabury.

Koestler, Arthur. 1964. *The Act of Creation.* New York: Macmillan.

Kotik, Yekhezkel. (Original work published 1913) 2002. *Journey to a Nineteenth-Century Shtetl: The Memoirs of Yekhezkel Kotik,* ed. David Assaf. Trans. Margaret Birstein. Raphael Patai Series in Jewish Folklore and Anthropology. Detroit: Wayne State University Press.

Kövecses, Zoltan. 2005. *Metaphor in Culture: Universality and Variation.* New York: Cambridge University Press. http://dx.doi.org/10.1017/CBO9780511614408.

Kowallis, Jon. 1986. *Wit and Humor of Old Cathay.* Beijing: Panda.

Kramer, Mark. 1983. *Invasive Procedures: A Year in the World of Two Surgeons.* New York: Harper & Row.

Kreppel, J. 1933. *Wie der Jude lacht: Anthologie jüdischer Witze, Satiren, Anekdoten, Humoresken, Aphorisen: Ein Beitrag zur Psychologie des jüdischen Witzes und zur jüdischen Volkskunde.* Vienna: "Das Buch."

Krikmann, Arvo. 2007. "Digging One's Own Grave." *Folklore: Electronic Journal of Folklore* 35:53–60. http://haldjas.folklore.ee/folklore/vol35/krikmann.pdf.

Krikmann, Arvo. 2009. "On the Similarity and Distinguishability of Humour and Figurative Speech." *Trames: A Journal of the Humanities and Social Sciences* 13 (1): 14–40. http://dx.doi .org/10.3176/tr.2009.1.02.

Kristol, Irving. 1951. "Is Jewish Humor Dead? The Rise and Fall of the Jewish Joke." *Commentary (New York.)* 12 (November): 431–36.

Kriwaczek, Paul. 2006. *Yiddish Civilisation: The Rise and Fall of a Forgotten Nation.* New York: Vintage.

Kuipers, Giselinde. 2006. *Good Humor, Bad Taste: A Sociology of the Joke.* Berlin: Mouton de Gruyter. http://dx.doi.org/10.1515/9783110898996.

Kuipers, Giselinde. 2008. "The Sociology of Humor." In *The Primer of Humor Research*, ed. Victor Raskin, 361–98. Berlin: Mouton de Gruyter. http://dx.doi.org/10.1515/9783110198492.361.

Kundera, Milan. 1969. *The Joke*. Trans. David Hamblyn and Oliver Stallybrass. New York: Coward-McCann.

Kyratzis, Sakis. 2003. "Laughing Metaphorically: Metaphor and Humor in Discourse." Paper presented at the Eighth International Cognitive Linguistics Conference, Logoño, Universidad de La Rioja. http://citeseerx.ist.psu.edu/viewdoc/summary?doi=10.1.1.132.9689.

Laineste, Liisi. 2002. "Take It with a Grain of Salt: The Kernel of Truth in Topical Jokes." *Folklore: Electronic Journal of Folklore* 21:7–25. http://www.folklore.ee/folklore/vol21/jokes.pdf. http://dx.doi.org/10.7592/FEJF2002.21.jokes.

Lakoff, George, and Mark Johnson. 1980. *Metaphors We Live By*. Chicago: University of Chicago Press.

Landmann, Salcia. 1962. "On Jewish Humor." *Jewish Journal of Sociology* 4:193–204.

Laplanche, J., and J.-B. Pontalis. 1973. *The Language of Psycho-analysis*. New York: W. W. Norton.

Larsen, Egon. 1980. *Wit as a Weapon: The Political Joke in History*. London: Frederick Muller.

Larson, Gary. 1989. *The PreHistory of The Far Side: A 10th Anniversary Exhibit*. Kansas City, KS: Andrews McMeel.

Latta, Robert L. 1999. *The Basic Humor Process: A Cognitive-Shift Theory and the Case against Incongruity*. Berlin: Mouton de Gruyter. http://dx.doi.org/10.1515/9783110806137.

"Laugh Break." n.d. Accessed 31 January 2011. http://www.laughbreak.com/lists/numbers_of_the_beast.html.

Leach, Maria, ed. 1949. *The Standard Dictionary of Folklore, Mythology, and Legend*. 2 vols. New York: Funk & Wagnalls.

Learsi, Rufus. 1961. *Filled with Laughter: A Fiesta of Jewish Folk Humor*. New York: T. Yoseloff.

Leary, James P. 1984. "Style in Jocular Communication." *Journal of Folklore Research* 21 (1): 29–46.

Lefcourt, Herbert M. 2001. *Humor: The Psychology of Living Buoyantly*. New York: Kluwer. http://dx.doi.org/10.1007/978-1-4615-4287-2.

Legman, G. 1968. *The Rationale of the Dirty Joke: An Analysis of Sexual Humor, First Series*. New York: Grove.

Legman, G. 1975. *The Rationale of the Dirty Joke: An Analysis of Sexual Humor, Second Series*. New York: Breaking Point.

Leitch, Thomas M. 1986. *What Stories Are: Narrative Theory and Interpretation*. University Park: Pennsylvania State University Press.

Levinson, Jerrold. 1998. "Humour." In *Routledge Encyclopedia of Philosophy*, ed. Edward Craig, 4:562–67. London: Routledge.

Levinson, Jerrold. 2003. "Philosophical Aesthetics: An Overview." In *The Oxford Handbook of Aesthetics*, ed. Jerrold Levinson, 3–24. Oxford: Oxford University Press.

Lévi-Strauss, Claude. 1955. "The Structural Study of Myth." *Journal of American Folklore* 68 (270): 428–44. http://dx.doi.org/10.2307/536768.

Lévi-Strauss, Claude. 1976. *Structural Anthropology*. Vol. 2. Chicago: University of Chicago Press.

Lewis, Paul. 1989. *Comic Effects: Interdisciplinary Approaches to Humor in Literature*. Albany: State University of New York Press.

Lifschutz, E. 1952. "Merry Makers and Jesters among Jews." In *YIVO Annual of Jewish Social Science*, ed. Koppel S. Pinson, 7:43–83. New York: YIVO.

Limón, Jose E. 1997. "*Carne, Carnales,* and the Carnivalesque: Bakhtinian *Batos,* Disorder, and Narrative Discourse." In *Situated Lives: Gender and Culture in Everyday Life,* ed. Louise Lamphere, Helen Ragoné, and Patricia Zavella, 62–82. New York: Routledge.

Lipman, Steve. 1993. *Laughter in Hell: The Use of Humor during the Holocaust.* Northvale, NJ: Jason Aronson.

Lipps, Theodor. (Original work published 1898) 1922. *Komik und Humor: Psychologish-Ästheticsche Untersuchung* [Comic and Humor: A Psychological-Aesthetic Inquiry]. Leipzig: Leopold Voss.

"List of Films about the RMS *Titanic.*" n.d. Accessed 26 September 2014. http://en.wikipedia.org /wiki/List_of_films_about_the_RMS_Titanic.

Loewe, Heinrich. 1922. *Reste von altem jüdischen Volkshumor* [Remains of Old Jewish Folk Humor]. Berlin: Privately printed.

Longenecker, Gregory J. 1977. "Sequential Parody Graffiti." *Western Folklore* 36 (4): 354–64. http:// dx.doi.org/10.2307/1499199.

Lukes, Steven, and Itzhak Galnoor. 1985. *No Laughing Matter: A Collection of Political Jokes.* New York: Routledge & Kegan Paul.

Macintyre, Martha. 1992. "Reflections of an Anthropologist Who Mistook Her Husband for a Yam: Female Comedy on Tubetube." In *Clowning as Critical Practice: Performance Humor in the South Pacific,* ed. William E. Mitchell, 140–43. Pittsburgh: University of Pittsburgh Press.

Maimon, Solomon. 1888. *Solomon Maimon: An Autobiography.* Trans. J. Clark Murray. Boston: Cupples & Hurd.

Marchese, David, and Willa Paskin. 2006. "What's Real in *Borat?*" Accessed 2 July 2014. www.salon .com/2006/11/10/guide_to_borat/.

Marsden, Norman. 1983. *A Jewish Life under the Tsars: The Autobiography of Chaim Aronson, 1825–1888.* Totowa, NJ: Allanheld, Osmun.

Martin, Mike W. 1987. "Humor and Aesthetic Enjoyment of Incongruities." In *The Philosophy of Laughter and Humor,* ed. John Morreall, 172–86. Albany: State University Press of New York.

Martin, Rod A. 2006. *The Psychology of Humor: An Integrative Approach.* Burlington, MA: Elsevier Academic Press.

Marzolph, Ulrich. 1988. "Reconsidering the Iranian Sources of a Romanian Political Joke." *Western Folklore* 47 (3): 212–16. http://dx.doi.org/10.2307/1499918.

McGraw, A. Peter, and Caleb Warren. 2010. "Benign Violation: Making Immoral Behavior Funny." *Psychological Science* 21 (8): 1141–49. http://dx.doi.org/10.1177/0956797610376073.

McGraw, A. Peter, Caleb Warren, Lawrence E. Williams, and Bridget Leonard. 2012. "Too Close for Comfort, or Too Far to Care? Finding Humor in Distant Tragedies and Close Mishaps." *Psychological Science* 20 (10): 1–9.

McGraw, A. Peter, Lawrence E. Williams, and Caleb Warren. 2013. "The Rise and Fall of Humor: Psychological Distance Modulates Humorous Responses to Tragedy." *Social Psychological & Personality Science* 20 (10): 1–7.

McGraw, Peter, and Joel Warner. 2014. *The Humor Code: A Global Search for What Makes Things Funny.* New York: Simon & Schuster.

Mead, Margaret. 2000. *And Keep Your Powder Dry: An Anthropologist Looks at America.* The Study of Contemporary Western Culture, vol. 2. New York: Berghahn.

"Medscape Physician Compensation Report." 2015. http://www.medscape.com/features/slideshow /compensation/2015/public/overview#page=3.

Mendelssohn, Moses. 1997. *Philosophical Writings,* ed. and trans. Daniel O. Dahlstrom. Cambridge Texts in the History of Philosophy. Cambridge: Cambridge University Press.

Mikes, George. 1971. *Laughing Matter: Towards a Personal Philosophy of Wit and Humor.* New York: Library Press.

Mikes, George. 1985. "Foreword." *No Laughing Matter: A Collection of Political Jokes,* by Steven Lukes and Itzhak Galnoor, vii–ix. New York: Routledge & Kegan Paul.

Miller, Saul. 1980. *Dobromil: Life in a Galician Shtetl, 1890–1907.* New York: Lowenthal.

Mio, Jeffrey Scott, and Arthur C. Graesser. 1991. "Humor, Language, and Metaphor." *Metaphor and Symbolic Activity* 6 (2): 87–102. http://dx.doi.org/10.1207/s15327868ms0602_2.

"Mistranslations We Love." n.d. Accessed 17 June 2015. http://www.alphadictionary.com/fun /mistranslation.html.

Mitchell, Carol A. 1977. "The Sexual Perspective in the Appreciation and Interpretation of Jokes." *Western Folklore* 36 (4): 303–29. http://dx.doi.org/10.2307/1499196.

Mizejewski, Linda. 1987. "The Erotic Stripped Bare: Romanians Are Prisoners of Sexlessness." *Harper's Magazine* 274 (March): 62.

Monro, D. H. 1951. *Argument of Laughter.* Carlton: Melbourne University Press.

Monro, D. H. 2006. "Humour." In *Encyclopedia of Philosophy,* 2nd ed., ed. Donald M. Borchert, 4:514–18. Detroit: Thomson Gale.

Morreall, John. 1981. "Humor and Aesthetic Education." *Journal of Aesthetic Education* 15 (1): 55–70. http://dx.doi.org/10.2307/3332209.

Morreall, John. 1983. *Taking Laughter Seriously.* Albany: State University of New York Press.

Morreall, John, ed. 1987. *The Philosophy of Laughter and Humor.* Albany: State University of New York Press.

Morreall, John. 1999. *Comedy, Tragedy, and Religion.* Albany: State University of New York Press.

Morreall, John. 2006. "Humor: Addendum." In *Encyclopedia of Philosophy,* 2nd ed., ed. Donald M. Borchert, 4:518–19. Detroit: Thomson Gale.

Morreall, John. 2008. "Philosophy and Religion." In *The Primer of Humor Research,* ed. Victor Raskin, 211–42. Berlin: Mouton de Gruyter.

Morrissey, Maureen. 1990. "Script Theory for the Analysis of Humorous Metaphors." In *Whimsy VII: Proceedings of the 1988 WHIM Conference,* ed. Shaun F. D. Hughes and Victor Raskin, 124–25. Tempe, AZ: International Society for Humor Studies.

Murstein, Bernard I., and Robert G. Brust. 1985. "Humor and Interpersonal Attraction." *Journal of Personality Assessment* 49 (6): 637–40. http://dx.doi.org/10.1207/s15327752jpa4906_12.

Nador, Georg. 1975. *Zur philosophie des jüdischen Witzes* [On the Philosophy of Jewish Jokes]. Publication der Academia Maimonideana, Kurzmonographien no. 3. Northwood, Middlesex: Bina Verlag.

"Nation." 1976. *Time,* 18 October, 23.

Neve, Michael. 1988. "Freud's Theory of Humour, Wit, and Jokes." In *Laughing Matters: A Serious Look at Humour,* ed. John Durant and Jonathan Miller, 35–53. New York: Longman Scientific & Technical.

Nevo, Ofra. 1991. "What's in a Jewish Joke?" *Humor: International Journal of Humor Studies* 4 (2): 251–60. http://dx.doi.org/10.1515/humr.1991.4.2.251.

Nevo, Ofra, and Jacob Levine. 1994. "Jewish Humor Strikes Again: The Outburst of Humor in Israel during the Gulf War." *Western Folklore* 53 (2): 125–46. http://dx.doi.org/10.2307/1500100.

Newcott, Bill. 2015. "The Paradox of Prayer." *AARP: The Magazine* 58, 2B (February/March): 44–47, 78, 82.

"New England Brewing Company." n.d. Accessed 11 February 2011. http://beeradvocate.com/beer /profile/357/58731.

Nicholson, Reynold A. 1977. *Containing the Translation of the Fifth and Sixth Books.* Vol. 6 of *The Mathnawí of Jalálu'ddín Rúmí edited from the Oldest Manuscripts Available.* London: Trustees of the E. J. Gibb Memorial.

Niger, Shmuel. 1972. "The Humor of Sholom Aleichem." In *Voices from the Yiddish: Essays, Memoirs, Diaries,* ed. Irving Howe and Eliezer Greenberg, 41–50. Ann Arbor: University of Michigan Press.

Nilsen, Alleen Pace, and Don L. F. Nilsen. 2000. *Encyclopedia of 20th-Century American Humor.* Phoenix: Oryx.

Nilsen, Don L. F. 1988. "The Importance of Tendency: An Extension of Freud's Concept of Tendentious Humor." *Humor: International Journal of Humor Research* 1 (4): 335–47. http:// dx.doi.org/10.1515/humr.1988.1.4.335.

Norrick, Neal. 2001. "Review of *Jokes: Philosophical Thoughts on Joking Matters* by Ted Cohen." *Humor: International Journal of Humor Research* 14 (2): 203–6.

Novak, William, and Moshe Waldoks, eds. 1981. *The Big Book of Jewish Humor.* New York: Harper & Row.

Noy, Dov. 1962. "Ha-kayemet bedihat-am yehudit" [Does a Jewish Folk Joke Exist?]. *Mahanayim* 67:48–56.

Nuñez-Ramos, Rafael, and Guillermo Lorenzo. 1997. "On the Aesthetic Dimension of Humor." *Humor: International Journal of Humor Research* 10 (1): 105–16. http://dx.doi.org/10.1515 /humr.1997.10.1.105.

"NY Businessman to Sue Borat." 2007. *The West Australian,* 8 June. Accessed 8 November 2007. http://www.thewest.com.au/default.aspx?MenuID 23&ContentID=3086.

Obrdlik, Antonin J. 1942. "'Gallows Humor'—A Sociological Phenomenon." *American Journal of Sociology* 47 (5): 709–16. http://dx.doi.org/10.1086/219002.

Olrik, Axel. (Original work published 1909) 1965. "Epic Laws of Folk Narrative." In *The Study of Folklore,* ed. Alan Dundes, 129–41. Englewood Cliffs, NJ: Prentice-Hall.

Omar, Ifran A. 2004. "Humor." In *Encyclopedia of Islam and the Muslim World,* ed. Richard C. Martin, 1:319–22. New York: Thomson Gale.

Omidsalar, Mahmoud. 1987. "A Romanian Political Joke in 12th Century Iranian Sources." *Western Folklore* 46 (2): 121–24. http://dx.doi.org/10.2307/1499930.

Ong, Walter J. 1982. *Orality & Literacy.* London: Routledge. http://dx.doi. org/10.4324/9780203328064.

Oring, Elliott. 1973. "'Hey, You've Got No Character': Chizbat Humor and the Boundaries of Israeli Identity." *Journal of American Folklore* 86 (342): 358–66. http://dx.doi.org/10.2307/539359.

Oring, Elliott. 1975. "Everything Is a Shade of Elephant: An Alternative to a Psychoanalysis of Humor." *New York Folklore* 1:149–59.

Oring, Elliott. 1976. "Three Functions of Folklore: Traditional Functionalism as Explanation in Folkloristics." *Journal of American Folklore* 89 (351): 67–80. http://dx.doi.org/10.2307/539547.

Oring, Elliott. 1981. *Israeli Humor: The Content and Structure of the Chizbat of the Palmah.* Albany: State University of New York Press.

Oring, Elliott. 1983. "The People of the Joke: On the Conceptualization of a Jewish Humor." *Western Folklore* 42 (4): 261–71. http://dx.doi.org/10.2307/1499501.

Oring, Elliott. 1984. *The Jokes of Sigmund Freud: A Study in Humor and Jewish Identity.* Philadelphia: University of Pennsylvania Press.

Oring, Elliott. 1986. "Folk Narratives." In *Folk Groups and Folklore Genres: An Introduction*, ed. Elliott Oring, 121–45. Logan: Utah State University Press.

Oring, Elliott. 1992. *Jokes and Their Relations.* Lexington: University Press of Kentucky.

Oring, Elliott. 1994. "The Arts, Artifacts, and Artifices of Identity." *Journal of American Folklore* 107 (424): 211–33. http://dx.doi.org/10.2307/541199.

Oring, Elliott. 1995. "Appropriate Incongruities: Genuine and Spurious." *Humor: International Journal of Humor Research* 8 (3): 229–35. http://dx.doi.org/10.1515/humr.1995.8.3.229.

Oring, Elliott. 1999. "Review of *The Basic Humor Process: A Cognitive-Shift Theory and the Case against Incongruity*, by Robert L. Latta." *Humor: International Society of Humor Research* 12 (4): 457–64.

Oring, Elliott. 2003. *Engaging Humor.* Urbana: University of Illinois Press.

Oring, Elliott. 2005–2006. "The Making of a Humorologist." *Studies in American Humor*, n.s. 3 (13):107–14.

Oring, Elliott. 2008. "Humor in Anthropology and Folklore." In *The Primer of Humor Research*, ed. Victor Raskin, 183–210. Berlin: Mouton de Gruyter. http://dx.doi.org/10.1515/9783110198492.183.

Oring, Elliott. 2011. "Still Further Thoughts on Logical Mechanisms: A Response to Christian F. Hempelmann and Salvatore Attardo." *Humor: International Journal of Humor Studies* 24 (2): 151–58. http://dx.doi.org/10.1515/HUMR.2011.009.

Oring, Elliott. 2012a. "Jokes on the Internet: Listing towards Lists." In *Folk Culture in the Digital Age: The Emergent Dynamics of Human Interaction*, ed. Trevor J. Blank, 98–118. Logan: Utah State University Press.

Oring, Elliott. 2012b. *Just Folklore: Analysis, Interpretation, Critique.* Los Angeles: Cantilever.

Orwell, Sonia, and Ian Angus, eds. 1969. *As I Please, 1943–1945.* Vol. 3 of *The Collected Essays, Journalism, and Letters of George Orwell.* New York: Harcourt, Brace, & World.

Ostrower, Chaya. 2014. *It Kept Us Alive: Humor in the Holocaust.* Jerusalem: Yad Vashem.

Otto, Beatrice K. 2001. *Fools Are Everywhere: The Court Jester around the World.* Chicago: University of Chicago Press.

Palencik, Joseph T. 2001. "Amusement and the Philosophy of Emotion: A Neuroanatomical Approach." *Dialogue* 46 (3): 419–34. http://dx.doi.org/10.1017/S0012217300001992.

Pancevski, Bojan. 2006. "Villagers to Sue Borat." *Los Angeles Times*, 20 November, Home Edition, Part E, 1.

Paolillo, John C. 1998. "Gary Larson's *Far Side*: Nonsense? Nonsense!" *Humor: International Journal of Humor Research* 11 (3): 261–90. http://dx.doi.org/10.1515/humr.1998.11.3.261.

"Paris en Amérique." 1864. *The Spectator* 37 (6 April): 910.

"Periscope." 2003. *Newsweek*, 19 May, 10.

Piddington, Ralph. 1933. *The Psychology of Laughter.* London: Figurehead.

Pinker, Steven. 2007. *The Stuff of Thought: Language as a Window into Human Nature.* New York: Viking.

Pi-Sunyer, Oriol. 1977. "Political Humor in a Dictatorial State: The Case of Spain." *Ethnohistory* 24 (2): 179–90. http://dx.doi.org/10.2307/481742.

Pollio, Howard R. 1996. "Boundaries in Humor and Metaphor." In *Metaphor: Implications and Applications*, ed. Jeffrey Scott Mio and Albert N. Katz, 231–53. Mahwah, NJ: Lawrence Earlbaum.

Pouivet, Roger. 2000. "On the Cognitive Functioning of Aesthetic Emotions." *Leonardo* 33 (1): 49–53. http://dx.doi.org/10.1162/002409400552234.

Provine, Robert R. 2000. *Laughter: A Scientific Investigation*. New York: Penguin.

Ramachandran, V. S. 1998. "The Neurology and Evolution of Humor, Laughter, and Smiling: The False Alarm Theory." *Medical Hypotheses* 51 (4): 351–54. http://dx.doi.org/10.1016/S0306-9877 (98)90061-5.

Rapp, Albert. 1951. *The Origins of Wit and Humor*. New York: E. P. Dutton.

Rappaport, Leon. 2005. *Punchlines: The Case for Racial, Ethnic, and Gender Humor*. Westport, CT: Praeger.

Rappaport, Roy. 1967. "Ritual Regulation of Environmental Relations among a New Guinea People." *Ethnology* 6 (1): 17–30. http://dx.doi.org/10.2307/3772735.

Raskin, Richard. 1992. *Life Is Like a Cup of Tea: Studies of Classic Jewish Jokes*. Aarhus, Denmark: Aarhus University Press.

Raskin, Victor. 1985a. "Jokes." *Psychology Today* (October): 34–39.

Raskin, Victor. 1985b. *Semantic Mechanisms of Humor*. Dordrecht, Holland: D. Reidel.

Raskin, Victor. 2008. "Theory of Humor and Practice of Humor Research: Editor's Notes and Thoughts." In *The Primer of Humor Research*, ed. Victor Raskin, 1–15. Berlin: Mouton de Gruyter. http://dx.doi.org/10.1515/9783110198492.1.

Raskin, Victor. n.d. "Review of *Inside Jokes: Using Humor to Reverse Engineer the Mind*," by Matthew M. Hurley, Daniel C. Dennett, and Reginald B. Adams Jr. *European Journal of Humor Research* 1(3):b55–57.

Raymond, Eric S., ed. 1996. *The New Hacker's Dictionary*. 3rd ed. Cambridge: MIT Press.

"Red Rider." 2007. Accessed 15 June 2014. http://www.doofclenas.com/forums/archive/index.php /t-132796.html.

Reik, Theodor. 1962. *Jewish Wit*. New York: Gamut.

Renwick, Roger de V. 2001. *Recentering Anglo/American Folksong: Sea Crabs and Wicked Youth*. Jackson: University Press of Mississippi.

Revel, Hirschel. 1943. "Wit and Humor." In *The Universal Jewish Encyclopedia*, ed. Isaac Landmann, 10:545–48. New York: Universal Jewish Encyclopedia.

"Review of Life and Opinions of Heinrich Heine." 1876. *Anthenaeum*, 15 January, 81–82.

Richman, Jacob. 1954. *Laughs from Jewish Lore*. New York: Hebrew Publishing.

Richter, Jean Paul. (Original work published 1813) 1973. *Horn of Oberon: Jean Paul Richter's School for Aesthetics*. Trans. Margaret Hale. Detroit: Wayne State University Press.

Ritchie, Graeme. 2006. "Reinterpretation and Viewpoints." *Humor: International Journal of Humor Research* 19 (3): 251–70. http://dx.doi.org/10.1515/HUMOR.2006.014.

Roberts, Robert C. 1988. "Is Amusement an Emotion?" *American Philosophical Quarterly* 25 (3): 269–74.

Robinson, Jerry. 1974. *The Comics: An Illustrated History of Comic Strip Art*. New York: Putnam.

Rohatyn, B. 1911. "Die Gestalten des juedischen Volkshumor I" [Forms of Jewish Folk Humor]. *Ost und West* 11:122–26.

Rose, Alexander. 2001–2002. "When Politics Is a Laughing Matter." *Policy Review* 110:59–71.

Rose, Margaret. 1993. *Parody: Ancient, Modern, and Post-modern*. Cambridge: Cambridge University Press.

Roskies, Diane K., and David G. Roskies. 1975. *The Shtetl Book*. New York: Ktav.

Rosten, Leo. 1970. *The Joys of Yiddish*. New York: Pocket Books.

Roth, Cecil, ed. 1972. *Encyclopaedia Judaica*. 16 vols. Jerusalem: Keter.

Roth, John K., ed. 2005. *Ethics*. 3 vols. Rev. ed. Pasadena, CA: Salem.

Rothbart, Mary K. 1977. "Psychological Approaches to the Study of Humor." In *It's a Funny Thing, Humour*, ed. Anthony J. Chapman and Hugh C. Foot, 87–94. Oxford: Pergamon. http://dx.doi .org/10.1016/B978-0-08-021376-7.50020-6.

Rothbart, Mary K., and Diana Pien. 1977. "Elephants and Marshmallows: A Theoretical Synthesis of Incongruity-Resolution and Arousal Theories of Humor." In *It's a Funny Thing, Humour*, ed. Anthony J. Chapman and Hugh C. Foot, 37–40. Oxford: Pergamon. http://dx.doi.org/10.1016 /B978-0-08-021376-7.50011-5.

"Rube Goldberg Machine." n.d. *Wikipedia*. Accessed 18 February 2008. https://en.wikipedia.org /wiki/Rube_Goldberg_machine.

Ruch, Willibald, Salvatore Attardo, and Victor Raskin. 1993. "Toward an Empirical Verification of the General Theory of Verbal Humor." *Humor: International Journal of Humor Research* 6 (2): 123–36. http://dx.doi.org/10.1515/humr.1993.6.2.123.

Sacks, Harvey. 1974. "An Analysis of the Course of a Joke's Telling in Conversation." In *Explorations in the Ethnography of Speaking*, ed. Richard Bauman and Joel Sherzer, 337–53. Cambridge: Cambridge University Press.

Sahlins, Marshall D., and Elman R. Service. 1960. *Evolution and Culture*. Ann Arbor: University of Michigan Press.

Samuel, Maurice. 1971. *In Praise of Yiddish*. New York: Cowles.

Sanders, Barry. 1995. *Sudden Glory: Laughter as Subversive History*. Boston: Beacon.

Sanders, Jacquin. 1962a. "The Seriousness of Humor." *East Europe* 11 (1): 21–29.

Sanders, Jacquin. 1962b. "The Tactful Satirists." *East Europe* 11 (2): 22–27.

Saunders, George. 2006. "*Borat*: The Memo." *The New Yorker*, 4 December. Accessed 2 July 2014. http://www.newyorker.com/archive/2006/12/04/061204sh_shouts.

"Scale Models 1." n.d. Accessed 2 February 2011. http://www.scale-models.co.uk/jokes/2775-dumb -blonde-jokes.html.

"Scale Models 2." n.d. Accessed 10 February 2011. http://www.scale-models.co.uk/jokes/4523 -another-blonde-joke.html.

Schaeffer, Neal. 1981. *The Art of Laughter*. New York: Columbia University Press.

Schammel, Michael. 1984. *Solzhenitsyn: A Biography*. New York: W. W. Norton.

Scheffler, Israel. 1991. *In Praise of Cognitive Emotions and Other Essays in the Philosophy of Education*. New York: Routledge.

Schiller, Paul. 1938. "A Configurational Theory of Puzzles and Jokes." *Journal of General Psychology* 18 (2): 217–34. http://dx.doi.org/10.1080/00221309.1938.9709976.

Schutz, Charles E. 1977. *Political Humor: From Aristophanes to Sam Ervin*. Rutherford, NJ: Farleigh Dickinson University Press.

Schutz, Charles E. 1995. "Cryptic Humor: The Subversive Message of Political Jokes." *Humor: International Journal of Humor Research* 8 (1): 51–64. http://dx.doi.org/10.1515/humr.1995.8.1.51.

Scott, James C. 1976. *The Moral Economy of the Peasant: Rebellion and Subsistence in Southeast Asia*. New Haven, CT: Yale University Press.

Scott, James C. 1990. *Domination and the Arts of Resistance: Hidden Transcripts*. New Haven, CT: Yale University Press.

Sebba-Elran, Tsafi. Forthcoming. "The Canonization and Censorship of the Modern Jewish Joke in Alter Druyanow's *Book of Jokes and Witticisms* (1922)." *Journal of Modern Jewish Studies*.

Seckel, Al. 2004. *Masters of Deception: Escher, Dali & the Artists of Optical Illusion*. New York: Sterling.

Seymour, Gerald. 1982. *Archangel*. New York: E. P. Dutton.

Shaftesbury, Third Earl of. (Original work published 1709) 1963. "An Essay on the Freedom of Wit and Humor in a Letter to a Friend." In *Characteristics of Men, Manners, Opinions, Times, etc.*, ed. John M. Robertson, 1:43–99. Gloucester, MA: Peter Smith.

Shapiro, Karl Jay. 1978. *Collected Poems, 1940–1978*. New York: Random House.

Sharpe, Robert A. 1975. "Seven Reasons Why Amusement is an Emotion." *Journal of Value Inquiry* 9 (3): 201–3. http://dx.doi.org/10.1007/BF00141031.

Sherzer, Joel. 1985. "Puns and Jokes." In *Handbook of Discourse Analysis*, ed. Teun A. Van Dijk, 3:213–21. London: Academic Press.

Sherzer, Joel. 1990. "On Play, Joking, Humor, and Tricking among the Kuna: The Agouti Story." *Journal of Folklore Research* 27 (1/2): 85–114.

Sherzer, Joel. 2002. *Speech Play and Verbal Art*. Austin: University of Texas Press.

Shifman, Limor, and Mike Thelwall. 2009. "Assessing Global Diffusion with Web Memetics: The Spread and Evolution of a Popular Joke." *Journal of the American Society for Information Science and Technology* 60 (12): 2567–76. http://dx.doi.org/10.1002/asi.21185.

Shredd, Travis. 2000. "The Neighbor of the Beast." Accessed 2 February 2011. http://www .cduniverse.com/search/xx/music/pid/1206548/a/668%3A+The+Neighbor+Of+The+Beast.htm.

Shusterman, Richard. 1997. "The End of Aesthetic Experience." *Journal of Aesthetics and Art Criticism* 55 (1): 29–41. http://dx.doi.org/10.2307/431602.

"Sick, Sick, Sick." n.d. Accessed 2 February 2011. http://www.traderskis.com/traderskis_zazzle /666_The_Humor_of_the_Beast.php (site discontinued).

Simon, Ernst. 1948. "Notes on Jewish Wit." *Jewish Frontier* 15 (October): 42–48.

Smyth, Willie. 1986. "Challenger Jokes and the Humor of Disaster." *Western Folklore* 45 (4): 243–60. http://dx.doi.org/10.2307/1499820.

Sohval, Daniel, and Salvatore Attardo. 2013. "Review of *Inside Jokes: Using Humor to Reverse-Engineer the Mind*, by Matthew M. Hurley, Daniel C. Dennett, and Reginald B. Adams, Jr." *Humor: International Journal of Humor Research* 26 (1): 177–79.

Solzhenitsyn, Aleksandr I. 1973. *The Gulag Archipelago, 1918–1956: An Experiment in Literary Investigation, I–II*. Trans. Thomas P. Whitney. New York: Harper & Row.

Spalding, Henry D. 1969. *Encyclopedia of Jewish Humor: From Biblical Times to the Modern Age*. New York: Jonathan David.

Sparshott, Francis. 1982. *The Theory of the Arts*. Princeton, NJ: Princeton University Press. http:// dx.doi.org/10.1515/9781400857012.

Speier, Hans. 1969. *Force and Folly: Essays on Foreign Affairs and the History of Ideas*. Cambridge, MA: MIT Press.

Speier, Hans. 1998. "Wit and Politics: An Essay on Laughter and Power." *American Journal of Sociology* 103 (5): 1352–1401. http://dx.doi.org/10.1086/231355.

Spencer, Herbert. 1860. "The Physiology of Laughter." *Macmillian's Magazine* 1:395–402.

Stecker, Robert. 2000. "Is It Reasonable to Attempt to Define Art?" In *Theories of Art Today*, ed. Noël Carroll, 45–64. Madison: University of Wisconsin Press.

Stein, Mary Beth. 1989. "The Politics of Humor: The Berlin Wall in Jokes and Graffiti." *Western Folklore* 48 (2): 85–108. http://dx.doi.org/10.2307/1499684.

Stokker, Kathleen. 1995. *Folklore Fights the Nazis: Humor in Occupied Norway, 1940–1945.* Madison, NJ: Farleigh Dickinson University Press.

Stolnitz, Jerome. 1961. "On the Origins of 'Aesthetic Distinterestedness.'" *Journal of Art and Aesthetic Criticism* 20 (2): 131–43. http://dx.doi.org/10.2307/427462.

Stowe, Debbie, and Paul Stump. 2007. *Who Is Borat? The Unauthorized Biography of Sacha Baron Cohen.* New York: Barnes & Noble for Kandour.

Strauss, Neil. 2006. "The Man behind the Moustache." *Rolling Stone,* 30 November, 59, 62, 64, 68, 70.

Suls, Jerry M. 1972. "A Two-Stage Model for the Appreciation of Jokes and Cartoons: An Information-Processing Analysis." In *The Psychology of Humor: Theoretical Perspectives and Empirical Issues*, ed. Jeffrey H. Goldstein and Paul E. McGhee, 81–100. New York: Academic Press. http://dx.doi.org/10.1016/B978-0-12-288950-9.50010-9.

Suls, Jerry. 1976. "Cognitive and Disparagement Theories of Humour: A Theoretical and Empirical Synthesis." In *It's A Funny Thing, Humour*, ed. Anthony J. Chapman and Hugh C. Foot, 41–45. Oxford: Pergamon.

Tallman, Richard S. 1974. "A Generic Approach to the Practical Joke." *Southern Folklore Quarterly* 38 (4): 259–74.

Taylor, Archer. 1943. "The Riddle." *California Folklore Quarterly* 2 (2): 129–47. http://dx.doi.org/10.2307/1495557.

"Ted Danson Is Criticized for Blackface Act at Friar's Club Roast of Whoopi Goldberg." 1993. Accessed 10 June 2015. http://articles.philly.com/1993-10-10/news/25936200_1_ted-danson-friars-club-racially-offensive-nature.

Telushkin, Joseph. 1992. *Jewish Humor: What the Best Jewish Jokes Say about the Jews.* New York: William Morrow.

Thomas, Caroline, and Victoria M. Esses. 2004. "Individual Differences in Reaction to Sexist Humor." *Group Processes & Intergroup Relations* 7 (1): 89–100. http://dx.doi.org/10.1177/1368430204039975.

Thomas, Dylan. 2003. *The Poems of Dylan Thomas*, ed. David Jones. New York: New Directions.

Thompson, Mark. 1996. "A Political Suicide." *Time,* 13 May, 44.

Thompson, Stith. 1955. *Motif-Index of Folk-Literature.* 6 vols. Rev. and enl. ed. Bloomington: Indiana University Press.

Thursby, Jacqueline S. 2006. *Story: A Handbook.* Westport, CT: Greenwood.

Tiupa, Valerii. 2009. "Communicative Strategy of the Anekdot and the Genesis of Literary Genres." *Russian Journal of Communication* 2 (3/4): 161–70. http://dx.doi.org/10.1080/19409419.2009.10756748.

Tolhurst, William. 1984. "Toward an Aesthetic Account of the Nature of Art." *Journal of Aesthetics and Art Criticism* 42 (3): 261–69. http://dx.doi.org/10.2307/429706.

Townsend, Mary Lee. 1992. *Forbidden Laughter: Popular Humor and the Limits of Repression in Nineteenth-Century Prussia.* Ann Arbor: University of Michigan Press.

"Tristan Café." n.d. Accessed 21 May 2011. http://www.tristancafe.com/forum/87331 (site discontinued).

Turner, Jonathan H., and Alexandra Maryanski. 1979. *Functionalism.* Menlo Park, CA: Benjamin/ Cummings.

"Two Pendejos." 2010. Accessed 15 June 2014. http://www.unexplained-mysteries.com/forum /index.php?showtopic=33684&st=1170.

Unger, Jim. 2007. *Herman: Living with Animals.* Toronto: ECW.

Untermeyer, Louis. 1946. *A Treasury of Laughter.* New York: Simon & Schuster.

Uther, Hans-Jörg. 2011. *The Types of International Folktales: A Classification and Bibliography.* 3 vols. Helsinki: Suomalainen Tiedeakatemia.

Veale, Tony. 2007. "Figure-Ground Reversal in Verbal Humor." Paper presented at the Tenth International Cognitive Linguistics Association Conference, 15–20 July, Kraków, Poland.

Veale, Tony, Kurt Feyaerts, and Geert Brône. 2006. "The Cognitive Mechanisms of Adversarial Humor." *Humor: International Journal of Humor Research* 19 (3): 305–39. http://dx.doi.org /10.1515/HUMOR.2006.016.

Veatch, Thomas C. 1998. "A Theory of Humor." *Humor: International Journal of Humor Research* 11 (2): 161–215. http://dx.doi.org/10.1515/humr.1998.11.2.161.

Vilaythong, Alexander P., Randolph C. Arnau, David H. Rosen, and Nathan Mascaro. 2003. "Humor and Hope: Can Humor Increase Hope?" *Humor: International Journal of Humor Research* 16 (1): 79–89. http://dx.doi.org/10.1515/humr.2003.006.

Warren, Claude. 1959. *Modern News Reporting.* 3rd ed. New York: Harper & Row.

Weininger, Otto. 1906. *Sex and Character.* London: William Heinemann.

Weisfeld, Glenn E., Nicole T. Nowak, Todd Lucas, Carol C. Weisfeld, E. Olcay Imamoğlu, Marina Butovskaya, Jiliang Shen, and Michele R. Parkhill. 2011. "Do Women Seek Humorousness in Men because It Signals Intelligence? A Cross-Cultural Test." *Humor: International Journal of Humor Research* 42 (4): 435–62.

Weitz, Morris. 1956. "The Role of Theory in Aesthetics." *Journal of Aesthetics and Art Criticism* 15 (1): 27–35. http://dx.doi.org/10.2307/427491.

Wengeroff, Pauline. 2010. *Memories of a Grandmother: Scenes from the Cultural History of the Jews of Russia in the Nineteenth Century.* Trans. Shulamit S. Magnus. Stanford Studies in Jewish History and Culture. Palo Alto, CA: Stanford University Press. http://dx.doi.org/10.11126 /stanford/9780804768795.001.0001.

Wertheim, Willem Frederik. 1965. *East-West Parallels: Sociological Approaches to Modern Asia.* Chicago: Quadrangle.

Wex, Michael. 2006. *Born to Kvetch: Yiddish Language and Culture in All of Its Moods.* New York: Harper Perennial.

"What Influences Medical Student and Resident Choices." 2009. Accessed 17 February 2016. http:// www.graham-center.org/content/dam/rgc/documents/publications-reports/presentations /student-resident-influence.pdf.

White, Christine Pelzer. 1986. "Everyday Resistance, Socialist Revolution and Rural Development: The Vietnamese Case." *Journal of Peasant Studies* 13 (2): 49–63. http://dx.doi.org/10.1080 /03066158608438291.

Wickberg, Daniel. 1998. *The Sense of Humor: Self and Laughter in Modern America*. Ithaca, NY: Cornell University Press.

Wilson, Christopher P. 1979. *Jokes: Form, Content, Use, Function*. New York: Academic Press.

Winick, Charles. 1961. "Space Jokes as Indications of Attitudes toward Space." *Journal of Social Issues* 17 (2): 43–49. http://dx.doi.org/10.1111/j.1540-4560.1961.tb01673.x.

Wisse, Ruth R. 2013. *No Joke: Making Jewish Humor*. Princeton, NJ: Princeton University Press. http://dx.doi.org/10.1515/9781400846344.

Wyer, Robert S., Jr., and James E. Collins II. 1992. "A Theory of Humor Elicitation." *Psychological Review* 99 (4): 663–88. http://dx.doi.org/10.1037/0033-295X.99.4.663.

"Yahoo Answers." n.d. Accessed 2 February 2011. http://answers.yahoo.com/question/index?qid =20110125135128AAYqcOP&grp_name=blondejokeplace&grp_spid=1601120663&grp_cat= /EntertainmentArts/Humor/Jokes/Blonde_Jokes&grp_user=0.

Yue, Xiao Dong. 2011. "The Chinese Ambivalence to Humor: Views from Undergraduates in Hong Kong and China." *Humor: International Journal of Humor Research* 24 (4): 463–80. http://dx.doi .org/10.1515/humr.2011.026.

Yurchak, Alexei. 1997. "The Cynical Reason of Late Socialism: Power, Pretense, and the *Ankedot*." *Public Culture* 9 (2): 161–88. http://dx.doi.org/10.1215/08992363-9-2-161.

Yurchak, Alexei. 2006. *Everything Was Forever, until It Was No More: The Last Soviet Generation*. Princeton, NJ: Princeton University Press.

Zakani, Obeyd-e. 2008. *Ethics of the Aristocrats and Other Satirical Works*, ed. and trans. Hasan Javadi. Washington, DC: Mage.

Zall, Paul M., ed. 1963. *A Hundred Merry Tales and Other Jestbooks of the Fifteenth and Sixteenth Centuries*. Lincoln: University of Nebraska Press.

Zan, Yigal. 1982. "The Text/Context Controversy: An Explanatory Perspective." *Western Folklore* 41 (1): 1–27. http://dx.doi.org/10.2307/1499722.

Zangwill, Nick. 2003. "Beauty." In *The Oxford Handbook of Aesthetics*, ed. Jerrold Levinson, 325–43. Oxford: Oxford University Press.

Zink, Sidney. 1954. "The Cognitive Element in Art." *Ethics* 64 (3): 186–204. http://dx.doi.org/10 .1086/290942.

Ziv, Avner. 1984. *Personality and Sense of Humor*. New York: Springer.

Ziv, Avner. 1986a. Introduction. In *Jewish Humor*, ed. Avner Ziv, 7–15. Tel Aviv: Papyrus.

Ziv, Avner. 1986b. "Psycho-social Aspects of Jewish Humor in Israel and in the Diaspora." In *Jewish Humor*, ed. Avner Ziv, 47–71. Tel Aviv: Papyrus.

Ziv, Avner, and Orit Gadish. 1990. "The Disinhibiting Effects of Humor: Aggressive and Affective Responses." *Humor: International Journal of Humor Research* 3 (3): 247–57. http://dx.doi.org /10.1515/humr.1990.3.3.247.

About the Author

ELLIOTT ORING is Professor Emeritus of anthropology at California State University, Los Angeles. He has written extensively about humor, folklore, and cultural symbolism. Professor Oring was editor of the journal *Western Folklore* and serves on the editorial boards of *Humor: International Journal of Humor Research* and *Journal of Folklore Research*. He was president of the International Society for Humor Studies and has served on the executive board of the American Folklore Society. He is a Woodrow Wilson Fellow, a Fellow of the American Folklore Society, a Folklore Fellow of the Finnish Academy of Arts and Sciences, and was a Fulbright Scholar at the University of Iceland in Reykjavík. He is the author of *Israeli Humor, The Jokes of Sigmund Freud, Jokes and Their Relations, Engaging Humor,* and *Just Folklore.*

Index

ALSO BY THE AUTHOR

Engaging Humor
Israeli Humor: The Content and Structure of the Chizbat of the Palmah
Jokes and Their Relations
The Jokes of Sigmund Freud: A Study in Humor and Jewish Identity
Just Folklore: Analysis, Interpretation, Critique

EDITED BY THE AUTHOR

Folk Groups and Folklore Genres: An Introduction
Folk Groups and Folklore Genres: A Reader
Humor and the Individual